HISTORY

OF

TENNESSEE

From the Earliest Time to the Present; Together with an Historical and a Biographical Sketch of Hamilton County, Besides a Valuable Fund of Notes, Original Observations, Reminiscences, Etc., Etc.

ILLUSTRATED.

NASHVILLE:
THE GOODSPEED PUBLISHING CO.,
1887.

This volume was reproduced from
An 1887 edition located in the
Knoxville Public Library,
Knoxville, Tennessee

All rights reserved. No part of this publication
may be reproduced, stored in a retrieval system,
transmitted in any form, posted on to the web
in any form or by any means without the
prior written permission of the publisher.

Please direct all correspondence and orders to:

www.southernhistoricalpress.com
or
SOUTHERN HISTORICAL PRESS, Inc.
PO BOX 1267
375 West Broad Street
Greenville, SC   29601
southernhistoricalpress@gmail.com

Originally published: Nashville, 1887
Reprinted with New Material by:
Southern Historical Press, Inc.
Greenville, SC 2018
New Material Copyright 2018 by
Southern Historical Press, Inc.
Greenville, SC
ISBN #0-89308-126-4
All rights Reserved.
Printed in the United States of America

PREFACE.

THIS volume has been prepared in response to the prevailing and popular demand for the preservation of local history and biography. The method of preparation followed is the most successful and the most satisfactory yet devised—the most successful in the enormous number of volumes circulated, and the most satisfactory in the general preservation of personal biography and family record conjointly with local history. The number of volumes now being distributed appears fabulous. Within the last four years not less than 20,000 volumes of this class of works have been distributed in Kentucky, and the demand is not half satisfied.

To him who has not attempted the collection of historical data, the obstacles to be surmounted are unknown. Doubtful traditions, conflicting statements, imperfect records, inaccurate private correspondence, the bias or untruthfulness of informers, and the general obscurity which envelops all events combine to bewilder and mislead. On the contrary, the preparation of statistical history by experienced, unprejudiced and competent workers in specialties; the accomplishment by a union of labor of a vast result would cost one person the best years of his life and transfer the collection of perishing event beyond the hope of research; the judicious selection of important matter from the general rubbish; and the careful and intelligent revision of all final manuscript by an editor-in-chief, yield a degree of celerity, system, accuracy, comprehensiveness and value unattainable by any other method. The publishers of this volume, fully aware of their inability to furnish a perfect history, an accomplishment vouchsafed only to the dreamer or the theorist, make no pretension of having prepared a work devoid of blemish. They feel assured that all thoughtful people, at present and in future, will recognize and appreciate the importance of their undertaking and the great public benefit that has been accomplished.

In the preparation of this volume the publishers have met with nothing but courtesy and assistance. They acknowledge their indebtedness for valuable favors to the Governor, the State Librarian, the Secretary of the State Historical Society and to more than a hundred of other prominent citizens of Nashville, Memphis, Knoxville, Chattanooga, Jackson, Clarksville and the smaller cities of the State. It is the design of the publishers to compile and issue, in connection with the State history, a brief yet comprehensive historical account of every county in the State, copies of which will be placed in the State Library. In the prosecution of this work they hope to meet with the same cordial assistance extended to them during the compilation of this volume.

THE PUBLISHERS.

NASHVILLE, October, 1887.

HAMILTON COUNTY.

HAMILTON COUNTY is situated in the southeastern portion of the State, and is separated from Middle Tennessee by Marion, Sequatchie and Bledsoe Counties, which bound it on the west. On the north Hamilton County is bounded by Rhea County, on the east by James County, and on the south by the State of Georgia. This county was established as a separate organization by an act of the Legislature, passed October 25, 1819, as follows:

SECTION 1. Be it enacted, etc., that the territory lying southwest of Rhea County, and south and east of Bledsoe and Marion Counties, shall constitute a county by the name of Hamilton in honor and to perpetuate the memory of the late Alexander Hamilton,* late Secretary of the Treasury of the United States.

SEC. 2. Be it enacted, etc., that the said county of Hamilton shall be bounded as follows: Beginning at a point at the foot of Walden's Ridge of the Cumberland Mountains, on the east side thereof; thence running to a point on the Tennessee River, two and a half miles below the lower end of Jolly's Island, so as to include Patrick Martin in the county of Hamilton; thence south thirty-five degrees east to the southern limits of the State; thence west to the point where Marion County line intersects said western boundary; thence northeastwardly with Marion County line to Bledsoe County line, to a point opposite the beginning, and thence to the beginning.

SEC. 3. Be it enacted, that for the due administration of justice, the court of pleas and quarter sessions, and the circuit court of the county of Hamilton, shall be holden at such place as shall be designated by Charles Gamble, Robert Patterson and William Lauderdale until otherwise provided for by law, etc.

Section 4 provided that an election should be held on the first Thursday and Friday of the ensuing March, for the purpose of electing field officers for the county, the militia of the county to compose the Sixty-fourth Regiment and part of the Seventh Brigade, and section 6 enacted that Hamilton County should be a part of the same district with Rhea in electing the governor, members of the Legislature, representative to Congress, and a President and Vice-President of the United States.

An act was passed November 20, 1821, to the effect that a line running between the counties of Rhea and Hamilton should commence at a point one-half mile below Blythe's Ferry, and run across the valley to the mountain, so as to run between the lands of Benjamin Jones and John Russell, "thence up the foot of the said mountain to the line of said county as now run and marked," and that the dividing line between Hamilton and Marion Counties, should be as follows:

---

*Alexander Hamilton died in 1804.

"Beginning on the southeast corner of Bledsoe County; thence along the extreme height of the mountain to the head of Duck Creek; thence down said creek to the mouth thereof; thence due south to the southern boundary of the State."

Omitting the laws of 1833 and 1836, an act was passed February 4, 1842, Sections 3 and 4 of which were as follows:

SEC. 3. That the first and second sections of "an act entitled an act to alter the dividing line between the counties of Marion and Hamilton," passed February 17, 1836, be and the same is hereby repealed.

SEC. 4. That the dividing line between the counties of Marion and Hamilton on the south side of the Tennessee River, as run and marked by the surveyor-general of the Hiwassee District, in pursuance of an act of the General Assembly, entitled " an act to extend the laws and jurisdiction of this State to her southern limits;" Chapter 16, passed November 8, 1833, shall hereafter be and remain the dividing line between said counties.

The next change in the county lines was made by an act passed February 4, 1850, Section 3 of which is as follows:

SEC. 3. That the dividing line between Rhea and Hamilton Counties shall be so altered as to commence on a black walnut and hickory on the eastern fork of said creek; thence forty poles down the creek to a stake; thence north seventy-five degrees west to the fork of said creek; thence westwardly with said road to the Bledsoe County line; thence with Bledsoe County line to Rhea County, so as to include Mr. John Gray and Robert Quarls in Rhea County.

On the 3d of April, 1881, an act was passed, section 3 of which was as follows:

SEC. 3. That the county lines between Bledsoe, Rhea and Hamilton Counties, shall be changed so as to attach the lands of James Sladen to Bledsoe County, beginning on the Hamilton County line, where said line crosses the head waters of McGill Creek; thence down the McGill gorge to the corner in the Roberts survey in said gorge; then with the same degree and line of the Roberts survey, running near a point in the old hard road known as the Stoney Battery, to the waters of Roaring River; thence with the waters of said creek to the original county line between Rhea and Bledsoe Counties.

A glance at the map will show that while the southern boundary coincides with the thirty-fifth parallel of latitude, none of the other boundary lines run east and west or north and south, the western and eastern lines running in a general northeasterly and southwesterly direction, corresponding mainly with the course of the Tennessee River above Chattanooga, and the northern boundary extending in a northwesterly and southeasterly direction. The area of Hamilton County is 380 square miles, or 243,200 acres. This has been its area since the organization of James County, by which there were taken from Hamilton County four civil districts to be incorporated into James County.

The topography of this county is exceedingly varied, the larger portion toward the northwest being mountainous and wild, while the valley of the Tennessee River, with the valleys of its tributaries from the northwest, occupies about one-third of the entire area. The principal valleys and ridges have a northeasterly and southwesterly direction. The elevation of the Tennessee River, where in its downward course it first touches Hamilton County, is about 700 feet above the level of the sea. The bridge of the Cincinnati Southern Railroad across the Tennessee River about seven miles above the Market Street crossing in Chattanooga is 698 feet above sea level, while low water at the same place is 635 feet above the same level. The signal service barometer bulb in the courthouse is 783 feet high. White Oak Mountains occupy a small space in the southeast corner of the county, while Raccoon Mountains extend into the southwest corner. Missionary Ridge commences at South Chickamauga Creek, near the Tennessee River, and rises to the height of about 500 feet above the valley, while on the opposite side of the Tennessee, Walden's Ridge rises to the height of nearly if not quite 1,500 feet above the valley, and Lookout Point, the highest point of Lookout Mountain, in the southwest corner of the county, rises to the height of about 1,600 feet above low water in the Tennessee.

The office of the United States Coast and Geodetic Survey, at Washington, D. C., kindly furnishes for publication in this work the following data regarding elevations in the vicinity of Chattanooga:

Gannett in his Dictionary of Altitudes, gives the elevation of the following points, based upon railroad levels: Knoxville, 900 feet; Loudon, 816 feet; Chattanooga, 684 feet. According to a plane table survey made in 1863, by Assistant Dorr, of this survey, Lookout Mountain, near Summertown, was found to be 1,580 feet above the level of the Tennessee at Chattanooga, which combined with Ellet's figures (Ellet gives the height of the Tennessee at Chattanooga as 643 feet), gives 2,223 feet as the elevation of Lookout Mountain. Assistant Webber computed the altitude of Point Lookout, of the Lookout Mountains, as 2,166 feet. His Gulf point, which is supposed to be on Missionary Ridge, he gives as 2,200 feet altitude. Prof. Buchanan computes the altitude of his station, Deadening, which lies on Wallen's Ridge, at 928.98 meters, equal to 3,048 feet. It is not known if the points selected as triangulation points are the highest on their respective ridges, but they are supposed to be very near the maxima.

B. A. COLONUS,
Assistant in charge of Office.

The following table, also kindly furnished for publication in this work, by G. B. Nicholson, chief engineer of the Cincinnati Southern Railway Company, will be found of special interest:

ELEVATIONS OF STATIONS.

Miles.	County.	Stations and Other Prominent Points.	Location of Elevation.	Feet Above Sea Level.
197.7	Scott	State Line	Kentucky and Tenn.	1350
200.6	Scott	Winfield	Depot	1323
204.4	Scott	Flat Gap	Top of Cut	1562
204.4	Scott	Flat Gap	Top of Tie	1514
206.5	Scott	Oneida	Depot	1445
209.0	Scott	Summit, South (highest point on line)	of Nigo Creek Top of Tie	1519
212.1	Scott	Helenwood	Depot	1392
215.7	Scott	New River	Depot	1206
216.0	Scott	New River	Top of Tie on Bridge	1222
216.0	Scott	New River	Low water	1095
219.0	Scott	Robins	Depot	1374
220.9	Scott	Rugby Road	Depot	1393
222.9	Scott	Glen Mary	Depot	1280
226.0	Morgan	Huffman's		1408
228.7	Morgan	Sunbright	Depot	1350
231.8	Morgan	Pilot Mt.		1339
233.6	Morgan	Annadell	Platform	1239
237.7	Morgan	Triplat's Gap	Top of Tie	1209
238.1	Morgan	Lancing	Depot	1188
243.3	Morgan	Nemo	Platform	908
248.2	Morgan	Melham	Platform	822
251.3	Morgan	Oakdale	Depot	805
255.2	Roane	Knoxville	Depot	793
255.4	Roane	Emory Gap	Top of Tie on Bridge	795
255.4	Roane	Emory Gap	L. wat. Emory River	725
257.0	Roane	Summit, south of Tunnel No. 27	Top of Tie	854
257.5	Roane	Emory Gap	Depot	832
264.9	Roane	Rockwood	Depot	876
270.0	Rhea	Glen Alice	Platform	816
273.0	Rhea	Roddy	Depot	775
277.5	Rhea	Lorraine	Platform	804
280.3	Rhea	Spring City	Depot	772
284.9	Rhea	Sheffield	County Road	844
290.6	Rhea	Dariom	Depot	758
296.9	Rhea	Richland Creek	Top of Tie	710
296.9	Rhea	Richland Creek	Low water	695
297.1	Rhea	Dayton	Depot	706
302.6	Rhea	Graysville	Road Crossing	734
304.0	Hamilton	Coulterville	Depot	703
306.7	Hamilton	Sale Creek	County Road	745
309.5	Hamilton	Retro	Road Crossing	738
314.1	Hamilton	Rathburn	Nar. Gauge Crossing	782
317.2	Hamilton	Daisy	Platform	718
318.0	Hamilton	Melville	Platform	702
321.6	Hamilton	Cave Springs	Springs	688
325.6	Hamilton	Hixon	Platform	683
328.5	Hamilton	Tennessee River	Top of Tie	698
328.5	Hamilton	Tennessee River	Low water	635
329.3	Hamilton	King's Point	Depot	687
335.4	Hamilton	Chattanooga	Market St. Crossing	675
		Georgia State Line		687

The distances in this table are from mile-post "O" at the south end of the Ohio River bridge.

The principal valleys in this county are the Tennessee, Lookout, Chattanooga, Chickamauga and the Back Valley, the latter lying between Walden's Ridge and a group of parallel minor ridges. The principal stream is the Tennessee which is about 1,500 feet wide, and is navigable within the county for steamboats all the year. After running between Hamilton and Rhea Counties about fifteen miles, it turns its course toward the southwest; and after running in this direction about fourteen miles, it strikes the base of Lookout Mountain, then pursues a northwest course about seven miles, when it breaks through the mountain range at the "Suck," and then follows a general, winding southwest direction through Marion County into Alabama. The other streams, all tributary to the Tennessee, are Lookout, Chattanooga, Citico and South Chickamauga Creeks from the southeast, and the Suck, Mountain, North Chickamauga, Soddy, Possum, Rocky and Sale Creeks from the northwest.

The geology of the county is very simple but very interesting, especially in an economical point of view, and although the entire series of formations is not present in this county, yet in describing the formations or strata that are present, it is necessary to commence very near the Azoic age. The lowest layer, found in the valley lands, is a chazy limestone, known in this State as the Knox dolomite, and then follow the Trenton and Nashville limestones in the valleys and Missionary Ridge, all of the above belonging to the Lower Silurian era. Then follow the dyestone or red iron ore in small ridges mainly, and Niagara limestone, belonging to the Upper Silurian, the iron ore belonging to the Clinton group. Black shale and St. Louis limestone are found next, belonging to the Devonian age, and last of all come the mountain limestone and the coal measures, belonging respectively to the Lower Carboniferous and Carboniferous eras. The coal measures cap Lookout Mountain, Raccoon Mountain and Walden's Ridge, in the last two the coal existing in great abundance and being exceedingly valuable for heating and smelting purposes. The veins usually lie in a horizontal position, or dipping more or less to the northwest, and varying in thickness from three feet to five feet. In Walden's Ridge one vein is said to be thirteen feet thick.

The iron ore above mentioned crops out near the bases of Walden's Ridge, of Lookout Mountain and of the Cumberland table-land, the dip of this ore varying from about twenty-five to nearly forty-five degrees. The strata containing this ore evidently extend, in the case of each ridge or table-land, entirely under such ridge from valley to valley on either side, the ridge or mountain appearing to have pressed or bent downward the strata upon which it rests, and thus to have formed for a permanent resting place, what geologists term a synclinal trough or valley, causing the edges of the underlying strata to turn up on either side. This ore extends in a northeast and southwest direction from near Birmingham, Ala., into and through the Tennessee Valley, in East Tennessee, through Pennsylvania, and into New York State, where the strata containing it are called the Clinton group. At many places it is called dyestone, being occasionally used in dyeing, and is unlike limonite; as it occurs in layers, its quantity can easily be determined. At Walden's Ridge it forms a stratum varying in thickness from eighteen inches to three feet, and is parallel with the slope of the ridge.

Missionary Ridge differs in structure from Walden's Ridge, being formed by outcroppings of the Knox dolomite, its eastern slope and contiguous territory toward the east of the ridge, being covered with flinty masses and gravel. Between Missionary Ridge and Chattanooga, this same dolomite and the Trenton and Nashville limestones form a wide, rolling valley. On the west side of Lookout Mountain, lies Will's Valley, in which mainly outcrops the same limestones, and, as has been said in another connection, on the west side of this valley the dyestone group again appears.

The uplands or ridges are in many places covered with a soil which is thin and poor, but which is less affected by drought than would naturally be supposed. This soil is well adapted to grazing and is capable of being fertilized to almost any desired richness. The first bottom lands are alluvial, with clay subsoil, and very valuable if drained and supplied with alkali. The second bottom lands are in some places of a clayey loam, in others of a sandy loam, and all either are or can be made exceedingly productive. As may be seen by the table given below, the climate is, generally speaking, mild and equable, the extremes of more northern and southern latitudes not being experienced.

The natural products of the forests are greatly varied. Oak grows nearly all over the county, and other kinds of timber are the ash, black walnut, beech, birch, cherry, red cedar, cypress, hickory, maple, holly, ironwood and locust, and white and yellow poplar abound. The short-leaf yellow pine is also found at the base of Raccoon Mountain, in Lookout Valley, on Soddy Creek, on Missionary Ridge and on the top of Walden's Ridge. It is of great value for bridge and car building, for flooring and joists and for interior finish and decorations, but does not work so easily as the long-leaf yellow pine of Georgia, Alabama and Mississippi. Timothy and other varieties of herdgrass, as also clover, grow luxuriantly; corn, cotton, wheat, potatoes, both Irish and sweet, broom corn, sorghum and tobacco, grow to perfection, and are cultivated with success. Garden vegetables of all kinds, and horticultural products, with the exception of the apple, find here a congenial atmosphere, and especially the grape, with the modified exception of the Catawba, the older vines of this variety being subject to oidium or mildew; but the Concord is most healthy and productive, and best adapted to this latitude. So far, however, agriculture is but indifferently or rather poorly conducted. Fertilizing is not appreciated at its true value; too much of the land is farmed by renters; deep cultivation and rotation of crops are too seldom practiced, and upstart weeds are permitted to grow to an inordinate extent and hight.

It is probable and is believed to be true that the first to settle in this part of the country were mainly Scotchmen, and that they came here almost immediately after the close of the Revolutionary war. Some of their names are here inserted: Daniel Ross, Daniel McNair, Daniel McCoy, Joseph Coody, Joseph Martin, Dick Taylor, Fox Taylor, Mr. Adair, Mr. Lowrie, Mr. McPherson and Mr. McDonald. Most of these married Indian wives and became incorporated into the Cherokee Nation. Daniel Ross married a half-breed Indian woman and became by her the father of John Ross, the Cherokee chief, who built the house at Rossville, Ga., now occupied by Thomas McFarland; of Lewis Ross, who, had it not been for his high cheek bones and straight, black hair, could not have been distinguished from a white man; of Andrew Ross; of Eliza Ross, a very beautiful and accomplished woman, who married a Scotchman and went to Scotland to live; and of the wife of Joseph Coody, who for a long time lived on the old Daniel Ross farm near the base of Lookout Mountain, and there carried on a deer skin tannery.

The reader will remember that by the act of the Legislature organizing the county, the boundary line was so run "as to include Patrick Martin in the county of Hamilton" and that "the court of pleas and quarter sessions and the circuit court of the county of Hamilton shall be holden at such place as shall be designated by Charles Gamble, Robert Patterson and William Lauderdale until otherwise provided for by law." It would seem reasonable to conclude therefore, notwithstanding the testimony of certain old settlers to the contrary, especially with reference to Patrick Martin and William Lauderdale, that all of these four persons were here previous to October 25, 1819. Robert Patterson came to this county as early as 1807, and settled on North Carolina grant No. 23, and Charles Gamble, who had been deputy sheriff in Rhea County, came to Hamilton in 1816, settled on the Tennessee River near the mouth of Sale Creek, and after the organization of the county became its first sheriff, and it is stated on apparently good authority that the first sheriff's sale was conducted near this creek, from which circumstances the creek received its name.

At the time of the organization of the county there were 821 inhabitants, 766 of whom were whites, thirty-nine slaves and sixteen free colored persons; hence it would be impracticable even if it were desirable to introduce a complete list of these early settlers. A portion only of the names of these, such as are now remembered or as appear on the county records can be given. Hasten Poe was one of these, and it was at his house, still standing (1886), not far from Melville Station on the Cincinnati Southern Railway, where the first term of the circuit court was held, having been selected by the commissioners, Gamble, Patterson and Lauderdale. Mr. Poe came to this county in 1818 and died in 1878. John Poe, his grandson, now owns the old place, from near which Poe's road, formerly "Poe's Turnpike," passes over Walden's Ridge. From Mr. Poe's house, known in early times as "Poe's tavern," the courts were transferred to that of Asahel Rawlings, who came to this county in 1817, and who had settled near the present site of "Old Dallas," Dallas having become by law the county seat. Nimrod Pendergrass settled on the Tennessee, about one mile above the mouth of Opossum Creek, in 1817 or 1818, having come from Rhea County. In about 1819 or 1820 James Smith came from Kentucky and settled also near Opossum Creek. James Cozby, with his sons, Woods and Robert, came to this county about the time the Cherokees were moved to the south side of the Tennessee, and in 1820 bought the place formerly owned by the Cherokee chief, James Brown, about ten miles above Chattanooga on the North Chickamauga. Andrew Johnson came early and still lives some distance above Hixson. William McGill came from Knox County, probably before the organization of the county, and lived near Robert Patterson. John Hanna came from Virginia in 1820, and lived on what was known as the Wallace farm. John Brown, James Varner and Gilbert Vandegriff were also early settlers, as was Nathan Shipley whose father was killed by Mitchell, near Joseph Paine's. Preston Gann and George Sawyers came about the same time and lived below what is now Hixson Station. They were neighbors of Ephraim Hixson, who came to Hamilton County from the Sequatchie Valley in 1830. John Russell was a very early settler and lived near Sale Creek. Thomas Coulter was here before 1820, for then he was dealing in lands. William Rogers lived near the present Coulterville, as did James McDonald, whose widow is now living at Benjamin McDonald's. This family are descendants of the celebrated Scottish chief, Roland McDonald. Elisha Rogers was one of the early settlers as was Jacob Hartman. Hugh, James and David Cunningham lived on Mountain Creek, near Daniel Sciveley. One of Jacob Hartman's grants from the State was so located that one of its boundary lines crossed a branch of Mountain Creek "at the place where Hugh Cunningham was drowned." Daniel Sciveley lived north of the Tennessee, near Walden's Ridge.

Thomas R. Russell was the first surveyor the county had, and judging from his work he was an educated and competent surveyor, as his lines can now be readily found and followed. George Williams was a very early settler living near the "Suck." Henry Rogers lived two and a half miles above Hixson; Joseph Rogers who came into the county in 1831 built a grist-mill on North Chickamauga Creek. David Beck, grandfather of the present county register, came to the county with his family of thirteen children in 1822, and Beryl Smith, who lived one-half mile below Hixson, came into the county in 1830, John Friar coming also about the same time. Abraham Thomas was a later comer, having lived originally in Virginia. He then moved to Bledsoe County, and finally to Georgetown, in what is now James County, in 1837, one year after John P. Long, at present the oldest living resident of Chattanooga, came to Hamilton County. Thomas Shirley, now living at the age of ninety in James County, came to Dallas at a very early day, and is probably the oldest of the early settlers of Hamilton County now living.

In the early part of the century John Walling with a *posse* of men, among whom were a Mr. Warren and a Mr. Green, came from Virginia to what is now Hamilton County, in pursuit of Indians who had captured and carried away as prisoners two white women. The *posse* overtook the Indians and recaptured the women on what is now generally called "Walden's Ridge," but which is sometimes named, as originally, "Walling's Ridge." Mr. Walling and his *posse*, after the recapture of the women, built a kind of fort on this ridge, which they occupied for some days, until, supposing the Indians had become reconciled to the loss of their captives, they returned home and restored the women to their friends. The Indians, however, followed and killed Mr. Walling while he was plowing in his field. From this circumstance the ridge was named originally "Walling's Ridge." In some unknown way the name was subsequently corrupted into "Wallen's Ridge," and it is now so known in some of the departments at Washington; and still later by another orthographical tergiversation it became "Walden's Ridge." It is believed, however, that B. B. Cannon, who was county surveyor from 1830 to 1837, is responsible for this last form of the word, as it is always spelled "Walden's" by him in his survey; and if this supposition be correct he was not without reason for its application, for a part of the old Walling family spell their name "Walden," but the majority adhere to the original form, Walling.

A very large grant of land was made in 1795 by North Carolina to Stockley Donelson in what is now Hamilton County. Nominally it was for 20,000 acres, but its boundaries as described contained within their limits nearly 150,000 acres. This grant extended from the mouth of Richland Creek in Rhea County to the mouth of North Chickamauga Creek, on what was then supposed to be the line between North Carolina and Georgia; up North Chickamauga Creek to the Cumberland Mountains (that branch now known as Walden's Ridge); thence along that ridge to Richland Creek, to a point where Dayton now stands, and thence down that creek to the beginning. Langdon Carter's grant was made in 1795, and Robert Patterson in about 1807 bought 300 acres of this grant lying on what is now known as Opossum Creek, then Mill Creek, and previously, Deep River, and so designated on grants and title papers. Mr. Patterson settled on his purchase about that time and resided thereon until after the extinguishment of the Indian title in 1819, when he was dispossessed in the following manner: In about 1821 William B. Carter and other heirs of Langdon Carter brought suit against Robert Patterson for the recovery of the land, founding their title upon a 640-acre grant to Langdon Carter, their father. In Hamilton County Mr. Patterson was so popular that the Carter heirs feared justice would not be done them there, and hence took a change of venue to Rhea, where they prevailed over Patterson, who thereupon moved a short distance above, and the place thus given to the Carters was occupied until within a few years by John Hughes.

The names of other early settlers with the approximate dates of their arrival in the county follow in connection with recorded land grants and deeds. The first deed registered in what are now the Hamilton County records was one by which Stockley Donelson conveyed to Charles McClung 640 acres for $200. The land was described as being "in the eastern district on the north side of the Tennessee River, on the first big creek above the mouth of Chickamauga Creek, called by some North Chickamauga, beginning some distance below a very large spring on the south side of the creek at a post oak and red oak trees and blazed black oak, running thence east 226 poles, crossing the spring branch at 24 poles; thence north 453 poles; thence west 226 poles, and thence south 453 poles to the beginning." This deed was dated October 23, 1799, and recorded April 11, 1820. Then follow five other deeds from Stockley Donelson to Charles McClung, all dated in July, 1797, each for 640 acres, except one for 600 acres, the price for the 600 acres being $100; for two of the 640-acre tracts, $107 each; for one, $150, and for the other, $200. Then follows the record of a grant, No. 166, by North Carolina to John Hackett for 600 acres of land for the consideration of £10 for each 100 acres, the grant being signed by "Richard Caswell, Esq., Governor, Captain-General and Commander-in-Chief," September 20, 1787. Then follows a deed signed by John Hackett, by which, on the same day, he conveyed to Richard Bearden this same grant, No. 166, together with 300 acres adjoining for $1,000. The first quit-claim deed registered was by James Cozby to Joseph Dunham, of a tract of land "lying in the eastern district on the north side of the Tennessee, a small distance above the Suck, and being a part of the 20,000 acres granted by the State of North Carolina to Stockley Donelson, No. 283, and dated July 20, 1795, and being the same land that John Hackett conveyed to Joseph Dunham February 23, 1809." This quit-claim deed was dated February 24, 1809. The above were all before the organization of Hamilton County. The first deed registered after said organization was dated February 23, 1821, and by it Richard Timberlake conveyed to James Brown a tract of land on North Chickamauga Creek of 640 acres for $3,000.

The first bill of sale recorded was by Jacob Roberson to John Brown for two negroes, one a woman named Elizabeth, about thirty-five years old, and the other a boy, named Joseph, about four years old, for $600, under date of May 6, 1820. The second was by John Russell to John Brown, under date of December 9, 1815, for two negroes, one a woman thirty years old, named Aney, the other a girl, Erager, twelve years old, for $530. Still earlier than this John Russell sold to John Brown, December 13, 1808, a negro boy, twenty-two years old, named Peter, for $500, and on the 19th of the same month John Brown bought of "Robert Brown, of the Cherokee Nation," a "male slave by the name of Cyrus," for $600. Robert Brown made his mark, as did also Susanna Brown, November 29, 1817, to a similar instrument, by which she conveyed to John Brown, for the consideration of $500, a yellow boy about fifteen years of age, by the name of Moses. According to the records John Brown appears to have been the principal slave buyer of those early days.

At the time of the arrival of the first settler in what is now Hamilton County the entire county was occupied by the Cherokees, but so far as is now ascertainable there were but few if any of these old settlers, who were slain by the red man's tomahawk or spear. The warlike spirit of the Cherokee, originally as fierce as that of any other Indian, had become to a great extent subdued by long contact and numerous disastrous conflicts with the superior skill of his white brother, who, though an intruder, was determined and destined to possess the soil. Though in the opening years of the nineteenth century this part of the Tennessee Valley was singularly free from hostile encounters, there had been previously an expedition undertaken, which had for its objective point a locality already famous, and since made more famous, in the military annals of the country. This was the expedition of Cols. Evan Shelby and John Montgomery against the irrepressible Chickamaugas, whose town, Chickamauga, was nearly a mile in length and extended up and down Chickamauga* Creek a few miles above its mouth. This expedition, which, under the pilotage of a Mr. Hudson, came down the Tennessee, in 1779, entered the Chickamauga Creek, and, disembarking on its bank, captured an Indian, whom they compelled to guide them to the town. The Chickamaugas were taken so completely by surprise that, making no resistance, they fled to the fastnesses of the hills and mountains, and were pursued. The number of the Indians thus attacked was about 500. They were commanded by the chiefs, Dragging Canoe and Big Fool, and were equal in numbers to the expedition under Shelby and Montgomery. Pursuit was made, a camp broken up on Laurel Creek, and Little Owl's Town and other towns taken and burned. The troops of Shelby and Montgomery were the first white men that had seen the rich lands of the Tennessee Valley, in what are now the counties of Hamilton, Rhea, Roane and Knox, and were the first to spread glowing accounts of their fertility and beauty; the consequence being that almost immediately a strong current of immigration was turned toward and into this fair and inviting region.

Subsequently to this expedition against the Chickamaugas, a battle was fought on Lookout Mountain between the Indians, commanded by the great chief Wynca on the one side, and Tennessee volunteers commanded by Gen. John Sevier, on the other. This was the first battle of Lookout Mountain of which there is any record or tradition, and was fought in 1782, Gen. Sevier being, as usual, victorious, compelling a truce and a surrender of prisoners and slaves. The second battle of Lookout Mountain was fought in 1788 by Gen. Joseph Martin, with Col. Robert Love commanding a regiment from Washington County, Col. Kennedy from Greene County and Col. Doherty from lower down. The forces under these officers were fired upon from every cranny and cliff and tree; three of their captains—Hardin, Fuller and Gibson—were killed, and Capt. Thomas Gibson wounded. This was six years before the famous Nickajack expedition, an account of which may be found in the general history, on page 97.

Until after the Hiwassee purchase, made in 1818, the Cherokees continued to live on both sides of the Tennessee River, but in 1819, according to the terms of the treaty under which the above named purchase was made, they moved to the south side of that river, and the north side was left to the exclusive occupancy of the white man. The territory

---

*Chickamauga means "dull, sluggish stream," according to John P. Long.

south of the Tennessee was then occupied by the Cherokees until 1838, when, under the provisions of the treaty of New Echota,* made by the Rev. J. F. Schermerhorn with a small fraction of the tribe, this portion of their lands was wrested from them. The Rev. Mr. Schermerhorn was selected by President Jackson to make this treaty by reason of his many previous successes as a treaty-maker among the Indians of the Northwest. In 1829 a fraudulent treaty had been forced upon the Choctaws by United States commissioners appointed for that purpose, and now those of the Cherokees who did consent to this treaty of New Echota did so under the conviction that removal, even if resisted and postponed, was ultimately inevitable, and that those who should first remove to their new home west of Arkansas would have numerous advantages over those who should move last. But while this treaty of New Echota was a sham and a fraud, yet there were many good reasons and some peculiar ones for desiring the removal of the Cherokees at that time. The nation, consisting of about 18,000 individuals, was entirely surrounded by white people, the lower stratum of which race was gradually but surely ruining the young men of the tribe by teaching them the vices of gambling and the use of intoxicating drinks, and was as certainly bringing the young women to ruin by inducing them to the crime of prostitution, and thus was threatened the destruction of the entire nation. Far west of the Mississippi they would be, for years at least, comparatively free from contaminating connection with these vices and crimes—these tantalizing sarcasms upon civilization.

The Rev. Mr. Schermerhorn made proclamation to the effect that he would meet the Cherokee nation at New Echota and with them make a treaty for their lands; but it was not until after the third attempt was made that this gospel messenger succeeded in getting up a treaty, and then in the absence of several of the head men of the Nation, who had gone to Washington to confer directly with the President and Secretary of War. The Cherokees were at that time divided into two parties, known respectively as the Ridge party and the Ross party. John Ridge, son of Maj. Ridge, and John Ross were the respective chiefs of these parties. The Ridge party, though numerically much the smaller, was in favor of removal and in favor of the treaty, while the Ross party was almost if not quite unanimously and very strongly opposed to the removal. This was especially the case with the young men, from whom the white settlers for some time, both before and after the conclusion of the treaty, expected warlike demonstrations, and whom it was exceedingly difficult for the old men to restrain. Through the wise counsels of the old men,

---
*New Town.

however, peace was maintained. The proportion of the Ridge party to the Ross party was about as 440 to 17,800, which numbers reveal in the clearest light the fraudulent nature of the "treaty" which was made in December, 1835, with the Ridge portion of the Nation and bitterly opposed by the Ross portion. These numbers are arrived at in the following manner: President Jackson, because of John Ross' opposition to the treaty, determined if possible to weaken his influence with his nation, and thus render them more tractable and facilitate their removal. With this object in view, some time after the ratification of the treaty, he caused to be called a convention of the tribe to decide upon a proposed change in the method of paying to them their annuities; that is to say whether the Government should continue to pay these annuities to the secretary of the council, who should also continue to apportion them out to the heads of families, or whether in future the Government agent should pay the respective shares directly to the heads of families. Chief Ross advised his people not to attend the convention; but notwithstanding this advice about one-half the voting population of his party attended, together with the entire voting population of the Ridge party. The vote upon the question having been taken, it was found that 110 votes had been cast in favor of the President's proposition and 2,225 against it. The voting population of the Ross party was therefore about 4,450, and of the Ridge party 110, and assuming that including women and children there were four members of the tribe to each voter, the entire number of the Ridge party is found to be 440, and of the Ross party 17,800. The treaty was made, according to the New American Cyclopedia, with three chiefs and about 600 men, women and children, and according to the Rev. W. Willey, with sixty men and no chiefs. The three chiefs who had sold their nation came to an untimely end. Maj. Ridge was waylaid and shot, John Ridge was taken from his bed and cut to pieces, and Elias Boudinot was decoyed from his house and slain with hatchets and knives. John Ross and his friends expressed the deepest regret at these barbarities, and the United States officers scoured the country for the murderers in vain.

The announcement having been made that the treaty had been ratified,* the Ridge party soon began to make preparations for removal, and before the two years of grace expired were safely settled in their new home; but the Ross party continued to struggle peacefully for their rights. In the winter of 1836–37 an effort for a new treaty was made, and in July, 1837, a delegation was chosen to visit Washington at the opening of the next Congress, and lay their cause before that body. This case, sustained

---

*The ratification occurred May 23, 1836.

by the signatures of almost the entire Cherokee Nation, and by numerous remonstrances from citizens of the United States, was presented in a most lucid and able manner, but no substantial modification of the treaty was ever effected. Still the Ross party could not believe that a treaty so iniquitous and oppressive would be carried into effect; and, acting under the advice of their great chief, made no preparations to go, simply waited to be removed, or rather made preparations to remain, as when, on the 23d of May, 1838, the soldiers under command of Gen. Winfield Scott, began to gather them in from their cherished homes to the rendezvous, their grounds had been planted for a larger crop than usual. The attitude of the entire tribe in this to them sorrowful emergency is well illustrated by that of a single individual, John Benge, a full blooded Cherokee Indian, who said that even then, when the time under the treaty had come to go, he would not move one step of his own accord; but that if a United States musket was presented, and he ordered to go, even though the musket were held and he ordered to move by a boy but ten years old, he would unresistingly obey. As a general thing in order to collect the Cherokees at the rendezvous, the lower end of Missionary Ridge near Rossville, it was necessary for the troops to quietly surround a portion of the tribe during the night, and the next morning bring to the appointed place all those thus surrounded, and even then it was always found that portions of families were absent, having either purposely gone away to such distances as not to be surrounded, or having evaded the detachments of troops so sent out, in order if possible to remain, instead of going with the rest of the tribe west of the Mississippi River. At length, after much difficulty and the exercise of much patience by the soldiers, about one-half of the Ross party were collected and for the most part loaded on flatboats and floated off down the Tennessee, others being marched overland. Owing to the lateness and increasing heat of the season, the other half were permitted to remain until the ensuing fall, when under a contract to that effect made by John Ross with the United States Government, Mr. Ross himself led them to their new reservation in the Indian Territory.

One of the incidents of the removal worthy of preservation is the following: A small party of Indians, consisting of Chief Bushyhead, his wife and their daughter and a young man, were coming through Rossville Gap in Missionary Ridge toward the rendezvous. The daughter becoming conscious of the immediate approach of an important epoch in her history, the young man was sent forward to the store at Rossville to await the coming of the rest of the little party. Upon arriving at the store the young brave was questioned as to when Bushyhead would arrive, and gave for reply that he would be at the store in about an hour, as he and his wife had simply remained in the timber with their daughter until she should be delivered of her expectant heir. In about an hour the remaining three, their number now increased to four, appeared in front of the store, the old people walking, the newly made mother riding upon a very poor and sharp-backed pony, apparently as unconcerned as if nothing unusual had occurred, and the newly born infant being tenderly carried and cared for in the arms of its grandmother. After remaining at the store a few minutes to purchase some calico or gingham out of which to make a new suit for the new comer, the young woman not having meanwhile alighted from her pony, the little party, Chief Bushyhead, his wife, daughter, grandson and the young brave, proceeded to the rendezvous, where to this narrative they are lost to view.

Missionary Ridge, made famous in later years by being the scene of one of the most important battles of the civil war, derives its name from having been the scene of the benevolent and pious labors of missionaries sent out to the Cherokees by the American Board of Commissioners for Foreign Missions. This mission on the ridge was established in 1817 on the south bank of Chickamauga Creek. The first missionaries to arrive were the Rev. Cyrus Kingsbury, a recent graduate from Andover Theological Seminary, the Rev. Ainsworth E. Blunt, and the Rev. John Vail. The mission being established was named Brainerd Mission, in honor of the Rev. David Brainerd, a celebrated American Missionary to the Indians, who died in 1747. The Rev. Loring S. Williams, accompanied by Moody Hall, arrived from New York State in March, 1817, a few weeks after the arrival of Mr. Kingsbury. The Secretary of War had been authorized by President Madison to instruct the Indian Agent to erect a schoolhouse, and a house for the teacher to be followed by others as occasion might require. The mission thus established was a compound of mission, boarding-school and agricultural college, and to conduct it imposed upon the missionaries immense labor and care. The government contractor failed to build the houses ordered by the President, and the missionaries themselves were soon busily engaged in making brick, burning lime, digging cellars and a well, and in conveying their corn meal a distance of forty miles. Houses being erected it then became a matter of economy to erect a mill in which to grind corn, and hence the erection of "Missionary Mill," on the west bank of Chickamauga Creek. To obtain water with which to propel the machinery of this mill, they dug a race three-fourths of a mile long to Spring Creek. The race though not in use is visible to the present day. The school established here for the education of the Indian youth was a great success, often having present at the same time 500 scholars. At the expi-

ration of about eighteen months the Revs. Kingsbury and Williams were transferred to the Choctaws in Mississippi, where they remained nineteen years. Mr. Kingsbury was succeeded by the Rev. Ard Hoyt, the Revs. Mr. Blunt and Mr. Vail remaining with Mr. Hoyt upon the Ridge. After the death of the Rev. Mr. Hoyt his place was filled by the Rev. Mr. Ellsworth who after the treaty of New Echota went West with the Ross party, Rev. Mr. Blunt settled down upon the "Blunt farm," whence he removed to Dalton where he died since the war. On the 27th of May, 1819, President Monroe, accompanied by Gen. Gaines, appeared unannounced at the door of the mission. He expressed himself as well pleased with all he saw, and ordered erected at the public expense a better schoolhouse for the girls. The mission was conducted until the removal of the Cherokees in 1838, the Lord's Supper being celebrated for the last time at Brainerd, August 19, 1838.

The postoffice at Rossville was established in 1827, James Coody being commissioned postmaster April 28. His successor was N. D. Scales, commissioned July 28, 1832. This postoffice was changed to Brainerd, February 6, 1834, when John C. Ellsworth became postmaster. Ainsworth E. Blunt was commissioned September 17, 1836, and the postoffice was discontinued February 20, 1838.

The mission property consisting of 160 acres of land together with the buildings, was sold by the Rev. John Vail to Thomas Crutchfield, and by him in 1852 was sold to Philamon Bird, who built a larger mill on the site of Missionary Mill, which since then has borne the name of "Bird's Mill." Mr. Bird constructed a dam across Chickamauga Creek, thus rendering useless the Missionary race. At this mill there are now three run of buhrs, a bolting apparatus and a saw mill, the capacity of the water-wheels being equal to seventy-five horse power. The old missionary house much reduced in size is now occupied by S. H. Bird, son of Philamon Bird, who died in 1871, and a frame church building known as "The Brainerd Church" stands about half a mile to the westward of the mill. In the old Mission Cemetery near the mill, now nearly overgrown with weeds and cedar trees is a small monument bearing the following inscription:

"Here lie the remains of SAMUEL WORCESTER, D. D., pastor of the Tabernacle Church, Salem, Mass., and first Secretary of the American Board of Commissioners for Foreign Missions: born in 1770 and died June 7, 1821."

His remains were afterward removed to Massachusetts for permanent sepulture.

The Rev. Loring S. Williams, mentioned above, writing from Iowa

March 4, 1878, to a friend in Chattanooga, inquired about the identification of a cave which he supposed was on Missionary Ridge near the bridle path from the mission to Ross' Landing. It was about 30 feet long, 25 feet wide and 15 feet high, and contained about 200 skeletons. His inquiry led to investigation by Gen. John T. Wilder and George W. Rider, who found the cave, not on the top of Missionary Ridge, but on the farm of Frank Gardenhire, about 100 yards from the mouth of Citico Creek. The opening leading to the cave was about 4 feet high and 6 feet wide, and inclined downward at an angle of about 30°. Frank Gardenhire's grandfather, who was the first man buried in Chattanooga Cemetery, told him that the Indians of the long ago attacked and killed the occupants of a flatboat from whom they caught the small-pox.* When the fever attacked them they would rush into the creek to cool off; many of them died in consequence, and a portion of their remains were deposited in this cave. Other remains for many years lay bleaching in the sun along the banks of the creek and in the woods until, during the civil war, they were carried away by army surgeons, officers and privates.

It has been recorded that the first sessions of the court of pleas and quarter sessions, and of the circuit court, were held at the house of Hasten Poe. They were next held at the house of John Mitchell, and then at Dallas, the first county seat of Hamilton County, named in honor of Alexander James Dallas, an American statesman who died in 1817. The county seat remained at Dallas until 1840, when it was removed to "Vann's Town," and soon afterward to Harrison, a town about twelve miles northeast of Chattanooga, named in honor of William Henry Harrison, ninth President of the United States. Here it remained until 1870, when an election held for that purpose decided its removal to Chattanooga. The building that had been used by the two courts at Chattanooga, from their establishment in 1858, was then used by the consolidated courts until 1879, when the new courthouse was completed. This building stands on the northeast corner of East Seventh and Walnut Streets. It is a fine structure and cost, with the real estate, as follows: Building, $39,000; ground, $16,000; architect, $1,800; bell, $775; clock, $1,750; furniture, $2,800; fence and grading, $2,500; total, $64,625. A. C. Bruce was the architect. The bell is 53 feet in circumference and 4 feet high, and, with its appliances, weighs 4,600 pounds. On the 17th of April a meeting of the bar of Chattanooga was held in the new building, which extended the thanks of the bar to the building committee for the production of such an elegant courthouse, the building committee consisting of W. D. Van Dyke, James W. Clift, W. P. Rathburn, Thomas Crutchfield and D. C. Trewhitt.

---

*See General History, pages 130–31.

On January 12, 1880, the committee to superintend the construction of the new jail held a meeting, the committee consisting of W. D. Van Dyke, W. P. Rathburn, R. M. Barton, M. H. Clift and J. H. Van Deman. A contract was made with Charles Sundquist for the purchase of his property across Walnut Street from the courthouse, and with T. J. Dolan & Son, of Fort Wayne, Ind., as architects. The new jail was completed in the spring of 1881, at a cost of $33,530.83, including the lot.

Because of the destruction by the war of the county and city records made previous to the year 1864, and also of most of the newspaper files, but a meager history of the county previous to that year can be given. The date of its division into civil districts can not now be recalled. However, a few of these can be and are here introduced. The Tenth Civil District of what was formerly Bledsoe County, which was attached to the county of Hamilton in 1856, was made the Fifteenth Civil District of Hamilton County, November 4, 1857, and the First and Second Civil Districts of Marion County, which were attached to Hamilton County at the same time, were by the same act of the Legislature, respectively constituted the Sixteenth and Seventeenth Civil Districts of Hamilton County, and the Seventeenth Civil District was afterward attached to the common law and chancery courts of Chattanooga.

The political complexion of the people of Hamilton County from 1832 to the breaking out of the civil war is shown by the following figures: Presidential vote, 1832, Andrew Jackson, 100; 1836, Martin Van Buren, 158; Hugh L. White, 215; 1840, Martin Van Buren, 473; William Henry Harrison, 606; 1844, James K. Polk, 624; Henry Clay, 644; 1848, Lewis Cass, 634; Zachary Taylor, 685; 1852, Franklin Pierce, 648; Winfield Scott, 774; 1856, James Buchanan, 1,051; Millard Fillmore, 1,064; 1860, John C. Breckenridge, 820; John Bell, 1,074; Stephen A. Douglas, 165. An examination of the above vote shows that while the two parties, Democratic and Whig, were sometimes very nearly equal in strength, yet the Whigs were uniformly in the majority. Following is the gubernatorial vote previous to the war: 1839, James K. Polk, 436; Newton Cannon, 622; 1841, James K. Polk, 560; James C. Jones, 628; 1843, James K. Polk, 621; James C. Jones, 628; 1845, Aaron V. Brown, 548; Ephraim H. Foster, 613; 1847, Aaron V. Brown, 721; Neill S. Brown, 628; 1849, William Trousdale, 601; Neill S. Brown, 750; 1851, William Trousdale, 601; William B. Campbell, 885; 1853, Andrew Johnson, 972; Gustave A. Henry, 786; 1855, Andrew Johnson, 1,044; Meredith P. Gentry, 966; 1857, Isham G. Harris, 890; Robert Hatton, 959; 1859, Isham G. Harris, 1,056; John Netherland, 1,121.

Following is a list of the members of the Legislature from Hamilton

County previous to the war: Senators—James Standifer, 1821; John Billingsly, 1823; James Preston, 1825; James I. Greene, 1829-31; Mills Vernon, 1833-35; Richard Waterhouse, 1841; J. M. Anderson, 1843; Isaac Robertson, 1845; J. M. Anderson, 1847; James W. Gillespie, 1851; John M. Havron, 1853; J. C. Burch, 1857; J. A. Minnis, 1859-61. Representatives—James C. Mitchell, 1821; Thomas Kelly, 1823-25; Thomas J. Campbell, 1831-33; Joseph M. Anderson, 1837; William J. Standifer, 1839; Daniel R. Rawlings, 1841; James A. Whiteside, 1845-47; John M. Havron, 1849-51; John C. Burch, 1855; J. W. White, 1857; Daniel C. Trewhitt, 1859.

The above figures and facts show that Hamilton County, after the election of Gen. Jackson to the presidency in 1832, was generally Whig, the exceptions being that sometimes the Democratic candidate for governor received a majority of her votes. It was natural that when the war came on for the perpetuation of American slavery, this county should be strongly opposed to uniting her fortunes with a new government based upon the principles of disintegration, and under which even if successful, the States would be professedly bound together only by a rope of sand. At the time of the breaking out of the war there were in this county about 1,500 slaves, the census of 1880 enumerating 1,419 and 192 free persons; yet, notwithstanding that numbers of Whigs owned slaves, when they were compelled to choose between secession and the abolition of slavery they chose abolition, and so far as was practicable remained true to the Union cause. Those who favored the government of the Confederate States enrolled themselves in companies which either joined the rebel army or remained at home to do duty as guards. Troops were sent into Hamilton County to overawe and subdue those of the people who favored the Union, and these, though organized and secretly holding themselves in readiness to rise at the approach of the Federal Army, were obliged, meanwhile, to hide their arms and ammunition in hollow trees and other places, and to communicate with each other often stealthily and by watchwords and signs.

One of the earliest episodes connected with the war was the visit of the Hon. Jefferson Davis to Chattanooga January 22, 1861, on his way home to Mississippi from his seat in the Senate of the United States. He delivered a speech in the Crutchfield House, denouncing the Government of the United States, and calling on the people of Tennessee to unite her destinies with her sister Southern States, pleading with them that he only wanted their influence and strength, that the cotton States would pay the debt to be created by the war, that Tennessee would never be called upon to pay one dollar of that debt, that the South must unite in a solid body, march upon the Northern States and lay their cities in ashes, for in them was the strength of the North, and the sure way to touch a Yankee's soul was to strike his purse. The speech of Mr. Davis closed with the celebrated sentiment of Patrick Henry, "Give me liberty or give me death!"

Among the numbers, Unionists and Secessionists, who listened to this speech was William Crutchfield, whose Union-loving heart was stirred to its inmost depths, and whose patriotic sentiments found expression in a rousing, denunciatory speech in reply. He stigmatized Davis as a traitor to his country, a perjured villain, as being now engaged in an attempt to overthrow a government he had sworn to protect and defend, and turning to the people pointed out to them their "future military despot." He denied that Mr. Davis had any right to dictate to the people what course they should pursue, and said they would fight for the Union, the constitution and the enforcement of the laws. This speech, being full of feeling, stirred up strong feeling on the part of the friends of the Southern cause, and it is generally believed that had not Mr. Crutchfield been compelled by his brother, Thomas Crutchfield, to cease speaking he would soon have been killed.

Great alarm was created throughout this part of the State by the simultaneous burning of the railroad bridges between Bristol and Chattanooga. This burning was done to assist the Union Armies in their expected advance into East Tennessee, and immediately three regiments were sent by the Confederate authorities to Chattanooga to punish all who might be found guilty of having participated in the bridge burning and generally to arrest and crush out the spirit of the "Lincolnites." Quite a large number of Union men were arrested upon the charge of bridge burning, who were placed in tents, strongly guarded and closely watched, and a Confederate spy apparently forced in among them for the purpose of ascertaining who were the guilty ones, but although there were two or three of the bridge burners among them the spy failed to make the discovery, and they were at length released upon taking the oath to support the Government of the Confederate States and upon giving bonds in the sum of $20,000.

The Confederate authorities had everything their own way in Hamilton County until the arrival of the Army of the Cumberland under Gen. Rosecrans, which, after the Tullahoma campaign, commenced crossing the Tennessee River on the 29th of August, 1863, and with the exception of Gen. Hazen's brigade was wholly across by September 4. The crossing of the river by the main body of Rosecrans' invading army was made below Chattanooga, and was rendered practicable by one of the most brilliant feints of the war, which largely contributed to Gen. Bragg's misconception of Rosecrans' aggressive strategy. This brilliant movement was made by four brigades, commanded respectively by Gens. Hazen, Wagner, Minty and Wilder, the four brigades numbering between 6,000 and 7,000 men. This force, under Gen. Hazen, took position on the north bank of the river, from William's Island to Kingston, but in heaviest force opposite Chattanooga and the mouth of South Chickamauga Creek. The extent of front, the show of strength and the vigorous shelling of Chattanooga by Wilder's and Wagner's artillery on August 21, the troops at Pikeville, and Crittenden's corps in the Sequatchie Valley—the bold expression of this whole movement, led Gen. Bragg to expect Rosecrans' army to cross the Cumberland Mountains to the north of Chattanooga, where he was prepared to receive it and where he could hold it in check for weeks, and perhaps for months. Under cover of this activity, Rosecrans effected the crossing of the Tennessee at four places, Caperton's Ferry, Bridgeport, the mouth of Battle Creek and Shellmound. This success of Gen. Rosecrans in crossing the Tennessee where he was least expected by Gen. Bragg caused this general to evacuate Chattanooga, which movement was completed by the morning of September 9, and as it was believed that Bragg was in full retreat before the army that had maneuvered him out of Chattanooga that army determined on a vigorous pursuit. Bragg, however, was not in full retreat; he was concentrating his army before Rosecrans, to save his own line of supplies, and also in the hope of striking the columns of Rosecrans as they separately debouched from the mountain gaps. Gen. Rosecrans' misconception of Bragg's intention nearly cost him his army, and in all human probability would have done so, had Gen. Bragg's subordinates been obedient to orders, and had Gen. Bragg himself been able to take advantage of his opportunities. On the 9th Gen. Crittenden, by command of Gen. Rosecrans, occupied Chattanooga preparatory to his participation in a general pursuit of the enemy by the whole army. In this pursuit, so ordered, the National Army moved forward in three columns, commanded respectively by Gens. Crittenden, Thomas and McCook, the distance from the extreme left of Crittenden's corps, the Twenty-first, to the extreme right of McCook's corps, the Twentieth, being about forty-five miles, Gen. Thomas with the Fourteenth Army Corps occupying the center. During the 10th the three columns moved in pursuance of orders, Gen. Crittenden on the Ringgold road, Gen. Thomas toward Lafayette, and Gen. McCook toward Alpine and Summerville. Upon reaching Alpine, McCook was in a state of complete isolation, and near Bragg's army, learning which, he judged it best not to march on Summerville, for at that place he would be in a position to be attacked and crushed by the entire rebel army. Gen. Crittenden had moved to the east on the Ringgold road, and Gen. Thomas was moving directly upon Bragg's army 50,000 strong, concentrated at and near Lafayette. Gen. Negley in the advance of Thomas's column, on the 9th, passed into McLemore's Cove, almost into the midst of Bragg's vast army, which movement Gen. Bragg rightly interpreted as meaning that a hurried pursuit was being made after his force under the idea that it was in full retreat, and he also quickly saw how the National Army was exposed to attack and defeat in detail. This was precisely the condition of things he had hoped for and now was his first opportunity. At midnight of that day he gave orders to Hindman to prepare his division to move against Negley, and gave orders to other of his generals to properly support Hindman. Buckner joined Hindman on the afternoon of the 10th, and Polk with his division was ordered to support Hindman during the expected operations in McLemore's Cove. The entire force disposed to crush Negley and Baird was 30,000 men. Bragg said in his orders sent by courier to Hindman, "Cleburne will attack in front the moment your guns are heard." About daylight of the next morning Bragg joined Cleburne and both generals impatiently waited nearly all day for the sound of Hindman's guns. Bragg was very urgent in regard to this movement, for he rightly anticipated that the National Army would concentrate as soon as its general should discover that he was not in full retreat. Van Horne, in his "History of the Army of the Cumberland," says: "Fortunately for Negley and the army there was delay." In point of fact, there were two delays, one caused by a proposed change of plan by Buckner and Hindman after their commands had united on the afternoon of the 10th, which proposed change Gen. Bragg did not approve, and at midnight repeated his original orders with emphasis; but during the night while awaiting his superior's reply to his proposition, Gen. Hindman and his staff remained at the widow Wallace's house, and imbibed too freely of her excellent wine, and when Gen, Bragg's peremptory order came to attack Negley early on the morning of the 11th, Gen. Hindman was in no condition to carry it into execution, and hence Bragg and Cleburne waited until long past noon in great anxiety for Hindman's attack, and when about the middle of the afternoon his first gun was heard, Cleburne at once pressed forward and to his great disappointment discovered that Negley had fallen back to Stevens' Gap. Thus failed the design on Gen. Thomas corps, and Gen. Bragg, still pursuing his original purpose of attacking and defeating the Union Army in detail before it could concentrate, on the evening of the 12th, ordered Gen.

Polk to move against and attack Gen. Crittenden's divided corps at daydawn, on the morning of the 13th, that the National Army was concentrating, and that it was "highly important that your attack in the morning should be quick and decided." But during the 12th, Gen. Wilder's mounted brigade, which had been pushed too far out toward Ringgold, discovering its error, made a brilliant attack upon Gen. Polk's position; and by the vigor of its movement, and the rapidity of its firing, created the impression upon that general that he was attacked by a very superior force, and hence at 11 o'clock that night he sent a dispatch to Bragg, stating that he had taken a strong position for defense and asking that he be heavily reinforced. Gen. Bragg again, as in the case of Hindman, sent Polk an immediate order not to defer his attack, and early on the morning of the 13th, at the head of Buckner's command, went to the front; and found that no advance had been made by Polk, and that Crittenden, having reunited his forces, had recrossed the Chickamauga. Thus, again, did Gen. Bragg's plans fail to strike and crush the National Army in detail.

After the first day's battle of Chickamauga, September 19, had ceased, with results generally favorable to the Union forces, Gen. Bragg, in making preparations for the battle of the 20th, divided his army into two commands: Gen. Longstreet to the left and Gen. Polk to the right. His plan of battle for the 20th was for Polk to assault in force on his extreme right at day dawn, after which the attack was to be taken up by the divisions to Polk's left, rapidly in succession, and when the entire line became engaged, to move forward vigorously and persistently throughout its entire length, at the same time wheeling on Longstreet's left as a pivot, and constantly pressing back Rosecrans' left, so as to obtain possession of the road to Chattanooga. Before daylight Bragg took his position in the rear of the center of his line and waited until after sunrise with increasing anxiety and disappointment for Polk to begin his attack. Bragg then sent a staff officer to ascertain and report the reason for this delay. The staff officer, finding that Polk had spent the night on the east side of Chickamauga Creek, rode over to him, found him at breakfast and delivered his message; meanwhile Bragg, impatient at the continued delay, himself rode over to the right wing and found the troops wholly unprepared for the attack. At length Polk appeared and he was urged to a prompt execution of his orders and a vigorous attack.

This delay on the part of Polk enabled Rosecrans to so adjust the forces of his left wing as to be partially prepared to receive the terrible assault of the rebel right when it was made, and it is entirely probable that the battle of the 20th, notwithstanding delays in the obeying of orders by some of Rosecrans' generals, would have been a magnificent victory instead of a partial defeat for the Army of the Cumberland, but for the conduct of Brig.-Gen. Thomas J. Wood, in the attempt to obey a part of a contradictory order sent to him at 10:45 A. M. directing him to "close up on Reynolds as fast as possible and support him." This was undoubtedly the pivotal point in that day's battle, but as it is presented with sufficient accuracy and fullness on page 557 of the general history, it is merely referred to here in the enumeration of the turning points of this battle fought magnificently by American soldiers on both sides under Gen. Rosecrans and Gen. Bragg. The next and last pivotal point in the battle of the 20th was when Gen. Rosecrans at Rossville took the advice of Gen. Garfield, his chief of staff, and himself retired to Chattanooga to re-form his retreating army, Gen. Garfield riding to the front to learn the position and condition of Gen. Thomas' army. It is now generally believed that had Rosecrans ridden to the front and found Gen. Thomas as Gen. Garfield found him, undefeated and refusing to be defeated, the portions of the Army of the Cumberland that had given way would have been rallied, returned to the field and turned partial defeat into complete victory. As it was, Gen. Thomas by his magnificent staying qualities won for himself that day the proud title of "The Rock of Chickamauga." Considering all things this was the hardest fought and most bloody battle of the Rebellion. Rosecrans had at no time during the two days' fighting more than 55,000 effective men, and his losses aggregated 1,687 killed; 9,394 wounded, and 5,255 missing—a total loss of 16,366.* Gen. Bragg, including his reinforcements from Virginia, Georgia and Mississippi had very nearly 70,000 effective troops, and his losses amounted to 2,673 killed, 16,274 wounded and 2,003 missing—a total of 20,950.

On the 21st Gen. Thomas advised Gen. Rosecrans to concentrate his army at Chattanooga, which was done as soon as practicable and the siege of Chattanooga commenced. The incipient fortifications left by Gen. Bragg when he evacuated Chattanooga on the 9th, were speedily strengthened as parts of a complete circumvallation to the east and south of the city. Gen. Bragg's lines extended from Lookout Mountain across Chattanooga Valley to Missionary Ridge and along its base and summit to the Tennessee River above the city. Bragg's object, acting contrary to the advice of Gen. Longstreet, was to interrupt Rosecrans'communications with Bridgeport, and thus starve into surrender the army he had failed

*The losses of this battle as compiled by Brig.-Gen. Richard C. Drum, adjutant-general United States Army, were as follows: General Headquarters—wounded, 2; missing 4; Fourteenth Army Corps—killed, 664; wounded, 3,555; missing, 1,925; Twentieth Army Corps—killed, 423; wounded, 2,698; missing, 1,215; Twenty-first Army Corps—killed, 322; wounded, 2,382; missing, 699; Reserve Corps—killed, 215; wounded, 976; missing, 631; Cavalry Corps—killed, 32; wounded, 136; missing, 300. Total number lost by the Army of the Cumberland 16,179

to annihilate at Chickamauga. His success was certain if he could maintain his hold on the roads to Bridgeport and the Tennessee River, for it would be, he knew, impossible to feed the Army of the Cumberland in Chattanooga by hauling supplies over the mountains from Bridgeport. The problem before Gen. Rosecrans therefore was, after having attained secure position in Chattanooga to open his communications with Bridgeport by the river and on the south side. From the 21st of September to the 28th of October, on the night of which day a steamboat (which had been captured at Chattanooga and had been repaired) passed the rebel batteries on Lookout Mountain, and a steamboat built at Bridgeport was soon in motion up the river loaded with provisions for the Union Army. But this siege of thirty-seven days was very trying to the army besieged. The raid of Wheeler's cavalry, though hotly pursued and finally driven again south of the Tennessee by Gen. Crook, resulted in the destruction of wagon trains bearing supplies for the Union Army, and the muddy and mountainous roads were an almost insurmountable obstacle against the transportation of food and clothing. The bad condition of the roads was owing to continuous rains falling earlier than usual, and these rains, while they caused much delay in the delivery of the needed supplies, also rendered both food and clothing more necessary by bringing on colder weather. The men were put on half rations of hard bread, and so kept for a considerable time, and the beef, driven from Nashville across a country affording but little food, was so poor when it reached Chattanooga, that the soldiers soon began to say that they were living on "half rations of hard bread and beef dried on the hoof." Everything within the Federal lines that could be utilized for fuel was exhausted even to the roots of stumps and trees, and among the trees so used was a noble oak, at least four feet in diameter, standing near the corner of Third and Market Streets, an ancient landmark, under the shade of whose wide-spreading branches were printed some of the first numbers of Parham's *Chattanooga Gazette*.

Early in October, the Eleventh and Twelfth Corps, commanded, respectively, by Gens. Howard and Slocum, with Gen. Hooker in command of the whole, reached Nashville and were disposed along the railroad from that city to Bridgeport, securing the communications between those points, and Gen. Grant, having been appointed to the command of the Military Division of the Mississippi, with his choice as to retaining the department commanders as they were, or to relieve Rosecrans and assign Thomas to his place, accepted the latter, assumed the command on the 19th of October, and arrived in Chattanooga on the 23d, Gen. Rosecrans having dictated a farewell to his army and left for Cincinnati before it was generally known that he was relieved.

Having become familiar with the topography of the surrounding country, the condition of the army and the plans for opening communications with Bridgeport, matured by Gen. Rosecrans, which plans were well under way upon his arrival, Gen. Grant permitted them to continue without modification, and on the 27th of October, four days after his arrival in Chattanooga, by a most brilliant combination by Gens. Hazen and W. F. Smith, the river was taken possession of at Brown's ferry, and by 10 o'clock on the morning of that day a pontoon bridge was successfully thrown across the river at that point, and on the afternoon of the 28th Hooker emerged into Lookout Valley at Wauhatchie. By the presence of Hooker's command the safety of the pontoon bridge at Brown's Ferry was assured, and it became an easy matter to float supplies up the river from Bridgeport to Kelley's ferry, thence haul them by wagon across Raccoon Mountains to Brown's ferry, and thence across Moccasin Point to Chattanooga. In a week from the time of Gen. Grant's arrival the troops were receiving full rations. With reference to the effect upon the soldiers, Gen. Grant in his "Memoirs" says:

"It is hard for any one not an eye-witness to realize the relief this brought. The men were soon reclothed as well as fed, an abundance of ammunition was brought up and a cheerfulness prevailed not before enjoyed for many weeks. Neither officers nor men looked upon themselves any longer as doomed. The weak and languid appearance of the troops, so visible before, disappeared at once."

But the opening of the road from Brown's to Kelley's ferry was a surprise and a disappointment to Bragg, and immediately a movement was set on foot by him to overwhelm the troops guarding it under Hooker. On the night of the 28th an attack was made on Gen. Geary at Wauhatchie by Longstreet's corps, and upon the commencement of the battle Gen. Hooker ordered Howard up from Brown's ferry to the assistance of Geary. Although Gen. Howard was only three miles distant he was three hours in reaching Geary, having fought and won a battle on the way, and Gen. Geary had maintained his position in the darkness, surrounded on three sides by a superior force, having successfully repulsed every rebel charge. Gen. Grant says that in the darkness and uproar the frightened teamsters deserted their teams, and the mules, becoming frightened, broke loose from their fastenings and stampeded directly toward the enemy, who doubtless took this for a charge and stampeded in turn. In this night engagement Geary lost 76 killed, 339 wounded, and 22 missing—a total loss of 437 (Grant says 416 killed and wounded); while the rebel loss was never known, but Geary buried 153 of their dead on his front alone, and 100 prisoners were captured, besides a large number of small arms. Gen. Thomas, in congratulating Hooker's troops on the defeat of Longstreet, said: "The bayonet charge of Howard's troops made up the side of a steep and difficult hill over two hundred feet high, completely routing the enemy from his barricades on its top, and the repulse by Geary of greatly superior numbers who attempted to surprise him, will rank among the distinguished feats of arms of this war." These detached actions for the defense of the road between the two ferries are known in history as the battle of Chattanooga, by the successful issue of which the siege of Chattanooga, by November 1, was fully brought to an end, so far as the supply of the army under Gen. Thomas was concerned.

But the gigantic task remained of driving away the besieging army. To accomplish this object it was necessary for Gen. Grant to await the arrival of Gen. Sherman, who, under orders from the general-in-chief of the army, left Vicksburg on the 27th of September and Memphis on the 11th of October for Corinth, on his way to Chattanooga, along the line of the Memphis & Charleston Railway. After passing through a hostile country, the people and the guerrilla bands infesting it destroying the railroad as fast as he completed it, he crossed the Tennessee River at Eastport November 1, and on the same day with his head of column reached Florence, Ala. On the 14th he reached Bridgeport with a large force, and on the 15th reached Chattanooga in person to confer with Gen. Grant. Gen. Bragg had sent Longstreet toward Knoxville to operate against Burnside, and Gen. Grant's plan involved Gen. Burnside's skirmishing with Longstreet, and falling back if necessary for the purpose of gaining time, so that when Gen. Sherman's army should arrive, he could throw a strong force between Bragg and Longstreet, thus preventing Longstreet's return and forcing him to the mountain passes to obtain his supplies.

Gen. Grant's plan of raising the siege of Chattanooga was a magnificent one and though slightly modified two or three times in accordance with subsequent developments was in the end brilliantly executed. It was for Sherman to attack Bragg's right flank, force it back, and form a line extending across South Chickamauga Creek, threaten or seize the railroad, and thus compel him to weaken his lines elsewhere or lose his communication with his base of supplies at Chickamauga Station. Gen. Hooker, who was then in Lookout Valley, was to get to Chattanooga Valley in the most expeditious way possible, cross this valley rapidly to Rossville, and form a line across Missionary Ridge facing north, and extending across Chickamauga Valley to the eastward, thus threatening Bragg's rear on that flank; and Gen. Thomas with the army of Cumberland was to march out from his entrenchments eastward from Chattanooga and assault the rebel center, weakened as it was hoped it would be, by strengthening his flanks. While other movements were proceeding under Gens. Sherman and Hooker, Gen. Thomas moved forward his entrenchments east of Chattanooga and secured a line fully a mile in advance of the one occupied in the morning, and the fortifications turned to face the east instead of the west, the loss in this preliminary action being probably about 1,100 killed and wounded on either side. On the morning of the 24th Sherman, having by daylight floated pontoons from North Chickamauga to South Chickamauga Creek, and by means of them and a steamboat crossed his entire army by about noon, at 1 o'clock started for his assault on the north end of Missionary Ridge, which by night he had carried, his right being at the tunnel and his left at Chickamauga Creek. On the same day Hooker fought his famous "battle above the clouds" on Lookout Mountain, captured 2,000 prisoners, and Grant's line was then a continuous one from the Tennessee at the mouth of South Chickamauga Creek up to and over the north end of Missionary Ridge, then to Chattanooga Valley, then to the mouth of Chattanooga Creek, and thence up the slope of Lookout Mountain to the foot of the upper palisade. Hooker, in order to gain his position in this line, had been obliged, as was said, to fight his famous "battle above the clouds," and and cross over the point of Lookout Mountain. His troops had been enabled to gain the plateau on the north slope of the mountain, in full view from the city of Chattanooga in clear weather, by a flank movement under Gen. Geary, who, unobserved, had crossed Lookout Creek near Wauhatchie, while Cruft and Osterhaus held the enemy's attention in crossing near the railroad bridge down below. The plateau was gained by all these commands about noon. A heavy mist had favored the movements of these troops, by rendering them to a great extent invisible to both armies; but the sound of their musketry and artillery was incessantly heard. And while the fighting on this plateau was going on, the citizens of Chattanooga and the soldiers of the Union Army were presented with a magnificent spectacle for hours—the innumerable flashes of musketry all up and down the mountain side being rendered more plainly visible by the darkness caused by the mist or fog which partially hid the soldiers themselves from view.

Having gained full possession of Lookout Mountain. Hooker's command encamped for the night, and early on the morning of the 25th started across the Chattanooga Valley for Missionary Ridge at Rossville, which he reached about 2 o'clock, having been detained from three to four hours at Chattanooga Creek because of the destruction of the bridges across that creek by the rebel soldiers in their retreat. At Rossville he captured large quantities of ambulances, wagons and stores, and after driving Stewart's soldiers out of the line of breastworks thrown up by Rosecrans' troops after the battle of Chickamauga, and capturing a large number of prisoners, encamped for the night with his line extending across the ridge, Osterhaus on the east side, Cruft on the ridge, and Geary in the valley west of the ridge.

While Hooker was getting across Chattanooga Valley, Sherman on the extreme left was doing some very heavy fighting, Bragg having massed the most of his forces in front of Sherman in order to drive him back and regain possession of the railroad to his base of supplies. All day up to 3 o'clock Sherman's troops, under Corse, Loomis and Morgan L. Smith, fought the rebels under Hardee, with Cleburne's, Gist's, Cheatham's and Stevenson's divisions, in a very stubborn struggle. The main part of the fighting up to this time had been Sherman's share. Hooker, failing on account of the burning of the bridges, and of the other obstructions placed in his way was unable to divert the enemy from Sherman's front as early as was designed, and a diversion must come from some quarter; Grant ordered Thomas to move out the four divisions constituting the center of the army, under Baird, Wood, Sheridan and Johnson, from left to right as named, and at a signal of six guns, fired in quick succession from Orchard Knob, to press forward, carry the first line of rifle pits at the base of Missionary Ridge, and there halt for further orders.

About half past three the troops in the center heard the six signal guns from Orchard Knob, and in an incredibly short space of time had driven the rebels from their lower line of rifle pits, Union and rebel soldiers going over the line at the same time, many of the rebels being captured and sent to the rear under the fire of their own friends higher up the hill. The Army of the Cumberland, thus held back for the main attack on the center of Bragg's position, had become very impatient at the delay, and now being permitted to advance, were not satisfied with having driven the rebels from the lower line of rifle pits, but while here awaiting orders, under a hot, galling fire from the upper lines of rifle pits, one-half way up, the other and much the stronger one on the crest of the ridge—first one regiment, then another started up the ascent with its colors, until soon the entire line seized, as it were, by the same spontaneous impulse, cheered by their officers and by each other, advanced as rapidly as the steep ascent would permit, over and around rocks, under, through and over fallen timbers, until within one hour from leaving Orchard Knob not only was the line of rifle pits midway up the ridge captured, but also the one on the crest. Sheridan's and Woods' divisions reached the crest almost simultaneously,* and just too late to capture Bragg, Breckenridge and a number of other rebel generals, who were carried away by their men, among whom the panic was so great that they could not be controlled. Many of the rebel soldiers, however, were captured and thousands of others threw away their arms in their retreat. Sheridan pursued the enemy in his front to Chickamauga Creek, meeting, however, with some resistance from troops occupying a hill in the rear of Missionary Ridge, whose position he flanked on both sides, causing them to retreat, leaving artillery, wagon trains and prisoners in his hands. Wood was unable to join Sheridan on account of heavy opposition under Hardee. About dark, however, after a sharp contest, Hardee withdrew, and Missionary Ridge was entirely under the control of the Union Army. Sherman's troops were held in check all day by Bragg sending column after column against them, and concentrating every gun upon them that could possibly be brought to bear, and thus the magnificent spectacle of Sherman's troops pursuing the rebel army from north to south along the top of Missionary Ridge was lost to the army of the Cumberland and Hooker's corps, and instead, Sherman's army, which had grandly maintained itself against great odds and repeated furious onslaughts and had fought one of the finest artillery duels of the war, was permitted to witness in part the rebel retreat on the 25th, and to learn on the 26th of the extent of the great victory won on Missionary Ridge. Pursuit was made next day and continued until the 28th, the pursuit being made by Hooker and Sherman, the latter's force strengthened by a portion of Thomas' command, the other portion having been attached to Granger's corps, and with that sent to the relief of Burnside at Knoxville. On the 28th, Sherman, after destroying the railroad between Dalton and Cleveland, and that from below Greysville back to the State line, made a reconnoissance to the Hiwassee, and on reaching Charleston took command of Granger's column and with all haste pressed forward to Knoxville, reaching there on the 6th of December, and finding that Longstreet had passed up into Virginia two days before. Leaving Granger's corps to aid in the pursuit of Longstreet, Sherman returned to Chattanooga, to which place Palmer had returned immediately after the pursuit ceased on the 28th. Howard and Davis, who had been detached from Thomas' command to aid in the pursuit of Longstreet, were ordered to report at Chattanooga, and Sherman marched to northern Alabama with his corps and placed them in winter quarters.

The losses in the battle of Missionary Ridge were as follows: In Sherman's command, including Howard's but not Davis', 295 killed, 1,402

---

*It is not easy, and perhaps not desirable to state which division was first on top of the ridge. Cist says Sheridan, Van Horne says Wood.

wounded, and 292 missing—a total of 1,989. This, however, includes the losses in Osterhaus' division (which, although belonging to Sherman, fought on the right under Hooker), which were 87 killed, 344 wounded, and 66 missing—a total of 497. Thomas' loss, including Howard's but not Davis' command, was 529 killed, 2,281 wounded, and 141 missing—a total of 3,951; Sheridan's division of Thomas' corps lost 135 killed, 1,151 wounded—a total of 1,256; while Wood's division of the same corps lost 150 killed, 851 wounded—a total of 1,001; none missing from either division. The Army of the Cumberland captured 40 pieces of artillery; 58 artillery carriages and caissons; 6,175 stands of small arms, principally English Enfield rifles, and 5,471 prisoners.

During the winter of 1863-64 but little was done by the army, except to remain quietly in camp around Chattanooga, and prepare for the spring campaign. The railroads through East Tennessee were repaired to and beyond Knoxville, and in the early spring of 1864 the Army of the Cumberland was so reorganized as to place Gen. O. O. Howard in command of the Fourth Corps, formed immediately after the battle of Chickamauga, by the consolidation of the Twentieth and Twenty-first Corps; Gen. J. M. Palmer was retained in command of the Fourteenth Corps, and Gen. Hooker was assigned to the command of the new Twentieth Corps, formed by the consolidation of the Eleventh and Twelfth. The cavalry was organized in four divisions under the command of W. L. Elliott. The Fourth was ordered to Cleveland; the Fourteenth in front of Chattanooga was well thrown forward toward the enemy's front at Dalton, and the Twentieth was stationed in Lookout Valley.

Chattanooga was then occupied until the autumn of 1865 by soldiers of the Union Army, the dates of the arrival of some of which are given under the head "Chattanooga." A hospital for the sick and wounded was established, and water-works were built to supply the hospital and the garrison.

Before the close of the war a beautiful location elevated about seventy-five feet above the surrounding valley was chosen for the last resting place for the soldiers of the Union Army in the various battles around Chattanooga, about one mile east of that place. It contains seventy-five and one-half acres of land and is surrounded by a heavy stone wall, just inside of which is a neatly trimmed hedge of osage orange. The ground rises gradually to the center, on the highest point of which float the stars and stripes. On each corner of a kind of central park is erected a cannon monument, at the base of each monument being four piles of five cannon balls each. On the cannon, standing on the southeast corner of this park, is the great seal of the United States, bearing the following inscription:

"United States National Military Cemetery, Chattanooga, established 1863; interments, 12,876; known, 7,947; unknown, 4,929." Since this inscription was made, additional interments have been made to the number of about one hundred, so that the entire number is now 12,983; the known being 8,020, divided among the States as follows: Alabama, 38; Connecticut, 20; Georgia, 11; Illinois, 1,088; Indiana, 1,317; Iowa, 185; Kansas, 53; Kentucky, 368; Maryland, 2; Maine, 1; Massachusetts, 73; Michigan, 488; Minnesota, 105; Missouri, 159; New York, 343; New Jersey, 32; Ohio, 1,798; Pennsylvania, 197; Rhode Island, 2; Tennessee, 137; Wisconsin, 237; West Virginia, 3; United States Regulars, 203; colored soldiers, 866; employes, 14; pioneers, 5; signal corps, 3; miscellaneous, 272. The total number of unknown is 4,963, the largest number being the "miscellaneous" class, 4,830.

The grand gate-way over the road leading from Montgomery Avenue into this cemetery, was completed about February 1, 1880. The arch-way from the base to the top of the blocking is about 32 feet, the arch, itself, being $19\frac{1}{2}$ feet high and the opening $10\frac{1}{2}$ feet wide. Above the keystone of the arch, on the outside, is the inscription: "National Military Cemetery, Chattanooga, 1863." On the inside in a similar position is the following: "Here rest in peace 12,956 citizens, who died for their country from 1861 to 1865." At the head of the grave of each soldier is a small marble slab, bearing his name and State, when known, and in addition to these and the four cannon monuments, is a tall white marble monument, erected in memory of the Fourth Army Corps, with the names of each regiment and battery composing that corps, classified by brigades and divisions, seventy-three regiments in all and six batteries, and besides is a smaller monument erected to the memory of Lieut.-Col. J. B. Taft, of the One Hundred and Forty-third New York Volunteers. Generally speaking, the cemetery, with its hills, its evergreen and deciduous trees of various kinds and sizes, its monuments of marble and cannon, and above all, the graves of its dead heroes, must remain through all coming time a most eloquent inspiration and incentive to love of country and the defense of the right.

Until 1867 this cemetery was managed by the quartermaster's department, but under the general law for the government of national cemeteries, passed February 22, 1867, superintendents have been appointed as follows: Frederick Buntley, 1867; James Murphy, 1880; John Trindle, in October, 1882, the present superintendent.

The Confederate Cemetery is located in the eastern part of the city of Chattanooga, adjoining the city cemetery. It was established during the war while the Confederate Armies held possession of Chattanooga.

In 1874 two associations, previously organized, were consolidated, viz.: The Memorial and Monumental Associations, and the new organization was named the Chattanooga Confederate Memorial Association. A constitution was adopted and signed by fifteen persons May 14, 1874; a few others signed later in that year and three in 1876. The object of this association was to collect the remains of the dead of the late Confederate Army and bury them in a cemetery in or near Chattanooga. Mrs. Penelope M. Cooke was president of this association from its organization to the time of her death, December 25, 1875. She was succeeded by Mrs. Anna F. Hight, who was succeeded in 1878 by Mrs. B. D. Lodor, who served until May, 1885, when Mrs. P. A. Brauner was elected, serving until May, 1886, when Mrs. L. T. Dickinson, the present presiding officer, was elected. The secretaries have been Mrs. P. A. Brauner, Tomlinson Fort, Mrs. W. G. Oehmig, Miss Mary Trigg, Miss Mary Cooke and Mrs. Louise G. Connor. About 2,500 bodies have been collected and laid to rest in this cemetery, and a fine monument, erected to their memory, was dedicated May 10, 1877, a day long to be remembered in the history of Chattanooga, as on that day the fraternal feeling, which had for some time been growing, first found public and glad expression. The exercises of dedication were participated in by soldiers of both the Confederate and Federal Armies, and by all classes of the people. The monument, designed by G. C. Connor, was erected at a cost of about $2,000.

Since the war the members of the Legislature from Hamilton County have been as follows:

Senators: A. M. Cate, 1865 and 1867; A. A. Pearson, 1869; E. A. James, 1873; L. S. Marye, 1875; R. P. Lloyd, 1877; John R. Neal, 1879; J. L. Gaston, 1881; H. L. W. Raulston, 1883; H. B. Case, 1885.

Representatives: James R. Hood, 1865; John Anderson, 1866 and 1867; E. A. James, 1869; C. C. Patton, 1873; George R. James 1875; S A. Key, 1877; H. M. Wiltse, 1879 and 1881; H. B. Case and Peter Bolton, 1883; W. C. Hodge and T. H. Davis, 1885.

Following is the presidential vote in Hamilton County from 1868 to 1884 inclusive: 1868—Ulysses S. Grant, 1,273; Horatio Seymour, 393; 1872—Grant, 1,630; Horace Greeley, 1,098; 1876—Rutherford B. Hayes, 1,888; Samuel J. Tilden, 1,613; 1880—James A. Garfield, 2,460; W. S. Hancock, 1,595; J. B. Weaver, 117; 1884—James G. Blaine, 3,829; Grover Cleveland, 2,439.

Gubernatorial vote: March 4, 1865, W. G. Brownlow, 705; no opposition; 1867—W. G. Brownlow, 1,480; Emerson Etheridge, 302; 1869—D. W. C. Senter, ——; —— Stokes, ——; 1870—W. H. Wisener, 1,364; J. C. Brown, 1,171; 1872—A. A. Freeman, 1,602; J. C. Brown, 1,161;

1874—Horace Maynard, 1,155; James D. Porter, 1,145; 1876—George Maney ——; James D. Porter, 1,627; Dorsey B. Thomas, 1,086; W. F. Yardley, ——; 1878—E. M. Wight, 1,103; A. S. Marks, 711; R. M. Edwards, 43; 1880—Alvin Hawkins, 2,440; John V. Wright, 1,428; S. F. Wilson, 346; R. M. Edwards, 114; 1882—Alvin Hawkins, 2,385; William B. Bate, 1,633; Joseph H. Fussell, 39; John R. Beasley, 22; 1884—Frank T. Reid, 4,263; William B. Bate, 2,366; W. J. Buchanan ——; 1886—Robert L. Taylor, 2,381; Alfred A. Taylor, 3,581.

Following is a list of the principal county officers from 1820 to 1876, since which time election returns are obtainable and are introduced in connection with most officers' names:

Asahel Rogers' name is signed as county court clerk to the first deed registered after the county was organized, to which he also affixed his "Privet seal," not having an official seal at the office that day, March 1, 1821. Asahel Rogers remained in this office until 1844, when he was succeeded by William T. Rogers. Subsequent clerks have been R. Henderson, 1847; James Clift, 1848; John H. Robertson, November 1848-56; George W. Arnett, 1856-60; Charles W. Vinson, 1860-64; R. H. Guthrie, 1864-70; J. H. Hardie, 1870-74; L. M. Clark, from 1874 to present time (1886).

Sheriffs: Charles Gamble, Terrill Riddle, A. M. Rogers, Matthew Anderson, John Johnson, J. C. Francis, James Roddy, James C. Connor, William Snow, Milo Coulter, G. W. Rider, A. B. Connor, William H. Bean, J. C. Connor, Charles B. Champion. The sheriffs collected the taxes up to 1840. From that time to 1876 there served the following as—

Tax collectors: James Rogers, Newton McGill, A. Selcer, Joseph Yarnell, W. H. Bean, M. Adams and D. B. Ragsdale.

Trustees: Thomas Stiff, William Rogers, Alfred King, A. P. Hunter, George W. Julian, Jesse Locke, W. H. Crowder, George Curry, F. Vaughn.

Registers: J. H. Jones, 1819; James S. Yarnell, 1836; A. G. W. Puckett, 1840; Resin M. Rawlings, 1842; John H. Torbett, 1843; A. A. Vinson, 1844; J. B. Peters, 1853; A. W. Moore, 1860; John F. Hamill, 1868; H. C. Beck, from 1874 to the present time.

Circuit court clerks: Daniel Henderson, Dr. P. H. Butler, B. C. Conner, B. B. Cannon, A. G. W. Puckett, E. A. Glass, William Rogers, C. W. Vinson.

The first surveyor of Hamilton County was Samuel R. Russell, who served from 1824 to 1828. He was followed by John Cummings from 1828 to 1830; B. B. Cannon, 1830-37; Noble J. Tounnel, a short time in 1837; Robert Tumall, 1837-47; Alexander T. Prowell, 1847-48; Presley

R. Lomenick, 1848-54; B. F. Clark, 1854-61; Presley R. Lomenick, 1861, killed during the war; — Lowe, first after the war, Robert L. McNabb, Alfred Conner, James W. Clift, R. C. McRee, Jr.; James Layman served five or six years; M. E. Dickens, six months in 1881; L. B. Headrick, from October 1881 to January, 1882; A. H. Rogers from 1882 to the present time.

The year 1870 is the first for which it is practicable to give tolerably accurate election returns for this county. In August an election was held at which the following votes were cast: Chancellor—D. M. Key, 1,032; D. C. Trewhitt, 806; John C. Gaut, 128; circuit court judge—John B. Hoyl, 979; W. L. Adams, 939; circuit court clerk—C. W. Vinson, 1,131; Stults, 831; county judge—A. G. W. Puckett, 1,056; Blackford, 670; Rogers, 136; county clerk—Hardie, 1,113; Guthrie, 928; Heaton, 72; register—Long, 911; Hamill, 894; Moore, 77.

In 1872 the vote was as follows: Sheriff—Bean, Republican, 1,591; Brown, Democrat, 953; tax collector—Adams, Democrat, 1,353; Carlile, Republican, 1,277; trustee—Crowder, Republican, 1,477; Selcer, Democrat, 1,114.

Hamilton County has been represented in the United States Senate by one of her citizens, David M. Key, who was appointed to the seat made vacant by the death of Andrew Johnson, which occurred July 31, 1875, and in the lower house of Congress by two of her sons—Reese B. Brabson 1859-61, and William Crutchfield 1873-75. Mr. Crutchfield was elected by a majority of 1,029 in a district which had usually been Democratic by about 5,000 majority, the vote of his opponent, D. M. Key, being 8,921. With reference to this election it was said that in 1871 the voting population of the district was 28,476, while in 1872, when Mr. Crutchfield was elected, only 19,068 votes were cast, of which Mr. Crutchfield received 9,950, Mr. Key 8,921. There were therefore 9,048 voters who did not vote, most of whom were whites. Mr. Crutchfield's success, therefore, was largely due to the colored men. His majority in Hamilton County was 301.

In 1876 the following votes were polled: For member of Congress—Dibrell, 1,615; Drake, 1,857; State senator—Lloyd, 1,624; Padgett, 1,853; floater—Shepherd, 1,693; Pryor, 1,780; representative—1,744; Munger, 1,735.

In 1878 the following was the vote: Chancellor—Bradford, 1,835; Mayfield, 1,543; circuit court judge—Trewhitt, 2,562; Hoyl, 1,084; Northrup, 43; attorney-general—Milburn, 1,957; Spears, 1,661; county judge—McRee, Democrat, 1,509; Headrick, Greenback, 680; Gowin,

Republican, 1,431; sheriff—Rogers, Democrat, 1,601; Springfield, Republican, 1,859; Conner, 233; circuit court clerk—R. M. Tankesley, Democrat, 2,076; C. W. Vinson, Republican, 1,587; county court clerk—Jones, Democrat, 1,380; L. M. Clark, Republican, 2,326; trustee—Ragsdale, Democrat, 1,662; Gahagan, Republican, 1,910; register—Coulter, Democrat, 1,547; Beck, Republican, 1,827; Catron, 222.

The Republican Congressional Convention for the Third District met August 17, 1880. T. L. Kennedy, of Warren County, was chairman; H. F. Griscom, of Hamilton County, and Foster V. Brown, of Marion County, secretaries. After the appointment of committees on credentials, organization and resolutions, Capt. W. Rule, editor of the Knoxville *Chronicle*, addressed the convention, and dwelt somewhat on the election of 1876. He said that the claims of the Democracy that they elected Tilden in 1876 were false, and no one knew it better than the Democrats themselves. The reason he knew they did not elect him was because they did not go to war, but tamely submitted to the result. In 1860 when they failed they went to war, and if they had thought they elected Tilden they would have gone to war again. Col. H. B. Case and G. A. Gowin were put in nomination, Col. Case receiving sixty-seven votes on the first ballot, thus becoming the nominee. The Democrats nominated G. G. Dibrell, and the Greenbackers John W. James. In the election Dibrell received in Hamilton County 1,509 votes, Case 2,386 and James 250. In the entire district Dibrell received 12,806 votes and Case 9,918. For the rest of the officers, Hamilton County polled the following votes: Sheriff—Springfield, Republican, 2,262; Champion, Democrat, 1,647; trustee—Gahagan, Republican, 2,651; Rogers, Democrat, 1,249; floater—Moon, 1,636; Kennedy, 2,412; Welch, 114; representative—Cowart, Democrat, 1,478; Wiltse, Republican, 2,354; Mannell, 311.

The voting population of Hamilton County in 1880 was 4,172. In 1881, according to a careful census, it was as follows: In the First, Second, Third, Eighth and Sixteenth Districts, 987; in the Fourth, Fifth, Sixth, Seventh, Fifteenth and Seventeenth, 1,479; in the Eleventh, 391; in the Twelfth, 447—total outside of Chattanooga, 3,304. In Chattanooga it was: Whites, 2,843; blacks, 1,387—total, 4,230; and in the entire county, 7,534, an increase in one year of 3,362.

In 1882 the vote of the county was as follows: Sheriff—J. E. Conner, 1,929; W. T. Cate, 2,393; circuit court clerk—R. M. Tankesley, 1,901; A. R. Jones, 2,319; county court clerk—W. J. Sawyer, 1,273; L. M. Clark, 2,994; trustee—J. H. Poe, 1,560; A. Shelton, 2,624; register—W. J. Ingle, 1,438; H. C. Beck, 2,817; member of Congress—Dibrell, 1,521; Trewhitt, 2,531; Parker, 7; State senator—Rankin,

1,654; Roulston, 2,353; Coppinger, 7; representative—Woodard, 1,658; Patterson, 1,669; Case, 2,284; Bolton, 2,347; Gillespie, 6; Stokes, 9, In the Third Congressional District Dibrell's vote was 11,403; Trewhitt's, 9,698. In 1884 the Congressional vote in Hamilton County was for Neal, Democrat, 2,249; H. C. Evans, Republican, 4,392, while in the entire district Evans' vote was 14,221, and Neal's 14,289. In 1886 the Congressional vote was for Neal, 2,300; John T. Wilder, Republican, 3,655; senator—Kennedy, Republican, 3,332; Whitice, Democrat, 2,632; representative—Stone, Republican, 3,485; Hutchins, Republican (colored), 2,742; Drumbar, Democrat, 2,734; Lloyd, Democrat, 2,525. In the entire district Wilder's vote was 13,818; Neal's, 14,115.

The first judges of the circuit court were Thomas Keith, George W. Rowles and John C. Gaut, the latter being the first to preside in this court since the war. The first records of this court are dated October 3, 1864, all previous to that time having been destroyed, the session being held at Harrison, with John C. Gaut, presiding. George W. Rider, sheriff, returned a *venire facias* executed upon the following persons: William Hickman, Moses Smith, McKinney Adams, A. Selcer, Caswell Hall, C. E. Shelton, James Childres, J. E. McKenzie, F. M. Capps, John A. Brownlow, Peter Munger, Alfred Bettis, W. R. Davis, Charles Newton, James Cannon, Jesse Shipley, Hiram Pendegrass, Henry Hickman, J. M. Watson, E. M. Cleveland, George Phillips, Washington Evans, Nathan Howard, Daniel F. Houser and William Vandegriff, all good and lawful men, and also summoned Joseph C. Given and R. C. Johnson to attend as constables. Charles W. Vinson, elected clerk of the court March 5, 1864, presented his bonds as such, in the sum of $10,000, to faithfully keep and preserve the records; $5,000, to account for all fines and forfeitures; $25,000, as special commissioner and $5,000 as tax collector. The grand jury was discharged on the same day from attendance on the court. The first case on the records was that of Joseph Yarnell vs. William Johnson, resulting in a stay of judgment for six months in order to allow the plaintiff time to file declaration, and quite a number of similar cases followed with similar results. The whole number of cases on this day was thirty-nine.

The court was next held September 2, 1865, George W. Bridges having been assigned to hold it, the Fourth Judicial District being then composed of the counties of Bradley, Polk, Rhea, Hamilton, McMinn, Meigs and Marion. A number of the cases of attachment held over until this court, were decided in favor of the plaintiffs, judgment being rendered in some of them for $10,000 and interest; but those cases to which attach the most and perhaps the only interest in a historic sense, were the indictments for treason. Following is the form of the indictment: The State *vs.* James Moore. The presentment was signed by all the grand jury and was to the effect that James Moore on the first day of May, 1862, and on divers other times, before and after that date in Hamilton County, traitorously, knowingly and wittingly, did aid and assist enemies at open war with the State of Tennessee and the United States, to wit: the pretended Government of the Confederate States of America, by procuring and persuading other persons to enlist in the armies of said enemy against the peace and dignity of the State; and the grand jury upon their oaths did further present that the said James Moore on the same day as above and before and after in Hamilton County, knowingly, wittingly and traitorously, did aid and assist enemies at open war with the State and the United States, to wit: the pretended Government of the Confederate States of America, by furnishing said enemy so at war, with arms, ammunition, provisions and other articles for their aid and comfort, against the peace and dignity of the State. The presentment was endorsed by Simeon Eldridge, George Phillips, Nathan Howard, Orson Shipley, James Ray, W. R. Brown, W. R. Mosy, James Allen, D. K. Kimbrough, George Varner, H. C. Alexander, Jonathan Jackson and Christian Spiteman. On October 5, 1865, twenty-one other individuals were indicted for treason, and on the 10th of February, 1866, George W. Bridges on the bench, several of these treason cases were brought on for trial, and were disposed of by quashing the indictments and setting the defendants at liberty.

Numerous indictments for felonious assault and murder committed during the years of the war, were brought, and for horsestealing, burglary, larceny, robbery, gaming, lewdness, retailing liquor without license and manufacturing liquor without bond, showing an exceedingly disturbed condition of society, during and immediately succeeding the war. On June 4, 1866, William L. Adams took his seat upon the bench and upon February 11, 1867, Daniel C. Trewhitt presided and was succeeded by John B. Hoyl, in 1870. The last day of this court in Harrison was December 5, 1870, when it adjourned to meet in Chattanooga on the second Monday in March, 1871. On the 6th of October, 1869, Elvira Yarnell was indicted for murdering her infant child, and upon trial was found guilty of murder in the first degree on February 8, 1870. Being recommended to the mercy of the court, the sentence, hanging, was commuted to imprisonment for life. In March, 1871, James Smith, colored, and Tabitha Davis, white, were indicted for living together as man and wife, found guilty, and sentenced to the penitentiary for twelve months, but on account of mitigating circumstances, the sentence was commuted to a fine and imprisonment in the county jail—Tabitha Davis to be imprisoned twenty days and pay a fine of $10, and Smith to be imprisoned forty days and pay a fine of $50.

For a few days, commencing November 19, 1873, Chancellor D. M. Key presided in this court by interchange with Judge John B. Hoyl, and also in April, 1874; and in September and November, 1875, W. M. Bradford presided similarly. The present judge of this court was elected in 1878. The most important trial during his term was that of Henry Lawson for having committed a rape upon the person of Miss Nancy Donaldson on the 4th of July, 1881. The jury in this case was composed of Henry Schwartz, C. H. Dyer, A. Poe, M. S. Brown, W. F. Montgomery, M. C. D. Bryant, James Clements, J. H. Brown, David Hartman, T. H. Dutton, John Kesterson and Peter Boltman. The attorneys for the prosecution were J. M. Robertson and Lewis Shepherd, and those for the defense were Otto Fischer and H. B. Case. The trial was hastened on by Judge Trewhitt, for fear that Lawson, being a colored man, would be taken from the jail and hanged by a mob. He was convicted July 25, 1881, sentenced July 27, and hanged September 2, 1881. The remarkable thing about this trial was that Lawson was probably innocent of the crime for which he was hanged, evidence to this effect transpiring after the hanging took place; but the community, incensed at the commission of so heinous a crime upon a white woman and believing her accusation to be true, would have hung the accused had time been given to produce evidence tending to prove his innocence. Other hangings in this county have been two since the war, at Harrison, and one in 1876, of Shade Westmoreland, for murdering his paramour's husband.

The most terrible tragedy in which this county has been directly interested, though committed outside of her limits, was the murder of William T. Cate, sheriff of Hamilton County, and his deputy, J. J. Conway. They were on their way to Knox County with three prisoners for trial in the supreme court, and both officers were assassinated while *en route* by brothers of one of the prisoners. At Sweetwater two men boarded the train, made furtive glances at and seemed to recognize one of the prisoners named Taylor, behind whom Deputy Sheriff Conway was sitting. One of the assassins sitting behind Conway deliberately drew his pistol, placed it behind Conway's ear and fired, killing him instantly. Almost at the same instant another man on the opposite side of the car opened fire upon Sheriff Cate, who was shot four times in all and soon after died of his wounds. The assassins were John, Bob and Andy Taylor. John was wounded in the arm but all temporarily escaped. After some time

Bob Taylor was killed three miles from Lebanon, Mo., by R. P. Goodall, sheriff of the county. John Taylor died about forty miles from the same place and Andy was hanged at Loudon, Tenn., November 23, 1883.

The county of Hamilton was originally in the Second Chancery Division of the State, and in 1858 held sessions in Harrison on the first Mondays of March and September. The first chancellor was Thomas L. Williams, who has been succeeded by T. Nixon Van Dyke, A. G. Welcker, Daniel C. Trewhitt, D. M. Key and William M. Bradford.

The first records of this court now in existence are dated at Harrison, then the county seat, February 7, 1865. D. C. Trewhitt, appointed by Andrew Johnson to fill the vacancy caused by the war, presided. Chancellor Trewhitt appointed as clerk and master Addison P. Hunter, who gave bonds in the aggregate to the amount of $40,000. D. C. Trewhitt held court until August 9, 1870, and was succeeded by D. M. Key, who presided at the December term at Harrison, which lasted one day, on which day, December 5, it adjourned to meet at Chattanooga. A special term of this court commenced at Chattanooga, January 23, 1871, D. M. Key, presiding, since which time there has been but one chancery court in the county.

The most important cases tried in this court have been the scrip case and that of the exemption from taxes of manufacturing establishments for a period of years. The history of each of these cases is briefly as follows:

In 1869 an ordinance was passed by the city council of Chattanooga, providing that all taxes due to the city, except the school tax, should be paid in scrip issued by the city, and that all labor employed by the city, including labor upon public works, should be paid in scrip. For three or four years there was very little friction resulting from this ordinance, because the scrip kept up to very nearly par, but about 1873 it began to depreciate, sinking to 75 or 80 cents, and before the year expired, to 50 cents and even 45 cents, one result of this depreciation being that the city had to pay for labor $2 per day in scrip, while private corporations were paying not over 90 cents or $1 per day in cash. Merchants refused to receive the scrip in payment for dry goods and groceries, and the laboring man receiving it could buy with it nothing to eat or wear. At length a little coterie of capitalists was formed for the purpose of buying up the scrip at heavy discounts and holding it for redemption by the city at par, or for appreciation in the market. Before tax-paying time would come, labor on public works was suspended, all the scrip issued would find its way into the hands of the ring, and the moment taxes were due, the authorities being prohibited by ordinance from receiving anything but scrip for taxes, the tax-payer would, from necessity, take his greenbacks, gold, or silver to these men and buy scrip at, say 90 cents on the dollar, and turn it over at par to the city in payment of his taxes. Thus the city was robbed right and left, causing great dissatisfaction; but the system was kept up until 1875, when about $240,000 was outstanding, and nearly as much more was issued during the fiscal year, 1875-76. In the beginning of the year 1876-77, Col. H. B. Case was elected city attorney, and the first question he was required to solve was as to the legality of the issuance of this scrip. After a careful investigation he was obliged to report that it was in violation of the constitution of Tennessee, and of the banking act of the United States. Upon this report being made, the Board of Mayor and Aldermen ceased the issuance of scrip and also its redemption, returning to a cash basis. Immediately the scrip ring, holding about $280,000 of it, began to bring suits against the city in sums under $500, before justices of the peace, with the view of getting judgments in small sums for the whole amount, and then by *mandamus* compelling the city to levy a tax for its payment. A bill of injunction was filed by the city attorney, setting up the unconstitutionality of purchasing the scrip below its face and selling it to the tax-payers at an advance, and that in equity they were entitled to receive no more than they had paid for it, and requiring all holders of scrip to come into chancery court and have an account taken and statement made showing the amount that each holder had paid, and also requiring him to receive that amount in such reasonable levies of taxes as the city could stand, suggesting one, two, three and four years as proper time. Chancellor Bradford issued an injunction in accordance with this bill, and ordered publication, enjoining all holders of scrip from bringing suit, and enjoining the mayor and aldermen from taking up any scrip, except upon order from the Court. Under this bill trial was had and injunction made permanent. An appeal was then taken to the supreme court, but about the same time a suit, brought by W. J. Colburn, *et al.*, against the mayor and aldermen, involving the legality of this same scrip was decided by the supreme court, declaring that all issues of orders by any municipality, which anticipated future taxation, were in violation of the constitution of the State, and of the charter of the municipality. Thereupon the Board of Mayor and Aldermen, under the permission of the chancery court, set aside a certain amount of the tax levy for the redemption of the scrip, and periodically as the levy was collected for that purpose, advertised for the lowest bids at which holders would sell their scrip to the city. Upon this principle in the course of some three years, all was purchased, except about $15,000, at prices ranging from 48 to 60 cents, and the balance redeemed at par.

In 1871 an ordinance was passed by the city council exempting from taxation any manufacturing property for a period of ten years from the time of its establishment. The second question proposed to City Attorney Case was as to the legality of this exemption. Col. Case reported that the ordinance was in violation of the constitution and laws of the State, and as the result of this report the Mayor and Board of Aldermen began the collection of taxes from that year on property previously exempt under the ordinance. Some of the manufacturers resisted the collection of the taxes, and the cases went to the chancery court and thence to the supreme court of the State, in which the position of the Mayor and Board of Aldermen was sustained. But no attempt was made to collect taxes for previous years.

The records of the county court were destroyed up to 1864, the first day's proceedings on record being April 4, 1864. Twenty justices presented their commissions, signed by Gov. Andrew Johnson. Peter Munger was elected chairman, and T. W. Spicer and A. J. Thomas were elected the other members of the "court of quorum." R. H. Guthrie gave bonds as clerk of the court in the aggregate sum of $25,000. Commissioners were appointed to repair the courthouse, the repairs being completed in 1866, and costing about $400. A. G. W. Puckett was then county judge. R. C. McRee became county judge in 1878, and Hugh Whiteside in 1886.

James A. Whiteside was one of the first lawyers in Hamilton County and one of the ablest that has ever lived in Tennessee. While exceedingly unostentatious, he was also exceedingly sagacious. His plans were laid with certainty and carried out successfully, and they were usually a success before the public knew of their existence. He was more of a lawyer than an advocate, was clear and logical in his argument, and as a consequence was more effective before a court than before a jury. He was a man of great reading and of much general information, and was the father of the railroad system of Tennessee. He was appointed by the Legislature, December 8, 1843, to assess the damages to the school lands in Hamilton County, caused thereto by the building of the Western & Atlantic Railroad, and authorized to demand and receive from the State of Georgia whatever damages said school lands might have sustained. Mr. Whiteside was of medium height, slender, well proportioned and straight. While he was at one time a member of the Legislature, he generally eschewed politics. He was a Whig until the election of James Buchanan to the presidency in 1856, when he became a Democrat. He was born in 1803, and died in November, 1861.

A. G. Welcker was a native of Roane County, Tenn., and was educated at the University of Tennessee. He was a splendid lawyer, but not so successful as an advocate. He came to Chattanooga about 1850, had a fine practice and was elected chancellor of this division, but when the Federal Army took possession he was ousted from his office and moved to Cleveland, where he died in 1867 or 1868. Hon. D. M. Key was his law partner from 1853 to the time of the war. Mr. Welcker was a Whig, but never ran for any office except that of chancellor.

Reese B. Brabson was a native of Sevier County, Tenn.; came to Chattanooga, having graduated from Maryville College, and became the law partner of James A. Whiteside. Mr. Brabson was especially strong before a jury, was very pleasant in his manners and was a very popular man. He was the Whig candidate for presidential elector in 1856, in opposition to Hon. D. M. Key, and was elected to Congress in 1858.

John A. Minnis was an early lawyer of Chattanooga, and had a full practice. He was elected to the Legislature, and at the close of the war settled in Montgomery, Ala., where he became city judge, and also United States District Attorney for the northern district of Alabama, holding court at Montgomery and Huntsville.

Gen. Francis M. Walker was an attorney at Chattanooga; was a good lawyer, but more of an advocate. He was a gentleman and very agreeable in his manners. He was a very brave soldier, became a brigadier-general in the rebel army and was killed at Atlanta.

George W. Lyle came to Chattanooga in 1856 from Clarksville, and married a daughter of Robert Cravens. He was a graduate of the law school of Cumberland University. He was a lawyer of great promise, and while a good speaker had no taste for politics, but his career was cut short by death in 1860.

The population of Hamilton County when organized has been elsewhere given. In 1860 it was as follows: Whites, 11,641; slaves, 1,419; free colored, 192; Indians, 6; total, 13,258. In 1870: Whites, 13,053; colored, 4,188; foreigners, 582; total, 17,823. In 1880: outside of Chattanooga, 11,516; Chattanooga, 12,938; total, 24,454. At this census the colored population in Chattanooga numbered 5,082; outside, 2,317. The voters numbered 6,017; males, 12,025, and females, 12,429. The assessed valuation of real estate in the county in 1880 was $4,156,465; of personal estate, $539,433. The taxes assessed in the year 1880 were, State, $13,895; county, $32,773; municipal, $75,619. The debt was, bonded, $21,000; floating, $95,264. The number of milch cows was 1,696; gallons of milk produced, 30,116; pounds of butter, 119,281; cheese, 20; pounds of wool, 10,690; number of farms, 930; acres of improved land, 55,854; value of farms, $1,948,175; of live stock, $245,893; of all farm products, $381,534; cost of fertilizers purchased, $487. The number of manufacturing establishments then was 58; amount of capital employed, $2,045,000; males employed above sixteen years old, 1,958; females above fifteen, 7; children and youth, 168; wages paid during the year, $568,508; materials used, $2,056,438; value of product, $3,230,006.

The public schools of Hamilton County are numerous and are improving. Previous to the establishment of the common-school system in the State, the people here, as elsewhere, depended upon private schools, but it would be very difficult to make even a tolerably accurate list of them. The most noted one that can now be remembered was Aldehoff's Institute, which was located on top of Lookout Mountain, about four miles south from the Point. It was so named from its founder, Prof. H. W. Von Aldehoff, a noted and learned teacher of *ante bellum* days. This institute was established in the fall of 1860, and was successfully conducted until some time during its third year, when owing to the advance of the Union Armies, it was suspended from force of circumstances. The building remained standing until within a few years, and was used in 1878 by refugees from the yellow fever scourge. At the present time nothing remains standing but the chimney, a monument to all that was peculiar in the Southern system of education.

The present common-school system was established by act of the Legislature in March, 1867, and under this act E. O. Tade became the first superintendent of public instruction in Hamilton County, at a salary of $700 per annum, serving four years. He was succeeded in 1871 by J. H. Hardie, who also served four years. At the beginning of Mr. Tade's term the county owned outside of Chattanooga three lots, but no school-house, and the school property remained in this condition until after W. M. Beene's election as superintendent in 1875. During his term of two years, four schoolhouses were erected, one in the Second Civil District; one in the Fourth, one in the Eleventh, and one in the Fifteenth. H. F. Rogers was elected superintendent in 1877, and during his term of two years, two schoolhouses were built, one in the First Civil District and one in the Twelfth. Under the administration of A. Shelton, who was elected in 1879, and served nearly four years, twenty-three schoolhouses were erected upon lots purchased by the county; and during the term of the present superintendent, H. B. Heywood, elected in 1883, there have been erected eleven more, so that at present the county owns forty schoolhouses, besides which it rents nine, making forty-nine in all in use. The salary of the superintendent was $700 per year until 1875, when it was reduced to $300, and remained at that figure until 1883, when it was raised to $600 per annum, its present figure.

At first the teachers were of a very inferior order; but Mr. Tade, although laboring under many discouragements, awakened considerable interest in the cause of education. During Mr. Beene's administration one teachers' institute was held; none was held under Mr. Rogers', but under Mr. Shelton's there were seven the first year, thirteen the second, ten the third and during the fourth under him there were two, and under P. A. Wall, appointed to fill out the unexpired term of Mr. Shelton, there were four institutes. Under the present superintendent, there have been four each year for white teachers, and two during his term for colored teachers, who have increased in numbers from one under Mr. Tade, to fifteen under Mr. Heywood. Teachers began to improve under Mr. Beene, and became decidedly better under Mr. Shelton who raised the standard of scholarship to which it was necessary to attain in order to obtain a certificate. Up to 1885, certificates were given for one year, when under an act of the Legislature, they were first, and have been since, granted also for three years.

The school fund of the county has slowly but steadily increased. In 1867 it was $1 per scholar; in 1871 it became $1.60; in 1875, $2; in 1879, $2.25; in 1882, $2.50; in 1884, $2.60, the highest figure it has yet reached. In 1886, on account of the abnormal increase of the scholastic population, the school fund dropped to $2.51 per scholar. The scholastic population of the county in 1876 was as follows: Whites—male, 1,751; female, 1,705. Colored—male, 715; female, 719; total, 4,890. In 1883 it was 8,423; in 1884, 9,618; in 1885, 10,454, and in 1886, at the close of the school year, June 30, 11,661. The schools were taught one month in the year under Mr. Tade; when Mr. Shelton became superintendent they were being taught three months in the year; at the close of his term, four and a half months, and in 1885, five months and one day. There are about fifteen good schoolhouses in the county, well furnished with seats, while the rest are of rather a primitive order. The forty belonging to the county are worth about $500 each, including furniture and land, though there are a few quite valuable properties—that in the Fifth District (No. 2), with its two acres of land, being worth about $12,000. Apparatus has been introduced into about six schools in the county. The salaries of teachers average about $33 per month. Satisfactory progress can not be made in the schools until a generous salary shall be paid teachers, thus attracting superior talent, and excluding that which is inferior, for, as a general thing, the people will not permit inferior talent to receive large pay.

The following schools have been incorporated under the "four-mile law:" Poe Spring Academy, August 15, 1879; Pleasant Grove Seminary, December 28, 1879; Soddy Preparatory and High School, February 13, 1880, and Bethlehem Academy, September 10, 1881.

Previous to the establishment of the present graded system of public schools in Chattanooga, private schools were the main dependence of the people. One of these was the Chattanooga High School for Girls, which was established in 1872, its second session opening September 2 of that year. H. H. Sneed was the rector; J. L. Cooper, professsor of mathematics and ancient languages; E. Krutch, professor of modern languages; Miss M. H. Shepard, principal of the preparatory and primary departments, and Miss Dismukes, assistant principal.

In the fall of 1872, under an ordinance passed the previous July, the graded system was established and went into operation the first Monday in January, 1873. The first members of the board of school commissioners were as follows, two from each ward: S. B. Moe and E. H. Price; J. F. Loomis and Willard Abbott; A. M. Johnson and H. C. Evans; W. D. Van Dyke and E. M. Wight; James Rollins and T. A. Hunt. Following are the names of the officers of the board: S. B. Moe, president; A. M. Johnson, vice-president; H. C. Evans, treasurer, and H. D. Wyatt, secretary and superintendent of schools. The city was divided into three districts, the first comprising the First and Fourth Wards; the second, the Second and Third Wards, and the third, the Fifth Ward. Besides a school in each ward there was the Howard Free School and later the Union Primary School. Some time previously a school for colored children had been opened under the auspices of the American Missionary Association, which in time passed under control of the board of commissioners. The schools remained in session five months the first year, having a total enrollment in the first district of 203; in the second of 288; in the third of 248; in the Howard School of 325, and in the Union Primary, of 88. The salaries paid ranged from $90 per month, paid to the principal of the Howard Free School, and $75 per month to each of the principals of the three district schools, down to $45 per month to each of seven teachers, $40 per month to each of three, and $35 per month to each of two. The entire number of white children, of school age, was 1,490; of colored, 897; of white children enrolled, 772; of colored, 415. The school board erected one new school building in the first district that year, and rented the rest of the room needed, with the exception of the Howard school building which was furnished by the American Missionary Association. The prime necessity of the schools then was buildings. The entire cost of establishing and maintaining the city schools for the first year ending July 31, 1873, was $8,824.80, including the salary of the superintendent which was $1,200. One remarkable thing about the text books introduced was that Quackenbos' History of the United States was used instead of Stephens'.

Three new school buildings were completed in the fall and early winter of 1878, and one, on McCallie Avenue, in 1879. At the present time there are three buildings used for white children and four for colored, two main buildings and two others. Statistics indicate the growth and development of the schools in the most concise form, hence the history of the schools in Chattanooga is mainly presented in figures. From 1874 to 1878, inclusive, the statistics are based upon a census of scholastic population from six to eighteen years of age, and since 1878 on a basis of from six to twenty-one. In 1874 the scholastic population of Chattanooga was, white, 1,471; colored, 908; in 1875—white, 1,474; colored, 812; in 1876—white, 1,390; colored, 927; in 1877—white, 1,538; colored, 883; in 1878—white, 1,652; colored, 870. In 1874 the number of different pupils enrolled was, white, 968; colored, 614; in 1875—white, 1,033; colored, 641; in 1876—white, 1031; colored, 599; in 1877—white, 1,067; colored, 642, and in 1878—white, 1,155; colored, 684. The per cent of attendance on number belonging was, in 1874, 92.86: in 1875, 95.44; in 1876, 92.47; in 1877, 93.24, and in 1878, 94.69.

The scholastic population since 1878 has been as follows: in 1879—white, 1,799; colored, 1,008; in 1880—white, 1,961; colored, 1,100; 1881—white, 2,058; colored, 1,166; 1882—white, 2,178; colored, 1,230; 1883—white, 2,544; colored, 1,385; 1884—white, 2,754; colored, 1,787; 1885—white, 2,999; colored, 2,059; 1886—white, 3,366; colored, 2,512. The number of different pupils enrolled was, in 1879—white, 1,225; colored, 662; in 1880—white, 1,357; colored, 828; in 1881—white, 1,480; colored, 854; 1882—white, 1,638; colored, 942; 1883—white, 1,478; colored, 666; 1884—white, 1,942; colored, 1,104; 1885—white, 2,095; colored, 1,363; 1886—white, 2,125; colored, 1,469. The per cent of attendance on number belonging was, in 1879, 94.41; in 1880, 94.48; 1881, 93.46; 1882, 93.62; 1883, 93.33; 1884, 93.15; 1885, 93.24; 1886, 91.58. The cost of tuition for each pupil belonging was in 1874, $11.87; in 1875, $16.75; 1876, $13.29; 1877, $11.07; 1878, $9.85; 1879, $9.42; 1880, $9.08; 1881, $10.12; 1882, $10.67; 1883, $16.09; 1884, $11.22; 1885, $12.11; 1886, $11.93. The average salary paid teachers was in 1874, $491.60; 1875, $596.60; 1876, $497.20; 1877, per month, $51.66; 1878, $51.96; 1885, $54.64; 1886, $51.70.* The entire cost of

---

*Years omitted, omitted from report of superintendent.

conducting the schools of Chattanooga, including purchases of real estate and improvements since 1873, has been as follows: in 1874, $21,378.55; 1875, $18,008.58; 1876, $17,620.25; 1877, $15,884.39; 1878, $19,182.74; 1879, $15,384.42; 1880, $17,834.06; 1881, $21,528.80; 1882, $24,722.08; 1883, $27,133.47; 1884, $28,478.73; 1885, $26,921.69; 1886, $———.

The common schools are divided into eight grades, four in the primary and four in the grammar department, the eighth grade being the lowest and the first the highest, the colored schools being graded the same as those for white children. In 1886 the number of white pupils in the first grade of the grammar schools was 65 and of colored pupils 12. The high school was established in 1874 with P. V. Livingston, principal. At the end of the first scholastic year the total enrollment was 35; in 1876 it was 40; in 1877, 33; 1878, 39; 1879, 39; 1880, 58; 1881, 64; 1882, 60; 1883, 65; 1884, 79; 1885, 94; 1886, 98. The course of study in the high school comprises three years of two terms each, during which six terms are devoted to Latin, three to algebra, two to geometry, four to German, one to rhetoric, one to geology and two to philosophy, elocution and music being pursued throughout the course. The first class graduated from the high school in 1879, consisting of 5 scholars. A class of 15 graduated in 1883, 13 in 1884, 14 in 1885, and 20 in 1886, one of whom was a colored girl. The entire number of graduates from the high school is 65.

The latest addition to the educational institutions of Chattanooga is the Chattanooga University. In 1871 the conception of a central university for the Holston, Central, Tennessee, Alabama, Georgia, Blue Ridge and Virginia Conferences of the Methodist Episcopal Church was formed in the minds of some of the leading divines of that church. In course of time this idea gained such force that a committee was raised to select a location for such a university. This committee visited Chattanooga, Knoxville and Athens, and after a careful examination of the advantages of each place expressed their preference for the three places in the order named, Chattanooga being the first choice, in part at least, because of its being the converging point of more railroads than any other city within the limits of the interested conferences. These conferences subsequently approved the choice of the committee and referred the whole matter to the Freedmen's Aid Society. However, the final decision was reserved until after the arts of coyness and coquetry, judiciously xercised by the locating committee upon all three of the cities, had sufficiently aroused the citizens of Chattanooga to the danger of losing the university, unless they should raise a sufficient amount of money to purchase at least a site for the institution. On October 6, 1881, a meeting of the citizens was held in the rooms of the Iron, Coal & Manufacturers' Association to take the necessary steps for the raising of this fund. Mayor Hart, who presided, announced that the university could be secured, provided the city would donate to its trustees from five to ten acres of ground. Committees in the different wards were appointed to solicit subscriptions of money for the purchase of the site and at length $15,000, the sum required, was raised. In December, 1882, the committee to finally locate the university held a meeting, and it was found that ten out of fifteen of the committee favored Chattanooga. At a meeting held at the Read House in July, 1883, the negotiations that had been pending for the purchase of a site were closed by the purchase for $30,000 of the "Sheffield Property," containing 10.85 acres of land. The land consisted of two parcels, the first bounded as follows: north by Vine Street, east by Baldwin, south by Oak and west by Douglas Street; and the second as follows: north by Oak, east by Baldwin, south by McCallie and west by Douglas Street. The property was purchased in 1867 by Joseph E. Sheffield, who in 1868 transferred it to his sons, G. S. J. and C. J. Sheffield, who sold it as above indicated to the Freedmen's Aid Society for the purposes of the university. The building erected upon this site is a handsome four-story brick structure with a stone basement, 120 feet long by 100 feet in depth, and contains over eighty rooms with every modern convenience, the entire cost being $90,000.

September 15, 1886, was the first day of the first term of the educational life of this institution, and the dedication occurred on October 25. Bishop J. M. Walden read the historical address, and Bishop W. F. Mallalieu, of New Orleans, delivered the dedicatory oration. On that day it was announced that there were 175 students enrolled, and the institution was looked upon as having attained a phenomenal success. The university is divided into five schools—academic, collegiate, theological, musical and art. The classical course in the collegiate school covers four years of study, while all the other courses in this and the other departments or schools require but three years. The first faculty of this institution was as follows: Rev. E. S. Lewis, A. M., acting president and dean of the college of liberal arts; Rev. J. J. Manker, D. D., dean of the theological school and professor of systematic theology; Wilford Caulkins, A. M., secretary and professor of ancient languages; Rev. W W. Hooper, A. M., treasurer and professor of natural science; Mrs. Mary M. Presnell, M. E. L., preceptress and professor of English literature; Edward A. Robertson, W. B., instructor in mathematics; Rev. Robert Steudel, B. D., professor of modern languages; Frank R. Adams, director of the musical department, and Mrs. R. G. Steudel, director of the art department.

Almost upon the threshold of its existence the faculty of this institution was confronted with a question of considerable importance, viz.: that of the right of colored students to matriculation and education within its walls. Two young colored men applied for admission and were refused and subsequently three young colored women applicants were likewise refused. The probability is that all were instigated to apply for the purpose of testing the position of the authorities of the university upon this question. The rejection of these colored applicants at once gave rise to earnest discussion of the question as to the right of the institution to use Freedmen's Aid Society property and funds for the exclusive education of white students, and the decision of this question must rest upon a correct understanding as to what were the objects or ends for which the Freedmen's Aid Society was established. These ends can be clearly perceived only by reference to the constitution and preamble thereto of the Freedmen's Aid Society. The preamble is in the following words:

WHEREAS: The usefulness and success of the Methodist Episcopal Church in the South requires the maintenance and success of various grades of schools among the freedmen; and

WHEREAS: There is no specific provision by benevolent organization in our church, to meet this special educational work of the freedmen; we, the "General Conference of the Methodist Episcopal Church, do therefore organize this Society under the following Constitution, with the name and for the purpose therein declared:

CONSTITUTION.

ARTICLE I.

This organization shall be known as the Freedmen's Aid Society of the Methodist Episcopal Church.

ARTICLE II.

Its object shall be to labor for the education and special aid of freedmen and others, especially in co-operation with the Missionary and Church Extension Societies of the Methodist Episcopal Church.

From the above preamble and Article II of the constitution, it is perfectly clear that the main object of the Freedmen's Aid Society is to educate the freedmen, and were it not for the presence in Article II of the words "and others," it is likewise perfectly clear that its educational work under its constitution would have been exclusively among the freedmen. If the words "and others" are applied without reference to the primary objects of the Society, they embrace all classes needing education, both black and white, and this is the construction placed upon Article II by those in charge of this institution. There is no doubt that this construction would hold if both races were admitted to the institution, but it is at least questionable whether an exclusively white school is authorized if at all only by an extremely strained and imaginary construction of the constitution. In 1884 the general conference of the Methodist Episcopal Church adopted the following resolution:

This General Conference declares the policy of the Methodist Episcopal Church to be that no member of any society within the church shall be excluded from public worship in any and every edifice of the denomination; and no student shall be excluded from instruction in any and every school under the supervision of the church, because of race, color or previous condition of servitude.

The conference, however, also resolved that the question of mixed schools was one of expediency to be left to the choice and administration of those on the ground and more immediately concerned and it is upon these slender threads of authority that the university is justified in excluding colored students. But there is no doubt that in the present state of public opinion regarding the coeducation of the two races, a university at Chattanooga for such purpose is an impracticability; hence the dilemma is presented of an exclusively white institution or none. The lesson to be learned from the initial experience of Chattanooga University is this—that in drafting rules, laws or constitutions, equivocal terms should be avoided.

The city of Chattanooga, although having no elegant church edifices before 1881, yet from 1840 has had church organizations with such modest and inexpensive structures as the members could afford to build, the first building ever used for religious service being the log schoolhouse at the corner of Fifth and Lookout Streets. The Cumberland Presbyterians now claim to have had the first church organization in Chattanooga, but the earliest exact date that is obtainable upon which a church was organized is June 21, 1840, when the foundations were laid of the First Presbyterian Church. Following are the names of some of the first members: W. W. Anderson, Robert M. Hooke, Henry Jones, Elizabeth Jones, John Vail, Lucy A. McFarland, William Smith, Caroline L. Smith, Mary L. Hooke, Ainsworth E. Blunt and John P. Long. A church building was erected at the corner of Third and Walnut Streets. This building, which was the first ever used in Chattanooga exclusively for religious purposes, was subsequently sold and the lot was exchanged about the year 1853, for a lot on the corner of Market and Seventh Streets, upon which a brick church was erected at a cost of $10,000, some of the largest contributors to this fund being Thomas McCallie, Dr. William S. Townsend, Robert M. Hooke, William Smith and James A. Whiteside. At that time this building was considered a large and elegant structure. In 1882 this property was sold and a new site secured on the corner of Georgia Avenue and Seventh Street, upon which an elegant and convenient church building was erected, the lot and church costing about $35,000. The dedication of this new edifice occurred September 28, 1885. Following is a list of the pastors of the church with the dates of the commencement of their pastorates: Rev. William Cunningham, 1840; Rev. William B. Brown, 1844; Rev. A. Blackburn, 1850; Rev. William Thompson, 1851; Rev F. A. Ross, D. D., 1853; Rev. J. N. Bradshaw, 1856; Rev. T. H. McCallie, D. D., 1862, and Rev. J. W. Bachman, D. D., present pastor, 1873.

The Second Presbyterian Church was organized with fourteen members, September 3, 1871. The first pastor was Rev. W. A. Rice. The Rev. J. C. Irwin was called April 1, 1875, and the present pastor, Rev. W. J. Trimble, began his labors April 1, 1879. The church building stands on the northeast corner of West Eighth and Chestnuts Streets, and is worth, with the lot upon which it stands, about $20,000. The church organization also owns a mission property worth $3,000. The Sunday-school was organized with thirty scholars in 1871, the superintendents having been Willard Abbott, T. C. Stewart, W. J. Trimble, William Powell and C. D. Mitchell in the order given. The membership of the church is now 205, and of the Sunday-school 175. The window in the church commemorative of the death of Miss Hattie Ackerman, a heroine and victim of the yellow fever epidemic, is a model of artistic skill and beauty.

The Cumberland Presbyterian Church was started probably in 1841, but the organization was not permanent, lasting only two or three years. The first pastors were the Rev. William B. Dawson and Rev. Aaron Grigsby, synodical missionaries. It was revived October 10, 1855, Revs. A. Templeton and Hiram Douglass being the prime movers. The following were the elders: Hugh McGill and Allen A. Kennedy. The Rev. A. Templeton remained as pastor until the breaking out of the war. Previous to 1858 the congregation worshiped in a little building on Cypress Street, between Sixth and Seventh Streets, at which time they moved to their present building on Chestnut Street, between Seventh and Eighth, which cost about $3,000. During the war they were without a pastor, and the church was occupied by the United States Army as a kind of arsenal. An attempt was made by a Southern soldier to blow it up while it was thus used, but the soldier was himself killed while making the attempt. At the close of the war, at the instance of W. L. Dugger, the Government repaired the damages to the building caused by its occupancy. The first pastor after the war was the Rev. E. J. Stockard, who came in 1867, remaining only a few months. He was succeeded in January, 1868, by the Rev. N. W. Motheral, who remained until 1870. The Rev. John Crisman then came and remained one year. The next was the Rev. William D. Chadick from 1871 to 1877; then the Rev. Thomas Toney, pastor, one year; then the Rev. Dr. William H. Darnall from 1880 to 1882; then, after the pulpit had been vacant about a year, the Rev. Charles Hyde was pastor about eight months in 1884 and 1885, when the present pastor, Rev. E. J. McCroskey, came, in April, 1885. The new lot of the church, corner of Oak and Lindsey Streets, was purchased in May, 1885, and the erection thereon of an elegant church commenced in March, 1886. The building is brick, with stone basement, 82x48 feet, extreme width of the towers, 55 feet; side walls, 18 feet high; stained glass windows, and an auditorium capable of seating about 600 people. The spire is about 175 feet high and the cost of the building was about $20,000. The membership of the church is about 200 and of the Sunday-school about 80. Dr. J. N. Lee is superintendent of the Sunday-school and G. H. Henson, assistant.

The Centenary Methodist Episcopal Church South was started about 1841 or 1842, the Methodists separating from other denominations, all of whom worshiped in the little log schoolhouse on Georgia Avenue near Fifth Street for some time after the laying out of the town. The first ten members were Jonathan P. McMillin, A. L. Edwards, James Warner and wife, Mrs. Bush, Mrs. Baldwin, Mrs. Faidley, W. J. Molleston, W. A. Caldwell and one other whose name can not now be learned. In 1847 a new church building was erected on the same lot on which stood the little log schoolhouse, fronting on Lookout Street, and this church then erected is now occupied by a colored Methodist organization. The first pastor of Centenary was the Rev. J. C. Pendergrass, and others following named in order were the Rev. W. H. Bates, Rev. Mr. Kelly, Rev. E. T. Sevier, Rev. Mr. Howell, Rev. David Sullins, Rev. W. E. Munsey, Rev. E. C. Wexler, Rev. Mr. Snapp, Rev. W. G. E. Cunnyngham, Rev. R. M. Hickey and Rev. Sewell Phillips, all before the war, which very much interrupted the work of the church. From 1865 to 1870 this organization leased and used the Cumberland Presbyterian Church, when a site for a new building was secured at a cost of $2,000 on Market Street extending back to Cherry Street. In time a portion of the lot was sold for $2,000, and with this sum was commenced the erection of a new church building on the other portion, which, when completed, cost $12,000, and was dedicated by Bishop George F. Pierce. In 1884 the church building became inadequate to the necessities of the growing congregation, and the Market Street Church property having been sold to D. B. Loveman & Co. for 35,000, a new location at the corner of Gilmer and A streets was purchased for $5,000, and the edifice now used by this congregation erected thereon. This edifice is of pressed brick, trimmed, capped and belted with Nashville sandstone, and rests on a basement of limestone in range work. It is 100x78 feet, the main gable is 61 feet high, the octagon tower 78 feet, and the main tower and steeple 220 feet, somewhat out of proportion to the size of the church itself. An elegant organ has been erected in the church at the cost of $2,500, the church itself having cost $30,250. The pastors of this church since the war have been the Revs. G. Taylor, C. T. Carroll, James Atkins, W. W. Bays, G. D. French, R. H. Parker, W. W. Bays, the second time, and the present pastor, Rev. G. C. Rankin.

The congregation of Centenary Church at the time of the dedication of the new building, June 14, 1885, numbered 407; the Whiteside Street Church, of which the Rev. T. R. Handy is pastor, numbered 220; the Cherry Street congregation eighty-one; the Wesley Chapel (colored) on Lookout Street about 500, and the First Methodist Episcopal Church 225, besides which there are the African Methodist Church, and the Zion Church, making the total number of Methodists in Chattanooga about 1,600.

The first Methodist Episcopal Church was started soon after the war, but for several years struggled along in poverty and obscurity. Though few in numbers, and beset with many difficulties, they continued to pursue their purpose to maintain and build up their congregation, and at length becoming conscious of success and of their strength they determined upon the erection of an elegant church edifice. The corner-stone of this building was laid on August 16, 1882. The platform erected for the occasion was occupied by several ministers, the choir, the mayor and board of aldermen, and officers of the Masonic Lodge of the city. Bishop Wiley delivered the principal address, and was assisted by the Rev. J. J. Manker, pastor of the church, who consecrated the corner-stone, which was then laid by the Masons, who in so doing performed a beautiful ceremony, and deposited therein King James' version of the Bible, the revised version of the New Testament of 1881, the Methodist hymnal and discipline, and a copy of most of the city newspapers. The church building stands at the corner of Georgia and McCallie Avenues, is entirely stone, and is therefore popularly known as the Rock Church. It is an elegant and expensive structure, costing in the aggregate, including the lot and organ, nearly $63,000. The organ which was first heard by the public September 26, 1886, has 1,000 pipes, and twenty-three stops. The Rev. J. J. Manker was pastor of this church four years, previous to the commencement of the pastorate of the Rev. T. C. Warner, D. D., who became pastor in the fall of 1884.

The entire number of Methodist Episcopal Church organizations in Hamilton County is now about thirty, having an aggregate membership of about 2,500, and twenty church buildings, the entire property of the denomination in the county being estimated to be worth $200,000. Following are the names of the preachers: T. C. Warner, D. D.; T. C. Carter, D. D.; J. J. Manker, D. D.; E. S. Lewis, J. J. Shingler, J. S. Jones, R. M. Marshal, I. V. Miller, S. Hawkins, W. W. Hooper and J. J. Robinette. Of the thirty organizations twelve belong to the colored people.

The Christian Church was established in 1871, by a small number of people collected by the Rev. Dr. Hopson, then of Louisville, Ky., who, on the 21st of November of the above named year, concluded a course of lectures, delivered with the view of organizing a church of that denomination in Chattanooga. The church at first contained twenty-one members, nine of whom had been converted and baptized by Dr. Hopson during his two weeks' stay in the city. The church thus organized held services at various places, at one time in a small school building in the rear of the Episcopal Church, on Eighth Street. At length in 1882 they bought a lot on Walnut Street, between Seventh and Eighth Streets, 50x82 feet in size, at a cost of $1,325, which is now worth $5,000, and in 1884 commenced the erection of a church, now completed, except the basement. This building was built at an expense of $10,000, at a great personal sacrifice to the members. It was dedicated November 10, 1886, by Elder R. Moffat, assisted by Elder T. D. Butler. The present membership of the church is 188. The following is a list of the pastors of this church: A. Allison, G. W. Abell, J. R. Biggs, F. M. Hawkins, A. G. Thomas, A. S. Johnson, D. T. Buck and T. D. Butler, who became pastor September 1, 1884, and retired from the church September 1, 1886. The Sunday-school contains 170 scholars. The present officers are, trustees, G. B. Woodworth, D. W. Chase and Mr. Post; secretary and treasurer, Dr. D. E. Nelson.

SS. Peter and Paul Catholic Church was established in Chattanooga in 1852, the first baptism of a child, occurring February 10 of that year, being performed by Rev. Henry Vincent Brown—this baptism indicating the time at about which the congregation was organized by this priest. The Rev. Mr. Brown visited the laborers along the railroads, most of whom were Irish, and was instrumental in encouraging them to congregate around his mission and to procure homes for themselves at the mere trifle at which they could then be procured. When the war came on it for the most part upset his plans. An Irishman named Daniel Hogan, filled with religious zeal, desirous of erecting a church building, gave to it the land now owned by this church, at the corner of Georgia Avenue and Gilmer Street. A stone structure was commenced and was built up to the eaves when work upon it was checked by the war, and the stones in the wall utilized in the erection of the stone fort. Since then no work has been done toward completing the edifice, the organization considering it best to wait until the final decision of the Government upon their claim for damages, which it expects will soon come in the form of an allowance, as on the 19th of March, 1886, the House Committee reported favorably upon the claim of $18,700. Rev. Father Brown was succeeded by Rev. Father J. T. Nealis, who remained but a short time and was followed by Rev. Father P. Ryan, who built the parsonage, and who died from yellow fever in 1878. Father Ryan introduced two Dominican Sisters from the St. Cecilian Academy at Nashville, in 1876, who in that year took charge of the Academy Notre Dame de Lourdes, which has been so successful that in 1886 a fine three-story brick school building was erected at a cost of $12,000, and the school contains about 250 scholars. Rev. Father P. J. Gleeson was transferred from Clarksville to this church in July, 1885, and since coming to Chattanooga he has purchased a site of forty-six acres on the east side of Missionary Ridge for a cemetery, to which were removed in November, 1886, the remains of Father Ryan. The church now (November, 1886) consists of about 200 families.

The Jewish Synagogue is located on Walnut Street near Fifth. For some years previous to 1882, there had been a Jewish congregation in Chattanooga, and in that year they completed their present synagogue, dedicating it in September. Rev. Julius Ochs, who was then the rabbi, delivered a very fine address, and was assisted in the dedicatory services by Rev. Dr. E. Schrieber, of Mobile, Ala., who delivered an able address on the theme, "Shema Israel." After a short address by Dr. R. M. Wise the exercises closed. The building is of brick, neatly and plainly constructed and will seat about 300 persons.

St. Paul's Episcopal Church is located at the southwest corner of Chestnut and West Eighth Streets, and St. John's Episcopal Church is located on the west side of Cameron Hill, near the Roane Iron Works. Both organizations are doing excellent work in the mission and hospital fields of labor. St. John's Church was consecrated February 19, 1882, by the bishop of Tennessee, assisted by the rector of St. Paul's Church and the Rev. J. H. T. LaRoche, of Sewanee. After the Bishop had delivered the sermon of consecration, he paid a deserved tribute to Miss E. L. Buckler, who had raised the money for building the church edifice upon ground given to the mission by the Roane Iron Company. The mission had been in existence four years, and had held services in a small chapel. The new building, which is capable of seating 300 people, together with the furniture and fixtures, cost $2,000. The chancel windows were presented by Grace Church, New York, and the font by Mrs. John Minturn, of New York, who also assisted Miss Buckler in raising the money to build the church.

The First Baptist Church is located on the southeast corner of East Sixth and Walnut Streets. It has a large and enterprising membership, and a commodious frame house of worship. The design is at present entertained of selling their present church property, and of building a more modern church, more on a par with the other newly erected church edifices in Chattanooga. The congregation was largely increased by the wise course of their late pastor, Rev. J. T. Christian, D. D., who was succeeded by the present pastor, Rev. M. M. Wamboldt, whose zeal, eloquence and excellent Christian character are fully appreciated by the church.

The Second Baptist Church is located at 1004 Cowart Street, in the manufacturing center of the city, and is a strong and growing congregation. The present pastor is the Rev. L. N. Brock, a man of piety, zeal and never-tiring energy.

The First Baptist Church (colored) is located at the corner of Tenth and B Streets. The building is not yet completed, the walls of stone being only partially erected and covered in with a temporary wood roof. The pastor is the Rev. W. M. Washington.

Shiloh Baptist Church (colored) is also making considerable progress.

The First Congregational Church (colored) is located on the west side of A Street, south of East Ninth Street. It was organized with sixteen members, June 9, 1867, with Rev. E. O. Tade, pastor, who remained six years. His successor was Rev. A. C. Ellis, who was followed in 1874 by Rev. E. B. Sellers, by Rev. Temple Cutler, in 1876, and by the present pastor, Rev. Joseph E. Smith, in 1879. The American Missionary Association aided this organization until 1883, since when it has been self-sustaining. It now has property worth $20,000. The colored people sustain numerous other churches in Chattanooga.

Chattanooga lies on the south of the Tennessee River (strictly speaking, on the east bank, as there the river flows in a southerly direction), not far from what might be termed the central point of converging mountain ranges—Walden's Ridge, Lookout Mountain and Missionary Ridge, or just above where the river breaks through between Walden's Ridge and Lookout Mountain, in longitude 85° 14' west from Greenwich and in north latitude 35° 4'. Previous to receiving its present name, it was known as Ross' Landing, Ross Warehouse, or Ross Ferry, these names having been applied indifferently for about twenty-five years, during most of which time the entire region in view from Lookout Point was a wooded wilderness, with only here and there an Indian's cabin and patch of truck. Rossville was for a long time the postoffice. When, in 1836, the Cherokee lands began to be settled by whites, and trade sprang up in the various products of their cultivated settlements, Ross' Landing, the principal landing on the river, became the nucleus of a town, and when, in 1838, the settlers were enabled to acquire titles to the lands they had held by the right of occupancy, a town was laid out at the Landing, lots were sold in April, 1839, and the future Chattanooga began her race for prosperity, wealth and renown.

Ross' Landing, besides becoming the center of trade for the immediate vicinity, also became the center of the salt trade for East Tennessee and north Alabama. The salt sold here was made at King's Salt Works, in Virginia, and at times of freshets, floated in flatboats down the north fork of the Holston, and so on down the Tennessee River to Ross' and other landings. This company, having a monopoly of the salt trade in this part of the country, sold salt at their own prices through agents stationed at the various landings along the river. In 1838, 1,500 barrels of salt were sold at an average price of $8 per barrel. Thus commenced the settlement and the commerce of Chattanooga—of the future greatness of which the early settlers had no prophetic vision, and while these small beginnings were being made, a "chief" was among them taking notes which he printed in the Chattanooga *Gazette*, but unfortunately the printed notes can not be rescued from oblivion. In 1836 a military post was established here, looking to the removal of the Indians at the expiration of the two years' grace given them by the treaty of New Echota. In April, 1837, a postoffice was established by the name of Ross' Landing, with John P. Long as postmaster. At first, not being on any post route, it was only a special office, the mail to be supplied from Rossville, Ga., by special contract. Some months afterward a tri-weekly line of four-horse post coaches, was established between Augusta Ga., and Murfreesboro, Tenn., which added so greatly to the mail facilities at Ross' Landing, that letters could be received from Washington in ten days, then considered remarkably quick time.

After the extinguishment of the Indian title to the land, the interest therein passed to the State of Tennessee for the use of the public schools, and to make the proceeds of this land available the Legislature, on the 29th of November, 1837, passed an act creating the Ocoee land district, and establishing a land office at Cleveland. According to the provision of this act lands in this district could be entered at $7.50 per acre and "whosoever was in possession of and residing upon any piece of land at the passage of said act should have a pre-emption or priority of entry for the term of three months over other persons, and if two or more persons were residing on the same quarter section, they should have a joint preference of entry on said quarter section.

At the time of the passage of this act there were residing upon the northeast quarter of Section 29, second fractional township, fourth range west, twenty-eight persons and upon the southeast fractional quarter (eighty acres of Section 20), twenty-five persons who were entitled to a joint preference of entry on their respective tracts of land. Those living on the quarter section were James W. Smith, John P. Long, Samuel Williams, William M. Davis, Matthew Frazier, Eliza Russell, Joseph Ellis, Abner Witt, John Keeney, John A. Porter, George B. Gwathmey, Samuel H. Davis, Ezekiel Price, Lewis Webb, Ailsey Cape, Abram Perry, Joseph Rice, Thomas W. Munsey, Berry Jones, Isaac Baldwin, E. H. Freeman, Charles Grigsby and six others. Those on the fraction were David G. Perry, Allen Kennedy, William Long, S. S. M. Doak, B. K. Hudgins, Matthias Williams, Matthew Hillsman, D. A. Wilds, William Hill, —— Cathey, I. T. Mathis, William Thurman, Nathan Harris, —— Thrailkill, Cary A. Jones, William B. Gilleland, James W. Tunnell, Jane Henderson, M. W. Legg, William G. Sparks and five others. All of those living on the quarter section or their assignees transferred their right of occupancy to three commissioners or trustees; A. M. Rawlings, John P. Long and George W. Williams, and most of those on the fraction transferred their rights to Allen Kennedy, R. A. Ramsey and Albert S. Lenoir, the duty of these commissioners being to enter the land, to have a town laid off, to make deeds to each respective occupant, to designate certain lots for the use of churches, to convey the lots so designated to the churches, and to sell the balance of the lots to the highest bidder and to divide the net proceeds among the interested parties.

In the summer of 1838 the town was laid off into lots by Josiah Patty of Roane County, and was bounded on the north by the Tennessee River, on the east by Georgia Avenue, on the south by James Street and on the west by the foot of Cameron Hill. The commissioners for those living on the quarter section entered said quarter November 7, 1838, by entry No. 98, on which a grant, No. 22, was issued by the State, December 3, following. The commissioners for the fraction also obtained a grant for that tract.

Soon after the survey and platting of the town several of the principal citizens assembled in the log schoolhouse standing on the corner of Fifth and Lookout Streets, for the purpose of naming the new town, soon to be much more than a mere landing. There were from fifteen to twenty persons present at the meeting, at which various names were suggested: Albion, because of the white cliffs on Walden's Ridge; Montevideo, because of the mountains in view from the location; Videopolis, suggested by James A. Whiteside, because of the city to be visible in the future from the mountains, and Chattanooga, by John P. Long, because this " was the name of a valley and a creek, and was said to have been the original name of Lookout Mountain, given to all these before the country was occupied by the Cherokees, and from antiquity the meaning had been lost." This name was adopted by the meeting and the future manufacturing center and historic city of the South thus became "Chattanooga." How Chattanooga became the manufacturing center and historic city of the South remains to be related. Mr. Long says the meaning of the name Chattanooga had been lost from antiquity. Some say the original signification of the word was "Hawk's nest," others say "Crow's nest," and still others "Eagle's nest." With reference to these meanings the following extract from Van Horne's "History of the Army of the Cumberland" is to the purpose.

"A somewhat similar name* was applied by the Cherokees to the cliffs, rising boldly from the river above the town, which was derived from Clanoowah, the name of a warlike but diminutive hawk, which was supposed to embody the spirit of the tribe. These cliffs were the private nesting-place of the bird, and hence a name was given which expressed this fact, and which perhaps has suggested the myth that 'Chattanooga' means "eagle's nest."

The same authority says that originally Chattanooga was the name of a small Indian hamlet situated near the base of Lookout Mountain, on the bank of Chattanooga Creek, and that in the Cherokee language it means "to draw fish out of water." It was therefore applied to their small hamlet on the creek, to the creek itself and to the valley. "The humble hamlet has disappeared, and its name, suggestive and appropriate at first, was inherited by the town of the white man with meaningless application," because the white man did not know its meaning. The acceptation of this explanation excludes the very plausible theory of John W. James, that the word, originally spelled "Chat-a-nu-ga," was suggestive of the general topography of the country, and meant "broken mountains."

The three principal landings along the river were Ross', Gunter's, and Ditton's. In December, 1838, the name of the postoffice at the former was changed to Chattanooga, and on the 20th of April, 1839, the lots on the quarter section were sold, except forty, the proceeds of the sale approximating $45,000. The sale of the lots on the fraction did not occur until after several years. Recurring to the early trade of the city it may be stated that the "Atlas" was the first steamboat that navigated the Tennessee above the Muscle Shoals. The Atlas was commanded by

---

*Similar to Chattanooga.

Capt. Dixon, made the trip to Knoxville and fully demonstrated the navigability of the Tennessee from the Muscle Shoals to Knoxville for several months in the year. The success of this experiment induced citizens of Knoxville to build a steamer named "Knoxville," which in 1831 or 1832 made regular trips on the river, and by the time Chattanooga was ready to engage in trade and commerce, she had by means of several boats regular communication with New Orleans by river, except a portage of forty miles around the Muscle Shoals, on which a railroad had been built, which was operated by horse power between Tuscumbia and Decatur. Thus Chattanooga was enabled to supply the northern counties of Georgia and Alabama, as far as the Coosa River, with groceries, etc., more cheaply than could any other point, and this together with her commerce with East Tennessee, gave her a growing and commanding trade.

Soon after the sale of lots in April, 1839, the necessity was felt for some form of town government, and in accordance therewith the Legislature on December 20, 1839, passed "an act to establish the town of Chattanooga in the county of Hamilton, and to incorporate the inhabitants thereof." The name and style of the new town established by this act, "on the south side of the Tennessee River, at the place now known as Ross' Landing," was "the mayor and aldermen of the town of Chattanooga," and this corporation was endowed with power, among many other things, to appoint a recorder, treasurer and town constable. The sheriff of Hamilton County was commanded to hold an election on the second Tuesday of January, 1840, for the purpose of electing seven persons to serve as aldermen for one year and these seven aldermen were required to choose one of their number to act as mayor of the town. The records of the town under this charter having been lost it is not easy to recall the names of the first aldermen, nor of the entire list of mayors under it; however the first mayor was James Berry, elected in January, 1840. Dr. Beriah Frazier was elected in 1841; Dr. Milo Smith, elected in 1842; Drs. Milo Smith, Joseph S. Gillespie and a few others whose names cannot now be ascertained filling the office during the years from 1843 to 1851 inclusive.

By this time Chattanooga had outgrown her primitive government, and the Legislature, recognizing the necessities of the situation, passed a second charter under the title of "an act to incorporate the city of Chattanooga, and for other purposes," the corporation being known under this act, by the name and style of the mayor and aldermen of the city of Chattanooga. The boundaries of the city as fixed by this charter were as follows:

Beginning at the northeast corner of the southwest fractional quarter of fractional section twenty-one, second fractional township fourth range west of the basis line in the Ocoee District; thence south twenty (degrees) west to the southeast corner of the northwest quarter of section thirty-three; thence north seventy (degrees) west to the middle of Tennessee River; thence up the middle of the river to a point opposite the beginning, thence in a direct line to the beginning.

The board of mayor and aldermen then serving was required to lay off the city into at least four wards, before the 10th of the following December and an election for a city council was required to be held on the last Thursday of that month, the city council to consist of a mayor, and a board of aldermen, the board of aldermen to consist of two members from each ward, and all to be elected by the qualified voters of the city. Section 12 of this act provided that the territory included in the boundary of the city of Chattanooga should constitute a civil district of the county and be entitled to three justices of the peace. By section 14, the corporation of the city was authorized to borrow money for any legal purpose in any sum not to exceed $20,000, which should not bear a higher rate of interest than six per cent per annum, but no authority was given to issue paper that should circulate as money; but the corporation was authorized to issue bonds as subscription to railroad or turnpike company stock in addition to the $20,000 loan authorized by section 14.

In accordance with the provisions of this act the first election was held on the last Thursday of December, 1851, and the board then chosen organized on January 5, 1852. Following are the names of the mayor and board of aldermen then organized: Mayor, Milo Smith; aldermen: First Ward—Larkin Hair, N. B. Parham; Second Ward—John P. Long, J. J. Bryan; Third Ward—Robert Cravens, William Crutchfield; Fourth Ward—D. C. McMillin, John A. Hooke.

The following is a complete list of the mayors elected under this charter: In 1853, Henry W. Massengale; 1854, William Williams; 1855, E. G. Pearl; 1856, D. C. McMillin; 1857, W. D. Fulton; 1858, W. S. Bell; 1859, Thomas Crutchfield, Sr.; 1860, Charles E. Grenville; 1861, J. C. Warner; 1862, Milo Smith; 1863, Milo Smith. The Federal Army took possession of the city in September, 1863, and as a consequence, the operations of the civil government were interrupted until October, 1865, when the following officers were elected: Mayor, Richard Henderson; board of aldermen, First Ward—A. Bohr, A. Kesterson; Second Ward—J. Mann, J. DeBeck; Third Ward—William Crutchfield, T. R. Stanley; Fourth Ward—Jacob Kunz, D. Hogan. The other mayors under this charter were Charles E. Lewis, elected in 1866; D. C. Carr, in 1867 and also in 1868.

Marshals: Thomas McMinn, 1852–54; N. P. Nail, 1855; Philip Simmerman, 1856–57; John J. Lowry, 1858–59; Jesse B. Allison, 1860–63; R. H. Croft, 1869; Jesse B. Allison, 1870; Charles Howell, 1871; N. W.

Wilbur, 1872; J. J. Lowry, 1874; D. M. Doty, 1876; J. J. Lowry, 1877; E. Balch, 1878; J. J. Lowry, 1879-80; N. W. Wilbur, 1881-82; —— Schwartz, 1885.

Recorders: Richard Henderson, 1852; John W. Ford, 1853; Daniel R. Rawlings, 1854; D. C. McMillin, 1855; Daniel R. Rawlings, 1856; William L. Rogers, 1857-59; John P. Long, 1860-63.

By the second charter of the city the mayor and aldermen of the city of Chattanooga were granted perpetual succession, as had also been done by the first. By the third charter, granted November 10, 1869, succession was given for ninety-nine years. By this charter the boundaries of the city were defined as follows: "Beginning at a point on the Tennessee River where the north line of the southeast fractional quarter of fractional section twenty-one, in the second fractional township, west of the basis line in the Ocoee District strikes said river; thence south 70° east to the northeast corner of said quarter section; thence south 20° west to the township line dividing the second and third townships; thence north 70° west along said township line to the middle of said river; thence up the middle of said river to a point opposite the beginning; thence in a direct line to the beginning."

The first election under this charter was held on the third Thursday in November, 1869, and under its provisions, non-resident freeholders were allowed to vote in the ward in which their freeholds were situated, but not elsewhere. The corporation was authorized to borrow money to any amount not exceeding $50,000, unless authorized to exceed that limit by a majority of the qualified voters of the city, and it was provided that the city marshal should be elected in the same manner as the mayor was elected, instead of being appointed as heretofore by the mayor and board of aldermen. In 1872 this charter was so amended as to increase the number of wards to five.

Following are election returns in the cases of mayor and aldermen from 1868 to the present time:

Mayors: 1868, A. J. Sharpe. 1869, W. P. Rathburn, 925; all others, 12. 1870, W. P. Rathburn, 963; B. S. Nicklin, 152; J. J. McGlohon, 408. 1871, John T. Wilder, 1,002; Thomas Webster, 812. 1872, E. M. Wight, 662; P. Foster, 568; R. Henderson, 179. 1873, P. D. Sims. 1874, John W. James, 1,025; S. A. Key, 808. 1875, Tomlinson Fort. 1876, E. M. Wight, 971; J. H. Ragsdale, 847. 1877, T. J. Carlile, 1,121; W. J. Colburn, 1,002. 1878, J. T. Hill, 1,134; John A. Hart, 994. 1879, H. F. Temple, 1,113; J. C. Stanton, 982. 1880, John A. Hart, 1,249; M. J. O'Brien, 1,127. 1881, H. C. Evans, 1,523; M. J. O'Brien, 1,003. 1882, H. C. Evans, 1,809; J. T. Shipp, 1,188. 1883, Hugh

Hon. H. Clay Evans

Whiteside, elected for two years. 1885, A. G. Sharp, 1,808; Clift, 1,696; Dean, 100.

Marshals: 1869, R. H. Kroft, 489; A. G. McLemore, 442. 1870, Jesse B. Allison, 474; J. R. Slayton, 276; R. H. Kroft, 272. 1871, Charles Howell, 920; B. B. Bell, 437; J. O. Farmer, 323. 1872, N. W. Wilbur, 968; J. J. Lowry, 680. 1874, J. J. Lowry, 1,018; D. C. Howell, 806. 1876, D. M. Doty, 926; J. J. Lowry, 890. 1877, J. J. Lowry, 1,090; W. Friedman, 1,033. 1878, E. Balch, 1,093; J. J. Conway, 1,005. 1879, J. J. Lowry, 776; J. A. Allen, 744; C. G. Davis, 507. 1880, J. J. Lowry, 1,251; W. P. Dale, 1,107. 1881, N. W. Wilbur, 1,292. 1882, N. W. Wilbur, 1,775; J. J. Lowry, 1,215. 1885, Schwartz, 1,835; Key, 1,657; Woodworth, 103.

On the 27th of March, 1879, the Legislature passed an act making the terms of aldermen in certain cities two years instead of one; and as the act applied to Chattanooga the mayor and aldermen adopted the provisions of the act by an ordinance passed September 16, 1879.

In 1883 an ordinance was passed under which the mayor should be elected for two years, and the Board of Aldermen reduced in number to six—one from each ward and one at large. The first Board of Aldermen after this change were as follows: First Ward, Henry Schwartz; Second Ward, C. H. Dyer; Third Ward, H. C. Evans; Fourth Ward, W. C. Hodge (colored); Fifth Ward, Newell Sanders; at large, J. W. Henderson. In the election of 1886, when there were three aldermen to be elected, the Democrats, in order to avoid being overwhelmingly defeated, withdrew their candidates and the result of the election was as follows: J. T. Williams, at large, received 1,438 votes; W. C. Hodge, Fourth Ward, 1,290; Howard, Fifth Ward, 1,353, other candidates receiving very light votes. The congressional vote in Chattanooga, November 2, 1886, was for Wilder, 2,495; for Neal, 1,477. For governor the vote stood for Robert L. Taylor, 1,557; Alfred A. Taylor, 2,420. For representatives: Stone, Republican, 2,405; Hutchins, Republican (colored), 2,061; Drumbar, Democrat, 1,793; Lloyd, 1,574. For senator: Kennedy, Republican, 2,283; Whitice, Democrat, 1,694.

Returning now to the business interests and growth of the city it may be stated that their development was comparatively slow before the war. But notwithstanding this the spirit of enterprise was abroad in the land. The railroad, although as yet not in view from Chattanooga, was yet to work a revolution, of which none even of the most sanguine in that city had ever dreamed. The history of the construction of the first railroad to reach Chattanooga is briefly as follows: South Carolina had built a railroad from Charleston to Augusta, and almost immediately the stupendous project was conceived and was being agitated of connecting Charleston with Cincinnati. In furtherance of this grand scheme a convention was held at Knoxville, July 4, 1836, at which delegates were present from Ohio, Kentucky, Tennessee, North Carolina, South Carolina and Georgia. The route favored by a majority of this convention was that through the Appalachian chain of mountains by the way of Knoxville and the Cumberland Gap, while the Georgia delegation, with Absalom Chappell at their head, contended for a more westerly route. Georgia was pushing her road northwest from Augusta to the Chattahoochee River, intending to continue that line northward to the Tennessee River, near Ross' Landing, thence up the Tennessee Valley to some suitable gap in the Cumberland Mountains, and thence to Cincinnati. This route was favored at Knoxville by the Georgia delegation, but the convention adopted the more direct route via Knoxville and the Cumberland Gap.

Upon the return home of the Georgia delegation they called a State convention to meet at Macon, which recommended a system of railroads for the State, and that the central point of this system should be east of the Chattahoochie River, now Atlanta, the Georgia Railroad to be continued to that point, as also the Central Railroad from Savannah, the Macon & Western from Macon, and a line not then built from Columbus; and the State was to build a single line from this central point to the Tennessee River. This general plan received the approval of the Legislature of Georgia, which passed an act in December, 1836, to build the Western & Atlantic Railroad from a point east of the Chattahoochee River to the northern boundary of the State at or near Rossville, and, with the consent of Tennessee, on to the Tennessee River. After many discouragements and much delay, the enterprise was completed, the road entered Chattanooga in 1849, and the first railroad train entered the town in December of that year. The tunnel, however, had not been built and passengers had to be transferred over the ridge at Tunnel Hill. The depot was located on Broad Street, according to an agreement with Thomas Crutchfield, who owned the land where the Read House now stands, and who as his part of the agreement was to build a hotel opposite. The hotel when erected was a small frame building and stood on the present site of the Read House. The depot then erected was used until 1858.

The entrance of this first train into Chattanooga was an event big with great possibilities, and it was celebrated in a becoming manner. L. P. Parham, editor of the Chattanooga *Gazette* made a speech in which he said: "I am full of this momentous occasion—too full for utterance. I have labored night and day for this enterprise. I was the first man in East Tennessee to agitate the building of this road, and now I am happy to know it has been completed to Chattanooga," etc.

The growth of Chattanooga was comparatively slow before the war. In December, 1851, E. R. Mills, who was located here as agent for the Central and Macon & Western Railroads "had the pleasure of informing the merchants and planters of North Alabama and Tennessee that the connection of the above roads at Macon is complete." In 1852 there were in business in Chattanooga the following individuals and firms: John H. Newton, dry goods; H. S. Abrahams & Co., dry goods, groceries and liquors, "the cheapest store in Chattanooga;" C. E. Grenville & Co., commission and forwarding merchants, who charged for forwarding cotton 25 cents per bale; oats, 2 cents; corn, $2\frac{1}{2}$ cents; and wheat, 3 cents per bushel; J. Mitchell had just moved in from Gainesville, Ga., and opened a new tin shop; Cohen & Barrett were there and had been for some years conducting the "People's Store;" Massengale, Avery & Co., general store; Joseph Ramsey & Son were pork packers and dealers in bacon and lard; L. L. Thomasson was a general commission merchant "on the upper wharf boat;" B. F. Tutt kept a drug store, and the "Tennessee River M. M. and Transportation Company's Express Line of Mail Steamers" ran daily between Chattanooga and Decatur, and were making tri-weekly trips to Knoxville. The city had become quite a commercial point, and at one time, in 1854, the accumulation of cotton over and above what the railroad could carry away was 10,000 bales. The city had then a population of about 4,000; there were four churches, and halls for the Masons, Odd Fellows and Sons of Temperance; but little had been done toward building up the schools.

In 1845 a charter was granted to certain persons to build a railroad from Chattanooga to Nashville, and after many obstacles had been encountered and surmounted by the projectors of the road it was completed about 1850. This is now the Nashville, Chattanooga & St. Louis Railway, which, including both main lines to Hickman, Ky., 321 miles, and branches, 198 miles, is 519 miles in length.

In 1853 what is now the Alabama Great Southern Railroad was chartered by Tennessee as the Wills Valley Railroad and by Alabama as the Northeast & Southwest Alabama. It was graded most of its length, and fifteen miles built and operated from Trenton, Ga., to Wauhatchie before the war, trains running into Chattanooga over the tracks of the Nashville, Chattanooga & St. Louis Railroad until 1868, when the original franchises were merged into a charter granted to the Alabama & Chattanooga Railroad Company. This company completed the line to Meridian, Miss., May 17, 1871. On the first of January, 1871, default was made on account of interest, and from that time to 1877, the history of this road is too intricate with lawsuits and sales, to find narration in this work. On January 22, 1877, it was sold to a company organized by the English holders of the bonds, and this company was fully organized as the Alabama Great Southern Railroad Company, November 30, 1877. Since then the roadbed has so improved that it is now one of the most substantial and safe in the country, and the entire length of the line is 296 miles.

The Memphis & Charleston was originally projected by leading capitalists of Tennessee, South Carolina and the North. John C. Calhoun, in company with capitalists from his own State and New York, visited Chattanooga and went over the route to Memphis in 1854. The road was constructed from Memphis to Stevenson, a distance of 272 miles; and trains run over the Nashville, Chattanooga & St. Louis, a distance of thirty-eight miles. This road was opened for business July 4, 1858.

In 1836 the Hiwassee Railroad was chartered from Chattanooga to Knoxville, and the East Tennessee & Virginia soon afterward from Knoxville to Bristol. About the year 1856, when both roads were completed, the name Hiwassee Railroad was changed to the East Tennessee & Georgia, and in 1869 or 1870 the two roads were consolidated under the name of East Tennessee, Virginia & Georgia Railroad. This road's branches and connections are the following: The North Carolina branch, connecting at Morristown; the Jellico Line, from Knoxville to the Cincinnati Southern Railroad; the Knoxville & Augusta, from Knoxville to Maryville; the Alabama division, from Chattanooga to Lauderdale, Miss., 389 miles, and the Georgia division, from Chattanooga to Brunswick, Ga., 431 miles.

The Cincinnati Southern Railway was the last to enter Chattanooga. It was projected and partly surveyed in 1836, the preliminary line being located that year through Kentucky and some distance into Tennessee by W. A. Gunn. In 1863 Col. J. E. McGowan commanded an engineer corps, which resurveyed Gunn's line of 1836, down to Burnside Point, and immediately after the termination of the war the question was agitated of connecting Cincinnati and Chattanooga by rail, and this agitation resulted in procuring, in 1869, legislation in Ohio authorizing the Board of Trustees of the Cincinnati Southern Railway to raise $10,000,000 for the construction of the line. After securing, in 1872, a charter for the company from the Kentucky Legislature, work began in earnest. The road was completed to Somerset, Ky., July 21, 1877, and to Chattanooga at 3:15 P. M., December 10, 1879, at which minute the last spike was driven, and an engine arrived in Chattanooga over the road at 9:40 P. M.

of the same day. The first engine to make the full run over the road arrived in Chattanooga December 13, and the first full train from Cincinnati arrived in Chattanooga at 2:30 P. M., December 18. The first freight train left Chattanooga for Cincinnati February 23, 1880, and regular passenger trains commenced running on March 7, the first regular passenger train arriving at Chattanooga at 11:15 A. M. Schedule time at first was as follows: Leave Cincinnati at 8:40 A. M., arriving in Chattanooga at 10:45 P. M.; leave Chattanooga at 4:20 A. M., arriving in Cincinnati at 6:20 P. M., distance 336 miles; time south, 14 hours and 5 minutes; time north, 14 hours; average speed, 24 miles per hour. At present the schedule time for the fastest express train is as follows: Leave Cincinnati at 8:05 A. M., arriving in Chattanooga at 6:00 P. M.; leave Chattanooga at 7:45 A. M., arriving in Cincinnati at 6:00 P. M., thus giving an average speed from north to south of 33.6 miles per hour. And it was over this road and the other two, all of which together now constitute the "Queen & Crescent Line," that on April 20, 21, 1884, the "Pythian train," ran from Cincinnati to New Orleans, a distance of 827 miles in 23 hours and 20 minutes, including stops; and excluding stops, in 19 hours and 1 minute, or in the latter case at the rate of 43.5 miles per hour, and including stops, of 35.4 miles per hour. In October, 1881, the road was leased for twenty-five years to the Cincinnati, New Orleans & Texas Pacific Railway Company at an average rental of $1,000,000 per annum.

About the year 1856 Chattanooga had become so large a city that the principal business of the county had centered there, but the county seat was at Harrison, twelve miles northeast. To relieve the citizens of Chattanooga from the necessity of attending court at Harrison, the Legislature on the 26th of January, 1858, passed an act establishing "The Law Court of Chattanooga," for the trial of cases originating in the Fourth and Fourteenth Civil Districts. This court was organized and held for the first time on the first Monday in June, 1858, the Hon. John C. Gaut, presiding, and Elbert A. Glass, clerk. Judge W. L. Adams presided at the June term in the absence of the judge of the court, John B. Hoyl, and until July 11, 1870. On the 14th of November, 1870, Judge Hoyl took his seat and presided in this court until its adjournment, December 2, 1870. During this time this court had jurisdiction over the Third, Fourth, Fifth, Fourteenth and Seventeenth Civil Districts.

On the 25th of February, 1858, an act was passed by the Legislature establishing a chancery court for Chattanooga, which was organized on the fourth Monday of July following, by Chancellor T. Nixon Van Dyke, with William I. Standifer, clerk and master, and Rufus G. Jones, deputy. When the county seat was moved to Chattanooga in 1870, this court was merged into the chancery court of the county, as the law court was merged into the county circuit court.

After the opening of the Western & Atlantic Railroad in 1849, Mr. Cravens, president of the East Tennessee Iron Manufacturing Company, moved from Roane County to Chattanooga and erected a foundry and machine shop for the manufacture of freight cars, and for doing general machine work. While conducting this enterprise he developed the fact that as good car wheels could be made from the cold blast charcoal iron of East Tennessee as could be made anywhere in the country. In time this establishment became the property of Thomas Webster. Other manufacturing establishments before the war were the following: I. G. Bynum's steam tannery, then the largest in the South; the pork packing establishments of Chandler & Co. and of Ramsey & Co.; the saw and planing-mill of McCallie, Marsh & Co.; Bell & Co.'s flouring-mill and distillery, the flouring-mill having a capacity of 150 barrels of flour per day, and the distillery of fifty barrels of whisky; C. E. Grenville's flouring-mill, with a capacity of fifty barrels per day, with others of minor note, until in 1860 there were twenty establishments in all employing a capital of $209,300. At this time the population of the city was 3,500, and for the next three or four years during the continuance of the civil war, the permanent population rather diminished than increased. The part taken by Chattanooga during that trying period is for the most part included in the account of Hamilton County's participation in the war of the Rebellion, in this connection only a few dates of the arrival of troops, etc., being introduced.

After the Tullahoma campaign, Gen. Bragg's army entered Chattanooga during the first week of July, 1863, and on the 21st of August, Gen. Wilder, in company with Gen. G. D. Wagner, shelled the city from the north side of the river, causing it to be evacuated by the rebel troops to points beyond range of Wilder's guns. On the 28th, William Crutchfield, a most intelligent, courageous, and useful scout, spy and guide for the Federal generals during their campaigns around Chattanooga, and a true blue Union man, having learned on the 26th of September, from the conversation of two rebel quartermasters, the strength of Bragg's army and his plan of campaign against Gen. Rosecrans, communicated this information to Gen. Wilder, who immediately telegraphed it by signal to Gen. Rosecrans who was about thirty miles below at Caperton's Ferry. On the 7th and 8th of September Bragg's army completed their evacuation of Chattanooga, and Gen. Wilder entered it on the morning of the ninth. After the battle of Chickamauga, Gen. Rosecrans entered Chattanooga on the 20th of September, and his army retreated to that place immediately afterward. By orders from the War Department, promulgated October 19, Gen. Rosecrans was relieved from the command of the Army of the Cumberland, Gen. Thomas promoted to that command, and Gen. Grant assigned to the command of the "Military Division of the Mississippi." On the 23d Gen. Grant arrived in Chattanooga taking command, and on the 24th he made a personal inspection of the positions occupied by the Army of the Cumberland. On the 23d of November, 120 pontons conveyed 3,000 men of Sherman's army corps down the Tennessee to the mouth of South Chickamauga Creek, Gen. Grant's headquarters being during that day and the next at Wood's Redoubt. On the 25th Gen. Grant's headquarters were in the morning on Orchard Knob, and in the evening after the victory of the Union Army on Missionary Ridge they were east of the crest of that ridge.

The Forty-ninth Ohio, Colonel Gibson, arrived in Chattanooga on Sunday, April 10, 1864, as also did the Seventy-fourth Ohio, Colonel Given, and the Eighth Iowa Cavalry, and on the 11th, the Twenty-third Indiana. The scout made by the Fourteenth Colored Regiment and then just completed, in which they had taken Pikeville, Sparta, Kingston and other places, was highly praised. The items in this paragraph are taken from the Chattanooga *Daily Gazette* of April 12, 1864, Volume I, No. 38, as is also the following partial statement of the dilemma which then presented itself to President Jefferson Davis, and the other authorities of the Confederate States:

>Unless they free the negro they have nothing left to fight with.
>If they free the negro they have nothing left to fight for.
>Ever since the Rebellion began negroes have been falling,
>Nevertheless their greatest fear now is that the negroes will rise.
>If Davis impresses food he turns the land into a desert;
>Unless he impresses food he turns his soldiers into deserters.
>If they fight they lose the day, and
>Unless they fight they lose every day.

Before the occupation of Chattanooga by the army of Gen. Rosecrans, a paper was published by Franc M. Paul, called the Chattanooga *Daily Rebel*. No. 247 of Volume 1 appeared May 22, 1863. In this number there was an editorial on "Jacobinism in the North" in which occurred the following paragraph:

>"So thoroughly is the Northern mind subject to the delusive principle that the support of the administration is the support of the Government, and so completely has the dominion of the bayonet subjugated the impulse of free thought which once animated the heart of the country, that little can be expected from the resistance of the people, leaderless, armless, objectless. There is no great chieftain among them. Judge Douglass is dead, but he was not a game man. Vallandigham has not the capacity nor the prestige; Horatio Seymour is an old woman; John Van Buren was bought for a trifle; Fernando Wood is only a local politician, and McClellan the great unhorsed, has proven himself to contain more of the "little" than of the "Napoleon." There is in fact no man among

them with a great mind and a burly heart, able to take up the banner of resistance and march against the monkeys who rule. At present, therefore, Jacobinism at the North is at a stand-still."

Chattanooga continued to be occupied by Union soldiers until after the President of the United States by proclamation, dated February 19, 1866, gave notice to the people that the civil war was at an end. At that time a brigade of colored troops was there which in a few months thereafter was mustered out of service and paid off. The final payment of these troops was the signal for the many army followers to vacate the place. At this time there were about 13,000 inhabitants in Chattanooga including "Africa," a settlement of negroes, discharged soldiers and the general riff-raff and hangers-on of the army, unpromising material out of which to rebuild and reconstruct a healthy and moral community. At this time there was no store room of any size in the place. The warehouses erected by government quartermasters and commissaries, were purchased and utilized for dry goods and grocery stores, and rooms in the rear of these were used for offices by professional men. The residences were for the most part dingy shanties, with here and there a low brick building, most of which have since been superseded by more tasteful and convenient structures. The only hotel worthy of the name was the Crutchfield House, which was burned down in the fall of 1871. The city itself was in a very dilapidated and repulsive condition, the streets being in wet weather extremely muddy and without walks at the sides. It was surrounded by two lines of heavy earthworks. Fort Sherman was located on the western slope of Brabson's Hill. On McCallie Avenue and Gilmer Streets, were two heavy redoubts, O'Meara and Jones. Fort Jones stood on the stone knob near the present East Tennessee depot, and was in part built from the walls of the Catholic Church then in course of construction at the corner of Georgia Avenue and Eighth Street. Fort Lytle stood near the corner of Carter and Hooke Streets. Fort Crutchfield stood at the right of the interior line. On the exterior line were Fort Wood and Fort Negley, otherwise called Fort Creighton and Fort Phelps. In February and March, 1866, the several lines connecting them were dismantled, and the cannon shipped away numbered something over 1,800. The forts and walls of circumvallation themselves have since, as necessity compelled, been razed to the general level or contour of their surroundings, and now in many places their sites are occupied by some of the finest residences in the city.

Gradually the most undesirable elements of the population sought other locations, the city government regained tolerable control of the criminal classes, and the burden of life in a lawless community became less grievous to be borne. From 1866 to 1870, the population diminished from 13,000, as estimated, to 6,093, as given by the official census of the latter year, but while the population was thus diminishing, the material interests of the city were being placed upon a permanent basis, and were improving, as is plain from the census report just mentioned. In this year there were in Hamilton County, mostly in Chattanooga according to that report, 58 manufacturing establishments, with 13 steam engines and 21 water wheels, employing 540 white males over sixteen years of age, and 1 white female over fifteen. The capital stock invested was $475,155, and the wages paid $253,133, the value of materials used $639,677, and the value of the product $1,012,335.

The first company incorporated after the war was the Chattanooga Gas Light Company, which was chartered by the Legislature January 23, 1866, with an authorized capital of $100,000, and with the privilege of increasing it to $200,000. The stock of the company was all required to be paid in within three years from the time of organization, but on January 19, 1869, the time was extended three years. The company was organized with officers as follows: President, J. B. Weaver; secretary, treasurer and superintendent, E. A. James. The present officers are J. A. Caldwell; president, and J. T. Lynn, secretary, treasurer and superintendent. The original price for gas was $5 per thousand cubic feet. The extreme limit was fixed by the charter at $10 per thousand feet. In 1878 the company built a new gas-holder, seventy feet in diameter and 20 feet deep, the lower 12 feet of which was blasted in the solid rock. October 1, 1886, the price per thousand feet was placed at $2, at which it still remains. Gas light served the purposes of public lighting until 1880, when the Chattanooga Electric Light Company was organized. The incorporators of this company were Hon. Xen. Wheeler, Gen. J. T. Wilder, Hon. Jacob Thornburg, William Baxter and H. S Chamberlain.

On the 26th of November, 1881, the Chattanooga Brush Electric Light Company was organized with the following charter members: H. S. Chamberlain, H. C. Evans, W. S. Marshall, S. A. Key and G. C. Conner. The light station was placed near the corner of Gillespie and Carter Streets. A Corliss engine of 125-horse power was set up, with a driving wheel twelve feet in diameter, making sixty-five revolutions per minute, and driving the dynamo 750 revolutions per minute. May 5, 1882, the passenger depot was lighted up with four lamps, and on Saturday night at 8 P. M. the works were formally inaugurated by Secretary G. C. Conner. The engine throttle was opened by W. S. Marshall and the circuit closed by Nellie Evans, daughter of H. C. Evans, and in an instant the white lights blazed out on top of the academy, from the Stanton

House, through the passenger depot and in various stores. Thousands witnessed the novel and unusual scene, and after one hour's illumination the engine was stopped. On Monday night the lights became permanent for the first time. Thus was this wonderfully powerful, brilliant and most injurious light—injurious to the eye because of its brilliancy and inconstancy—introduced into Chattanooga. In April, 1883, the city council erected gasoline lamps as follows: In the first ward, thirteen; in the second, fifteen; in the fourth, fourteen, and in the fifth, sixteen.

The Citizens' Mutual Gas Company was incorporated in July, 1884, with a capital of $100,000. On the 1st of October, 1886, the two gas companies, finding it impossible for both to prosper, were consolidated. During the existence of both companies the price of gas was $1 per thousand cubic feet.

The works of the Lookout Water Company were commenced in 1864, bp the Federal Army. Subsequently they were sold to E. Yardly & Co., who consolidated with a company organized under an old charter obtained before the war. This organization was short-lived, failing in 1866. Litigation over the assets consumed two years, the works being finally sold by order of the chancery court. The present company became the purchasers, and organized as the Lookout Water Company, under a charter obtained March 11, 1868, with A. M. Johnson, president, and J. W. James, secretary. The only assets coming into their hands was about two miles of pipe laid by the army, much of which had to be removed, being laid on private property. The water had been distributed from wooden tanks on the side of Cameron Hill. The present reservoir and pumping site was purchased in 1870, but although considerably improved by putting in valuable machinery, a 4,000,000 pump being the latest addition, it is only a temporary location. The company owns a permanent pumping location at the mouth of Citico Creek, above all posble sewerage; and it also owns Fort Wood for a permanent reservoir. The first pump used to supply the city with water is now used to pump out the dry well containing the machinery. Its suction was five inches and discharge four, and its daily capacity was 250,000 gallons. The company now has three duplex Worthington pumps, two of them having a capacity of 2,250,000 gallons each, and the other of 4,000,000 gallons, all discharging through a twenty-four inch pipe into the reservoir. The consumption has grown from 50,000 gallons per day to 3,000,000 gallons. The present pumping capacity is 8,500,000 gallons each twenty-four hours. There are now twenty-five miles of main pipe and the capital stock is $100,000. The officers of the company at present are A. M. Johnson, president; J. W. Thornton, secretary, and

Nisbet Wingfield, superintendent and engineer. These, with T. G. Montague and F. F. Wiehl, constitute the board of directors.

The Roane Iron Company was started in 1865 by Gen. John T. Wilder and H. S. Chamberlain, who in that year bought 1,000 acres of coal and iron ore lands in Roane County. The property was stocked and the company organized in 1868, with the following additional members: W. O. Rockwood, A. R. Forsyth, D. E. Rees, John M. Lord and Henry C. Lord. The incorporation of the company was also effected in 1868, with a capital of $25,000, and furnace No. 1 was erected in 1869. It is 56 feet high, 14 feet bosh, and closed top; the second furnace was erected in 1872, the stack being 65 feet high, with 16 feet bosh, closed top. At the present time these furnaces are supplied with five blast engines, and furnish employment to 800 men in mining, coking and smelting. At Rockwood, where these furnaces are located, this company owns 12,000 acres of land, and it was here that they made the first coke iron, made south of the Ohio River.

In 1865 the Government erected a mill for the purpose of re-rolling rails, and soon afterward sold it to the Southwestern Iron Company, which operated the mill until 1870, when they sold the property to the Roane Iron Company. This company enlarged and greatly increased the capacity of the plant, which was and is located on the Tennessee River, west of Cameron Hill. Up to 1878 they manufactured iron rails exclusively; in 1878 they introduced the manufacture of steel rails by the Siemen's process, and from that time to 1882 manufactured both steel and iron rails. From this time to 1886 the mills were closed for want of iron ore of the desired quality for manufacturing steel rails by the Bessemer process. This want being supplied the mills were reopened about December 1, 1886, receiving the ore from the Crystal mines in Carter County, Tenn., adjoining the Cranberry mines in North Carolina. The capacity of these mills is 75,000 tons of steel rails annually, and the total number of men employed by this company is 1,600—800 at the Rockwood furnaces, and the same number at the Chattanooga mills. The capital stock has been increased from the original $25,000 to $1,000,000.

The original directors and officers of the company were as follows: W. P. Rathburn, president; H. S. Chamberlain, vice-president and manager; H. C. Evans, secretary; S. B. Strang, assistant manager; Hon. Xen. Wheeler, D. M. Key, S. M. Winchester, Dudley Baldwin, M. C. Younglove, W. O. Rockwood, A. R. Forsyth and Abram S. Hewitt. The present directors and officers are H. S. Chamberlain, president; H. C. Evans, secretary; Abram S. Hewitt, C. M. McGhee, A. R. Forsyth,

W. E. Rockwood, D. B. Rees, J. E. Line, T. G. Montague and M. C. Younglove. In Chattanooga this company, besides their works, own sixty acres of land, and two miles of railroad connecting with the Nashville, Chattanooga & St. Louis Railway.

The Lookout Iron Company was started as the Tennessee Iron & Steel Company in 1876, commencing to make iron bar on October 5 of that year. The officers of the company were L. Schofield, president and manager; O. L. Packard, treasurer and general agent, and L. Schofield, Jr., secretary and assistant manager. In 1879 the company was reorganized and the name changed to the Lookout Rolling Mill Company, with Col. G. H. Hazlehurst, president, and A. M. Johnson, secretary and manager. Col. Hazlehurst died in 1883; the works closed in 1884, and were sold, in March, 1885, to A. M. Johnson and J. N. Hazlehurst, and in the following July the present company was organized with A. M. Johnson, president; J. N. Hazleton, vice-president, and J. W. Thornton, secretary. In June, 1886, J. N. Hazleton became president, Mr. Thornton being retained as secretary. The capital invested is $56,000, and the number of men employed is 165, about 120 skilled laborers and 45 common laborers. The company manufactures merchant bar iron, fish and angle bars and round edge tire, and in 1886 they commenced the manufacture of wrought iron butt-weld tubing. The value of their annual output is $350,000.

Wason Car & Foundry Company was organized in 1873, with Charles Wason, president; W. H. Parker, vice-president, and F. F. Morrill, secretary and treasurer. The business of the company is to manufacture railroad cars, car wheels and castings. Their facilities are excellent, and when running to their full capacity they employ 250 men. They had, in 1876, at the corner of Carter and Catharine Streets, eight commodious brick buildings—a two-story framing shop, 58x122 feet; a two-story pattern shop, 52x122 feet; a second two-story pattern shop, 52x55 feet; a one-story erecting shop, 42x265 feet; one-story blacksmith shop, 47x133 feet; one-story machine shop, 47x61 feet; one-story boiler room, 21x47 feet; one-story foundry, 60x133, and one one-story annealing room, 52x53 feet. The capacity of the works is eight cars and sixty-four car wheels per day. On the 31st of December, 1879, a fire caused by spontaneous combustion resulted in a loss of $50,000. In 1886 the works were sold at assignee's sale to H. C. Evans, and the company was reorganized with S. M. Carpenter, president, and H. C. Evans, vice-president, secretary and treasurer. Their capital is now $175,000, and the value of the annual product $100,000.

The Chattanooga Iron Company was incorporated in 1874, as a joint stock company, one-half of the stock being owned in Chattanooga. Their works were completed in September and furnaces put in blast in October of that year. They are located on the south bank of the Tennessee River, near the Roane Iron Mills, and have a capacity of twenty-five tons of pig-iron per day. The capital stock paid in in 1881 was $120,000; the value of the annual product was $200,000, and the cost of producing iron $12.50 per ton. The capital stock of this company at the present time is $120,000, and the officers are J. E. Brown, Atlanta, Ga., president; W. C. Morrill, Atlanta, vice-president and secretary, and L. L. Colyar, treasurer and general manager.

Wilder's Machine Works were started in 1880 by Gen. John T. Wilder. They were located at the corner of Carter and James Streets, and comprised a foundry 48x96 feet, and a machine shop 48x110 feet, and were established for the purpose of manufacturing Wilder's patent turbine wheel. The iron front was placed in position February 23, 1880, and the machinery was started May 15, following. In November, 1881, these works were leased to Col. S. B. Lowe and W. A. L. Kirk, and the name changed to the Lowe Machine Works. Subsequently they were leased by the Kirk Machine Company, who, until within a few months, were operating them, employing a capital of $20,000 and producing $50,000 worth of turbine wheels, cotton presses, Watts' patent self-oiling car wheels, Little Giant hydraulic nozzles, general machinery and mill work and castings, each year. In 1884 the original building and location were sold, and a new building erected immediately north of the Wason Car Works.

Woodworth & Winchester. G. B. Woodworth, formerly of Pennsylvania, purchased the saw mill of Waters & Clippinger, near the Roane Iron Company's works. This saw mill had been running two or three years. Mr. Woodworth sold S. M. Winchester a half interest, and in 1881 they sold the property to Hughes & Marquet, having purchased of Treece & Gilmour their Market Street mill. After running this mill until 1882 Mr. Woodworth sold out to Mr. Winchester, and after serving as manager one year for Hughes & Marquet formed the firm of G. B. Woodworth & Co., and ran a lumber yard near the Roane Iron Works. In January, 1884, the firm of Woodworth & Winchester was formed, and continued until 1886, when the former bought out the latter's interest in the saw mill, but both continuing together in the lumber business, having one yard on the river near the foot of Market Street, and another on Cowart Street near the railway. This firm employs about twenty-five men during the sawing season and saws 3,000,000 feet of lumber annually.

The firm of Temple & Shipp was originally the Southern Pump & Pipe Company, which was established in January, 1874, with a capital of $25,000. H. F. Temple, of the Chicago firm of J. F. Temple & Sons, in the year above named met J. F. Shipp, of Atlanta, who was the Southern agent of the Chicago house, and with him formed a partnership, and located in Chattanooga in preference to Atlanta. The business of the new company was the manufacture of the improved porcelain lined farm pump, patent wood pipe for gas and water mains, pump material, tubing, etc. In 1880 they added the manufacture of furniture to their business, and have since conducted this portion of their manufactures under the name of the Chattanooga Furniture Company. The present location of their factory is at the corner of Frank and Boyce Streets. They own 3,000 acres of timber lands in the Sequatchie Valley, mainly covered with hickory, oak and poplar. The capital invested in the manufacture of pumps and pipes is about $40,000, and in the manufacture of furniture, about $75,000.

The Etna Foundry & Machine Works were started in 1874 in a small way by G. W. Wheland, who came here from Ohio. The works are situated between Sidney and Boyce Streets near the South Tredegar Iron Works. The business consists in the manufacture and repair of circular saw and grist-mill machinery, general castings, steam engines, and the Todd new improved turbine water wheel. As his business has increased Mr. Wheland has added to his building and facilities until at the present time he employs on the average about fifteen men, and turns out about $40,000 worth of work each year.

The business to which the South Tredegar Iron Company has fallen heir was commenced in 1860 by S. B. Lowe and others, under the name of the Vulcan Iron Company, and was conducted by them on a moderate scale until the war put an end to business in Chattanooga. After the cessation of hostilities the company reorganized and continued under the old name until 1873. In 1875 Hazleton & Harrison took up the business, and were succeeded in 1880 by the Powell Iron & Nail Company, who ran about one year. In 1881 the South Tredegar Iron Company was incorporated with a capital of $200,000. The officers were H. L. Fox, of St. Louis, president; J. M. Duncan, formerly of Ohio, vice-president, and C. E. Rubedeaux, secretary. In 1880 thirty nail machines were in operation, in 1881 thirty more were added and in 1882, fifteen, making seventy-five as the present complement. Iron nails were made up to June 1, 1884, when the company commenced making steel nails, having on the 19th of the previous April made their first blow of Bessemer steel, the first Bessemer steel made south of the

Ohio River. Since this time they have made their own steel. In 1883 they commenced the manufacture of railroad spikes, and during the same year built a large cooperage establishment for the manufacture of their own kegs. In their foundry they make iron, brass and steel castings, and they also have a blacksmith shop. They employ on the average about 450 men, the spike plant has a capacity of twenty tons per day, and the nail plant about 160,000 kegs of nails per annum.

The Enterprise Machine Works were established by Benjamin Truxall in 1870, on Market Street between Eighth and Ninth. In 1872 Louis Dunmeyer was admitted to partnership, and the firm became Truxall & Dunmeyer, with a capital of $500. In December, 1885, they moved to their present location, the corner of Montgomery Avenue and Boyce Street, where they manufacture steam engines, shafting, pulleys, and carry on a general repairing business. They employ on the average ten men, and turn out about $20,000 worth of work per year.

The manufacture of brick was begun in Chattanooga, by Abbot & Golden, in 1866, and continued by them in a small way until 1870, when (L. E. & D. P. Montague) purchased the business and at once erected new buildings and added largely to the business. Besides ordinary and fire brick they manufacture sewer pipe and white goods, flue pipe and flue linings, and grind clay to be manufactured into china-ware, and also make farm drain tile, this branch of their business being added in 1885. The capital invested is about $70,000, and the number of men employed in Chattanooga about 125, while in Alabama where they own a fire-brick and china-ware clay mine, it is fifteen.

When the Fayweather & Ladew Tannery was first established in Chattanooga in 1876, it was by the name of J. B. Hoyt & Co., the great leather and belt house of New York City. It was composed of J. B. Hoyt, D. B. Fayerweather and H. S. Ladew. In 1883 Mr. Hoyt retired from the firm, disposing of his interest to the present proprietors, both of whom are New York gentlemen, the first named never having been in Chattanooga, and the latter but once. The business has been conducted ever since its establishment by David Woodworth, Jr., originally from New York. The property consists of forty acres of land, and fifty-two dwellings for the employes, foreman and superintendent, and the buildings necessary for the tanning of the hides, and storing of the bark. The tanning is limited to belting and sole leather, New York slaughtered hides being used almost exclusively. About 300 men are employed the year round, and in the barking seasons sometimes as many as 4,000. While this tannery with its two main yards and beam-house buildings, its two dry houses, seven bark sheds, and other necessary buildings, has not the capacity of some Pennsylvania establishments, yet it probably tans more hides than any similar institution in this country. Neither the amount of capital invested nor the annual amount of business done, could be obtained from the superintendent.

Plow-making was begun in Chattanooga, by Newell Sanders, from Indiana, in a small way in 1879. His first factory, a frame building on Fort Street near Montgomery Avenue, was not much larger than a large dry goods box, costing about $100. After working two or three years he admitted to partnership George W. Wheland, the firm then becoming Newell Sanders & Co. In 1883 it became the Chattanooga Plow Company, a joint stock company with $40,000, taking in C. C. Bloomfield, of Jackson, Mich., and C. D. Mitchell. Mr. Sanders was elected president of the company, and Mr. Mitchell, secretary. This company purchased the block of ground between Fort and Carter Streets south of Montgomery Avenue, and upon it erected a machine shop 60x150 feet, a foundry 60x120 feet, and a warehouse and office building 60x150 at an aggregate expense of $10,390, and put in $12,000 worth of machinery. The capital stock is now $60,000. This company employs about eighty men, one third colored with satisfactory results. The articles manufactured are chilled plows, cane-mills, self-skimming evaporators, portable furnaces, a Scotch harrow, and a cotton seed and grain crusher, with which it is claimed farmers and planters can with great advantage crush corn into hominy, and also cotton seed into an exceedingly economical fertilizer. The annual output of this factory is about $175,000.

The Chattanooga Steam Marble & Stone Works (Daly, Smith & Hill) was established by P. C. Daly, in Chattanooga, in 1872, at the corner of Cherry and Eighth Streets. In 1880, C. E. Smith, having sold his marble business in Cleveland, Tenn., came to Chattanooga, and purchased a one-half interest in Mr. Daly's business for $600, and soon in addition to the manufacture of monuments and tombstones, furnished dressed stone for buildings. In 1884 their business had so increased that they found it necessary to move from the corner of Market and Eighth Streets to more spacious grounds; so purchased nine lots at the corners of Cowart, Alabama and Williams Streets, and put up two sets of gang saws, propelling them by steam, and since the spring of 1885 have since been conducting a general marble and building stone business. In September, 1885, J. T. Hill was admitted into the firm, and the capital increased to $40,000, and the volume of business in 1885 was $50,000. The firm employ about sixty men, and manufacture monuments mainly from Georgia marble, and furniture pieces mainly from Tennessee marble, both varieties being variegated, but the latter much darker in color

C. E. James

than the former. Their oölitic limestone used in buildings is obtained near Bowling Green, Ky.

The Chattanooga Foundry & Pipe Works were established in 1877 by David Giles and C. P. Isbester, both of them originally from Pennsylvania. One building was erected that year in which the business of manufacturing cast iron gas and water pipe was commenced, also general castings. Two additions have since been made to the building, one in 1884 and one in 1886, until now it is 95x250 feet in size. A machine shop was erected in 1886, three stories high. The company was incorporated July 13, 1882, and officers elected as follows: D. Giles, president; C. B. Isbester, vice-president. At the present time the officers are D. Giles, president; C. B. Isbester, vice-president, and M. Llewellyn, secretary and treasurer. This company employs about 150 men, 100 colored and fifty white, the latter being skilled laborers.

The Chattanooga Stove Company was incorporated December 19, 1881, and the first meeting of the incorporators was held January 18, 1882. The incorporators were J. T. Hill, Theodore Richmond, J. H. Warner, S. A. Key, T. A. Snow, J. P. Smith and W. E. Baskette. The first president of the company was John A. Hart, and first secretary, W. E. Baskette. The capital stock was $50,000. A building was erected between Whitesides, Catharine, Sidney and Akin Streets, which together with the land cost $30,000, the main part being four stories, the molding room one story. Business was commenced January 19, 1883, and amounted the first year to $35,000; the second year to $65,000, and it is estimated that the third year it will reach $85,000. One hundred and thirty different styles of stoves are made, mostly for the burning of wood and soft coal, hard coal being as yet, in the Chattanooga market, too expensive for general consumption. Colored men are exclusively employed as molders with eminently satisfactory results.

Wagner's Foundry & Machine Works were started in 1878 by Casey & Wagner, and run by them one year, since which time they have been managed by Ambrose Wagner alone. The capital invested is about $8,000, and the number of men employed about twenty-five. The work done consists of the manufacture of castings and a line of mining cars, car wheels and mining tools and general repairing, and amounts to about $35,000 per year.

The Alabama Great Southern Shops were established in Chattanooga in 1880, and are located on Montgomery Avenue and Hooke Street. They consist of a machine shop, planing mill, blacksmith shop, pattern shops and round house. The work done here is mainly the repair of locomotives and cars, the only manufacturing yet done consisting of two six-wheeled switch engines, Nos. 111 and 121, the former being completed February 1, 1883, and the latter subsequently. No. 111 was the first locomotive built south of Louisville, Ky. The largest locomotive on the Alabama Great Southern Railway is a Mogul (eight-wheeled) freight locomotive, weighing 95,000 pounds.

The Cincinnati Southern Railway Shops were located in Chattanooga in 1880, on the Boyce estate near the Stanton House. They consist of a blacksmith shop, machine shop and round house. Chattanooga contributed $100,000 in bonds to their establishment. About 125 men are employed, the work done consisting in the repairing of passenger and freight cars and locomotives. A few caboose cars have been built here, but no other new work.

The business of D. W. Hughes' Planing Mill, Saw Mill and Lumber Yard, was started in 1870, by Smith & Childs, with a small planing mill on King Street where the E. T. V. & Ga., freight depot now stands. Here they remained until 1875 when they moved to the present site of the C. S. Ry. Shops. In 1880 they removed to Cowart and Louisa Streets where they were succeeded by Hughes & Marquet, who conducted the business in partnership three years when they were succeeded by the senior member, D. W. Hughes. The planing mill and lumber business have been carried on since 1870, but the saw mill was erected in 1883. The planing mill has a capacity of 10,000 feet per day, the saw mill of 40,000 feet per day, and the lumber carried amounts to 3,000,000 feet. The capital invested amounts to $150,000, and the number of men employed to 125. Mr. Hughes established branches of his lumber business in Knoxville, Tenn., and Birmingham, Ala., in 1886, in the latter place paying $300 rent for property that cost the owner $90,000. The total annual value of his business, including the manufacture of doors, sash and blinds, is $200,000.

The business of the Willingham Lumber Company was started in 1872 by Willingham & Dunn at Forsythe, Ga. In 1876 they moved to Columbus, Ga., and upon a dissolution of partnership in 1885 W. A. Willingham moved to Chattanooga and located on the corner of Boyce Street and Montgomery Avenue. In May, 1886, the Willingham Lumber Company was incorporated by W. A., W. G., J. T. and E. G. Willingham, with a capital stock of $100,000. They erected a planing mill three stories high, 88x80 feet in size, and put in a 125-horse-power engine. The capacity of their mill is 40,000 feet per day, and the annual product of their establishment at Chattanooga is $180,000; at Atlanta, $70,000; and at Columbus, $50,000; in the aggregate, $300,000. They employ 70 men in Chattanooga, 15 in Atlanta, and 10 in Columbus—in all 95 men.

The business of Morrison & Woodward was started by Gillespie & Co. (John M. and John C. Gillespie) in 1870, and conducted by them until 1881, when it was purchased by Morrison & Woodward, who largely increased it and introduced much finer work. The capital of Gillespie & Co. was about $15,000; that of Morrison & Woodward is nearly $100,000. J. B. Nicklin became a member of the firm in 1885. The company manufacture sash, doors and blinds, and deal in lumber on an extensive scale, carrying a stock of about 1,500,000 feet. The entire annual volume of their business amounts to about $125,000, seventy-five being the average number of men employed.

The firm of Ristine, Campbell & Co. was first established in 1870 as Ristine, May & Co., at Loudon, Tenn., where they remained until 1876, when they removed their business to Chattanooga, locating on King Street near the E. T. V. & Ga. Railway. Here they erected a factory, staining-room and warehouse at an expense of about $5,000, and commenced the manufacture of furniture on a large scale, about $75,000 worth each year being made. In —, the firm was reorganized by the retirement of E. F. May and S. H. Kennedy, and the addition of J. A. Campbell and G. N. Hensen, when the name became Ristine, Campbell & Co., and at this time the capital of the company was increased from $15,000 to $26,000. On the 16th of October, 1886, Mr. Ristine retired from the firm and his place was taken by W. A. Campbell, cashier of the bank of Sweetwater, Tenn., and the capital was then increased to $30,000.

The Chattanooga Boiler Works (Alfred Webb & Co.) were started in 1877 by J. M. Wilson at their present location, and were purchased in 1879 by the present proprietors, Alfred Webb and E. I. Stone. The brick building occupied by these works is 50x75 feet in size, and was built by Mr. Wilson at a cost of about $1,500. The present company has a capital of about $12,000, $10,000 being invested in machinery. The business consists in the manufacture of boilers, stand pipes and tanks; thirty-five men are employed, and the annual production amounts to about $100,000.

The Lookout Boiler Works were started by the present proprietors, Friedel & Strahle, in 1881, on the corner of Water and Chestnut Streets, where they erected a frame one-story building costing about $700, and put in about $1,500 worth of machinery. They make boilers, tanks, stacks and do a general repairing business; employ ten men, and turn out about $25,000 worth of work each year.

The Phœnix Foundry was started in 1882 by D. T. Carpenter and W. S. French, who erected a building sixty feet square on Boyce Street between Catharine and Henry Streets. This foundry does work on orders, employs about twenty men and the annual product amounts to about $35,000.

The Citico Furnace Company was organized as a joint stock company in 1883, with a capital of $150,000, since increased to $175,000. The original directors and officers were as follows: H. S. Chamberlain, president; Edward Doud, superintendent and treasurer; John A. Hart, J. F. Loomis and D. P. Montague, secretaries. They bought thirty acres of land at the mouth of Citico Creek, and built a stack sixty-nine feet high with sixteen feet bosh, put in three Whitwell fire brick hot blast stoves and two Corliss engines. The furnace was first put in blast in April, 1884; makes pig iron, Citico brand, and has a capacity of 30,000 tons per annum. The present officers are the same as at first, except that H. S. Chamberlain is president and treasurer. The ores used are obtained along the Tennessee River in the vicinity of Chattanooga, and in northern Georgia, and are of the red fossil, brown hematite and magnetite varieties, the latter variety being obtained in Carter County, Tenn. The iron made finds a market in the adjoining Southern States, and as far north as Cleveland, Detroit, Chicago and St. Louis, and at intermediate points.

The Vetter Beer & Ice Company was started in 1883, by J. W. Vetter, as the J. W. Vetter Ice Company. The factory was located on Broad Street, near Ninth, and manufactured four tons of ice per day, which was sold at about 60 cents per 100 pounds. J. W. Vetter sold his factory to the present proprietors in 1886, who manufacture about five tons per day. The company is composed of F. E. Marquet, manager, and A. G. Reynaud, secretary and treasurer. The company on October 13, 1886, completed the boring of an artesian well in the rear of their factory, which is 476 feet deep. At the depth of 460 feet, water was struck, which immediately filled the well to within thirty-four feet of the surface of the ground, above which height it still refuses to rise.

The Lookout Ice Company was started by Samuel Blair in 1885. He organized a company with an all paid up capital of $40,000, with the following officers: Samuel Blair, formerly of Cincinnati, Ohio, president; Dr. D. G. Curtis, of Chattanooga, vice-president; Charles W. Biese, Chattanooga, secretary and treasurer; J. S. Blymyer, Cincinnati; Mr. Huntington, New Orleans, and M. H. Ward. The company erected, on Market Street and the Tennessee River, a two-story fire-proof building, at a cost of $4,000, and put in this building $32,000 worth of machinery and fixtures. The first ice was made in July, 1885, the factory having a capacity of fifteen tons per day, and the storehouse of 2,200 tons. The well is thirty feet deep, and from the bottom of this well a tunnel 365 feet long extends out into the Tennessee River.

C. C. Shelton's flouring-mills were erected on the corner of Market and Second Streets in 1877, containing then two sets of buhrs. In 1881, Mr. Shelton, yielding to the progressive spirit of the times, put in a complete outfit, sixteen sets, of gradual reduction rollers, and now has in addition to these rollers, two sets of stones for grinding corn. The mill is three stories high, 42x100 feet, and the wareroom 42x80 feet. Fifteen men are employed, and the capacity of the mill is 150 barrels of flour per day of 24 hours, or $150,000 worth of flour each year. Mr. Shelton was the first miller in the South to introduce the roller process of making flour.

Julius F. Loomis and John A. Hart established themselves in the lumber business in Chattanooga in 1876, as Loomis & Hart. In 1877 they built their planing mill and in 1878 added their furniture business. In November, 1884, A. J. Gahagan, J. T. Arnold, F. L. Winchester were admitted to the firm, and the present firm name (Loomis, Hart & Co.) adopted. These latter gentlemen have full charge of the business which amounts to $200,000 per annum, and furnishes employment to 120 men.

Chattanooga is well supplied with excellently managed street railroads, and a line of street cars runs to the base of Lookout Mountain, which in connection with the cable incline railway, completed by Maj. W. R. King, provides easy and cheap means of transportation to the top of Lookout Mountain. There is also an excellent dummy railway from the city to Missionary Ridge, completed in October, 1886.

The wholesale trade of Chattanooga has become very large, as has the lumber trade. The manufacture of cotton goods has not as yet, however, met with the success its founders hoped for. The present condition of the business interests of the city is shown by the following enumeration of the various individuals and firms carrying on the different departments of trade: Dealers in agricultural implements, 8; architects, 4; artificial stone, 1; bakers and confectioners, 7; blacksmiths and wagon-makers, 14; bookstores, 2; boots and shoes, 9; brick manufacturers, 3; carriage and wagon-makers, 3; china, glass and queensware, 3; civil engineers and surveyors, 4; clothiers, 9; coal, coke and wood, 7; coal, 4; commission merchants, 2; contractors and builders, 9; dentists, 7; drugs, 15; dry goods, 7; express companies, 2; flour and grist-mills, 3; furnishing goods, 2; foundries and machine shops, 8; furniture stores, 12; general stores, 5; grocers—wholesale and retail, 107; hardware, 6; harness and saddles, 5; jewelers, 7; lumber, 11; meat markets, 12; medicine companies, 2; lawyers, 43; physicians, 44; music teachers, 14; plumbers, 5; printers and binders, 5; produce and commission merchants, 7; publishers, 9; real estate agents, 11; sewing machine agents, 4; shoemakers, 29; stoves and tinware, 5; tailors, 9; wines, liquors and cigars, 46; undertakers, 3; besides numerous other dealers in many other kinds of goods and wares.

The banks in Chattanooga before the war were the Bank of Chattanooga, Bank of Tennessee, a branch of the Union Bank of the State, and the Lookout Savings Bank, the latter commencing business in 1866 and voluntarily closing in 1869.

The City National Bank was organized in 1871, with P. M. Craigmiles, president; John Craigmiles, vice-president, and D. C. McMillin, cashier, and with a capital of $170,000. This organization built the banking house at the corner of Seventh and Market Streets. Earnings not being satisfactory to the stockholders, the business was discontinued in 1875, all claims being paid in full.

The Discount & Deposit Bank opened its doors for business in 1867, with John King, president; Tom Crutchfield, vice-president, and Allen C. Burns, cashier. The capital at first was $10,000. In 1868 Thomas Calloway and David N. Bell became stockholders, and the capital was doubled. This small capital was soon tied up in unproductive real estate, and the expenses of management and interest paid on deposits exceeded the earnings. After the death of the cashier in 1881 the bank ceased business.

A branch of the Freedmen's Savings Bank was opened in Chattanooga by Rev. E. O. Tade in 1867. Having no capital and a very small line of deposits the business was soon abandoned.

The Mechanics and Traders Bank of Chattanooga was chartered July 1, 1877. The first officers were J. C. Vance, president; C. T. Wilson, cashier. The directors in addition to Mr. Vance were R. G. Houston, John B. Keely and M. H. Clift. The business was carried on in the City National Bank building, but not being very prosperous, it was soon voluntarily closed.

The First National Bank was organized October 25, 1865, and opened its doors for business December 26, of that year, with a capital stock of $200,000. In 1866 the capital and surplus were $210,000, and in 1886 they were $410,000. In 1866 the loans and discounts amounted to $1,223,000, and in 1885, $3,830,000. The first officers of this bank were W. P. Rathburn, president and T. G. Montague, cashier. Upon the death of Mr. Rathburn, January 10, 1884, Mr. Montague became president. The other officers at present are H. S. Chamberlain, vice-president; H. C. Squire, cashier, and Joseph H. Rathburn, assistant cashier. The business of this bank is managed in a cautious, conservative and safe manner by able business men.

The Third National Bank was organized in September, 1881, with a capital of $125,000. The first directors and officers were William Morrow, president; J. H. Warner, vice-president; J. L. McCullom, W. D. VanDyke, J. P. Smartt, S. A. Key, A. M. Johnson, J. C. Griffin, J. T. Hill and D. E. Rees, and T. D. Flippin, cashier. In 1882 D. E. Rees was elected president; J. P. Smartt, vice-president; and W. E. Baskette, cashier; and in January, 1885, John A. Hart was elected president; D. E. Rees, vice-president, the cashier remaining the same. The only change since then has been the election of C. R. Gaskill, assistant cashier. In September, 1885, the capital stock was increased to $200,000, and July, 1886, to $250,000, the surplus fund being then $22,500, and the undivided profits $19,250. No interest is paid on deposits subject to check, but four per cent is paid on time deposits.

The City Savings Bank was started in December, 1885, by R. B. Hillas, D. Satterlee, and G. W. Thompson, all from Dunlap, Iowa, and C. E. Stivers of Chattanooga, who had been in the employ of the First National Bank of Chattanooga fifteen years. The business was conducted as a private partnership until October, 1886, when the bank was incorporated with a subscribed capital of $200,000, with the following officers: G. W. Thompson, president; G. H. Jarnagin, vice-president; and C. E. Stivers, cashier, and with other directors as follows: J. F. Loomis, J. B. Merriam, W. A. Willingham and A. J. Gahagan. Interest is paid on all sums of $5 and upward at the rate of four per cent per annum, the right of requiring thirty days' notice being reserved, and six per cent interest is paid on certificates of deposit for one year.

The Mountain City Fire & Marine Insurance Company was incorporated March 3, 1870, with an authorized capital stock of $500,000. It commenced business June 1, 1885, with $100,000 subscribed. Its resources, December 31, 1886, were $104,255.70, of which there was credited to the reserve fund on the books of the company $4,729.08, leaving $99,526.62. The losses paid in 1886 amounted to $3,972.68. The reasons for this low loss ratio are that the risks are judiciously scattered and small policies issued. The officers of the company are J. C. Griffiss, president; J. A. Hart, vice-president, and W. J. Colburn, secretary. The directors in addition to the president and vice-president are D. A. Carpenter, H. S. Chamberlin, M. H. Clift, W. O. Peeples, J. P. Smartt, H. F. Temple and R. L. Watkins.

The Coal, Iron & Manufacturers Association made application for a charter on October 22, 1876, which was granted in the following language: "Be it known that W. P. Rathburn, J. T. Wilder, S. B. Lowe, M. D. Vanhorn, L. Schofield, L. L. Thomasson, C. E. James, L. Schofield, Jr., H. F. Temple, W. E. Rockwood, V. A. Gaskell, C. P. Robertson, A. G. Sharp, Edwaid Doud, Louis L. Parham, Lucius P. Bright, M. L. Chapman, Tomlinson Fort, E. G. Eaton, M. H. Clift, Xen. Wheeler, J. F. James, J. C. Hazleton and H. S. Chamberlain are hereby constituted a body politic and corporate by the name of the Iron, Coal & Manufacturers' Association, for the purpose of encouraging, promoting and fostering the mineral, manufacturing and commercial interests of the city of Chattanooga and the surrounding country, and with this object in view to establish in Chattanooga an office or bureau for the collection and systematic arrangement of specimens of iron, coal, and other minerals, with the product of the manufacturer's and mechanic's art; also specimens of scientific and historic interest; also for the purpose of collecting facts statistics, maps, books, and information of interest and advantage to society, and especially to various interests and occupations represented in said association, one of the objects of this association being to establish an iron, coal and general exchange after the nature of a board of trade or chamber of commerce, to facilitate and increase the traffic in iron, coal and other minerals and their products." The officers provided for were a president, secretary and treasurer. In order to make the support of the association light for each member the effort was made to secure a large membership.

The officers have been as follows: Presidents—W. P. Rathburn, 1876; J. T. Wilder, 1877; H. S. Chamberlain, 1878; W. D. VanDyke, 1879; John C. Griffiss, 1880; S. B. Lowe, 1881; D. E. Rees, 1882; H. Clay Evans, 1883; M. J. O'Brien, 1884; Marcus Grant, 1885; G. C. Connor, 1886. Vice-presidents—H. S. Chamberlain, 1876 and 1877; W. D. Van Dyke, 1878; John C. Griffiss, 1879; S. B. Lowe, 1880; D. E. Rees, 1881; H. C. Evans, 1882; M. J. O'Brien, 1883; Marcus Grant, 1884; J. L. McCullom, 1885; D. B. Loveman, 1886. Secretaries—M. L. Chapman, 1876, 1877, 1879 and 1885; T. J. Carlile, 1878; G. C. Connor, 1880 to 1884 inclusive; H. M. Wiltse; 1886. Treasurers—C. P. Robertson, 1876 and 1877; L. P. Bright, 1878 and 1879; R. M. Barton, Jr., 1880; E. F. Sevier, 1881 to 1886, inclusive.

Some of the important work accomplished by this association has been as follows: In 1877 it entertained the Association for the Advancement of Science; in 1878 it entertained the American Association of Mining Engineers; in 1879, secured a signal station and observer for Chattanooga; in 1880, inaugurated a course of lectures, organized a system of flood warnings, secured an appropriation for a road from Chattanooga to the National Cemetery, and the establishment of the United States District Court at Chattanooga; in 1882, entertained the charcoal iron workers of the United States, raised a committee to secure a customs house, and had the United States take charge of the flood warnings; in 1883, assisted to secure the Methodist University for Chattanooga, and in 1886 raised another committee to secure a custom house.

The Board of Trade was organized originally on the 31st of August, 1881, as the "Merchants' Union," at a meeting held in the circuit court room. The cause of the movement resulting in this organization was the discrimination in freight rates practiced against the city of Chattanooga by all the converging railroads, and the organization had for one of its objects the termination of this unjust discrimination. P. C. Wilson said that as secretary of the committee on transportation of the Iron, Coal & Manufacturers' Association, his attention had been called to this unjust discrimination, and that he was of opinion that united action on the part of the merchants of the city was the only remedy. A committee of citizens was then appointed to organize and suggest permanent officers. All who were willing to become members of the "Merchants Union" signed their names as follows: W. O. Peeples & Bros., L. L. Thomasson & Son, J. W. Harris, J. B. Merriam, D. J. Pierce, Smartt & Oehmig, Wassman Bros., W. F. Peak, D. B. Loveman & Co., J. B. Pyron, J. W. Butler & Co., Thomas W. Miller, M. J. O'Brien, Nixon & Wester, P. C. Wilson and R. M. Tankesley, these being all that were present.

Officers were elected as follows: M. J. O'Brien, president; William Nixon, first vice-president; W. O. Peeples, second vice-president; P. C. Wilson, secretary; D. J. Pierce, treasurer. A committee on transportation was appointed as follows: C. P. Robertson, D. B. Loveman, J. H. Warner, John A. Martin and P. C. Wilson. A second committee was appointed to draft a constitution and by-laws, and a third to visit all the merchants to secure membership. The committee on transportation was then given power to act and the Union was committed in advance to sustain any contract said committee might make. On September 5, seventy additional members were added to the list.

The "Merchants' Union" was changed to the Board of Trade of Chattanooga, January 17, 1882. On February 14, the committee on transportation reported that although they had not succeeded in making satisfactory arrangements with the railroads, they hoped to do so before long. The committee made quite an encouraging report on April 12, and on October 2, reported that Chattanooga was then more on an equality with other towns as regarded freight than ever before. On March 5, 1885, the board of Trade in obedience to a request from the Iron, Coal & Manufacturers' Association, agreed to defray one-half the expense of securing the location of the Methodist University at Chattanooga, and on July 6 the transportation committee reported with regard to freight rates that the rate from New York to Memphis and to Decatur, Ala., was 40 cents per 100 pounds, while to Chattanooga it was 80 cents, and advised merchants purchasing in New York to ship goods to Decatur, and then to Chattanooga by river.

The officers of the Board of Trade elected January 1, 1883, were W. O. Peeples, president; C. P. Robertson, first vice-president; W. E. Carlile second vice-president; J. N. Trigg, secretary, and D. J. Pierce, treasurer; on January 7, 1884: W. M. Nixon, president; W. R. Carlile, first vice-president; Fillmore Gibson, second vice-president; J. N. Trigg, secretary, and T. V. B. Miller, treasurer. January 5, 1885: W. R. Carlile, president; J. P. Smartt, first vice-president; Joseph Wassman, second vice-president; Prosper Lazard, secretary, and T. V. B. Miller, treasurer, and on January 4, 1886: J. P. Smartt, president; Prosper Lazard, first vice-president; J. N. Trigg, second vice-president; Gordon Lee, secretary, and T. V. B. Miller, treasurer.

The healthfulness of Chattanooga is generally superior to that of most other Southern cities, and when compared with that of foreign cities it does not suffer. The death rate from 1870 to 1880 among the white people was 22 per 1,000, and among the colored people 36 per 1,000. The excess of death rate among the colored people was doubtless caused by poverty, hard labor, poor pay and poor living. In 1885 the death rate was 23 in Chattanooga, while in other cities in this country it was: in Knoxville 23; in Cincinnati 25; in Baltimore 22; in New York 30; in Brooklyn 25; in Boston 24, and in San Francisco 22. The climate has much to do with health. For 1884 the average height of the barometric column was 29.258 inches, the highest point reached being January 26, 29.819, and the lowest being on November 28, 28.725 inches. The temperature for the year averages 60°. The thermometric column in the signal service office seldom reaches 100°. In 1881 the hottest day was August 12, when the mercury reached 105°. In 1884 the maximum temperature was 91.8°, on August 27, while July was the hottest month of the year, the average temperature being 76.6°; August, 74.4°; June, 71.5°. The lowest point reached in 1884 was on January 6, 1° below zero. In 1878, the yellow fever year, great interest was felt as to the date of the first frost in the fall, and it was ascertained that beginning with 1869 these first frosts had fallen on the following days: In 1869, October 16; 1870, November 1; 1871, October 12; 1872, October 15; 1873, October 21; 1874, October 14; 1875, October 12; 1876, October 3; 1877, October 23. In 1878, when an early frost was needed more than ever before in the history of the city, it did not come until November 2, though on the 19th of October ice formed to the thickness of one-twelfth of an inch under the north and west windows of the office of the United States engineers, which caused Henry W. Darling in an announcement of the fact in the *Times* to exclaim: "Thank God for His thrice blessed frosts." Some time previously, when the entire population was either suffering from or fearing they would suffer from the scourge, the following invocation to "Jack Frost," the natural enemy of yellow fever, appeared in the public prints:

> Whole cities wail his deadly stroke;
> Trade bends beneath his rod;
> Palsied our every interest lies;
> Tears, bitter tears, suffuse our eyes;
> Our bosoms burst with groans and sighs.
> Come, then, thou angel of the skies,
> Thou messenger of God!

The first death from yellow fever that year was that of Mrs. Schwartsenburg, trom Memphis, which occurred during the last week in August. The next death was on the 19th of September, and from that time until the termination of the epidemic 366 in all had died therefrom. At first the physicians hoped it was not, and would not admit that it was yellow fever, and reported numerous deaths as produced by malignant malarial fever, pernicious, inflammatory and bilious fever, so that the exact number of yellow fever deaths is not known. An approximate estimate, however, is as follows: Whites—male, 152; female, 101; blacks—male, 71; female, 42; whole number, 366. The Catholics did noble work in caring for the sick. They opened a *novena* for prayers, October 4, at their church, in order to obtain from Almighty God the cessation of the scourge. The services commenced at 3:30 P. M., and lasted nine days. Proper instruction was given by Father John. The Dominican sisters took charge of the hospital October 7—Sisters Angela and Bernadin. Father John in his instructions to the hospital workers said that there were no "Protestants" among the sick—nobody but suffering men, women and children. Many of the people, in order to escape from danger, retired to the hills and mountains, and to considerable distances. As late as October 20 these refugees were advised not to return to their homes, as to do so would impose additional burdens upon the relief committee, which was then spending $1,000 per day. One of the latest victims of the scourge was Mayor Thomas J. Carlile, who died October 29, aged forty-five years. At a meeting of the board of health, held November 2, a resolution was passed to the effect that, in the opinion of the board, yellow fever was over and that all absent persons might, with safety, return to the city. The year 1878 had been exceptionally free from thunder storms, and the physicians believed that while their non-occurrence and the occurrence of yellow fever at the same time might be only a coincidence, yet electric concussions in the atmosphere produce ozone, and ozone is believed to be a peculiarly health-giving substance.

The question of high and low water in the Tennessee is also one of peculiar interest to Chattanooga, as in times of high water considerable portions of the city are overflowed. Low water mark was established in 1839, and since then the only times the water has reached low-water mark were four days in September, 1881, and on September 19, 1883. High water since 1867 has been as follows: March, 1867, 58 feet ⅝ of an inch; January, 1879, 38 feet; March, 1880, 38 feet, 4 inches; February, 1881, 22 feet 5 inches; January, 1882, 40 feet 4 inches; January, 1883, 38 feet 8 inches; March, 1884, 43 feet; November, 1885, 30.4 feet; April 3, 1886, 51.1 feet.

The only other serious epidemic that has visited this city is the small-pox, which raged with exceptional virulence in 1882 and 1883. The first death from this disease occurred in January, 1882, and the last in June, 1883. The epidemic fairly began in May, 1882, when there were fifteen deaths. In December the greatest number of deaths occurred, 103—twenty-six white persons and seventy-seven colored; and the total number of deaths for the eighteen months of the epidemic was 334, 110 whites and 224 blacks, while the number of deaths from all other causes during the same time was 570; total number of deaths for the eighteen months, 904. This was a most remarkable thing, an epidemic in the latter part of the nineteenth century, in one of the most healthful cities in the South, more fatal than any one of the four great epidemics of the eighteenth century. But there had been no general systematic vaccination since 1873; those who suffered from small-pox were mostly poor people, and the deaths were very largely among the colored people, the population of the city then being composed of 14,000 whites and 7,000 blacks—two whites to one black; while the deaths were almost precisely in the opposite proportion, two blacks to one white. Vaccination was begun in December, 1882, in which month the number of deaths was 103; in January, 1883, there were only seventy-four, and in February, eighteen, while in March there was but one. In a few months cases of and deaths from small-pox entirely ceased, either because of vaccination or because the disease had spent its force. Two things are now wanting in Chattanooga in order that there may be no excuse for a recurrence of this plague: First, an ordinance excluding from the public schools unvaccinated children, and second, improved methods of living among the poorer classes, both white and black.

The Chattanooga *Gazette* was founded in 1837 by F. A. Parham as the Hamilton *Gazette* at Ross' Landing. The material was floated from Knoxville down the Tennessee River on a flatboat, on which, after arriving at the landing, the first week's issue was printed. Soon after arriving at the landing the publisher built a substantial office on Walnut Street, between Fourth and Fifth Streets, which is now used as a dwelling. After Chattanooga was thus named, the paper changed its name to the Chattanooga *Gazette*. The *Gazette* constantly urged the building of railroads, and supported the principles of the Whig party from its establishment to its suspension in 1859, though strenuous efforts were made in the days of Know-nothingism to convert the editor to the views of that party. From 1859 the *Gazette* remained suspended until 1864, when it was revived, Joseph Ruohs furnishing the money and James R. Hood and Elbert A. James being the editors. It was the only paper published within eighty miles of the place, and the army in possession of the city found in its columns great relief from the monotony of camp life. It was finally suspended soon after the close of the war.

A number of other papers have been published in Chattanooga, and have been discontinued. Among them were the following: The Daily *Republican*, the first number of which was issued November 3, 1867; the Daily American *Union*, the first number being dated March 4, 1866; the Chattanooga *Daily Rebel*, mention of which has been elsewhere made, and the Chattanooga *Daily Herald*, the first number of which appeared February 20, 1872. The *Herald* was a seven-column folio paper; was published by Samuel Bard, and favored the re-election of U. S. Grant to the presidency. The Chattanooga *Advertiser* was published some time by Ramage & Co.

The Chattanooga *Times* was founded by Kirby & Gamble in the fall of 1869, the first number appearing December 15. In April, 1874, this firm sold the plant for the benefit of creditors, and it was purchased by Patten & Payne, J. C. Payne conducting the paper from that time to October 1, 1876. It then passed into the hands of Cunningham & Crandall, a firm which soon dissolved, Crandall retiring, and Cunningham with several different partners. continuing its publication until June 30, 1878, when he sold a half interest and leased the other half to Adolph S. Ochs. The property was in a very bad condition, and the weekly edition had been suspended, and the yellow fever broke out within two months of the purchase. By November the expenses of running the paper were over $600 above receipts, but about this time the weekly edition was revived, and since then the growth of the paper in circulation and influence has been steady. From less than 200 in 1878, the circulation of the *Daily Times* has grown to 4,000, and of the *Weekly Times* to 10,000, and the business of the paper has many times doubled since 1880. The entire plant is worth about $50,000. It is owned by a stock company, and since 1878 has been edited by Col. J. E. MacGowan. The total number of employes on the paper and in the publication office is about forty.

The Chattanooga *Commercial* was started in 1872 by a stock company, with George M. Doak as editor. In 1876 the paper was suspended, and in 1877 it was revived by George M. Drake and H. F. Griscom. Mr. Drake retired in about five months, and the publication of the paper was continued by H. F. Griscom & Co., Mr. Griscom, editor, continuing thus until September, 1884, when the present company was organized, and a morning daily paper started. On April 19, 1886, the morning daily was changed to an evening daily, the weekly edition continuing to be issued on Sunday. The officers of the present company are J. M. Vernon, president and general manager; D. W. Chase, vice-president, and H. F. Griscom, secretary and treasurer.

The *Methodist Advocate* was established in Atlanta, Ga., in 1868; Dr. E. Q. Fuller was appointed editor, and was retained in this position until 1872, when Rev. N. E. Cobleigh, D. D., was elected editor. On Dr. Cobleigh's death in 1874, Dr. Fuller was appointed to again fill the place, and was elected editor by the general conference in 1876. He was re-elected in 1880, and held the position until 1883, when the paper ceased to be published by the book concern. At this time Rev. T. C. Carter, D. D., purchased the material, moved the enterprise to Chattanooga, and issued the first number in that city January 24, 1883. Dr. Carter has since continued its publication. It is recognized by the General Conference, and is the organ of the Methodist Episcopal Church in the South. Its circulation is now 4,000. J. H. Bowman is the associate editor.

The *Baptist Reflector* was founded in 1874, at Morristown, by O. C. Pope, D. D., and was moved to Nashville in 1876, where its publication was continued by W. D. Mayfield & Co. until 1879, when they sold out to J. B. Cheeves, who continued its publication until July, 1881. In January, 1881, J. M. Robertson, D. D., purchased the *Baptist Sun*, at Rome, Ga., and the *Baptist Beacon*, at Knoxville, and concentrated them at Chattanooga. In July, 1881, he bought the *Reflector*, and removed it to Chattanooga. In November, 1885, the Baptist Publishing Company was chartered with a capital of $10,000, and the paper sold to this company, by whom Dr. Robertson was elected editor. The stock of this company is held in most of the counties of the State, and the paper has a large circulation in Georgia and Alabama, but it is especially large in Tennessee.

The *Chattanooga Sunday Argus* was started November 1, 1885, by G. Allison Holland as proprietor and editor, and C. S. E. Holland as local editor and assistant business manager. Mr. Holland started this enterprise with the design of publishing a straight Democratic paper. It is an eight-column folio, circulates in all the adjoining States to the number of about 3,000 weekly, at the annual subscription price of $1.50. A specialty is made of double numbers; about twenty of these being issued each year.

The first number of the *Tradesman* was issued March 3, 1879, by the Tradesman Publishing Company. It is a Southern trade journal, contains thirty-six pages, is issued semi-monthly at $2 per annum, and is devoted to the manufacturers, merchants and industrial classes of the South. The company was incorporated with George H. Hazlehurst, president; H. F. Temple, vice-president, and Adolph S. Ochs, secretary and treasurer. William Yonge was first business manager, and Col. J. E. MacGowan, editor.

There are two other papers published in Chattanooga, one devoted to the interests of the laboring man, the other to those of the colored man, the latter being edited by colored men.

The Young Men's Christian Association was chartered November 8, 1876, the charter members being William Morris, H. D. Wyatt, J. L. Morrison, G. M. Sherwood, Paul Kamerer, W. J. Colburn and L. P. Thatcher. But little was effected, however, by the association before 1882, in February of which year it was reorganized with about one hundred members and officers, as follows: L. M. Elder, president; F. Gibson, vice-president; W. B. Strang, first secretary; C. E. Ensign, recording secretary; C. O. Lindsay, treasurer. These same persons have ever since held these offices. The present membership is 325. This association constantly keeps open a free reading room, and has a free circulating library of about 1,000 volumes. Its most important work is in the evangelical field; its objects are the physical, mental, moral and religious education of the young; it has four rooms in the Adams Block, rent free, which have been furnished with sufficient elegance by the ladies of the city without cost to the association, and its missionary work extends to the criminal and otherwise neglected classes.

The Chattanooga Orphans' Home was established in February, 1878, and incorporated in the following July. It is under the auspices of the Women's Christian Association of Chattanooga, an organization representing all the Protestant denominations of the city. The first meeting that led to its organization was called by the Home Mission Society of the First Presbyterian Church in October, 1877, the motive leading to it being the desire of the ladies of the city to rescue the unprotected young, especially the girls, from a future life of crime. The home was to be a temporary shelter from which they could be placed permanently in Christian homes, the work having been a most gratifying success. One year after the organization of the home Rev. T. H. McCallie donated to it a lot upon which, through the liberal contributions of other citizens, furniture, board and wages of the ten northern ladies having charge of its various departments, lights, fuel, bedding and clothing of all the children have since been supplied. Mrs. Steele chose a board of trustees and deeded to them as a chartered body the property after paying for the land, and the buildings which were destroyed by fire in November, 1885. Citizens of Chattanooga paid about $8,000 toward the erection of the new building, and without any solicitation on the part of Mrs. Steele, her friends and acquaintances and the public contribute to the necessities of the institution as they feel inclined, and these voluntary contributions have thus far very largely met its running expenses. Mrs. Steele is from Revere, Mass., and is conducting this noble charity wholly upon her own responsibility, except as indicated above.

The Associated Charities of Chattanooga was organized October 1, 1881. The directors and officers of this association are as follows: H. S. Chamberlain, president; C. A. Hoyt, secretary and superintendent; Leonard Boice, treasurer; Rev. J. W. Bachman, chairman of the executive committee; C. P. Robertson, J. C. Griffiss, Tomlinson Fort, D. J. Chandler, C. S. Peak, R. M. Barton, C. D. McGuffey, Joseph Wassman, D. Woodworth, Jr., S. P. Breckinridge and D. B. Loveman,

The secret organizations in Chattanooga are so numerous that a history of each one cannot well be given in accordance with the plan of this work. A list of them, however, is here introduced. Of the A. L. of H., there is the Chickamauga Council. Of the A. O. U. W., Benefit Lodge, No. 6; of F. L., Lookout Camp, No. 33; of the G. A. R., Lookout Post, No. 2, Mission Ridge Post, No. 45, and Chickamauga Post, No. 22 (colored); I. O. O. F., Chattanooga Lodge, No. 45, and Guttenberg Lodge, No. 158; K. of H., Schiller Lodge, No. 158; K. of L., Lookout Assembly No. 2270, Eureka Assembly No. 4375 (colored), Central Assembly No. 5589, Phœnix Assembly No. 5726, and McDevitt Assembly No. 6883; K. of P., Damon Lodge No. 2, Keystone Lodge No. 35, Endowment Rank Section No. 337, and Uniform Rank, Anchor Division No. 3; Masons—Lookout Commandery No. 14, K. T.; Hamilton Chapter No. 49, R. A. M.; Chattanooga Lodge No. 199, F. & A. M.; Temple

Lodge No. 430, F. & A. M.; Royal Arcanum, Chattanooga Council No. 137. The S. of T. are represented by the Chattanooga Division No. 111; U. O. G. C., Chattanooga Commandery No. 77. Colored organizations: P. G. M. Council, G. U. O. F.; Eagle Star Lodge No. 1777, G. U. O. F.; Xenophon Lodge, No. 1995, G. U. O. F.: Household of Ruth, No. 121; Lookout Lodge, No. 10; Phœnix Lodge, No. 14, F. & A. M.; Mt. Moriah Lodge, No. 21, F. & A. M. The Confederate Veterans have N. B. Forest Camp, C. V. No. 3, organized September 1, 1885.

Besides the two cemeteries mentioned in the history of the county, there are, in Chattanooga, the City Cemetery, Forest Hills Cemetery, the Hebrew Cemetery and the Catholic Cemetery.

The postoffice at Chattanooga was established at Ross' Landing with John P. Long as postmaster, March 22, 1837. The name was changed to Chattanooga November 14, 1838. John P. Long remained postmaster until October 4, 1845, on which day David J. Carr was appointed. Since Mr. Carr's term the following have been postmasters: William F. Ragsdale, appointed April 9, 1852; Henry T. Phillips, July 15, 1853; James R. Hood, March 27, 1861; E. A. James, July 18, 1865; Robert S. Kendrick, April 5, 1869; Samuel Bard, December 12, 1872; Robert S. Kendrick, March 20, 1873; William T. Cate, March 2, 1875; Thomas Taylor, July 3, 1776; John T. Wilder, July 17, 1877; Harry F. Griscom, March 29, 1882, and George W. Martin, July 15, 1885. The postoffice became presidential February 21, 1856, and the letter-carrier service was established September 1, 1883.

The Chattanooga Orphans' Home for white children was established in February, 1878, and incorporated in July following. It is under the auspices of the Women's Christian Association of Chattanooga, a body representing all the Protestant denominations of the city. The first meeting that led to its organization was called by the Home Mission Society of the First Presbyterian Church in October, 1877. Years of labor in relieving the necessities of the poor showed no permanently good results. Little children were growing up from street-begging to lives of crime, and this was especially true of girls. The need to rescue them was great and the question was "How can it be done?" Nothing short of complete removal from parental influence was practicable. The object of the Home was indirectly to provide for temporal wants but the chief end in view was the "winning of souls." Hence the Home was to be a temporary shelter and training school from which children could be placed permanently in Christian homes. In 1879 Rev. T. H. McCallie donated a valuable lot, and through the liberal contributions of citizens a building was erected at a cost of $6,500. By additional labor and the appreciation of real estate the value of the property is now about $18,000. The number of orphans cared for by sending to homes is about 125, but a number of others have been taken as boarders. The first officers of the institution, elected in February, 1878, were Mrs. E. D. McCallie, president; Mrs. E. E. Loomis, vice-president; Mrs. S. D. McCorkle, secretary, and Miss S. E. Shaffer, treasurer. Mrs. McCallie continued president until February, 1886. At the election in February, 1887, Mrs. E. D. McCallie was again elected president; Mrs. S. E. Nelson, first vice-president; Mrs. D. Woodworth, second vice-president; Mrs. J. P. Wilkinson, third vice-president; Mrs. S. D. McCorkle, secretary, and Mrs. M. M. Wight, treasurer. The executive committee now consists of Mrs. G. A. Wood, Mrs. A. Hyde, Mrs. Woodburn, Mrs. Crouch, Mrs. G. C. Conner and Mrs. S. C. Dodge. Mrs. C. A. Reed is matron and Mrs. Kemp assistant matron. The total number of beneficiaries of the institution, direct and indirect, is about 200.

The Steele Home for colored children was opened April 26, 1884. It was designed as a home for needy children where they could be trained to perform the various kinds of housework, receive the rudiments of an English education and have good foundations laid for living upright, honest lives. It is located at the corner of Strait Street and the East Tennessee, Virginia & Georgia Railroad, and the property, consisting of four lots and the buildings, is worth $15,000. It opened with three children and has received in all 149, varying in age from infancy to fourteen years. Upon arriving at this last named age the children are sent to the industrial school established by the American Missionary Association. The Home receives $50 per year for feeding each child belonging to the county, Mrs. Steele herself, the founder of the Home, being responsible for the building.

The origin of the trouble over the city charter was in 1883, when, on account of a strong Republican majority in the city council, colored men were placed upon the police force. This was very distasteful to a portion of the Democracy, and they conceived the plan of having a charter passed by the Legislature, which was Democratic, giving the governor power to appoint all the city officers except the mayor and board of aldermen, who were to have no power except to levy taxes and to pay out the funds upon the order of the police commission which was to be appointed by the governor. There were only about thirty Democrats in the secret, all of them ex-rebels. The proposed charter was brought before the Legislature and passed by the Lower House by an almost solid Democratic vote, only three or four voting with the Republicans against it. By this time the people of Chattanooga became thoroughly aroused and sent up to the Legislature an enormous petition against the proposed legislation signed by most of the Republicans and liberal Democratic voters of the city. The bill, however, passed the first and second readings in the Senate. By this time, Col. Case, senator from Hamilton County, had organized a strong working force against the bill, and went before the Senate committee before whom, as attorneys for the bill, were — Snodgrass and T. M. McConnell. The burden of the argument in favor of bill was that the Republican party of Chattanooga was so strong that the Democrats could have no voice in the government of the city, and that the Republicans put negroes on the police force. Snodgrass, during the course of his speech in favor of the bill, said in substance: "If any of you gentlemen will come over to Chattanooga and get on a little bender, we will furnish a nigger to arrest you, a nigger to lock you up and a nigger to take care of you after you get into jail. Pass this bill and it will end the occupation of that gentleman (pointing to Case) and he and all of his northern Yankee friends in Chattanooga will leave the State." Influenced by such arguments as this the Senate committee, composed of thirteen Democrats and two Republicans reported the bill on its third reading. It came up on Thursday before the final adjournment of the Legislature. In the meantime Col. Case had prepared a table of statistics showing the wholesome management of the city's affairs by the Republicans, and also showed that several times when the Republican conventions had nominated incompetent men for important offices they had themselves as a party, elected a Democrat in preference because of his superior qualifications and higher standing. He also showed that there was no mismanagement of the city's affairs, that the money had all been judiciously and economically expended, and that under Republican administrations, Chattanooga had the best system of schools in the Southern States. These figures and facts were all placed in the hands of Senator Patterson of Savannah, Tenn., who, in his argument against the bill, said that the Democratic party should not be the only party in the world to oppose local self government; that this bill contemplated the placing of the government of Chattanooga in the hands of the governor of the State, and that the Democratic party was belying its history in attempting to pass any such enactment. Senator Patterson held the floor two hours, when adjournment for dinner was had. After convening again he took the floor and was so melting away the support of the measure that the Democrats favoring it became alarmed, and did not dare to bring it to a vote, and about 3 P. M. moved to postpone further consideration of the bill until the next Tuesday. During the postponement the measure was beaten in the Senate. As a result, the managers of the affair in Chattanooga, in concert with a few Republicans, fixed up a compromise measure by which the government was to remain unchanged except that the governor should appoint a police commission, to consist of three men not more than two of whom should be of the same party, and that this commission should have the appointment and control of the entire police force of the city. The mayor was to hold his office for two years instead of one, and the number of aldermen was reduced from ten to six, one from each ward and one at large. This act also provided that all voters, as a precedent to voting, should register at least ten days before the election, and pay his poll tax at the time of registration. The operation of the act was such that the Republicans gained every alderman and the mayor. The registration operated in such way as to create a corruption fund, candidates for office having, in many cases, to pay the poll tax for voters. Although this was a compromise measure, those most active in its procurement were not satisfied to abide by it, but went back to the Legislature asking that body to pass a measure eliminating the board of mayor and aldermen from any participation in the government of the city except to levy taxes and pay them out upon the order of the board of public works, a board of school commissioners and a board of police commissioners, all to be appointed by the governor of the State, and made it obligatory upon the mayor and board of alderman to levy the tax upon estimates furnished by these several boards. This act passed the Lower House of the Legislature, and two readings in the Senate, and was recommended for its third and final passage by the committee on corporations. Col. Case in the discussion of the question made a very vigorous fight against the measure on the ground of its unconstitutionality in depriving the tax-levying power of the discretion as to what tax should be levied and expended, and succeeded in converting five or six Democratic senators to his views and they refused to vote for the measure, unless an amendment were adopted to the effect that the act, if passed into a law, should not take effect until after having been first submitted to a vote of the people of the city of Chattanooga, and adopted by a majority of the voters casting their votes at such election, and that if a majority of the voters should be found opposed to the law going into operation, it should remain as if it had not been passed. In this condition the bill was passed by the Senate, and the House concurred in the amendment, but the parties who were pressing the measure, have never yet dared to submit it to a vote of the people, thus tacitly admitting that in their opinion the people of Chattanooga, if given a chance to do so, would certainly vote it down.

The people of East Tennessee were highly gratified by the appointment of the Hon. D. M. Key to the postoffice portfolio in the cabinet of President Hayes. A meeting of the citizens of Chattanooga was held March 17, 1877, to give expression to their views and sentiments. W. A. Hoskins was president of the meeting. In the fall following, President Hayes, having accepted an invitation to visit Chattanooga, arrived in that city September 20. The party consisted of the President, Mrs. Hayes, and their two sons, Burchard and Webb, Postmaster-General Key, William M. Evarts, and others. An address of welcome was delivered by Col. J. B. Cooke, a prominent ex-Confederate officer. Wade Hampton then made an address, as also did Gen. Key. An address was delivered for the colored people by Rev. G. P. Milton, and for the workingmen by R. V. Brennan.

Three years later another visitor, equally distinguished with President Hayes, but in different ways, arrived upon invitation in Chattanooga—Thomas Hughes from Rugby. On the 15th of September, 1880, Mr. Hughes reached Chattanooga, on the 16th visited Lookout Mountain, and in the evening held a reception at the Stanton House. In the course of his reponse to the toast: "Our Guest, Author, Statesman, Philanthropist, Chattanooga welcomes him to the inner sanctuary of her admiration and popularity," he said:

"From the top of Lookout Mountain I admired the superb richness of the country, but there is a higher and more human side to the sights afforded a stranger in your town. I refer to that most beautiful cemetery in which are gathered together those who fell in the war, now twenty years ago. To all the advantages of your city is added the most inspiring one that you are here in the center of the greatest events of our day. One feels that the greatest crisis that the world has yet gone through took place on these hills. The lines in "Childe Harold" apply more fully to these fields than to Waterloo, or any other battle-field celebrated among the nations. The crisis at Chattanooga was more important to the human race than the crisis at Marathon or Tours. The only sentiment that will find utterance in the hearts of all true Americans is expressed in the words: 'Union and freedom now and forever.'"

Coulterville is situated on the Cincinnati Southern Railway, thirty-three miles from Chattanooga. At the time this railway was constructed there was here but one house, that of John J. Coulter, besides the church, both of which were erected in 1852. The church was built by subscription by the people living in the surrounding country. Mr. Coulter gave the railroad company two and one-fourth acres of land, and sold them about three and two-thirds acres more upon which to erect the depot, and the church authorities also sold the railway company the church property, which added to the other makes about six acres owned here by the company. Sale Creek Lodge, No. 280, A. F. & A. M., then united with the church and erected a building 50x40 feet in size, and two stories high to be used both for religious and educational purposes, standing about 300 yards above the depot, and costing about $1,000, Four stores have been kept in this village: the first by W. L. Pahmyer, in 1877, the second by Spivey & Martin, the third by D. W. & W. H. Wilson, and the fourth by J. J. Kelley. At the present time there are two stores, kept respectively by J. M. Martin and John R. Hickman, who has been postmaster since June 3, 1879, when the postoffice was established.

Sale Creek is on the Cincinnati Southern Railway. The Welsh Company came here in 1867, and leased the coal mine of Lusk, Pearl & Co.; commenced mining coal and carried the coal on a tram railroad to Sale Creek, a distance of one and a half miles, where it was loaded into flatboats until 1875, when work was suspended and a railway graded from the mines to connect with the Cincinnati Southern Railway. When this railway was built the place had about 300 inhabitants. The first store was started here in 1868 by Peter Bolton, who sold out in 1875 to the Welsh Company. A blacksmith shop was opened here in 1868. G. W. Branham started a store in 1877 and is still keeping it. The school has been in operation here since 1850, when it was known as the Masonic Academy, the building having been erected by the Masonic lodge aided by private subscription. The first teacher here was J. N. Aiken. The present board consists of Dr. V. J. Kennedy, Peter Bolton and Joseph McReynolds. The upper story of the present schoolhouse was put on in 1885, during which year the school was graded. There are five religious denominations here: the Presbyterian, Cumberland Presbyterian, Baptist, Methodist Episcopal, Methodist Episcopal South. Coke ovens were built here in 1882, which now turn out about three carloads of coke per day, the amount of coal mined being about 100 tons per day. The first coal mined here was in 1845, by Robert Jack on his own farm. The postmasters at Sale Creek have been Thomas Coulter, appointed October 26, 1841; John R. Hickman, April 16, 1855; Thomas Coulter, February 19, 1856; Abel A. Pearson, March 18, 1856; Gideon T. Morgan, January 10, 1866; John R. Hickman, March 19, 1866; Peter Bolton, January 11, 1871; William B. Bolton, December 29, 1882, and Jacob A. N. Patterson, April 2, 1886.

Soddy is situated on the Cincinnati Southern Railway, the station here being named Rathburn in honor of W. P. Rathburn. The place was very small until the Soddy Coal Company commenced mining coal here in 1867. Some coal had been mined here previously by Col. William Clift and Maj. R. C. McKee, the former having settled on Soddy Creek two miles east of the present postoffice, in 1826. After the starting of the coal nine the town began to grow. The Soddy Coal Company built the first houses, and opened the first stores, and there was also one small grocery and a drug store, besides those owned by the company. The Soddy Company consisting of about fifteen Welshmen made an assignment in 1874, and most of the stock was purchased by J. T. Williams, J. W. Clift, A. Lloyd and M. H. Clift, a portion of it remaining in the hands of Lewis. This company now employ about 500 men, and mine about 150,000 tons of coal each year. They commenced making coke in 1881, and now make about 36,000 tons per year. Besides good common schools, Soddy has a graded school in which Latin and the higher English branches are taught. Of this school P. A. Wall is the principal, and Mary McDonald assistant. The postoffice of Soddy was established in 1829, and William Clift appointed postmaster December 15 of that year. It was discontinued December 3, 1845. On April 10, 1850, it was re-established, John M. Watson being on that day appointed postmaster. His successors have been George Card, appointed September 13, 1867; Edward S. Card, September 6, 1869; William H. Card, November 27, 1874; J. T. Lloyd, January 17, 1882, and Abraham Lloyd, Feburary 6, 1882.

Daisy is situated on the Cincinnati Southern Railway. The place was named after Daisy Parks, a daughter of Thomas Parks, vice-president of the Tabler-Cleudup Coal & Coke Company. The Daisy Coal Company was organized April 16, 1881, the first members being Thomas Parks, J. T. Wilder, Maj. Dodan, R. M. Barton and L. B. Headrick. This company continued on as such until July, 1885, when the Tabler-Cleudup Company was organized with Maj. J. H. Tabler, president; Thomas Parks, vice-president, and D. G. Cleudup, treasurer. The capital stock of this company is $400,000. The average output of coal is about 50,000 tons and of coke, which they commenced making in November, 1885, about 10,000 tons per annum. They employ about 150 men, own 7,000 acres of land with four veins of coal from three and one-half to seven feet thick. This company opened the first store in the place in 1883, in addition to which there are now two small stores, one started by Puckett & Roe in 1884, the other by J. T. Jones in 1886. The town of Daisy contains two churches, Poe Springs Academy and about 600 inhabitants. A postoffice was established here, named Poe's Cross Roads, June 30, 1846, with Samuel P. Poe, postmaster. It was discontinued

October 21, 1847. Daisy postoffice was established December 12, 1883, with Robert H. Maddox, postmaster, still retaining the position.

Melville is a small station about one mile south of Daisy. It was named after Melville Adams, who gave a piece of land to the railway company with the understanding that a station should be built thereon. The postoffice at Melville was established as Chickamauga, March 14, 1850, and changed to Melville, January 15, 1878, with Mr. Adams postmaster. George S. Card was appointed March 14, 1881, and the name of the office was changed to Daisy December 12, 1883. One of the most remarkable natural phenomena in Hamilton County is the "Sunken Lake" or "Lake Llewellyn," near the top of Walden's Ridge, opposite Melville. It is oval in form, the top of the opening being in extent equal to about five acres of ground, the distance from the surface of the ground to the water being about one hundred feet and the depth of the water, which is as clear as crystal, being also about one hundred feet. The surface of the water is equal in extent to about three acres. On the west side the rocks rise perpendicularly from the water to the surface of the ground, on the north they slightly overhang, and on the other two sides they slope down to the water's edge. How this opening, nearly 200 feet deep in the solid rock, was made is as yet an unsolved problem.

Cave Spring Station is on the Cincinnati Southern Railway, and is so named because of the large spring flowing out of a cave. As yet there is nothing here but the tank and the saw-mill of J. M. Long. Falling Water postoffice, half a mile westward is to be moved to Cave Spring Station. The postmasters at Falling Water have been William C. Hale, appointed August 11, 1874; Richard F. Selcer, October 9, 1877, and Henry Barker, April 19, 1880.

Hixson is a small town on the Cincinnati Southern Railway, originally named Lookout for the reason that it was at this point that the civil engineer corps in surveying the line of the railway first caught a glimpse of Lookout Mountain. This was in 1878. The name was changed to Hixson in January, 1884. The first store was started here, March 1, 1881, by E. F. and E. Hixson, and the second during the same year by H. and G. W. Hixson. A blacksmith shop was also started here that year by Ephraim Rogers. The Methodist Episcopal Church South, which is one mile and a half distant, was started in 1866 and now has about sixty members. The postoffice here is named Lakeside and was established March 24, 1880, with Ephraim F. Hixson, postmaster.

King's Point was named after John King, who sold 500 acres of land to the King's Point Town Company, upon which to build a town. At that time there was one farm house on this land occupied by Alexander Milliken. The Allins, real estate agents in Chattanooga, built a store, the only one now in the place, which contains about one hundred inhabitants. The school and church occupy the same building which cost about $1,000. The postoffice here, named King's Point, was established March 1, 1883, with John B. Allin, postmaster. He has been succeeded by Richard M. Kerley, June 15, 1883; William S. Huffine, February 14, 1884; Alexander Milliken, May 21, 1885; Edward M. Brooks, June 15, 1885, and Orson Ames, September 8, 1886.

Boyce is at the junction of the Cincinnati Southern Railway and the Western & Atlantic. The station is one-half mile above the old station, which is now occupied as a residence. There is one store here, opened by James Squires in 1884. The postoffice here was originally named Boyce Junction, and was established September 24, 1879. The name was changed to Amnicola October 29, 1879, to Boyce August 5, 1880, and to Amnicola August 24, 1880. The postmasters have been A. C. Taylor, appointed September 24, 1879; Tom Crutchfield, October 29, 1879; A. C. Taylor, September 5, 1881; William Higgins, May 12, 1882 and James Squires, September 10, 1885.

Dallas, old Dallas, as it is now called, because it is not any longer a town, was started about 1830. Asahel Rawlings had a store there about this time and was the first postmaster, having been appointed in 1822, when the place was named Hamilton C. H. In 1840 the town was in its prime, having then two or three stores, about half a dozen houses and a few cabins, a blacksmith shop, a good hotel and a population of about sixty. When the county seat was moved to Harrison in 1840 Dallas soon declined. Asahel Rawlings was appointed postmaster at Hamilton C. H., May 11, 1822. The name was changed to Dallas, February 20, 1833; the postoffice was discontinued March 23, 1846; was re-established June 29, 1848; was again discontinued October 2, 1849; was again re-established September 4, 1866, and finally discontinued September 13, 1872. Since Mr. Rawlings the postmasters have been Aaron M. Rawlings, appointed July 24, 1833; Samuel S. M. Doak, July 21, 1836; James S. Yarnall, March 21, 1837; Samuel T. Izen, May 27, 1837; Thomas Stiff, October 26, 1838; Albert W. Beddo, May 1, 1844; George R. Cannon, December 3, 1845; Clinton A. Jones, June 29, 1848; John H. Bradfield, September 4, 1866; Daniel B. Brayfield, November 4, 1869.

Harrison was located about thirteen miles northeast of Chattanooga, was named after President William Henry Harrison, was the county seat of Hamilton County from 1840 to 1870, and at the time of its greatest prosperity contained about 1,000 people. After 1870 it rapidly declined and now there is left scarcely a vestige of its former glory. A list of its postmasters could not be obtained.

Tyner, at first called Tynerville, is located ten miles from Chattanooga, on the East Tennessee, Virginia & Georgia Railway. It was founded by Capt. Tyner, and received his name in 1858. The first store, established by Lafayette Varnell, was continued until the war, after which N. L. Rawlings started a store and H. J. Springfield & Bro. ran a grocery and saloon. There is a Baptist Church and a Cumberland Presbyterian Church, a Masonic lodge, and Pleasant Grove Academy located at House's camp-ground, named after G. W. House. Foster Carper in early days ran a tannery here, then the largest in the country. At the present time Tyner contains about one hundred inhabitants. The postoffice was established as Tynerville, with Washington Evans postmaster, February 1, 1860, the name being changed to Tyner September 13, that year. Robert L. Gamble was appointed postmaster April 22, 1865; James Allen, June 26, 1867; James Milliken, January 21, 1868; John T. Rawlings, July 23, 1868; John C. Gamble, December 15, 1870; Robert L. Gamble, June 13, 1872; Henry J. Springfield, November 6, 1873; Henry B. Springfield, August 26, 1878; Thomas B. Varnell, November 4, 1880; Allen Thornbrough, March 27, 1884, and Thomas B. Varnell, December 17, 1885.

Chickamauga was started in 1858 as "Pull Tight," so named because of the extreme tenacity of the mud. Then there was simply the depot and a saloon. In 1859 Ellis Bros. started a general store, which they continued until the war, and which they reopened after the war, continuing it until 1880, and then selling out to Worley & Co., who in 1884 sold it to its present proprietors, Varnell Bros. The second store was started by M. J. Gilliland in 1880; G. R. Phillips, the third, and J. W. Finley, the fourth, who sold his to Ellis Bros. The oldest citizen in the vicinity is Rev. H. S. Moore, pastor of the Baptist Church, which was built in 1884. The postoffice was established here as Chickamauga Station, January 16, 1867, and the name was changed to Chickamauga November 29, 1882. The postmasters have been Thomas C. Holley, appointed January 16, 1867; Robert McCrary, January 7, 1868; John F. Kincheloe, June 10, 1872; John M. Ellis, March 27, 1878; George R. Phillips, October 4, 1881, and Winfield T. Worley, November 27, 1885.

Fairmount is a pleasant village of about 150 inhabitants, on Walden's Ridge. The postoffice was established in 1872, the postmasters having been James P. Sham, appointed April 19, 1872; Miss M. J. Bohanan, March 20, 1873; George N. Rogers, July 18, 1873; Joseph F. Mayhew, February 3, 1874; Helena M. Scales, November 20, 1876; Green A. Brown, March 13, 1877; Helena M. Scales, January 3, 1879; John S. Scales, May 2, 1884, and Wilson B. Connor, April 27, 1886.

Summertown is located on top of Lookout Mountain and is inhabited chiefly in summer. The postoffice is named Lookout Mountain, the first postmaster having been Charles C. Carpenter, appointed June 11, 1867; followed by Ewing O. Tade, July 22, 1872; G. W. Arnold, December 10, 1872; Esther A. Waters, May 16, 1873; Willey J. Drinnon, December 9, 1873; Hannah Hill, August 23, 1875; postoffice discontinued April 11, 1876, and re-established June 5, 1877, George S. Ruble appointed that day; John E. Grimer, June 21, 1881; Eliza B. Carlile, November 18, 1881; Marion A. Carlile, December 15, 1881; Sue E. Reade, November 6, 1883, and Harry E. Stoops, February 23, 1886.

Wauhatchie is situated in Lookout Valley, on the Nashville, Chattanooga & St. Louis Railway. But little is here besides the station, one store and the postoffice, which was established in 1866, discontinued June 12, 1867, and re-established November 12, 1868. The postmasters have been Isaac C. Rowden, January 2, 1866; Samuel Rowden, January 20, 1879; Walter M. James, February 19, 1879; Franklin A. James, December 15, 1879, and Samuel E. Rowden, December 2, 1885.

Other postoffices in Hamilton County with the dates of their establishment are as follows: Brays, July 24, 1885; Bunch, April 23, 1880; Divine, May 18, 1881; Hill City, established as Harveytown, December 4, 1883, and changed to Hill City, March 27, 1884; Igou's Ferry, April 6, 1871; Kirklin, August 15, 1882; Mission Ridge, September 29, 1884; Poeville, December 20, 1883; Retro, June 23, 1880; Red Bank, December 9, 1875; Suburba, November 17, 1885; Trewhitt, June 1, 1883, and Williams' Landing, May 2, 1878. Besides these a large number of postoffices have been established and discontinued.

HAMILTON COUNTY.

D. M. & J. W. Agey. The Mountain City Business College was established, in June, 1886, by J. W. Agey, a native of Beaver County, Penn., born March 21, 1855. He was joined in the enterprise by his elder brother, D. M. Agey, who was born March 4, 1853, and who is also a native of Beaver County, Penn. Both brothers had good educational advantages. The elder received his higher education in Mount Union College, Ohio, and the younger at Valparaiso, Ind. Having taught for some time in Ohio they went to Missouri, where both held prominent positions as instructors until 1886. The elder brother studied law while in Ohio, and was admitted to the bar, but circumstances brought him into a nobler calling. Calvin and

Susan (Beam) Agey are the parents of our subjects. Some time after marriage they moved to Ohio, where they remained until 1886, when they came to Chattanooga. Both J. W. and D. M. Agey, as well as their parents, are members of the Christian Church. J. W. is a Mason, and D. M. is a member of the I. O. O. F. and of the Knights of the Maccabees. In 1881 D. M. married Miss Carrie McKee, a native of Ohio, who bore him two sons: Hoite M. and Thomas G. His wife is also a member of the Christian Church.

Paul R. Albert, manager of the new opera house, and a member of the wholesale firm of J. Seeman & Co., was born December 13, 1841, in France, and his father, Paul, was also a native of France. His mother, Sophia Gurhauer, was born in Berlin, Germany. When only six years of age our subject came with his parents to Cincinnati, Ohio. His father, a merchant, died some time after the removal, and the mother married Dr. George Kuhlmann. Young Paul, the only son by the first marriage, was educated in the public schools and at Woodward College, Cincinnati, Ohio, and the Urbana University. His step-father wished him to prepare for a professional life, but he secretly took a commercial course preparatory to entering the business world. When his step-father decided to send him to Yale College, our subject concluded to run away from home. He engaged with a Cincinnati firm at $1.50 per week and at last arose to the chief clerkship. Having received a better offer from a large Cincinnati firm to enter a Nashville branch of the house he came South in 1862, and such was the confidence and esteem in which he was held by the firm that he was soon taken in as a partner, and three years later was given charge of three branch houses in which he was also a partner. The failure of the Cincinnati firm involving the branch establishment swept all the fruits of his labor away, and in 1872 he came to Chattanooga, and engaged in the confectionery business with J. Seeman, on very small capital. Gradually they arose until in 1876 they began an exclusively wholesale business as tobacconists and manufacturing confectioners. Mr. Albert is connected with the Star Jelly Works, is president of the Chattanooga Canning Company, is one of the directors of the Chattanooga Building and Savings Association, is a director of the Handel Musical Society, also of the Chickamauga Guards, is secretary of the Chattanooga Opera House Company, is Trustee of the Burris Syndicate and president of Lookout C. M. Association. He was Grand Dictator of the K. of H. for the State of Tennessee, and is now Supreme Representative of the State. He is a Mason, and a prominent officer in several benevolent fraternities besides.

J. A. Allen, chief of police of the city of Chattanooga, was born

January 16, 1833, at Columbus, Ky., but was reared to manhood in East Feliciana Parish, La. At the commencement of the late war he was an overseer of a plantation in that State, but this he resigned to enlist in the Sixteenth Louisiana Regulars (Company A), and in 1862 was ordered to Chattanooga on detached duty. He remained at this point until the evacuation of the city by the Confederates, then went to Macon, Ga., and in 1865, at the close of the war, returned to Chattanooga, which has since been his home. Mr. Allen is a carpenter by trade, and this occupation he followed until appointed on the police force in 1876. Prior to his election as chief of police in April, 1883, he officiated for one year as county jailer. In 1863 he was united in marriage with Mrs. Travers, and to their union six children have been born, only one now living. He and family are members of the Methodist Episcopal Church South. He is a son of Louis and Lucy (Feltz) Allen, who were natives of South Carolina and Tennessee, respectively, the former dying in Louisiana in 1860, preceded by his wife in Arkansas in 1840.

John C. Anderson, agent for Western & Atlantic Railroad at Chattanooga, was born in Dalton, Ga., November 27, 1853, and is the son of John W. and J. S. (Chester) Anderson, natives, respectively, of Georgia and Tennessee. Our subject was reared and educated in his native city, came to Chattanooga in December, 1870, and entered the employ of the Western & Atlantic Railroad as clerk, where he has remained since. He is one of the organizers, and is president of the Empire Lumber Company, established in Chattanooga in 1882, secretary of the South Chattanooga Land Company, president of the Chattanooga Real Estate Company, and has been prominently identified with the real estate interests in the city. March 27, 1879, he wedded Miss Fannie I. Woodruff, of Griffin, Ga. He is a Democrat in politics, a member of the First Presbyterian Church, and is recognized as one of the enterprising and reliable business men and citizens of Chattanooga. He has been a resident of that city since 1870, with the exception of three years, from 1878 to 1881, when he was in Georgia in charge of large lumber operations for the Georgia Land & Lumber Company.

Hon. James T. Arnold, of the firm of Loomis, Hart & Co., Chattanooga, was born in Greenville, Ohio, April 5, 1845, and here reared and educated. In 1866 he engaged in mercantile pursuits in Bluffton, Ind., until 1871, when he went to Montpelier, Ind., and engaged in the same business until 1885. In February of that year he came to Chattanooga and became a member of the above-named firm, being superintendent of the main office and furniture department. In 1871 he wedded Miss Elizabeth Johnston, who died in September, 1883, leaving three children, all sons. In July, 1886, he married Lettie Cleveland, of Indiana. Mr. Arnold is a Republican in politics and represented his district in the Indiana Legislature in 1879-80. He is a prominent man and is well respected. His parents, William and Margaret (Folkerth) Arnold, are natives, respectively, of South Carolina and Maryland.

C. H. Baldwin, secretary, treasurer and local manager of the Chattanooga Stove Company, was born at Town Line, N. Y., November 10, 1855, but removed at an early age to Cleveland, Ohio, where he was educated in the excellent public schools of that city. Having a liking for mechanics he early engaged in the stove manufacturing business at Cleveland, but from 1878 to 1884 he took charge of branch foundries of the Cleveland Co-operative Stove Company located at Black River, Ohio, Indianapolis, Chicago, and St. Louis. In January, 1884, the Chattanooga Stove Company began operations, and Mr. Baldwin was appointed manager, a position he has since retained with entire satisfaction to the stockholders, besides being a stockholder in the Cleveland Co-operative Stove Company, of Cleveland, Ohio. The father of our subject, W. W. Baldwin, is a native of Vermont, and is now a resident of Cleveland, Ohio, being the general manager, secretary and treasurer of the Cleveland Co-operative Stove Company of that place, and general manager of the Chattanooga Stove Company of Chattanooga. The mother of C. H. Baldwin, whose maiden name was A. A. Johnson, of New York, died in November, 1886, leaving three sons and two daughters living from a family of seven children.

John C. Banks is a native of Olney, Ill., born September 29, 1852, and the son of John and Martha (Pulliam) Banks, both natives of Indiana. At the close of the late war our subject removed with his parents to Cynthiana, Ky., where he was reared and educated. He assisted his father in the stove and tin business until 1870 when he left home and went to Vincennes, Ind., there worked at his trade (tinner) for Smith & Sons until January, 1872. He married Miss Laura Snyder, and by this union became the father of one son named Charles H. In 1881 he removed to Chattanooga, Tenn., and was in the employ of Gibson, Lee & Co. until 1884, when he engaged in business for himself at 304 West Ninth Street. Upon the completion of the Adams Block he secured a large and commodious store room at 120 East Eighth Street, where he carries one of the largest and best selected stocks of stoves, crockery and house furnishing goods in the city, doing a wholesale and retail business (with one man on the road), and employing about twenty tinners. Mr. Banks is a Democrat, a member of the I. O. O. F. and K. of P., and of the Methodist Episcopal Church.

Hugh R. Banks, of the well known firm of Chapman & Banks of Chattanooga, was born in Charleston, S. C., September 27, 1843, where he was reared and educated. While securing a good collegiate education the stirring events of the war put a stop to further study. He entered the Confederate service paymaster's department for North Carolina, South Carolina and Georgia, serving through the entire war. After cessation of hostilities he went to Texas, and engaged in the cotton business as factor until 1878, when he returned to his native city and resided there until December, 1884, when he came to Chattanooga, and engaged in his present real estate business with Mr. M. L. Chapman. May 20, 1873, he was united in marriage to Miss Ella Hammond, of Robertson County, Tex., who bore him two living children, both daughters, named Aviline and Caroline. Mr. Banks is a Democrat in politics and an enterprising citizen.

George A. Barnes, agent at Chattanooga for East Tennessee & Virginia, and Georgia, Memphis & Charleston Railroads, is a native of Massachusetts, born July 26, 1841. He was reared and received a fair education in his native State. He has been in the railroad business since 1870, was secretary and treasurer of Springfield, Jackson & Pomeroy Railroad, Ohio, for some time, and was for a number of years in the employ of the Cleveland, Columbus, Cincinnati and Indianapolis Railroad, at Springfield, Ohio. He came to Chattanooga in December, 1885, and has since been agent for both of the above named roads at this point. November 11, 1881, he was united in marriage to Jeannette Fellers, of Ohio, who bore him one child, a son named Clarence A. Mr. Barnes is a Republican in politics and a member of the Masonic fraternity.

Thomas E. V. Barkley, A. B., M. D., was born in Winchester, Ky., January 7, 1858, and is a son of Capt. Hiram Barkley, a native Kentuckian, and Martha Betty (Campbell) Barkley, also a native of Kentucky, where they are now living. Of their family of four children, our subject was the eldest. He was educated in the high school at home and at Washington and Lee Academy, and finished his education at Bethany College in 1877. He then took a medical course at Miami Medical College where he graduated in 1880. He came to Chattanooga and became a partner of Dr. Berlin. He is a member of the K. of P., and K. of H., Fraternal Legion, and also of the Christian Church. He is a member of different societies, and is much esteemed by all who know him.

G. A. Baxter, A. M., M. D., is a son of George W. and Catherine (Alexander) Baxter, both born and reared in North Carolina. While growing up the father received a good literary and legal education, and made the profession of law his pursuit in life. He died in 1854, and later the mother married his brother, Hon. John Baxter, lately United States circuit judge. The mother lived until 1865. To the second marriage there were no children, and only one, the Doctor, to the first marriage. He was born in Buncombe County, N. C., November 28, 1851, and his higher education was received at Earlham College, Indiana, from which he received the degree of A. B. He then attended Kenyon College, and later graduated from Hobert College of Geneva, N. Y., from which also he received the degree of A. M. The East Tennessee University conferred upon him the honorary degree of A. M. In 1873, he graduated from Belleview Hospital Medical College, and thereupon accepted the position of assistant surgeon on the Erie Railroad, the surgical department of which he organized. In 1875, he came to Chattanooga and has practiced his profession here since. In 1879, he married Miss Ellen Douglas, of Nashville, who bore him three children, two of whom are living: Douglas and Bruce. The Doctor has held the position of vice-president of the State Medical Society, is a member of the city board of health, Royal Arch Mason, K. of P., K. of H., and both he and wife are members of the Episcopal Church.

Henry C. Beck, the efficient and affable register of Hamilton County, was born on the 10th of March, 1853, in the county where he now resides, and which has been his home through life. His father, Joshua Beck, was a native of North Carolina and immigrated to this county at the early period of 1822. He here wedded Margaret Hixon, a native of Hamilton County, Tenn., and they became one of the county's best and most respected families. They followed agricultural pursuits until the death of the father, August 5, 1886, since when the widow has lived a retired life near Chattanooga. Henry C., the immediate subject of this biography, was reared and mostly educated in his native county, although, for a time, he attended school at Athens, Tenn. He first began his public career in August, 1874, when he was elected to the office of county register; so efficiently did he fill the requirements of this position that he was re-elected at the end of his term, and twice thereafter re-elected, and is now serving his fourth term in that office. Mr. Beck also fills the positions of secretary of the Northside Steamboat & Ferry Company, secretary of the Grandview Cemetery, and is a director in the Mutual Real Estate and Home Building Association. To his marriage with Miss Rhoda D. Wexler, a native of Sullivan County, this State, there have been born two sons and one daughter, one son being now deceased.

A. Shelton

Dr. J. T. Bell, physician and surgeon of Soddy, was born in Rhea County September 15, 1850, and is the son of William H. and Nancy (Rainy) Bell. The father was born in Green County and died February 19, 1876. He was a minister of the gospel in the Cumberland Presbyterian Church of which he was first to establish in East Tennessee. He organized congregations and built churches all over East Tennessee. A few of the many churches he was the means of building were at Cleveland in Bradley County, at Jasper in Marion County, and at New Bethel in Bledsoe County. He was taken sick while preaching in the Presbyterian Church at Cleveland during the session of the synod, was taken home and died shortly afterward. He was a charter member of Washington Masonic Lodge and was very active in the furtherance of every interest, pertaining to the prosperity of the lodge. The mother was born in Bledsoe County and died in May, 1883, in Cook County, Tex. Dr. Bell received his literary education principally at Sequatchie College in Bledsoe County, where he graduated in the mathematical and English course of study. He is also a graduate of the medical department of the University of Nashville and the Vanderbilt University. At each of these institutions of learning he acquitted himself in a highly creditable manner, taking rank with the best of the students in attendance. After attending his first course of lectures he located at Dayton, Tenn., where he remained but a short time. He was at Coulterville two years and then moved to Soddy in June, 1883, and has been quite successful as a practitioner. Dr. Bell is a young man, but his prospects seem very bright for the future. He married E. L. Abel, of Dayton, Tenn., daughter of Perry and Mary Abel. The Doctor is a descendant of purely Irish ancestry. Mrs. Bell is a member of the Methodist Episcopal Church South, and of Dutch descent. The Doctor is a Democrat and a member of the Cumberland Presbyterian Church.

Dr. H. Berlin is the son of H. and C. H. (Peters) Berlin, both natives of Mechlinburg, Germany, where they now live. The father was a farmer and manufacturer of fishing tackle. Of their family of two children our subject was the youngest. He was born May 8, 1851, also in Mechlinburg, Germany, and secured his education, both literary and professional, in his native country. After practicing medicine there for two years he came to the United States in 1879, and located in Chattanooga. He was for a time engaged in the general practice of medicine, but of late years has devoted his entire energy to surgery and female diseases, wishing to familiarize himself more with the ideas and practice of the profession in this department he became a student of the University of Tennessee. In 1875 he married Miss Mary Von Podiwils, of

Germany, by whom he has two children: Charlotte and Henry. The Doctor is a correspondent for several medical journals on subjects pertaining to the profession and science. He is a member of both State and county medical societies, being vice-president of the latter. He is a Mason and a member of the K. of P. Mrs. Dr. Berlin is a member of the Episcopal Church.

Charles W. Biese, secretary and treasurer of the Lookout Ice and Cold Storage Company, of Chattanooga, was born in Holstein, Germany, November 8, 1835; came to the United States in 1860 and located at Chicago, where, in 1861, he enlisted in the Federal Army, serving through grades of private, sergeant, lieutenant and captain in the Eighty-second Illinois Regiment until 1865. He then opened one of the first coal mines in this locality which he operated three years. He was then connected with Cherokee Mining & Manufacturing Company, and later was connected with the Georgia Coal Company. In 1869 he assisted in building bridges and trestles on the Great Southern Railroad, Alabama. Later he engaged in the same business with the Alabama Grand Trunk Railroad, with office at Mobile, Ala. and was engaged in the commission business for two years. In 1875 he returned to this place and engaged in the agricultural implement business which he lately sold to his son Robert and a Mr. Dickinson. In 1883 Mr. Biese had a company formed to engage in the manufacture of artificial ice, but owing to competition it proved a failure. In 1884 he again formed a company of which the present company is the outcome and of which he is secretary. In 1864 he married Narcissa H. McDonald, of Dade County, Ga., who died in 1873, leaving four children, all of whom are living. In 1875 he married his present wife, Miss Eliza A. Pryor, of Jasper, Tenn., who has presented him with two sons, only one living. Mr. Biese is a Republican, a Knight of Labor, a Mason, and a member of the G. A. R., was Post Commander of Lookout Post, No. 2, during 1886. He is also a member of the K. of P., K. of H., and of the Methodist Episcopal Church South, of which he is a steward.

U. D. Billmeyer, D. D. S., whose birth occurred March 14, 1853, is a son of Joseph and Margaret (Carnahan) Billmeyer, who were born, reared and married in Pennsylvania. After living in that State for some time they then moved to Michigan about 1852. In early life the father was a contractor and builder and later a farmer and fruit grower. Both are living in Michigan at the present time. Of their family of seven children our subject is the eldest. He graduated in the Michigan State Normal School in 1876, and, after teaching a year, entered the dental department of Michigan University, completing the course in 1879. The following year he accepted the position of demonstrator of operative dentistry in the same institution, which position he held in a highly creditable manner four years. On account of failing health he was obliged to resign his position in the middle of a session. In 1884 he came to Chattanooga, and, without the assistance of relatives or friends, succeeded in building up an excellent practice. In 1882 Miss Lida Wallace, a native of Michigan, became his wife. They are both members of the Methodist Church. He is a member of the East Tennessee Dental Association, is a Royal Arch Mason and president of the Union Wood Dish Co.

Samuel Blair, of Chattanooga, was born in Harrison County, Ky., December 2, 1816, where he was reared and educated. In 1840 he went to Cincinnati, Ohio, and engaged in the ice business, and is still a member of the Cincinnati Ice Company. He came to Chattanooga in 1883, and a year later organized the Lookout Ice Company of which he has been principal stockholder and president. In December, 1886, the company began the erection of cold storage warehouses, and have changed the name to Lookout Ice and Cold Storage Company, with increased capital. In April, 1843, he was united in marriage to Miss Mary A. Lafferty, of Cincinnati, Ohio. The fruits of this union were five living children—three sons and two daughters. Mr. Blair is a member of the Methodist Episcopal Church, a member of the I. O. O. F., also of the encampment of the I. O. O. F. and is a Democrat in politics. He is an honest and well respected citizen. He has lately organized a stock company of $50,000 and is now boring for natural gas and oil in Hamilton County, Tenn., near Luck Creek.

Dr. M. Block, wholesale druggist, is a native of France, born in 1832. He received his literary education in Metz, Lorraine. In 1857 he immigrated to the United States, spending his first two years in New York as clerk in a wholesale notion house. In 1859 he went to Chicago, where he taught French, while attending two courses of lectures at the Chicago Medical College, where he graduated in 1863, and at once entered the United States Army as acting assistant surgeon. In 1866 he was mustered out of the service as assistant surgeon, located in Chattanooga, engaged in the practice of his profession, in which he met with much success. Excessive labor broke down his health, which forced him to give up the practice. In 1868 he embarked in the drug business in copartnership with his brother-in-law, Mr. Prosper Lazard, under the firm name of M. Block & Co. The combined capital of the partners being $22,500. In 1872 Dr. Block commenced traveling in north Alabama and Georgia in the interest of his house, laying the foundation of the wholesale drug business, in which the firm has met with such remarkably good success since. The firm keeps now two traveling salesmen on the road, has a regular laboratory in charge of a competent chemist, and owns several valuable propriatory articles, among others the well known Bee Hive Cough Syrup, a valuable expectorant that meets with large sales. In April, 1885, Mr. Lazard, owing to ill health, withdrew actively from the business. The firm name of M. Block & Co. is still retained, but will soon be changed (about July 1, 1887,) in that of the M. Block Drug Company, under a recent charter obtained from the State of Tennessee. The new company will remove into larger quarters, and with an increase of capital will correspondingly increase its operations. Dr. Block married in 1865, and is the happy father of two daughters and two sons, one of the latter, Master Leo Block, a promising lad of seventeen, being order-clerk at his father's store. The remarkable success of the firm is mainly due to the principle of strict honesty and rule of promptness adopted from the start. The Doctor enjoys a well merited social and professional reputation, has at one time been president of the board of education. He is now president of the Chattanooga Druggist Association, and vice-president of the East Tennessee Pharmacy Association.

Hon. Peter Bolton, mechanic and magistrate, was born February 27, 1824, in Rhea County, Tenn., about five miles north of where he now lives. He is the eldest of nine children, born to the union of Robert and Annie (Holt) Bolton, and he and two brothers are the only surviving members of the family. The father was a native Virginian, who came to Tennessee at a very early day, and settled in Rhea County in 1816. He died in 1869. Mrs. Bolton was born in Williamson County, Tenn., and died in 1870. Her father was a soldier in the war of 1812. Mr. Peter Bolton, grandfather of our subject, came to Granger County, Tenn., some time before the Indians were moved out of East Tennessee, and was quite an extensive tobacco raiser. Our subject came to Hamilton County about 1839, made his home with his uncle, and was educated in the subscription schools of Hamilton County. He worked at the blacksmith's trade until twenty-five years of age, after which he worked at the carpenter's trade, which he had learned in connection with the blacksmith's trade. He was postmaster at Sale Creek twelve years, but resigned the office after his election as representative from Hamilton County. He was elected justice of the peace of the Eleventh District in 1864, and has been elected each successive election since that time. During the years 1868 and 1869 he was tax collector for his district and served as deputy sheriff at the same time. During the late war his warmest sympathies were with the stars and stripes. Previous to the war, in 1852, he married Miss Selena L. Merriman, of Bledsoe County, Tenn., daughter of Bryant and Martha (Ferguson) Merriman, who came from Wilkes County, N. C., to Bledsoe County, Tenn., in 1834. Mr. and Mrs. Bolton are members of the Missionary Baptist Church, of which Mr. Bolton is now Deacon, In politics Mr. Bolton has been a life long Republican, casting his first presidential vote for Abraham Lincoln.

Samuel Born, superintendent of Forest Hill Cemetery, was born in 1835, in Switzerland, where he grew up and married Miss Fannie Kellyhouse, by whom he had two sons. His wife died in the old country, and he then married Elizabeth Icely, by whom he had two daughters. In 1870 he came to this country, and three years later his wife also came over. She died of cholera in 1873. He afterward married Minerva Carden who bore him one son. After her death he married Mrs. P. M. Bennett who had one daughter by a previous marriage. Mr. Born worked at gardening until 1881 when he took charge of the cemetery. He owns eighty-five acres of land four miles from Chattanooga for which he has been offered $16,000. He is a good citizen and well respected. He and his wife are members of the Methodist Episcopal Church.

William M. Brundage, farmer, is a native of New York, born November 11, 1831, and the son of Jonathan W. Brundage and Permelia (Mills) Brundage, both natives of Orange County, N. Y., and both of German descent. The father was one of the most successful physicians of Susquehanna County, Penn.; he died in 1864, at the age of sixty-five, and mother in 1861, at the age of sixty-one. Our subject received a fair education in the common schools of Pennsylvania. He began life a poor man after the late war, but now owns a good farm on Mission Ridge, four miles from Chattanooga. The farm is well cultivated, is very fertile and productive, is estimated to be very valuable, as compared with the valuation of land sold near him. In 1858, Mr. Brundage married Miss Sarah J. Bennett, a native of Pennsylvania, born May 22, 1841, and the daughter of L. G. and Maria J. Bennett. To our subject and wife were born two daughters: Georgie V. and Nora E. Previous to the war Mr. Brundage was a Whig in politics but since that event has voted with the Republican party. He is an honest, industrious man and is respected by all. Mrs. Brundage is a member of the Methodist Episcopal Church.

James D. Buttolph, is a native of Liberty County, Ga., born October 24, 1858; son of David L. and Laura (Maxwell) Buttolph, natives respectively of New York and Georgia. Our subject was reared and educated in Georgia, but removed to Marietta of the same State in 1868. In 1873 he entered the employ of his present partner, Mr. Thomas H. Cheek, being head miller for five years of the Kennesaw mills. He traveled one season, 1885, for Milnan Kerr Dust Collector Co. He came to Chattanooga in January, 1886, and in May entered the firm of Eakin Cheek & Co. In April, 1880, he married Miss Bessie Elliott, of South Carolina, niece of Bishop Elliott, of Georgia; two sons blessed this union. Mr. Buttolph is a Democrat in politics and a member of the Presbyterian Church.

William A. Campbell, of the firm of Ristine, Campbell & Co., was born in Meigs County, Tenn., February 3, 1843, and is the son of Andrew and Sarah (Shiflett) Campbell, natives, respectively, of North Carolina and Virginia. Our subject was reared to manhood in his native county, and in 1862 enlisted in the Federal Army, Company G, Third Regiment, Tennessee Cavalry, and served through the grades of private, lieutenant and captain of his company until the close of the war, after which he engaged in merchandising in his native county until 1871, when he went to Charleston, Tenn., and followed the same pursuit, in connection with the grain business, until 1884. He then went to Sweetwater, Tenn., and organized the Bank of Sweetwater, of which he was cashier until November, 1886. He then came to Chattanooga, and became connected with the present business, although still connected with the bank and other enterprises at Sweetwater, Tenn. April 20, 1869, he married Miss Mary J. Henninger, of Pikeville, Tenn., who bore him four children. Mr. Campbell is a Democrat, a Royal Arch Mason, council degree, a member of the American Legion of Honor, and also a member of the Cumberland Presbyterian Church. John A. Campbell, a brother of William A. Campbell, also a member of the firm of Ristine, Campbell & Co., of Chattanooga, was born in Meigs County, Tenn., August 3, 1848, and in this county was reared and educated. In 1871 he engaged in merchandising with his brother, William A., in his native county, and also engaged in business in Loudon County, Tenn. In September, 1885, he became a member of the firm of Ristine, Campbell & Co., and has continued as such up to the present. He removed to Chattanaoga in April, 1886. December 10, 1875, he married Miss Mollie B. Boggess, of Meigs County and to them were born three children. Mr. Campbell is a Democrat and a Royal Arch mason.

John T. Cahill, proprietor of Cahill's Architectural Brass and Iron Works, was born in Lynchburg, Va., in 1855, and is the son of William and Margaret (Maher) Cahill, natives of Ireland. Our subject removed to Chattanooga with his parents before the war, and here he was reared, learning the molders trade. In 1875 he established his present business on a capital of $3,000, but has increased the business from time to time. In 1880 he erected his present foundry on the corner of Boyce and Hook Streets. The dimensions of this immense structure is 200 x218 feet. They make a speciality of architectural work (building castings) and also do a general foundry work, handling and manufacturing grates and mantels. They employ eighty men on an average, and the business sales amount to $100,000 per annum. Mr. Cahill is a stockholder and director of the Dowling Furnace Company. In 1881 he married Miss Ellen Burchell, of Knoxville, Tenn. He is independent in politics, and he and his family are members of the Catholic Church.

M. Cary, manufacturer of carriages and spring wagons, 812 Cherry Street, and 813 Georgia Avenue, was born May 21, 1844, in Bucyrus, Ohio. He is the second of four children born to Aaron and Nancy (Myers) Cary. Aaron Cary was born in 1814, in Bucyrus, Ohio, and is of Scotch descent. His ancestors came to America at the time the Pilgrims landed at Plymouth Rock, and his father, Lewis Cary, was the first settler at Bucyrus, Ohio, having built the first house at that place. The mother of our subject was born in 1821, in Carlisle, Penn. Her great-grandfather came from Holland about the time the Hollanders settled on the Hudson River. Mr. Cary was reared in the Quaker Church, but at present he is a member of the Second Presbyterian Church. His son, Dr. Cary, was appointed medical missionary to Siam, by the board of missions of the Presbyterian Church. M. Cary, the subject of this sketch, received his education in the graded schools of Defiance, Ohio. At the age of eighteen he went to Monroeville, Ind., and bought staves for his brother. The following year he accepted a position as general agent for Reiley & Robertson, of Allegheny City, Penn., and Cleveland, dealers in oil barrel cooperage. He had the supervision of thirteen points throughout Indiana and Ohio. The firm failing in 1869 threw Mr. Cary out of employment but he secured a position as drummer from Carnahan, Hannah & Co., wholesale dealers in boots and shoes, at Fort Wayne, Ind., where he remained two years. He then took charge of a general store at Maples, Ind., which he had previously owned. The style of the firm being M. Cary & Co. He was also engaged at the same time in the stave business and in manufacturing patent barrel hoops. At the end of six years he moved to Fort Wayne, Ind., and traveled one year for Burgert & Hart, of Toledo, Ohio, wholesale boot and shoe dealers. In 1880 he purchased and ran the Mayer House, at Fort Wayne, Ind., a short time, and then began settling up his business preparatory to coming South. In the fall of 1881 he moved to Chattanooga, and followed various occupations until the fall of 1886, when he purchased an interest of the M. F. Drake Carriage Manufactory, and afterward purchased the whole business. He married Miss Nancy Simpson in the winter of 1867 and the fruits of this union were five children: Alberta (deceased), Arthur M., Estella E., Winifred Alice and Hugh Aaron. Mr. and Mrs. Cary are members of the Mission Ridge Presbyterian Church in which Mr. Cary is an elder. He is a Republican in politics and an excellent citizen.

D. T. Carpenter, farmer and molder in the Ninth District, was born July 9, 1827, in Grafton County, N. H. When twenty-six years of age he went to Cleveland, Ohio, where he remained one year, and then went back to New Hampshire and married Miss Miranda Parkhurst, of Andover, Vt., daughter of John and Hannah (Johnson) Parkhurst. Mrs. Carpenter was born in Vermont in 1831, and by her marriage became the mother of nine children, viz.: Ella (Mrs. W. S. French), Clarence A., Clara E., Flora B., George E. (deceased), Grace L., Jettie A. and George E. Mrs. Carpenter is a member of the Presbyterian Church. D. T. Carpenter is a son of Asa and Anna (Turner) Carpenter. The father was born in New Hampshire and died in 1863. The mother was also a native of New Hampshire and died in 1843. They were both of English descent. The father was a descendant of one of three brothers who came to Connecticut from England about the time of the Revolutionary war. He was a captain of State militia for many years, and he and his wife were zealous Christian workers in the Congregational Church. After marriage our subject moved to Chicago, where he worked at molding in a foundry for three years. In 1856 he moved to Cleveland, Ohio, where he was foreman in a foundry for the next sixteen years, after which he moved to Columbus, Ohio. He came to Chattanooga in 1873 to look for a suitable place to locate, and in 1874, moved his family down, settling in Chattanooga, where he secured an appointment as foreman in a foundry, in which capacity he continued until 1883. Here he with others organized what is known as the "Phœnix Foundry Co.," of which Mr. Carpenter is president and his son, C. A. Carpenter, and Mr. French are managers. They have enjoyed excellent success, continuing to run during the entire time of the stagnation in business of the past three or four years. Mr. Carpenter began life in very limited circumstances, but by economy and judicious management is now in a very comfortable condition. Besides the interest he owns in the Phœnix Foundry he has a fine farm of 100 acres, nicely located on Mission Ridge near East Lake Station, on the Belt railroad. He enlisted in Company H, One Hundred and Fiftieth Ohio National Guards in 1864, and served as one of the 100 days' men. He was fifth sergeant of his company, and at the end of the 100 days was brought home sick. Mr. Carpenter's grandfather, Jesse Carpenter, was a soldier in that mighty struggle for independence.

Hon. Halbert B. Case, attorney at law, of Chattanooga, was born May 3, 1838, in Mecca, Trumbull Co., Ohio. His father was Joseph L. Case, and his mother's maiden name was Eliza P. Bidwell. The former was born and reared in Simsbury, the latter in Canton, Conn., and both came from early Puritan stock. They moved to Trumbull County, Ohio, about 1832, and settled in the dense forests upon the farm upon which the subject of this sketch was born, and where, with the exception of about four years during which he resided in the State of New York, he was reared to manhood. As a boy and young man he was both industrious and studious. He made the best use of the common schools of his neighborhood until he was nine years old, after which, during the spring, summer and autumn, his services were required in the management of his father's farm, upon which he was always faithful and efficient. Notwithstanding the long hours of severe toil upon the farm, he found recreation during the early hours of the night in the pursuit of useful knowledge, his reading being usually of an historical character, and the winter months were well improved, first in the common and then in the select or high schools, then so numerous on the Western Reserve. By the time he arrived at the age of fourteen he had well mastered the branches of study peculiar to the common school, and then entered upon higher grades of study. When sixteen years old he entered the Western Reserve Seminary at Farmington, with a view to preparing for college. Being without wealth he earned the money with which to pay for his own education. In his eighteenth year he had his first experience as a teacher, and thereafter until the close of his literary studies, he taught in various localities part of the year, and devoted the rest of the time to study. After nearly two years in the seminary he began a course in Oberlin College, where he continued to study until shortly before the breaking out of the war of the Rebellion. Believing that the institution of slavery was a national curse, a curse to the slaveholder as well as to the slave, and believing that the war was caused by that institution, and was to be carried on in its interest by the one side, and hence that the war must necessarily result in its destruction, or in the overthrow of the Government, he deemed it his duty to abandon his studies in the midst of his course and respond to the call of his country. Accordingly he was one of the first to volunteer from his native county, enlisting as a private soldier on the 18th of April, 1861, in Company H, Seventh Regiment, Ohio Volunteer Infantry. In the organization of the company he was elected orderly sergeant. The company went at once to Camp Taylor, in Cleveland, Ohio, where the regiment was made up and sent thence to Camp Dennison. In the reorganization of the regiment for the three years' service, young Case was elected second lieutenant, and about six months afterward was promoted to first lieutenant. In these various positions he served through the arduous campaigns in West Virginia, participating in nearly all the engagements, until the spring of 1862, when he resigned and raised a company of which he became captain—Company C, of the Eighty-fourth Regiment, Ohio Volunteer Infantry. This was a four months' regiment, but it served a little over five months at Cumberland, Md. Capt. Case was appointed provost-marshal and commandant of the post which included a territory some twelve miles square, and in which was located a hospital, occupied by from 10,000 to 15,000 sick and convalescent soldiers. All the troops of the little department thus fell under his command, and it included officers ranking him in grade, as high as colonels, but so well did he perform his duties that Gov. David Todd, having sent ex-Gov. Dennison to Cumberland to ascertain who was a proper person to recruit the Eighty-fourth Regiment for the three years' service, upon the mustering out of the regiment from the four months' service, handed Capt. Case a commission as colonel to recruit the regiment for the three years' service. This appointment was wholly unsolicited and unexpected. Col. Case entered upon the work with ardor and enthusiasm, continuing some two and a half months, when, upon the order of the Governor, his regiment and the One Hundred and Twenty-fourth were consolidated, he ordered to assume command and to report at once to Cincinnati. But at the solicitation of Col. Oliver Payne, an arrangement was made by which the latter took command and led the new regiment to the field, and Col. Case ordered to continue recruiting the Eighty-fourth Regiment. However, being somewhat tired of the service, he obtained consent to retire, and at once entered upon a law course at the University of Michigan, from which he graduated March 29, 1864, taking the degree of LL. B. On the 23d of June, 1863, he married Miss Caroline E. Kibbee, taking her with him to Ann Arbor during his last year in the University. The vacation was largely spent in a course of analytical chemistry in the laboratory of the University. After graduation he spent some time in special work in the army in the South, but did not re-enter active service. He began the practice of his profession at Youngstown, Ohio, where he lived until March, 1869, when he removed to Des Moines, Iowa, where he led an active life as vice-president of the State Insurance Company, which, under his energetic management, met with phenomenal success. But here came to him dark days and full of trouble, the most trying ordeal of his life. His young wife, a son of seven years and a son of four months, all apparently in the vigor of health, were suddenly stricken with disease, and all died within the short space of five days, and all lay dead in his house April 28, 1872. The effect of this blow was so great that, after struggling for twenty months to recover from it, he deemed it necessary to change the scene of his labors, and removed to Chattanooga about May 1, 1874. Here he married Janie M. Spooner, a friend of long standing, with whom he has since lived in most happy relations. In Chattanooga he has earnestly pursued his chosen profession, and he is universally recognized as an able lawyer and useful citizen. In his adopted city he held the office of city attorney from November, 1876, to November, 1878, to the satisfaction of the authorities and the people. He was the candidate for Congress on the Republican ticket in the Third Congressional District, in 1880, and received nearly 10,000 votes, the largest vote given a Republican in the district up to that time, the result of the most brilliant canvass ever made by any candidate in the district. In 1882 he was elected to the Lower House of the State Legislature, and in 1884, he was elected to the State Senate, and declined a renomination in 1886, on the plea that politics made him poor. In all of his official positions he has been active, attentive and faithful in the discharge of his duties, and his record is exceedingly creditable to him. Open and frank in disposition, he shirks no duty, and is untiring in its pursuit and unsatisfied until it is performed. He is a deliberate, argumentative and convincing speaker, and has the moral courage to express his convictions without fear or favor. Once convinced that a measure is right he stands by it on principle, if need be, against the world. Earnestly believing in universal education and in universal civil and political rights, he boldly proclaims his views, oftentimes in defiance of popular sentiment, and yet with due regard to the right of others to entertain contrary convictions. By his first wife Col. Case has one son living, Frank Luther Case. He was born in Youngstown, Ohio, December 10, 1866. He went through the graded schools in Chattanooga, and graduated in the high school in June, 1883. He then spent two years in the Grant Memorial University, Athens, Tenn., and since then has been two years in Oberlin College, Ohio. He will enter the senior class in that institution in June, 1887. As a sophomore he was elected one of nine in a class of eighty-five to represent the class in the junior oratorical exercises which occured about May 15, 1887, in which he acquitted himself with credit. He has also been elected one of six of his class for the senior oratorical contest to occur in June, 1888. He is a fine musician and a fine German and classical scholar.

Wilford Caulkins, A. M., late professor of ancient languages in Chattanooga University, is a son of John G. and Nancy (Lee) Caulkins, both natives of New York. The mother was a cousin of the noted philanthropist, George I. Seney, of Brooklyn, N. Y., and also a cousin of Mary Ingraham, wife of the late Bishop Gilbert Haven. After her marriage to Mr. Caulkins they lived in their native State until 1869, when they moved to Knox County, Tenn., where the mother died in 1877. For a livelihood the father followed merchandising and farming. He has been a life-long worker in the Methodist Episcopal Church, as was also his wife. He is now living in Knoxville, Tenn., and is seventy-four years of age. Their family consisted of six children. Dr. Douglas Caulkins, of Knoxville, is one of this family. Our subject was born July 30, 1852, in Duchess County, N. Y., and was the oldest child born to his parents. His preparatory education was received in a private school in his native State. At leisure hours he assisted his father in the store, and, after coming to Tennessee, he worked on the farm and was also clerk in a store in Knoxville for a number of years. He entered the East Tennessee Wesleyan University in 1876, from which institution he graduated in 1880 with the first honors of his class. Rev. Richard J. Cooke, D. D., author of a celebrated theological work on the "Doctrine of the Resurrection," was a member of the same class. While in college he was tutor in Latin and Greek, and after graduating was elected professor of Latin in his *alma mater*. Later he was also placed in charge of the department of Greek. In May, 1886, he resigned at that place to accept the chair of ancient languages in Chattanooga University. In January, 1887, after the inauguration of Gov. R. L. Taylor, Prof. Caulkins' name was urged for the position of State superintendent of public instruction by several of the leading journals of the State, including the Chattanooga *Times*, the Knoxville *Journal*, the Knoxville *Tribune* and the Athens *Post*. He was not, however, an applicant for the position and made no effort to secure it. In 1877 Miss Laura D. O'Brien, a native of Greenville, Tenn., became his wife, and to them were born three daughters. Both Prof. and Mrs. Caulkins are Methodists. The Professor is a man of superior endowments and culture and one whose services the university was considered fortunate in securing. His professional services were eminently satisfactory to the authorities of the university, but in March, 1887, finding himself not in harmony with the proposed policy of the institution in educating white and colored students together, he resigned his position. He is now conducting a private school in Chattanooga.

James A. Caldwell, attorney and president of the Chattanooga Gas Light Company, is a native of Hamilton County, but was reared principally in Monroe County, Tenn. He was educated in the University of Virginia, and served four years in the Fifty-ninth Tennessee Infantry (which was mounted part of the time). After the war he came to Chattanooga in 1867, and practiced law alone until 1870, when he was elected clerk and master, and held this position until 1876, after which he resumed the practice of law alone. In 1873 he was united in marriage to Elizabeth S. Gillespie, a native of Roane County, Tenn., and the daughter of Gen. George L. Gillespie. The fruits of this union were four children, three of whom are living. In 1884 Mr. Caldwell formed a partnership with H. L. Turney, whose death occurred in 1885, since which time our subject has conducted the practice alone. He has been president of the gas company since 1873, and was director of that company previous to that date. He assisted in the organization of the Forest Hill Cemetery Company, being at different times director, secretary and treasurer of the same. Mr. Caldwell and family are members of the First Presbyterian Church, of which he is an elder. His parents, O. H. P. and Jane (Johnston) Caldwell, are natives of Monroe County, Tenn. The father's death occurred in Georgia in 1854. The mother, now Mrs. William M. Stately, is living in Alabama.

A. C. Carey, city engineer, was born in the Keystone State, but was reared in Cincinnati, Ohio, and received his education in the public schools of that city. While in the city of Cincinnati he practiced civil engineering for several years prior to coming to Chattanooga, and was well qualified to fill the position of city engineer in this city. He accepted his present position February 1, 1881. He has stock in several business enterprises of Chattanooga. His father, E. H. Carey, was also a native of Pennsylvania, where he followed the harness-maker's trade. He afterward came to Cincinnati and superintended the construction of several different street railroad lines until his death, which occurred in 1883. The mother, A. M. (Juvinal) Carey, was also born in the Keystone State, and is now a resident of Cincinnati.

J. B. Cash, principal of high school and Second District of Chattanooga, is a son of Henry and Eunice (Brown) Cash, both natives of the Buckeye State. The mother died in 1854, but the father is still living in Ohio, engaged as a farmer and stock grower. He has been married twice since the death of his first wife. Our subject is the eldest child by the first marriage, and was born in Belmont County, Ohio, January 16, 1849. He was educated in the common schools and at Mount Union College, located in Mount Union, Ohio, having graduated from that institution in 1880. By teaching and going to school alternately, he worked his way through college, and is considered a first-class educator. Previous to coming to Chattanooga in 1886, he was principal of the Bellaire

(Ohio) High School and also of the high school at Atchison, Kas. He is an excellent citizen and a member of the Methodist Episcopal Church.

Hiram S. Chamberlain was born at Franklin, Portage Co., Ohio, August 6, 1835, the fourth in a family of eight children born to Leander and Susanna (Willey) Chamberlain. The parents were natives of Vermont, the father's birth occurring in Addison County, April 16, 1804, as were also his father, Leander, born in 1766 and his grandfather, Peleg, who was born in 1736. The mother was a native of New Haven; she died in March 1887. In the year 1840 the family moved to Cuyahoga County, Ohio, where the father died in August, 1884. Hiram S. received his education at what is now Hiram College, attending that institution during President Garfield's tutorage. He taught school winters during his stay at Hiram, but left college in order to go to the front to fight for the preservation of the Union. In July, 1861, he enlisted as a private in the Second Ohio Volunteer Cavalry, and remained at Camps Chase and Dennison until December of that year, when his regiment was ordered to the front. The first month after his enlistment he was appointed quartermaster-sergeant; in October, 1862, was commissioned second lieutenant, and February 26, 1863, he was promoted to first lieutenant and regimental quartermaster. He was quartermaster of Carter's cavalry division under Gen. Burnside at Knoxville, when it was captured from the Confederates in September, 1863. May 24, 1864, he was commissioned captain and assistant quartermaster by President Lincoln, and during the remainder of the war served in that capacity. At the close of the war, Capt. Chamberlain engaged in the iron business, to which he has since chiefly devoted his attention. He resided at Knoxville until 1871, then removed to Chattanooga, and is at present president and manager of the Roan Iron Company, also president and leading stockholder of the Citico Furnace Company, and vice-president of the First National Bank. Capt. Chamberlain is one of the best posted men on mineralogy in the South, and it is to his knowledge of this valuable science that his present financial prosperity is largely due. September 4, 1867, he married Miss Amelia I. Morrow, who was born at Knoxville, December 3, 1841. Six children have been born to them, all at Knoxville except the youngest two, who were born at Chattanooga: Minnie Morrow, born January 28, 1869; Mary Hattie, born July 9, 1871, died November 9, 1873; Susie Willey, born June 4, 1874, Louise A., born May 23, 1877; Morrow, born December 12, 1879, and Hiram Sanborn, born June 26, 1882.

Milton L. Chapman, a native of Elyria, Ohio, was born February 3,

1853. He was reared and educated in the Buckeye State. In December, 1870, he came to Chattanooga, and engaged in the milling business with his father, Henry Z. Chapman, until February, 1874, when he engaged in the real estate business at this place, which he has continued successfully to the present time. He is president of the Chattanooga Chair Company, and was secretary of the Iron & Coal Association of Chattanooga for four years, and at present is one of the board of managers of the same. He is now one of the directors of the Gadsden (Ala.) Land & Improvement Company, and is also identified with other enterprises in the city. He is manager of Spring Lake Improvement Company. This lake is situated four miles southeast of Chattanooga, in Georgia. The object of the company is to make the lake a pleasure resort, and supply Chattanooga with water in the future. In 1871 Mr. Chapman married Miss Carrie B. Gibbs, of Ohio, and three living children are the result of this union—one son and two daughters. Mr. Chapman is a Republican in politics, and a wide-awake business man.

Thomas H. Cheek was born in Rappahannock County, Va., October 20, 1836, and is a son of Elijah and Mary (Holtzman) Cheek, both natives of Virginia. The subject of this sketch removed with his parents to Memphis, Tenn., in 1848, where he resided until 1861, and then entered the Confederate service, being in the ordnance department under Col. Hunt for four years. After cessation of hostilities he established a flour-mill in Macon, Ga., and also followed the same business in Marietta until May, 1886, when he came to Chattanooga, but is still interested in the flour business in Georgia. In 1859 he wedded Mary M. Reid, a native of Courtland, Ala., who presented him with three children, only one, a daughter, living. Mr. Cheek is a good citizen, and a member of the Presbyterian Church.

J. J. Clift, farmer, and clerk in the Soddy Coal Company's store, was born May 28, 1838, in Hamilton County, where he now resides. He is the youngest of seven children born to William and Nancy A. (Brooks) Clift. William Clift was born December 5, 1795, in Greene County, Tenn., and came to Hamilton County about 1828. He organized the Seventh Tennessee Regiment, of which he was colonel, enlisted in the fall of 1861, and was a very warm supporter of the stars and stripes. Hearing that they were threatened by the Confederates, this regiment disbanded and fled to Kentucky. He was captured while returning from carrying some dispatches from Gen. Burnside to Gen. Rosecrans. He was taken to Atlanta, where he was retained in captivity about four months. He then made his escape in February, 1864, and reached home the same month. He was magistrate of his district eighteen years, and was also colonel of the State militia. He was greatly harassed by the Confederates during the late war, but to the last remained a stanch Union man. He was also a very fine business man, and when he died his effects were estimated to be worth $1,000,000. He died February 17, 1886, aged ninety. Mrs. Clift was born February 22, 1795, in East Tennessee; she died August 17, 1847. Our subject received a fair education in the common schools of Hamilton County, and finished at Sale Creek Academy. He married Miss Elizabeth L. Reveley, of Dayton, Tenn. Mrs. Clift was born February 12, 1843, and died February 12, 1870, leaving three children: Nancy A., W. Robert, and Elizabeth J., now attending the Female College, at Rogersville, Tenn. Mr. Clift and family are members of the Presbyterian Church. In politics Mr. Clift is a Democrat, casting his first presidential vote for John Bell. He was elected justice of the peace in 1876, and still holds that office. He has given universal satisfaction in the discharge of the duties of this office. He has been deacon of the church to which he belongs for the past eight years.

J. H. Cleage, manager for A. G. Rhodes & Co., furniture dealers, 111 and 113 West Eighth Street, Chattanooga, is a native of McMinn County, Tenn., and was reared and educated at Athens, Tenn. He followed agricultural pursuits until he came to Chattanooga in 1880. He then engaged in the grocery trade at this place until he accepted his present position in 1882. In 1875 he was united in marriage to Miss Tipton Bradford, a native of Jefferson County, Tenn., and the fruits of this union were four children, only two of whom are living. Alexander and Jemima (Hurst) Cleage, the parents of our subject, were natives of Virginia and Tennessee, respectively. The father died at Athens, McMinn Co., Tenn., in 1875; the mother is now residing in Chattanooga. The individual members of the firm of A. G. Rhodes & Co. are A. G. Rhodes, Atlanta, and A. C. Scuddy, Nashville. They began business in Chattanooga in 1881, and handle furniture on the installment plan. They are live, wide-awake men, and are doing a good business.

J. W. Clift, bookkeeper and manager of the Soddy Coal Company store since 1874, and one of the principal stockholders of the same, was born in 1828. He is a son of William and Nancy A. (Brooks) Clift, and was born and reared in Hamilton County. He was educated principally at the common schools, and attended two terms at Harrison Academy. In 1849 he married Miss McKenzie, a daughter of Samuel and Elizabeth F. (Huston) McKenzie. Nine children were the fruits of this union, six of whom are living: Nancy E. (Mrs. Miles); William, bookkeeper for the Soddy Coal Company; Nina Wallace, Joseph W.

H.J. Springfield

Aldine, Wingenund (deceased), Bruce and James. Mr. Clift is of Scotch-Irish descent. In 1861 he enlisted in the war and served almost continuously until the final surrender. He was made captain of Company A, Thirty-sixth Tennessee Infantry, and upon the reorganization he came home for a short time. He enlisted shortly after in Capt. Starne's company, Fourth Tennessee Cavalry, and was promoted to a lieutenancy, and shortly thereafter detached and placed upon duty in the adjutant-general's department where he served until the close of the war. He was paroled at Meridian, Miss., May 13, 1865. Mr. Clift is actively engaged in several mining and manufacturing enterprises. He is one of the principal stockholders in the Soddy Coal Company, Waldou's Ridge Coal Company, of Sale Creek, Tennessee, and in the Owita Coal Company, of Arkansas, and he is also connected with the rolling mill, at Chattanooga. The Soddy Coal Mines were first opened by a company of Welshmen from Ohio in 1867. Mr. Clift is a Democrat in politics, and he and wife are members of the Presbyterian Church.

M. H. Clift, attorney, of the firm of Cooke, Clift & Cooke, is a native of Hamilton County, and the son of Col. William Clift, a native of Greene County, Tenn. The father was reared in Knox County, and came to Hamilton County about 1825, residing at Soddy until his death in 1866. He was colonel of the State militia many years, and during the war was colonel in the Federal Army. From 1848 to 1855 he was commissioner of improvement for the United States Government. The mother, Nancy (Brooks) Clift, was a native of Knox County, and died in this county in 1847. Our subject was reared and educated in Hamilton County, and at the commencement of hostilities enlisted in the Fourth Tennessee Confederate Cavalry. He was paroled at Columbus, Ga., being at that time on Debrill's staff. He was admitted to the bar just prior to the war, and at its termination came to Chattanooga and began practicing his profession in the firm of Wallace & Clift, where he remained one year. After practicing alone for a few months he became a member of the firm of Clift & McRee, then Clift & Bate, then Clift, Bate & Cooke, then Clift & Cooke, and finally, January 1, 1887, the firm of Cooke, Clift & Cooke was formed. Our subject is president of the Soddy Coal Company and Walden Ridge Coal Company, also director in the Mutual Gas Company and the Home Insurance Company. In 1867 he married Miss A. C. Cooke, who bore him two children; she died in 1876. In 1883 he married Miss Florence Parrott, of Cartersville, Ga., and to this union have been born two children, both living. Mr. Clift is a member of the Masonic fraternity and of the K. of P.

Webster J. Colburn, of Chattanooga, was born in Chatauqua County

N. Y., November 26, 1840; son of Albert T. and Betsey (Older) Colburn, natives of New York. They removed to Michigan and from there to Wisconsin, where our subject was reared and educated. In 1861 he enlisted in Company K, First Wisconsin Infantry, and served over five years, first as a private in the above company, then re-enlisted in the Third Battery of Wisconsin Light Artillery as sergeant; was promoted to second lieutenant; in 1864 was appointed captain and assistant quartermaster of volunteers, and was breveted major in 1865 for meritorious service. In the final report of the quartermaster-general, at the close of the war, he was one of the officers specially mentioned for good service. He was on duty eighteen months during the war at Chattanooga, and was mustered out at Memphis as chief quartermaster of West Tennessee in 1866. He then engaged in the insurance business at Memphis, but came to Chattanooga in 1867 and engaged in the same business, which he has continued successfully up to the present, representing the Phœnix Fire, of Hartford; the Phœnix Assurance, of London; the Imperial, of London; the New York Underwriters' Agency, and the Georgia Home. In 1885 he was instrumental in organizing the Mountain City Fire and Marine Insurance Company of Chattanooga, of which he has since been the efficient secretary. September 13, 1866, he married Miss Ada E. Brabson, a native of Tennessee, and a daughter of the late Hon. Reese B. Brabson, a member of Congress from this district. This union resulted in the birth of eight children—three sons and five daughters. Mr. Colburn is a Democrat in his political views, a Mason, a K. of H., and a member of the A. L. of H., besides being a member of several military orders and societies. He and family are members of the Episcopal Church.

J. E. Conner, the present sheriff of Hamilton County, Tenn., was born, reared and educated in that county. He came to Chattanooga in 1876 and occupied the position of constable for six years, after which he was engaged as foreman in the retail department with J. H. Warner & Co. He remained with this firm until his election to his present office in August, 1886, being sworn in September 1 of the same year. Mr. Conner is a member of the K. of P., the K. of L., and is a worthy member of the Methodist Episcopal Church South. His father, Wesley P. Conner, is a native of Marion County, Tenn., and came to Hamilton County in 1848, where he followed agricultural pursuits. He died in April, 1858. The mother of our subject, Mrs. Jane (Smith *nee* Maysey) Conner, is a native of Campbell County, Tenn., and previous to her marriage with our subject's father was married to Mr. Smith. She died in September, 1874, and of the two children born to this union our subject is the only surviving member.

S. C. Cook, D. D. S., is a son of John and Anna (Collins) Cook, natives of Pennsylvania and North Carolina, respectively. In early life they came to Tennessee and here were married. By occupation the father was a mechanic and school-teacher. He died in 1860, but the mother is still living. Of their family of eight children all were sons. Our subject was born in Monroe County, Tenn., May 2, 1849, and educated in the common schools and at Wesleyan University, Athens, Tenn. Having followed the mercantile business for some time he began the study of dentistry. He then practiced at Sweetwater, Tenn., until 1880, when he took a full course at the Ohio College of Dental Surgery, graduating in 1881, taking the prize of the college for operative dentistry. After graduating he was appointed clinical instructor in Vanderbilt University. In 1886 he came to Chattanooga and is having a good practice at that place. He is a member of both the State and East Tennessee Dental Associations, and has been vice-president of the first and president of the second. He is a Royal Arch Mason and is a member of the Methodist Episcopal Church South.

Charles H. Coolidge, purchasing agent for the Dade Coal Company of Cole City, Dade Co., Ga., is a native of Maine where he was reared and educated. In 1868 he went to Chicago and engaged in the grain trade, in which business he remained until January 1, 1884, when he came to Chattanooga, and accepted his present position. In 1870 he married Miss Ella Parlin, also a native of Maine, and this union resulted in the birth of four children. The above company was organized in 1870, with $500,000 capital. They employ 500 Georgia convicts and 200 free laborers, and have an output of about fifty car loads of coal per day. Mr. Coolidge's parents, Elisha and Hattie (Bayes) Coolidge, were both natives of Maine, and died in the same State in 1862 and 1877, respectively. They were honest and well respected citizens.

Hon. William Crutchfield, farmer and extensive fruit grower in the Chattanooga Valley, two miles south of the Tennessee line, was born November 16, 1826, in Greenville, Greene Co., Tenn., where he resided until 1840. In August, 1844, he moved to Jacksonville, Benton Co., Ala., where he became an extensive grain grower, introducing improved methods and astonishing every one by his successful farm management. He was soon elected captain of the militia, by acclamation, in a district strongly Democratic, while he openly worked for and voted the Whig ticket. He moved to Chattanooga in 1850, and was soon looked upon by all as an uncompromising, strong advocate of the Union cause. On the night of January 22, 1861, while on the way to his home in Mississippi after resigning his seat in the United States Senate, Hon. Jefferson Davis made a speech in the Crutchfield house denouncing the Federal Government in most bitter terms, and called upon the people of Tennessee to join the balance of the South in their attempts for secession. In answer to this speech Mr. Crutchfield denounced him as a traitor to his country and a perjured villain, and in most sarcastic, measured tones painted Mr. Davis out to the people as their future military despot. Great excitement followed Mr. Crutchfield's speech, but bloodshed was prevented. Reports of both speeches were printed the following morning in the Chattanooga *Gazette*. Mr. Crutchfield was guide and captain under Gen. Wilder through the Chickamauga campaign, with Gen. Thomas through the siege of Chattanooga, went as guide to Gens. Grant, Thomas and Hooker the day after Brown's Ferry was carried, and on many occasions furnished the generals of the Union Army of the Cumberland very valuable information and assistance. Fifteen of his blood relatives fought against him during the Chickamauga battle, besides his father-in-law and brother-in-law. The generals of the Union Army appreciated his services fully, but the Government has not shown him justice. When once Mr. Crutchfield forms an opinion and adopts a resolution he is unyielding and exceedingly firm in maintaining and carrying them to completion. He represented this congressional district in the XLIII Congress, and acquitted himself in a highly creditable manner while a member of that body. He was elected to the office by 1,500 majority, and was the first Union man sent to Congress from this district since the enfranchisement. He refused the urgent entreaties of his friends to accept another nomination. Through his shrewd and able manipulations $600,000 was appropriated to the improvement of the Tennessee River and $10,000 and $15,000 to the Little Tennessee and Hiawassa Rivers, something that all previous representatives had failed to do. The last two appropriations were never used and were returned to the Government. Mr. Crutchfield accumulated a vast amount of wealth before the war, but that event and treachery of pretended friends despoiled him of the most of it. He moved to his present place of residence in 1876, where he owns 500 acres of splendid farming and fruit-producing land. He is passionately fond of fruit culture and has some very fine fruit orchards. His farm is nicely improved, and Mr. Crutchfield, while not a Rothschild in wealth, is certainly well prepared to enjoy life. He is a firm believer in the doctrine of Henry Clay, is a stanch Union man and votes the Republican ticket. He is the second of four children born to Thomas and Sarah (Cleage) Crutchfield. The first known of the Crutchfield family in America were Oscar and Stapleton Crutchfield, prominent Protestant refugees from England. They settled in Richmond, Va., and were among the first settlers. Thomas Crutchfield, father of our subject, was born in Rockbridge County, Va., in 1808, and immigrated to Greenville, Tenn., at a very early period. He died in Chattanooga March 5, 1850. He was the contractor and superintendent of the building of many of the most prominent public buildings in Tennessee and other adjacent States. Mr. William Crutchfield married Nancy Jane Williams, August 15, 1859. She was born October 22, 1833, at Chelikee, Ga., and is a daughter of Thomas R. and Sarah (Sparks) Williams. Jeremiah Williams, father of Thomas, was captain of a company and took an active part in the Revolutionary war. Mrs. Crutchfield is a descendent of a very prominent French family that left France and came to Carolina to escape religious persecution during the time the Huguenots were so bitterly persecuted by the Catholic Church. To Mr. and Mrs. Crutchfield were born eight children: Sarah (deceased), Thomas Williams, Frances A., Mary Jane (Mrs. A. W. Poe), Medora (Mrs. J. W. C. Henderson), Mrs. Mary Keele, Courtney, the deceased, Emmalin.

Samuel A. Cunningham was born in Jonesboro, Tenn., March 6, 1835, and is a son of the late Dr. Samuel B. Cunningham of Jonesboro, Tenn. In 1860 he married Alice, daughter of the late Judge Thomas R. Nelson of the supreme bench of Tennessee. The result of this union was the birth of four children. Our subject was president of the East Tennessee & Virginia Railroad for some time, and in 1868 engaged in the agricultural implement business in Carter County, Tenn. Mr. Cunningham is a Democrat in politics and a member of the Presbyterian Church. In 1873 he entered the employ of C. Aultman & Co. This company is one of the largest and wealthiest implement manufactories in the United States. The home factory is at Canton, Ohio, and they also have a branch house at Chattanooga. They manufacture engines, separators, saw mills, mowers, reapers, selfbinders, etc. The company have had an agency in Chattanooga since 1856. The branch house was established in 1876 under the management of R. A. Kirk, but in 1880 Mr. Kirk was succeeded by Mr. Cunningham, who has since been the efficient manager. This branch house supplies the entire Southern States east of the Mississippi River and south of North Carolina. The ware house and office are located at 914 and 916 Market Street. They carry, besides their own manufacturing, a full line of agricultural implements, also wagons, buggies, corn-mills, etc., and employ six men in the house, also have six men on the road. They have an agency in every important county seat in this territory and are doing an extensive business.

Dr. David G. Curtis is the son of H. W. and Eleanor Eames Curtis, natives of New York and Massachusetts, respectively. They were married in Jamestown, N. Y., where they lived until the death of the father, which occurred in 1871. After the death of the father the mother came to Chattanooga to reside with her children, three of whom had preceded her to this place. She died in 1887 at the advanced age of eighty years. The subject of our sketch was born in Jamestown, Chautauqua Co., N. Y., on the 20th of July, 1836. During his youth and minority he had very fair educational advantages, his father, though not rich, being a merchant, possessed liberal means and gave his son David, with his other children (of whom there were four besides David—two sons and two daughters), fair opportunity for the acquisition of knowledge and intellectual training. At the age of twenty our subject began the study of medicine and finished his course in 1858, graduating from Berkshire Medical College, Massachusetts. Desiring to study the diseases of the Mississippi Valley, he attended the Hahnemann Medical School of St. Louis, and afterward located in southwestern Missouri to practice his profession. In 1863 he volunteered in the United States Navy at Mound City, Ill., serving as assistant surgeon on the United States steamer, "Carondolet," until the close of the war. In 1865 he married Miss Sarah R. Edmiston, of Huntsville, Ohio, who has borne him three children, two of whom are living—both boys. He practiced his profession in Ohio until 1871, when he came to Chattanooga, where he has since resided, practicing medicine. He has been a member of the board of health nine years and is now its vice-president. He went through the various epidemics that have scourged our city since his arrival in it, the cholera in 1873, the yellow fever in 1878, and the small-pox in 1883, rendering heroic and efficient service in them all. He is now a member of the city school board and has been for some time. He has also been quite successful in real estate deals as well as an able practitioner. He is one of the original number who established the Ice & Cold Storage Company of Chattanooga, and is now its vice-president and one of its directors. The Doctor is a man of rather radical views on most questions and has the courage of his convictions. He always talks "from the shoulder out" and his position on any question can be easily ascertained. He believes in the Darwinian theory of the "survival of the fittest." He is destined to make his impress on the community, in which he lives.

Warren A. Dewees, agent of the Southern Express Company, is a son of Thomas and Wilhelmina (Pennypacker) Dewees, the father a native of Pennsylvania, and the mother of Virginia. After marriage they settled in Ohio, where the father followed the bricklayer's trade. Of their family of seven sons, our subject is the fifth. He was born January 27, 1853, in Stark County, Ohio, was educated in the public schools, and while growing up learned his father's trade. In 1869, he came to Chattanooga, and worked at his trade until 1872, when he engaged as driver for the Southern Express Company, and has held all the positions in the office up to the highest, having fourteen men under his supervision. He is a Mason, a Knight Templar, a Knight of Honor, and is an excellent citizen.

Hon. William Henry DeWitt, whose name and fame are alike familiar to all residents of Hamilton County and to a large portion of the State, and whose portrait adorns this work, is a native Tennessean, born in Smith County October 24, 1827. His father, Rev. Samuel DeWitt, was born in South Carolina in 1792, and was an officer in the war of 1812 under Gen. Jackson. His mother was a McWhirter, and both branches of the family were of old Revolutionary war stock. The early years of the subject of this sketch were passed upon the farm, his few hours spared from work being employed in the laudible effort of trying to secure an education. So limited were his advantages that he had to master the lower branches of mathematics and the first books of Latin without the aid of an instructor. For ten months he attended Berea Academy, near Chapel Hill, Tenn., under the tuition of Rev. John M. Branes, one of the old time educators of the State. After attaining manhood he resided at Gainsboro for two years as an instructor in the Montpelier Academy. The succeeding two years he passed in Jackson County as teacher, and from 1850 to 1856, he lived at La Fayette where he taught school one year and practiced law five years, having acquired the latter profession entirely by his own exertions. For about one year he practiced his chosen profession at Lebanon, and from 1858 to 1875, continued the same at Carthage, in his native county, where he achieved much success. Both before and since the war some of the most able men of Tennessee have been made lawyers under his instructions, and for which he never asked compensation. In 1855-56 he was the representative to the Lower House of the State Legislature from the counties of Smith, Macon and Sumner, a position for which he declined the renomination. In 1861 he was an opponent of the constitutional convention of the State which was defeated, and the same year was elected to a seat in the Confederate Congress. Gov. Brown, in 1862, appointed him special chancellor of the Fifth Chancery Division of Tennessee pending an election contest. In politics he was a Whig, faithful and ardent, but when the war came on he espoused the cause of the Confederacy and has since affiliated with the Democratic party. At Nashville, in 1876, he was chairman on resolutions in the State convention which sent delegates to the National convention at St. Louis, which nominated Gov. Tilden for the presidency, and in 1878 was a member of the State Judicial Convention. May 30, 1847, Miss Emilia, daughter of Thomas Price, became his wife, and to their union five children have been born, two dying in infancy and only one now living. His second marriage occurred May 30, 1867, to Miss Elizabeth Wilson, a direct descendant of Daniel Boone, and two children are the fruit of their marriage. Mr. DeWitt is a Mason, an Oddfellow and a Methodist. He is justly regarded as one of the ablest lawyers of the State, and is possessed of the highest sense of honor and justice. His friends are legion, his enemys few, if any.

L. J. de Sabla, farmer and gardener, was born June 11, 1832, at Pointe a Pitre, Guadeloupe, West Indies. He is the third of five children born to Marquis de Joly de Blayon de Sabla and Eugenie Gallois. The father was a soldier in the 100 days' service under Emperor Napoleon Bonaparte. He died in 1865, in Panama, where he was buried. The mother was born in 1812 in Pointe a Pitre, Guadeloupe, West Indies; she died in Panama in 1870. Our subject had most excellent educational advantages, and finished at Henry IV College, at Paris, France. He also secured a good medical education, and practiced his profession one year in Pointe, Guadeloupe, West Indies. In 1849, he went with his father to Panama and engaged in civil engineering on the Panama Canal. In 1853, he came to New Orleans, La., and from there went to a health resort, on the Cumberland Mountains, for the benefit of his health. He married Miss Paulene Nancy Narramore, daughter of Judge Narramore, of Cumberland County, Tenn. Mrs. de Sabla was born January 4, 1841, in Cumberland County, Tenn., and by her union with our subject, became the mother of six children: Catherine Helen, Joseph Ernest, Mary Octavia (Mrs. George H. Cushman), James Theodore, Fielding Eugene and Matilda Alice. Mr. de Sabla was elected and served as civil engineer of Cumberland County, Tenn., eight years, was also county court clerk of the same county for several years, and served as clerk and master under Hon. D. McKey. Mr. de Sabla has been quite successful, and owns 120 acres of fine land just beyond the city limits on the south; 170 acres in Georgia, and 3,700 acres in Cumberland County, Tenn. Mrs. de Sabla and children are members of the Methodist Episcopal Church, and Mr. de Sabla is a member of the Catholic Church. He was formerly a Whig, but since the war he has voted with the Republican party.

W. M. Dorsey, farmer, is the youngest of eight children, four of whom are now living, born to D. and A. (Duckworth) Dorsey. The father was born about 1776, in Burke County, N. C., and came to McMinn County in 1829, where he died about 1876, upward of one hundred years old. The mother was born in 1780, also in Burke County, N. C., and died about 1856. They were both active Christian workers in the Presbyterian Church. Mrs. Dorsey's father, John Duckworth, was a soldier in the Revolutionary war, and was wounded at the battle of King's Mountain. Her grandfather came from Ireland to America some time before the Revolutionary war. Our subject was born in 1824, in McMinn County, Tenn., and came to Hamilton County in 1869, received an average education in the schools of McMinn County, and lived with and assisted his father on the farm until thirty-five years of age, when he married Miss Barbara L. Wilkins, daughter of A. S. and Lavina (Wallick) Wilkins, both natives of North Carolina. They came to Hamilton County about 1840, where they still reside. Eleven children were the results of our subject's marriage: John and Mary (twins), Louvina (Mrs. Varnell), Dimmon A., Hattie, Willie N., Charles S. and four who died in infancy. Mr. Dorsey is a Democrat in politics, and cast his first presidential vote for Franklin Pierce in 1848. He began life a comparatively poor man, and what he is now worth was gotten by his own industry and good management. He owns a good farm of 160 acres on the Western & Atlantic Railroad. It is well improved and located eight miles east of Chattanooga. He is a Master Mason, joining the order in 1856, and he and wife are members of the Missionary Baptist Church.

J. D. Dobbs, farmer, was born February 2, 1840, in Cobb County, Ga. He came to Hamilton County in 1855, and has resided here ever since. He was educated in the military school at Marietta, Ga., also at the Chattanooga High School, and was a short time in attendance at Burrell College, Spencer, Tenn. In 1858 he married Miss Nancy Roberts, daughter of Commodore and Jane (Bunch) Roberts. Mrs. Dobbs was born in October, 1839, in Sequatchie Valley, Tennessee, and her marriage resulted in the birth of eight children: Joseph D. (deceased), Anna, Maria (Mrs. F. M. Gossett), James M., Minnie S. (deceased), John, Gorden, and Lewis David (deceased). Mr. Dobbs is a Democrat in politics. May 10, 1861, he enlisted in Company H, Second Tennessee Cavalry, and was orderly sergeant of the same. He served two years. He is one of the heirs to 175 acres of land adjoining the city limits. His parents, James M. and Maria (Stanley) Dobbs, are of English and Irish descent respectively. The father was a major of Cobb's company of Georgia Rangers during the Mexican war. He was a brave soldier and participated in all the principal battles of that war. He was born in Elbert County, Ga., December 24, 1818, and died September 10, 1869. The mother was born in Cobb County, Ga., and died when the subject of this sketch was but eighteen months old. His grandfather, David Dobbs, was born and reared in Elbert County, Ga., and commanded a regiment in the Seminole war. His maternal grandfather, Dr. Lewis Stanley, was born in South Carolina and was among the first emigrants to Cobb County, Ga. He was a successful medical practitioner in that county.

G. W. Drake, M. D., a successful practitioner of Chattanooga, is the son of Samuel B. and Sarah J. (Ball) Drake, both natives of Virginia, where they were reared and married. In early life the father was a lawyer, afterward a merchant and lastly a farmer; he died about 1848. The mother is still living and is about seventy years of age. Of their family of five children, three of whom are living, our subject is the eldest. He was born April 4, 1842, in Powhattan County, Va., and received a classical education in Richmond College of the same State. In 1861 he enlisted in Powhattan Troops Confederate Cavalry, being the first troops at Manassas Junction. In 1864 he was wounded in the right arm near Spottsylvania which disabled him from further duty. After the war he taught school and studied medicine, graduating from Vanderbilt University in 1876 as M. D. Soon after this he came to Chattanooga. He is vice-president of the State Medical Association, having held that position two years, and was vice-president of the Chattanooga Medical Association. By his union to Miss Elmira Wood he became the father of two children—one son and one daughter. His first wife died, and in 1873 he married Miss Laura Whitehead, who bore him two children, both deceased. Dr. Drake is a successful physician and has practiced his profession for about eleven years. He is a Royal Arch Mason and a man well respected.

Louis Dunmeyer, of Chattanooga, was born in Hardy County, Va., August 11, 1842, son of Jacob and Catherine Dunmeyer, both natives of Germany. He moved to Pittsburgh, Penn., with his parents in 1846, where he was reared and educated. In 1863 he enlisted in the United States Navy, serving as fireman in this department under Admr. Dahlgren until the close of the war. In 1869 he married Miss Lottie Sayles in Buffalo, N. Y.; she died in 1871 without issue. In 1872 Mr. Dunmeyer came to Chattanooga where he became a partner in the Enterprise Machine Works, and has continued in that capacity ever since. He is a Republican, a member of the I. O. O. F., the K. of P., and is a successful business man.

Harry W. Durand, attorney and counsellor at law, is a native Hoosier, Jackson being the county of his birth. He received his early education from the excellent system of public schools for which Indiana is noted, and later attended the graded schools of the city of Bloomington, in Monroe County. He thus acquired an uncommonly good academical education which he still further bettered by a course at the State University, situated at Bloomington, which graduated him in 1876. Later he studied law in that city, and practiced his chosen profession there until 1881 when he came to Chattanooga, and until 1886 was connected with the firm of Wheeler & Marshall. Since that time he has prosecuted his profession alone, and is justly regarded as one of the brightest attorneys at the bar of Hamilton County. October 3, 1883, he united in matrimony with Miss Jessie Lee Vincent, and their union has been blessed with the birth of one daughter. The father of the subject of this biography, Dr. J. J. Durand, is a native of Ohio and is a successful practicing physician of this county. His mother, whose maiden name was See, is a native Indianian.

A. S. Dunlap, M. D., is a son of James and Margaret (Stewart) Dunlap, who were born, reared and married in the State of Ohio. The father was a Presbyterian clergyman. The Dunlaps came from Scotland at an early day, and settled in Virginia, and removed from there to Kentucky; a branch also settled in Ohio. Our subject, the eldest of a family of seven children, was born in Madison County, Ohio, May 7, 1836, and graduated from Miami University in 1857, with the degree of A. B., and five years later with the degree of A. M. Previous to entering the university he attended Salem Academy, South Salem, Ross Co., Ohio, to prepare for college. In 1867 he graduated in medicine from the University of Michigan, having taught in the meantime, and read medicine with Dr. A. Dunlap of Springfield, Ohio. From 1870 to 1886, he held the position of first assistant surgeon of the National Military Home near Dayton, Ohio, and from 1871 to 1885 was United States pension examiner and secretary of the pension board. He has been a member of the American Medical Association since 1869, and was also a member of Clark & Montgomery Counties (Ohio) Medical Societies. In December, 1886, he came to Chattanooga to enjoy a milder climate, he having become acquainted there some six years ago. He is an active member of the Presbyterian Church, and is esteemed by all who know him.

Rev. George W. Dumbell, rector of the Episcopal Parish, has three churches under his charge, namely: the Parish Church, St. Paul's, St. John's, West Chattanooga, and the Grace Memorial Church, in South Chattanooga. He was born in the Isle of Man, and educated at Rugby and Trinity College, Cambridge, England. Dr. Dumbell, previous to coming to Chattanooga, was successively rector of Jackson, Tenn., and St. James', Milwaukee. He married, in 1857, Georgiana Mary, daughter of Hon. Austin Cox, one of the Puisne judges of British Honduras, by whom he has had fifteen children, eleven of whom are living. The eldest son, George William, is a banker at Los Angelos, Cal., and the second son, Howard Murray, is in holy orders, and one of his father's curates.

John McK. Dunscomb, manager of the telephone office at Chattanooga, is a native of New York City, born November 15, 1860. He was educated at St. Aloysius' Academy and at Xavier College. At the age of fourteen he engaged in the harness business with his father. Having taken a trip to the Northwest, he returned and kept books. He organized the United States Disinfectant Company, becoming vice-president of the same. In 1884 he engaged with the East Tennessee Telephone Company, and in 1886 took his present position, in which he has proved very efficient. Our subject was the eldest of four sons born to Alexander H. and Anna M. (Shelley) Dunscomb, both natives of New York City, where they passed their days. The father followed the occupation of a harness manufacturer. He died in 1880, and the mother previous to this, in 1871.

C. H. Dyer, justice of the peace, is a native of Maine, but was reared and educated at Boston, Mass. At the commencement of hostilities between the North and South he enlisted in the Boston Light Artillery, and was mustered out at Burlington, N. Y. In the year 1864 he was united in marriage to Miss Adda Francisco, a native of New Orleans, to whom four children have been born. In the year 1870 our subject and family removed to Tennessee and settled in Chattanooga, where Mr. Dyer followed his trade, being a mechanic and builder. During the years 1876 and 1877 he was engaged in the coal trade, and later was in the agricultural implement trade until his election to his present office in 1880. He was a member of the board of mayor and aldermen in 1883. His parents, David B. and Catherine (Bryant) Dyer, were natives of Maine, but the father was reared in Vermont. They afterward moved to Massachusetts, where the mother's death occurred in 1876.

William H. Eagar, agent for the Cincinnati, New Orleans & Texas Pacific, and Alabama & Great Southern, was born in New Orleans, February 14, 1851. He was reared in Selma, Ala., where he removed with his parents when a child. In 1872, he engaged in the railroad business in the employ of the Alabama Central Railroad (now East Tennessee, Virginia & Georgia), and continued with that road as clerk, paymaster and conductor until 1874, when he entered the employ of the Alabama & Chattanooga (now Alabama & Great Southern Railroad), and has been with this road ever since. August 21, 1874, he united his fortunes with those of Miss Sarah J. East, a native of Alabama, and the result of this union was the birth of three children—two sons and one daughter—all of whom are living. Mr. Eagar came to Chattanooga in 1877, and in February, 1880, was made agent for the Alabama & Great Southern, and November 1, 1881, he was made joint agent for both roads. He is a Democrat in politics, a member of the American Legion of Honor, and also a member of the Episcopal Church.

Albert Eakin, of the firm of Eakin & Co., grain dealers of Chattanooga, was born in Bedford County, Tenn., July 13, 1843, and is the son of John and Lucretia (Pearson) Eakin. The father was of Scotch-Irish lineage, and was one of the most successful citizens of Bedford County, and reputed one of the wealthiest citizens of the State at the time of his death, which occurred in 1849. The mother was a native of South Carolina. Our subject was educated in New Haven, Conn., and prepared for Yale, but the war breaking out, he came home and enlisted in Company F, Forty-first Regiment Tennessee Infantry. He was captured at Fort Donelson, and imprisoned eight months, after which he re-entered the service, acting as commissary to the brigade of cavalry under Gen. Joseph Wheeler until the surrender. In October, 1865, he married Miss Cyrena Buford, who died in June, 1880, leaving one daughter. In 1868 Mr. Eakin entered the grain business in Shelbyville, Tenn. In 1881 he went to Nashville and followed the same business. In July, of the same year, he married Laura Dayton, of Shelbyville, who bore him two children—a son and daughter. Mr. Eakin is a Democrat, and a member of the First Baptist Church. In June, 1882, he came to Chattanooga, and engaged in the grain business. In May, 1886, he engaged with the above mentioned firm, whose individual members are Albert Eakin, Thomas H. Cheek and James D. Buttolph, in the grain business. They erected their present elevator on the Nashville, Chattanooga & St. Louis Railroad, corner of Boyce and Cravens Streets. The elevator is ninety feet high, four stories, and is 48x110 feet, including platforms, storage capacity of bulk and sack grain, 100,000 bushels. They have all the latest combined improvements in elevators. Has Caldwell's conveyors and Barnett & Lee's separators, and has a capacity of handling and cleaning twenty car loads of grain per day. They give employment to twelve men on an average, do a general storage business, and also buy and sell about $400,000 worth of grain per year at present. They ship to nearly all points in the Southern States. In connection with this business, they have a mill for the manufacture of chopped feed, which is becoming a popular stock feed in the South.

L. M. Elder, a legal practitioner of the firm of Elder & White, is a native of Trenton, Tenn., and a graduate of the University of Virginia in 1873. He then returned to Trenton, where he was admitted to the bar the same year. He practiced law alone for about one year, after which he was a member of the firm of Jones & Elder until the date of his coming to Chattanooga, November, 1876. In 1875, he married Miss Mary Saffarans, a native of Memphis, who bore him five children—one son and four daughters. Mr. Elder practiced in the firm of Elder & Elder until 1882, after which he practiced alone until June of the same year, when the present firm was formed by our subject and George T. White. Our subject was president of the Y. M. C. A. of Chattanooga during 1880 and 1881, and is now a member of the board of directors. His father, John W., is a native of Murfreesboro, Tenn., and is at present president of the Gibson County Bank at Trenton, Tenn. The mother of our subject, Martha G. (Houston) Elder, was a native of Blount County, was reared in Alabama, and died at Trenton in 1878.

John W. Elder, Jr., of Chattanooga is a native of Trenton, Tenn., born August 2, 1853, and a son of Henry L. and Harriet N. (Houston) Elder, natives of Tennessee. Our subject was educated in the University of Tennessee, and graduated from that institution in 1874. He studied law under ex-Supreme Judge T. J. Freeman and practiced law from 1876 (the time he came to Chattanooga) until 1881, when, on account of failing health, he relinquished the profession, and has since been actively engaged in the real estate and insurance business, representing Queen of England, Sun, Fire of London; Equitable, of Nashville; Washington Fire and Marine, of Boston, and Fire Insurance Association, of London. May 18, 1881, he married Miss B. McMillin, of Chattanooga, a daughter of D. C. McMillin, Sr. Mr. Elder is a Democrat, a member of the Royal Arcanum and present Commander of American Legion of Honor (local lodge) and also a member of the Methodist Episcopal Church South.

Hon. H. Clay Evans, a gentleman whose name is synonymous with the business interests and prosperity of Chattanooga, is a native of Juniata County, Penn., his birth occurring in 1843. His parents, Jesse B. and Anna (Shingle) Evans, were also natives of the Keystone State, but removed from there to Wisconsin in 1846, where the subject of this sketch was reared and educated. In 1849 the father became infected with the gold fever, and leaving his family crossed to the Pacific Slope, where he engaged in mining. He died in Montana Territory in 1869. As a member of the Union Army, H. Clay Evans participated in its various fortunes until 1864, when he arrived in Chattanooga which has since been his home. For some time he was connected with the Alabama & Chattanooga Railroad, and was one of the active promoters of the interests of the great Roane Iron Company. From 1874 to 1884 he served as secretary, treasurer, vice-president and general manager of the last named corporation, but in the latter year was elected cashier of the First National Bank which position he resigned to accept the Republican candidacy for Congress in the Third Congressional District. Mr. Evans entered this contest with a Democratic majority of about 1,700 votes against him, but his known ability and personal popularity cut down the opposing majority to only sixty-eight votes. Besides being the present sole owner of the Anchor Flouring Mills, the largest in the South, Mr. Evans is the chief stockholder and manager of the Chattanooga Car & Foundry Company, and is a large stock owner of the Lookout Mountain Inclined Railway Company. He served as city mayor two terms and is now a member of the board of mayor and alderman. He is a member of the Electric Light Company of Chattanooga, is the owner of one of the finest residences in the city (built at a cost of about $20,000) on East Terrace Street, and is, in every sense of the word, a Chattanoogan, with Chattanooga ideas and with the proverbial enterprise of Chattanooga. Mr. Evans is a Sir Knight in Masonry. He married Miss Addie Durand, of Chautauqua County, N. Y., and their union has been fruitful in the birth of three children.

P. Fleming, plumber, steam and gas fitter and dealer in plumber and gas fitters' supplies, etc., is a native of Ireland, born in 1851. He immigrated to the United States in 1864, and passed several months in New York and Ohio, after which he came to Tennessee and located at Nashville. He remained in that city until 1872, when he removed to Chattanooga, and here followed the plumber's trade until 1875, after which, in connection with this he added his stock of supplies. He keeps ten men employed, and has a large trade in the city. In the year 1874 he was united in marriage to Miss Anna O'Donnell, a native of Chattanooga, who bore him one son, Martin, who was born in 1877. Mrs. Fleming's death occurred in 1878. Our subject's parents, Andrew and Mary (Karrigan) Fleming, were both natives of the Emerald Isle, where the mother still resides. The father died in 1855.

James B. Frazier, of the legal firm of Shepherd & Frazier, is a native of the Sequatchie Valley of Tennessee, but was reared principally in the city of Nashville where he had exceptionally good school advantages. He pursued the regular course of study at the University of Tennessee, located at Knoxville, from which institution he graduated in 1878, and then began the study of law under the tuition of his father who is recognized as one of the ablest attorneys at the Nashville bar. He was admitted to practice in 1879, and the year following removed to Chattanooga and embarked in the practice of his profession, where he has acquired a good and steadily increasing practice. He continued alone until January 1, 1884, when the present firm of Shepherd & Frazier was formed. Mr. Frazier is a member of the Masonic fraternity, is an able attorney and a first-class citizen in every respect. In 1883 he wedded Miss Lou Keith, who is a native of Athens, Tenn. His father, Thomas M. Frazier, is a native of Greene County. this State, but since 1869 has been a resident of Nashville, where for twelve years he served as judge of the criminal court. The mother of our subject was Margaret M. McReynolds, a native of Bledsoe County, Tenn.

Dr. J. M. Fraer, a successful practitioner of Chattanooga, is the son of Peter and Celia (Bennett) Fraer. The father was born in New York and the mother in Liverpool, England, and when eight years of age was brought to Canada where she and Mr. Fraer were married. Having lived there about ten years they moved to Lewiston, N. Y., afterward to Niagara Falls and still later to Erie County, Penn., where both died. He was a manufacturer and inventor. Of the four children born to them only one is now living, our subject. He was born January 1, 1846, near Dundas, Canada. He received an academic education and a medical education at the Homœopathic Hospital College of Cleveland, Ohio, at Detroit Homœopathic Medical College and at New York Homœopathic Medical College, graduating at Detroit and taking a post graduate course at New York. He also took private instructions in surgery under William T. Helmuth. After practicing until 1872 he came South and soon after established himself in Chattanooga. In 1883 he married Miss Julia Williams. For fourteen years he has been in the practice of his profession and has met with evident success as a physician. He passed through the several epidemics, but stood at his post through all. He is a Knight of Pythias and an influential citizen.

Walter Scott French, of the Phœnix Foundry Company. Our subject was born in Warren County, near McMinnville, Tenn., May 12, 1854, and is the only son of John H. and L. Virginia (Smith) French of three children born to them, his sisters being Jessie V. and May L. (Noel) French. His mother, of whom he is very proud, was born in Accomac County, Va., was educated in Washington County, Penn., began her literary career in Memphis, Tenn., and was married to John H. French, his father, in 1853, a native of Virginia and a resident of Tennessee, whose writings are too well known to need comment here. His early life was spent on his father's farm, where, under the tutorship of his excellent mother and a few local teachers, he received his primary education, and laid the foun-

H. WHITESIDE

dation of a character for a useful life. In October, 1872, at the age of eighteen, he entered the Eastern Tennessee University, where he applied himself diligently to master the scientific course of the institution, stood high in his classes, and soon won the esteem and confidence of his instructors and fellow students by his gentlemanly deportment. Owing to sickness in January, 1874, he was obliged to give up his studies and seek rest, which was much needed. Having regained his health, in October, 1875, he entered Frank Goodman & Company's Business College, at Nashville, Tenn., where in February, 1876, he graduated with honors, and in April of the same year entered upon active life, as bookkeeper for the manufacturing firm of T. F. Burroughs & Company, of his native town, at a nominal salary. Longing for a wider sphere of activity, and wishing to see more of the world, he decided to sever his connection with the firm, and on December 17, 1877, left for Chattanooga, Tenn., where without means and among strangers he began life anew. Disappointed in not finding ready employment, though by no means discouraged, his efforts were at last successful, and on January 8, 1878, he was taken into the employment of Mr. P. C. Wilson, glass dealer—a business entirely new to him—over many worthy applicants, at $20 per month, which was afterward increased as he became more proficient. As an appreciation of his services, his kind employer allowed him to represent the firm at the great banquet tendered by the citizens of Cincinnati to the merchants of the cities of the South, upon the formal opening of the Cincinnati Southern Railroad, where nearly 2,000 guests dined at Music Hall on March 18, 1880. In March of the next year he was called home to attend the bedside of his dying mother, where after a long illness she breathed her last on April 1, and was laid to rest. Two weeks after this event found him again at his business, and in August of the same year, at the earnest solicitations of his first employer, Mr. T. F. Burroughs and his father, he was induced to take a half interest in the firm. On September 7, 1881, he was married to Miss Ella M. Carpenter, a native of Indiana, and a former resident of Cleveland, Ohio, whose parents came to Chattanooga in 1874, and left for McMinnville, his old home, and immediately entered upon his duties in his new sphere. After eighteen months of patient and unceasing labor, and seeing that he was falling behind in meeting his payments, he at once determined to sell his interest, either to his partner or father, and return to Chattanooga. This he did, although he received no financial benefit in the transaction, except to clear himself of a debt of $8,000. The transfer was made to his partner on March 15, 1883, and with a light heart he returned to his adopted city. In July of 1883 he, in conjunction with his wife's father and brother, organized the Phœnix Foundry Company, of which he was made secretary and treasurer, and owing to whose good management and devotion to its affairs brought the company safely through the depressing period of 1884-85. From the investment of $500 in this company, saved up by the severest economy and the frugal habits of his young wife, he is slowly gaining a place of honor among his fellow-citizens. Two children were born of this marriage—boys. Independent in politics, Presbyterian in his religious faith, a good citizen, energetic, conscientious and courageous, we leave him to bravely fight the battle of life set before him.

S. J. A. Frazier, of Hill City, Hamilton Co., Tenn., is a native of the eastern division of the State, his birth occurring in Rhea County, in 1840. Graduating at the East Tennessee University at Knoxville, just before the war, he entered the Confederate service, and arose to the rank of captain in the Nineteenth Tennessee Regiment. At Chickamauga he was shot through the windpipe and captured, and confined at Johnston's Island, until the close of the war. In 1870 he was elected attorney-general for the Fourth Judical Circuit of Tennessee; moved to Hamilton County in 1882, and became one of the earliest settlers and chief founders of Hill City. To his marriage with Annie Keith, which was solemnized in 1871, two children have been born, Alleck and Sallie. In the last Democratic convention Mr. Frazier was a prominent candidate for Congress.

Charles B. Freeman, justice of the peace, was born in Dalton, Ga., November 25, 1858, and is a son of Judge J. P. Freeman of that place. His early life was spent in various occupations until a railroad accident caused him to be a cripple for life. He then began the study of law under Hon. W. C. Glenn, of Dalton, Ga., and was admitted to the Dalton bar in 1880. Two years later, he came to Chattanooga, and practiced his profession in that city until January, 1884, when he was elected justice of the peace, at a special election, to fill the vacancy caused by the resignation of G. M. Sherwood. Mr. Freeman is a notary public and commissioner of deeds for New York, Michigan, Illinois, Indiana, Kentucky, North Carolina, Alabama, Geor8ia and Louisiana.

C. R. Gaskill, president of the Chattanooga Iron Fence & Screw Company, secretary of the Chattanooga Street Railroad Company, and assistant cashier of the Third National Bank of this city, is a native of Georgia, and was educated at the capital of that State. In 1872 he came to Chattanooga and commenced reading law. In 1873 he accepted a position in the First National Bank as collector, which position he filled acceptably until 1877. Having in the meantime kept up his study of the law, he was then admitted to the bar and pursued the practice of the profession until 1881, when he returned to the banking business by accepting the position of book-keeper in the Third National Bank, and has been connected with that corporation until the present time, having served as assistant cashier since 1883. Mr. Gaskill is a member of the Masonic brotherhood, in which order he attained the rank of Knight Templar. He wedded Sallie Lee, a native of Crawfish Springs, Ga., and by her is the father of one daughter, Annie Lee. He is the son of V. A. and M. A. (Battle) Gaskill, who were natives of Rutland, Vt., and Georgia, respectively. The father is yet living at his birthplace in New England, but the mother died in 1867.

Joseph L. Gaston, M. D., is a son of Mitchel and Jane (Wilson) Gaston, both natives of East Tennessee, where they were married and have since passed their days. They now reside near Chattanooga, and the father cultivates the soil. Joseph L. was born in McMinn County, Tenn., January 26, 1848, and passed his youthful days on the farm. He received his literary education at the Grant Memorial University, at Athens, Tenn., from which institution he graduated in 1871. He then taught school and read medicine for two years. He then entered the University Medical College of New York, and graduated there in 1875. He practiced medicine at Harrison, James Co., Tenn., until 1880. Then on account of failing health he virtually relinquished the practice of medicine and was elected State senator. In 1882 he resigned that office to accept the position of collector of customs at the port of Chattanooga, which position he held until the change of administration in 1885. In January, 1885, he was elected city treasurer for the city of Chattanooga, and served his time—one year—in that capacity. Having by this time regained his health, he again resumed the practice of medicine in Chattanooga. He is now, in 1887, city physician and secretary of the Board of United States Pension Examiners. In December, 1878, he married Celestia Lamon, and to them have been born two children, Fred and Harry. He and Mrs. Gaston are both members of the Methodist Episcopal Church.

Andrew J. Gahagan, of Chattanooga, was born in Madison County, N. C., February 23, 1844, son of George W. and Mary E. (West) Gahagan, natives respectively of South and North Carolina. Our subject was reared and educated in North Carolina, and at the breaking out of the war enlisted in Company D, First Tennessee Cavalry (United States Volunteers), and during service was promoted to the rank of second and first lieutenant. During the last year of the war he served as quartermaster of his regiment. In 1867 he engaged in mercantile pursuits in

Chattanooga, but retired from this in 1878 and was elected trustee of Hamilton County, serving by re-election two terms or until 1882, when he was elected assistant cashier of the First National Bank. In 1884 he became a member of the firm of Loomis, Hart & Co., having charge of the finances of said firm. On the 1st of March, 1871, he married Eliza J. Dugger, of Chattanooga, and to them were born three children—two sons and one daughter. Mr. Gahagan is a Republican in politics, and as such was elected to the office of trustee. He served as a member of the board of mayor and aldermen several terms. He is a member of the Masonic fraternity, of the K. T., of the G. A. R. and of the Methodist Episcopal Church North.

William Gillaspie, farmer, was born June 27, 1842, in Knox County, Tenn., and is the second of eight children born to Marcus and Eliza Jane (Simpson) Gillaspie. Marcus Gillaspie was born in Knox County, in 1809, and died in 1861. His wife was born May 16, 1818, in Ireland. She came with her parents to America when about nine years of age and settled first in Philadelphia. In 1830 they moved to Claiborne County, Tenn., and from there to Knox County, in 1833, where Miss Simpson married Marcus Gillaspie. She is still living and makes her home with her son, William. Both Mr. and Mrs. Gillaspie were members of the Methodist Episcopal Church, from the time they were first married. Our subject received a fair education in the schools of Hamilton County, and assisted his father on the farm until the breaking out of the war, when he enlisted in Capt. White's company, Fifth Tennessee Cavalry, and served three months. His father died, and he was released and returned home. In the fall of 1862 he volunteered again, this time joining Capt. Roger's company, the Fourth Georgia Cavalry. He was sergeant of his company until the winter of 1865, and the company was escort for Gen. Walker during the battles of Chickamauga and Missionary Ridge. After the war Mr. Gillaspie returned to agricultural pursuits, which he has since continued. In January, 1887, he was elected road commissioner of his district. He was married in 1885 to Miss Maggie Castle, a native of Hamilton County, born in 1861, and the daughter of Samuel and Mary (Dody) Castle. Mrs. Gillaspie is a member of the Catholic Church, and Mr. Gillaspie of the Methodist Episcopal Church. He commenced life a poor man and is now in very comfortable circumstances. He owns 190 acres of excellent land located on the Bird's Mill road, four and a half miles east of Chattanooga. Mr. Jacob Gillaspie, grandfather of the subject of this sketch, was a soldier in the struggle for independence. He resided in North Carolina previous to the Revolution, but after that event he moved to Knox County,

Tenn., settling first in a fort near where Campbell's Station now is. He was of Irish descent.

David Giles, president of the Chattanooga Foundry and Pipe Works, was born in Pittsburgh, Penn., February 27, 1836, son of Thomas and Mary (Evans) Giles, natives of Wales. David Giles was reared to manhood in his native State and in Ohio. He learned the iron business in Pennsylvania, being a practical molder by trade. In 1857 he came South and accepted a position as foreman of a foundry at Nashville, where he continued until 1866, when he established a foundry in that city and conducted it successfully for one year, when Mr. C. B. Isbester became a partner, and these gentlemen, in 1877, moved the foundry to Chattanooga. Mr. Giles has been president of the present stock company since its organization as a stock company in July, 1882. He is a Republican in politics, a Knight of Honor, and is recognized as a reliable and enterprising business man and citizen.

Rev. Patrick J. Gleeson, pastor of the Roman Catholic Church of SS. Peter and Paul, was born in Ireland in April, 1846. Having received a thorough classical and English education in his native country, he came to America in the fall of 1868. He taught the catholic school of Knoxville, Tenn., soon after his arrival in the country to the close of the school year. In September, 1869, he resumed his studies for the priesthood, entering Mount St. Mary's Seminary of the West, Cincinnati, Ohio. Here he continued the usual course of study of philosophy and theology, and received minor orders, sub-deaconship and deaconship from the Most Rev. John Baptist Purcell, archbishop of Cincinnati, on the Ember Days, in December, 1872. He was ordained priest on January 23, 1873, in the cathedral of Nashville, Tenn., by Most Rev. P. A. Feehan, the bishop of Nashville, now archbishop of Chicago. A week later he was sent on his first mission to Clarksville, Tenn. He labored in Montgomery and adjoining counties until transferred to his present charge, arriving in Chattanooga July 18, 1885.

J. C. Guild, inspector of mines for Tennessee, and member of the firm of Dickerson & Guild, civil and mining engineers and analytical chemists, is a native of Sumner County, Tenn. He was reared and educated in Nashville, and graduated from Vanderbilt University in 1883. He was in the service of the State as assistant geologist, during which time he collected all the minerals sent to the Southern exposition at Louisville, and also arranged the mineral cabinet for the State at Nashville, and assisted in collecting the specimens for the same. As inspector of mines he makes semi-annual reports to the State commissioner of agricultural statistics, etc., besides many private reports of individual mines. He located in Chattanooga in 1886, and October of the same year married Miss Mary Orr, a native of Nashville. Mr. Guild is a member of the Greek Society, "Beta Theta Pi." He is also grandson of Jo. C. Guild, author of "Old Times in Tennessee." His father, George B. Guild, an able attorney at Nashville, is a native of Nashville, and was a member of the Legislature in 1872, was also formerly county court clerk of Sumner County. The mother's maiden name was Georgie Thompson. The parents are both living, and our subject, two brothers and one sister are the surviving members of a family of five children.

Green & Walker, hardware merchants of Chattanooga, established their business August 1, 1886, at their present quarters, 828 Market Street. They carry a large and well selected stock of general hardware and mechanic's tools, and control a large share of the trade in city and county. The individual members are William T. Green and Frank M. Walker. Mr. Green was born in Knox County, Tenn., in 1849, and is a son of the late Augustus P. Green of this city, who died in this county in 1878. William Green was reared and educated in Hamilton County. In 1874 he engaged in mercantile pursuits near Memphis, Tenn.; in 1880 returned to Chattanooga, and for four years has been engaged in the hardware business. He has been quite successful in this occupation. He is a Democrat, a Mason, and is one of Chattanooga's reliable business men. Frank M. Walker (other member of the firm), was born in Rogersville, Hawkins Co., Tenn., April 3, 1863, and is the son of the late Gen. Frank M. Walker who was killed during the late war. Frank M. Walker, Jr., was educated in Rogersville, and in 1880 came to Chattanooga, where he learned the hardware business with J. H. Warner & Co. In 1886 he engaged in his present business with Mr. Green. June 2, 1886, he married Miss Maggie Whitman, of Georgia. Mr. Walker is a Democrat in politics, and is a wide-awake thorough-going business man.

D. R. Griffiths, merchant and farmer at Sale Creek, was born in South Wales, November 20, 1834, and came to America in 1864. He first settled in Steubenville, Ohio, but in a short time removed to Shamokin, Penn., and from there to Hubbard, Ohio, in October of the same year. In March, 1868, he came to Sale Creek, where he has since resided. Previous to this, in 1866, he, with nineteen others, then living in Ohio, organized a company to come to East Tennessee and lease some coal mines. They opened up the mines in the same year, and continued very successfully, considering the poor market they had, until 1880, when the company sold out to the present owners. Mr. Griffiths began working in the mines at the early age of seven, and continued this up to 1880. He then opened a store at Sale Creek, and has engaged in this business, in connection with farming, up to the present. He also deals very extensively in tan-bark; and in 1883 they handled $16,000 worth of the same, averaging per year about $5,000. What education Mr. Griffiths has was picked up by the family fireside. He began working for himself at the age of seventeen, and has accumulated considerable property by his own exertions. In 1854 he married Miss Ruth Richards, who was born in January, 1836, and who is the daughter of William and Margaret Richards, of Aberdare, South Wales. To our subject and wife ten children were born, of whom four boys and two girls are now living: William, David, Thomas, Richard, Annie (Mrs. Reese), and Ruth (Mrs. Thompson). Mr. Griffiths is a Republican in politics, and he and wife are members of the Union Church at Sale Creek, although reared Baptists.

John A. Hart, of the well known furniture and lumber firm of Loomis, Hart & Co., was born in Greenville, Ohio, on the 1st of March, 1845. He received his early education in the schools of his native town, finishing his schooling at college in Delaware, Ohio. During the early part of the war he espoused the Union cause, and enlisting from school served until the close of the civil war as a private. The war over he settled in Alabama and engaged in the lumber business, but later settled permanently in Chattanooga. He here has indentified himself closely with the business prosperity of the city, and in 1879 and 1880 served creditably in the capacity of mayor. January 13, 1885, he was elected president of the Third National Bank, a position he yet retains. He is the present president of the Chattanooga Stove Works which he organized, also vice-president of the Mountain City Fire Insurance, and besides is a stockholder in many of the most important and successful manufacturing enterprises for which Chattanooga is noted. As a business man Mr. Hart has been very successful, and he is recognized as one of the most enterprising men of Hamilton County.

James N. Hazlehurst, president and manager of the Lookout Iron Company, was born in Hancock County, Ga., January 15, 1864. He was reared in his native State and finished his education at Sewanee University, Tenn., in 1883. His parents, George H. and Irene W. (Nisbet) Hazlehurst, natives of Georgia, had in the meantime removed to Chattanooga. Our subject was in the Western States and Territories from 1878 to 1881 as civil engineer on the Texas Pacific, New Orleans & Pacific, and Louisville, New Orleans & Texas Railways. Upon the organization of the Lookout Iron Company, in 1885, he became its vice-president, and one year later its president. He has officiated in the latter capacity in a faithful and highly efficient manner up to the present time. Mr. Hazlehurst is also a partner in the mercantile business of

A. B. Wingfield & Co., of this city. October 6, 1886, he married Miss Mary E., daughter of John C. Griffis, of Chattanooga.

J. F. Hamill, farmer, of the Second District, was born February 29, 1828, in Blount County, Tenn., and is the seventh of nine children born to the union of Samuel and Catherine (Best) Hamill. The father was born in Blount County, Tenn., about 1789, and came to Hamilton County February 14, 1832. He was elected justice of the peace in 1836, and held this office until his death in May, 1856, with the exception of a few months, caused by his removal from the Second to the Fifth District. He was a very devoted and active member of the Old Line Presbyterian Church, and was one of the founders of the same at the Baker Creek Meeting House. The mother was born in Buncombe County, N. C., and died in 1840. Her parents came to Blount County in an exceedingly early day. Our subject attended school but nine months in his life, but his father was a school-teacher, was well educated, and kept his household bountifully supplied with papers, magazines and the best books circulating at that day, which afforded our subject an excellent opportuuity to store his mind with the general news of the day and with historical facts. J. F. Hamill, in 1852, was elected justice of the peace and served until 1858. He was then elected coroner of the county and served until 1860. He also farmed, and ran a ferry boat at Chattanooga until the breaking out of the war. He was then captured as a political prisoner and carried first to Knoxville, then to Nashville, then to Tuscaloosa, then to Mobile, and from there to Macon, Ga., where he was released. In July, 1863, he returned home, and until December of the same year worked as a hired hand. He then made his escape, to avoid the Conscript Act, went to Lexington, Ky., where he struck the Federal Army, going the entire distance on foot. After the war he returned to Chattanooga, where he was made first sergeant of police and served in this capacity twelve months. In the spring of 1868 he was elected register of the county, and served about six years. In 1874 he moved to the farm where he has since resided. Previous to the war, in February, 1852, he married Miss Rachel Ford, who bore him seven children: Samuel (deceased), Benjamin, Lizzie (Mrs. Williams), James Buchanan, Mollie J. (deceased), John (deceased) and Catherine. Mrs. Hamill died in February, 1864, at Nashville, and on May 19, 1868, Mr. Hamill married Mrs. Mary Smith, formerly Miss Kirklen, and to this union four children were born: Mollie John, Daniel, Samuel and John. Mrs. Hamill is a member of the Methodist Episcopal Church South, but Mr. Hamill is not a member of any church, but is a Quaker in principle. He was a Whig before the war, but since that event has voted the Republican ticket. His first presidential vote was cast for Z. Taylor. His grandfather, David Hamill, came from Belfast, Ireland, to Pennsylvania. His wife also came from Ireland and settled in the same locality, where, after the Revolutionary war, they were married. They immigrated to Blount County some time before 1800, and our subject's father was born in a stockade. J. F.'s maternal grandfather, Daniel Best, came from Holland to America and settled in Buncombe County, N. C., but afterward immigrated to Tennessee.

G. M. D. Heard, crockery merchant at Chattanooga, Tenn., was born July 21, 1844, in Cleveland, Ohio. He is the eighth of ten children born to Charles W. and Caroline (Goldsmith) Heard. Mrs. (Goldsmith) Heard was a daughter of Mrs. Abigail (Jones) Goldsmith, of Painesville, Ohio, where the latter now lives, and was one hundred years old the 29th of April, 1887. She is a native of Berkshire Hills, Mass., and came from there to the city where she now resides, early in this century. Mr. Charles W. Heard was born in Onondaga County, N. Y. in 1806, and came to Ohio at quite an early day. He was a prominent architect of Cleveland, Ohio, where he built some of the oldest houses and superintended the building of some of the most prominent public buildings now standing. He was a consistent Democrat, maintaining his opinions against bitter opposition and prejudice which existed in that section during the late war. He was of Scotch descent. Mrs. Heard was a descendant of the famous Oliver Goldsmith family. Our subject secured a fair education in the schools of Cleveland, Ohio, and ran away from them and entered the army in 1862. He enlisted in Company E, Eighty-fourth Ohio Volunteer Infantry. He came to Chattanooga in 1870, where he has since resided, engaged in his present business, the style of the firm being Brooks & Heard, 122 Market Street, Chattanooga. He was elected and served as school commissioner of Chattanooga one term. He married Miss Lillie Tutt in 1875. She was born in Chattanooga, Tenn., in 1857, is the daughter of Benjamin F. and Lizzie (Rawlings) Tutt, and a descendant of the Tutt family of Augusta, Ga. Four children were the result of our subject's marriage: Clio, Rawlings Walton, Charles Wallace and Lois Goldsmith. Mr. Heard is a Republican in politics, and he and wife are members of St. Paul's Protestant Episcopal Church at Chattanooga, of which Mr. Heard is a vestryman. He purchased, in 1884, Beauclair, at the head of Whiteside Street in St. Elmo, the most beautiful natural location for a residence in the county.

Caspar H. Hensel, manager for the John Kauffman Brewing Company (Cincinnati) at Chattanooga, and principal owner of the Chattanooga Ice & Bottling Company, is a native of Prussia, Germany, born

January 23, 1846. He came to the United States in 1865, and located at Cincinnati, where he engaged in mercantile pursuits. In 1883 he entered the employ of the John Kauffman Brewing Company, and in August, 1885, came to Chattanooga as their representative. In November, 1885, he established the Chattanooga Ice & Bottling Company, with Mr. A. R. Blair. Since November, 1886, he has been principal owner and manager of the same, bottling ale, beer, carbonated waters, ginger ale, etc. The business amounts to from $25,000 to $30,000 per annum. He also does an equally large business in ice, being simply dealers in manufactured ice. In June, 1876, Mr. Hensel married Amelia Schuein, of Cincinnati, Ohio, and they have two living children by this union, both daughters. Mr. Hensel is a Democrat in politics, a K. of H. (Cincinnati Lodge), and a member of the German Lutheran Church.

Jesse T. Hill, of Chattanooga, was born in Nashville, Tenn., March 18, 1850, and is a son of Robert T. and Catherine (Stout) Hill, natives of Nashville, where our subject was reared and educated. In 1868 he came to Chattanooga and entered the employ of the Southern Express Company, where he remained four years. He was then deputy clerk and master of chancery court about ten years, after which he became secretary of the Etna Coal Company. In September, 1885, he engaged in the marble business as a member of the firm of Daly, Smith & Hill. Mr. Hill has been director of the Third National Bank, of Chattanooga since its organization, and is also director of Citico Furnace Company. He is president of the Tennessee Marble & Railroad Company, with headquarters here, and quarry in Monroe County, Tenn., March 16, 1878, he was united in marriage to Miss Alice B. Woodward, a native of Ohio, and to them were born three daughters. Mr. Hill is a Democrat, and was mayor of Chattanooga during the years 1878-79. He is a Mason, was a member of the Chattanooga school board four years, and himself and family are Episcopalians. His partner, Patrick C. Daly, was born in Ireland in 1836, and came to the United States in 1849, where he learned the marble cutter's trade in New York City. He worked at the same in Northern cities until 1872, when he came to Chattanooga in April of that year and engaged in the marble business. He is a Royal Arch Mason.

J. W. Hoagland, M. D., is a son of E. M. and Cynthia (Smith) Hoagland. The father was born in Ohio and the mother in Westmoreland County, Va., being of the same family as the famous John Smith, of Virginia. When a girl she moved to Ohio, where she and Mr. Hoagland were married. After moving to Indiana the mother died, and the father afterward returned to Ohio and married Mrs. Mariah

State. He was a farmer by occupation, and became the father of nine children by his first marriage. Our subject was born in Richland County, Ohio, July 16, 1845, and received a good common school education. At the age of fourteen, he began the carpenter's trade. He taught school for some time, by which calling he made enough to take him to college and to Worcester University. During the last year of the war, he served in the Federal Army, after which he took a medical course at the Columbus Medical College, from which he graduated in 1876, and has practiced continuously ever since. In 1885 he came to Chattanooga. Previous to this, in 1883, he married Amelia Wiggins, a native of Noble County, Ind., and a daughter of Rev. Charles F. Wiggins.

Rev. W. W. Hooper, A. M., professor of natural science in Chattanooga University, was born in Licking County, Ohio, October 18, 1843. His father, Jacob Hooper, was born in Maryland, and his mother, Mary (Watson) Hooper, was a native of Virginia. In early life both went to Ohio, where they were married and became the parents of six children—two sons and four daughters. In 1852 the mother died, and afterward Jacob Hooper married Elizabeth Lewis, who bore him two sons and one daughter. Both Mr. and Mrs. Hooper are now living in California. In early life the father was a farmer, but afterward followed mechanical pursuits. In 1861, our subject entered the Ohio Wesleyan University, but the stirring events of the war caused him to throw aside his books and volunteer, in 1862, in Company A of a battalion of United States Infantry, and participated in the deadly conflict at Shiloh and Murfreesboro. Having served eighteen months he was taken sick, and after recovery was detailed in the United States medical department at Louisville, Ky. After the war he spent some time in the Central Ohio Normal and in the Illinois State Normal, after which he taught school and went to college by turns. In 1872, he graduated from the university, and three years later received his degree of A. M. After conducting the high school at Buckley, Ill., a short time, he was elected vice-president of Rust University at Holly Springs, Miss., and three years later became president of the same, which position he held ten years. In 1886 he took his present position. In connection with his profession, he has been working in the ministerial field. In 1874, he married Miss Mattie Green, a native of Ohio, and a graduate of the Ohio Wesleyan Female College. To them were born two children: Frank and Mabel. The Professor is a Mason, and his wife is also a member of the Methodist Episcopal Church.

William T. Hope, M. D., was born December 26, 1850, in Roane County, Tenn. He graduated from the literary department of Cumberland University in 1870. Having read medicine for two years, under Dr. B. B. Lenois, he took a course of lectures at the University of Virginia, and graduated from Bellevue Hospital Medical College, New York, in 1873. After practicing two years in his home county, he came to Chattanooga, where he has remained ever since. He has been city physician, president of the board of health, and is a member of the Chattanooga Medical Society, State Medical Society, the American Medical Association and the American Public Health Association. For many years a member of the Masonic fraternity, he was elected Eminent Commander of Lookout Commandery of K. T. in 1887. In November, 1886, he was married to Miss Lizzie L. McIlroy, a native of Pike County, Mo. Both are members of the Cumberland Presbyterian Church. His parents, W. B. and Mary A. (Foute) Hope, were both natives of Roane County, Tenn. They had three children of whom W. T. and M. M. Hope are now living. The father has generally followed farming and merchandising, was a major during the days of militia, and an enrolling officer during the late war. The mother died about 1855, and W. B. Hope was again married in 1862, to Mrs. Kate Welcker Robinson. Nine children have been the result of this union of whom seven are now living.

H. D. Huffaker, county superintendent of public instruction in Hamilton County, was born November 18, 1860, in Hamilton, now James, County, Tenn., and is the eldest of a family of nine children born to Jesse T. and Sarah (Holland) Huffaker. The father was born in Alabama in 1838, and came to Hamilton County, Tenn., when but twelve years of age. In 1861 he enlisted in Company I, East Tennessee Cavalry, and was sergeant of his company. At the termination of the war he received his discharge at Knoxville. He is an ordained minister of the gospel in the Missionary Baptist Church, and has charge of three churches at the present time. He is of Dutch-Irish extraction as is also his wife, who was born in Monroe County in 1841, and died March 12, 1882. She was the daughter of Rev. H. P. Holland (deceased). Mr. Holland was a prominent citizen of Hamilton, now James, County, and was also of Dutch-Irish lineage. Our subject received his education at Sumach College in Murray County, Ga., and at Coosawattee Seminary, Gordon County, Ga. He is a graduate of Behm's Commercial College at Chattanooga, and since then has been engaged in teaching and bookkeeping. January 4, 1887, he was elected superintendent of the county schools. He has made teaching a success, and his salary was increased each successive term taught. He is one of five in Hamilton County who hold five year certificates, and he is also president of the Hamilton County Teachers' Institute. December 29, 1885, he married Miss Addie Varnell, of Tyner, Tenn. She was born September 29, 1864, in Hamilton County, and is the daughter of G. W. and Lizzie (Hughes) Varnell. Mr. Varnell was born September 15, 1829. He served during the late war as first lieutenant in Company F. At the termination of the war he received his discharge at Nashville. He is of Dutch-Irish extraction, as is also his wife, who was born December 23, 1842 and died February 1, 1878. She was the daughter of William Hughes (deceased). Mr. Hughes was born October 6, 1806, and served as captain in Company F. He was a prominent citizen of Hamilton County until his death, February, 7, 1878. Our subject and his wife are members of the Missionary Baptist Church, which he served as secretary at his former home in north Georgia. He is a Democrat in politics and a strong Prohibitionist. He is a very promising young man. He is at present principal of the Daisy Academy, but intends at the end of this term to give up school teaching and devote his entire time to the duties of his office. Mrs. Huffaker is his assistant teacher in the academy.

David W. Hughes, former proprietor of the planing and saw mill and also former lumber dealer at Chattanooga, was born in South Wales, September 17, 1857, came to the United States in 1866 and to Chattanooga in 1867. He entered the lumber business here as employe for other firms. In 1878 he engaged in the business for himself in partnership with Childs & Co., and in 1880 the firm became Hughes & Marquet. In 1883 Mr. Hughes became sole proprietor of the business. The present works were built in 1878 and the dimensions of the planing mill are 80x120 feet, is two stories high, with one shed 20x200 feet and another 30x200 feet. The saw mill is 70x120 and the planing mill, grounds and buildings cover an entire block between Cowart and Whiteside. Louisa and Catherine Streets saw mill is on the Tennessee River, adjoining Roane Iron Works. The saw mill and lumber yard cover sixteen acres of ground. The entire business employs about 200 men when in operation. Mr. Hughes is president of the Brush Electric Light Company, and has a branch lumber business in Knoxville, Birmingham and in Atlanta, Ga. March 1, 1887, he sold out to the Hughes Lumber Company, an incorporated company who succeeded him in the business. He was elected president and manager of the company. Mr. Hughes is independent in politics, a K. T., a Mason, a K. of P., Royal Arcanum, and a successful business man.

Caleb B. Isbester, vice-president of the Chattanooga Foundry and Pipe Works, was born in Scotland December 31, 1828, and is a son of Caleb and Elizabeth (Newton) Isbester, both natives of Scotland. Our subject came to the United States in 1832, was reared in Pittsburgh and Allegheny City, Penn., where he learned the pattern maker's trade (iron business). He came South in 1852, and in 1868 engaged in the foundry business with Mr. Giles, after which, in 1877, they moved the foundry to Chattanooga. He has been vice-president since the organization of the present stock Company. He was united in marriage to Miss Virginia Thornton of Tennessee, and to them were born two children—a son and daughter. Mr. Isbester is a Republican in politics, and an excellent citizen.

J. J. Jackson, farmer and stock raiser in the Second District, was born September 10, 1834, in Hamilton County, and received his education in a log schoolhouse with no "chinking" about it and a dirt floor. After assisting his father on the farm until of age he married Miss Rebecca Gann in 1855. She was born December 14, 1837, and is a daughter of Preston and Mary (Laymen) Gann, who were among the earliest settlers of Hamilton County. Mr. Gann was born in Hawkins County, Tenn., and Mrs. Gann in Washington County, Tenn. The former was of Scotch-Irish descent, and the latter of German. Our subject's union was blessed by the birth of eight children, four of whom are still living: Martha A. (deceased), James La Fayette, Ardelia (deceased), Sophronia (Mrs. James A. Hunter), Rufus (deceased), Mary Ann (deceased), Tennessee and Willie. Mr. Jackson enlisted in the Federal Army, Company A, Sixth Tennessee Mounted Infantry, but previous to this he was captured several times and made his escape each different time. He was mustered out of service at Nashville, Tenn., at the close of the war. In politics Mr. Jackson is an ardent Republican, but before the war was a Democrat. Although not members of the church yet Mr. and Mrs. Jackson are liberal in their support of all church and educational enterprises. They have given each of their children a good education, and one son, J. L., is now a practicing physician and surgeon in Chattanooga. He received his literary education at Athens University, and his medical education at the Old School Medical College at Cincinnati, Ohio, completing his course at the latter institution in two years. He is a very successful practitioner, especially so in surgery. Our subject was the eldest of eight children born to Jonathan and Nancy (Rodgers) Jackson. The father was born in North Carolina about 1809, and moved to Marion County with his parents about 1812. In 1822, or near that time, he moved to Hamilton County and settled near Hixon Station. He was a successful farmer and a highly respected citizen. He died in 1876. The mother was born in West Tennessee, and came with her parents to Hamilton County about 1820. She died in 1880, on the day of the November election. Mr. Jonathan Jackson was of Welsh and his wife of Irish descent. They were highly respected people, and were active members of the Methodist Episcopal Church South. Our subject's grandfather, Ephraim Jackson, was a soldier in the Revolutionary war.

Charles E. James, whose name figures largely and prominently in the business interests of Chattanooga, is a native of East Tennessee, born at Blountville, near the Virginia State line, December 12, 1851. When but five years of age his parents removed to Chattanooga, and he was here reared and educated. In 1870 he embarked actively in business pursuits in the iron brokerage business, at which he continued until the year 1877, when he removed to the city of Montgomery, Ala., there assisting in the construction of the water works of that place. The year following he returned to Chattanooga, and established his present extensive business in iron and railway supplies, which is mentioned more fully in the history of the present business interests of Chattanooga in another part of this volume. He assisted in the organization of the Chattanooga Gas Light Company, of which he was the efficient superintendent five years. He was also one of the principal movers in the establishment of the Union Railway Company, of Chattanooga, of which he is now president. Mr. James is a Democrat in politics; is a Knight Templar in Masonry, and is the father of one son by his marriage with Miss Kate R. Webster, to whom he was wedded in November, 1876. He is the son of Jesse J. and Sarah M. (Vincent) James.

M. L. Jenkins, superintendent of the Soddy Coal Mines, was born in December, 1842, and is one of twelve children born to John and Ann (Lewis) Jenkins. The parents were both inhabitants of Wales. The father is still living, and is eighty years old. The mother died about 1855, while still quite young. Our subject received his education in the subscription schools of Wales. He began mining as a day laborer at the age of twelve, and by his own energy and ability has arisen to his present position. He came to America in 1868, and located first in Pennsylvania, where he remained three years, and then went to Mahanoy City. In 1872 he came to Soddy, where he has since remained. He married Miss Elenor Lloyd in Wales. She is the daughter of Evan and Catherine Lloyd. Mrs. Jenkins was born about 1850, and by her marriage became the mother of six children: Evan (deceased), Hester, Catherine, Maggie (deceased), Abram and John. Mr. and Mrs. Jenkins are members of the Congregational Church. Mr. Jenkins is a Republican in politics, a Master Mason, a K. of H. and a member of the I. O. O. F.

H. A. Johnson, manager and only resident member of the firm of Taylor, Crote & Johnson, saw mill men and lumber dealers, is a native of Buffalo, N. Y., where he grew to manhood, and where he was engaged in the lumber business until he came to Chattanooga in 1881. He was then engaged in buying and shipping walnut lumber, until 1884, at which date he located permanently here. In 1872 he was united in marriage to Miss Rosa Wright, a native of Fredonia, N. Y., to whom one child, a daughter, has been born. Our subject's parents, Amasa and Delpha (Smead) Johnson were natives of Vermont. The mother died in 1865, and the father is now a resident of Michigan. The mill owned and operated by Taylor, Crote & Johnson was built in 1881 by Treice & Gillmore, which firm was succeeded by Woodward & Winchester in 1883, and by Treice & Johnson until the present firm was formed in the fall of 1885. About forty hands are employed by this firm, and they saw 4,000,000 feet annually.

Hon. David M. Key, judge of the United States District Court for the eastern and middle divisions of Tennessee, is a native of Greene County, this State, his birth occurring January 27, 1824. He is a son of Rev. John and Margaret (Armitage) Key who were also natives of Greene County, their respective deaths occurring in Monroe County, Tenn., in 1854 and 1882. The father was a minister in the Methodist Episcopal Church. In the year 1826 the family removed to Monroe County where David M. was reared and educated, having graduated from Hiwassee College in 1850. He selected the legal profession as his vocation through life, and the same year of his graduation was admitted to the bar. For two years he practiced law at Madisonville, then a short time at Kingston, and in February, 1853, came to Chattanooga, which has ever since been his home. Until the commencement of the war he practiced his profession in the firm of Welcker & Key, then enlisting in the Forty-third Confederate Tennessee Regiment of Infantry, served until the close of the war, and was mustered out as lieutenant-colonel. He then resumed the practice of law in the firm of Welcker & Key until 1868, then in the firm of Key, Eakin & Key. He was a member of the constitutional convention of 1870, and in August of the same year was elected chancellor of the Chattanooga division. This position he resigned in 1875, to accept the appointment of United States Senator tendered him by Gov. Porter. In March, 1877, he was appointed Postmaster-General by President Hayes, and filled the office until August 25, 1880, when he accepted his present position. In 1857 Mr. Key wedded Elizabeth Lenoir, a native Chattanoogan, and to their union nine children have been born, eight of whom are yet living.

Thomas S. King, secretary and treasurer of the Vehicle Spring Company, is a native of Wales, and came to the United States in infancy. His parents, Thomas and Mary (Morgan) King, located in Illinois in 1848, where our subject was reared and educated at McKendree College, Lebanon, Ill. At the time of the breaking out of hostilities between the North and South our subject enlisted in the One Hundred and Fiftieth Illinois Infantry and served until the close of the war. He then returned to Illinois, but at the end of one year moved to Georgia and engaged in the mercantile business for a short time. He was then engaged in the railway mail service of the United States until he accepted his present position in December, 1884. The Vehicle Spring Company was organized in the year 1884, and has $5,000 invested. He is a member of the Masonic fraternity and the G. A. R. Mr. King's parents were natives of England and Wales respectively. The father was a local preacher of the Methodist Episcopal Church for more than thirty years before his death; died August 30, 1886. The mother is still living.

Elisha Kirklen, merchant at St. Elmo, was born March 9, 1832, in Bledsoe County, and is one of ten children born to Elisha and Susan (Hixon) Kirklen. The father was born in North Carolina in 1802, and came to Bledsoe County at a very early date. He served as justice of the peace for many years, and was a very successful farmer and merchant. He was of English descent and died in 1866. The mother was born in Bledsoe County in 1804. She was an active Christian worker, and died December 17, 1886. She was of German descent. Our subject received a fair education in the common schools of Bledsoe County. He assisted his father on the farm, and in 1852 married Miss Nancy Stockton. She was born December 18, 1833, and was the daughter of William and Charlotta (Reckter) Stockton. Nine children are the result of our subject's marriage: Mary S. (Mrs. Ashley), Martha J. (Mrs. Shultz), Laura L. (Mrs. Adams), Abraham, Lizzie (Mrs. Jackson), William, Elisha, Joseph and George. Mrs. Kirklen is a member of the Methodist Episcopal Church South. Our subject farmed in the Second District until 1884, when he moved to St. Elmo and engaged in merchandising. He has a fine farm of 800 acres in the Second District, also four and a half acres in St. Elmo. Mr. Kirklen is a Democrat in politics, and was postmaster at Hamilton postoffice for several years.

Rev. E. S. Lewis, A. M., acting president of Chattanooga University, was born in Natick, Mass., August 24, 1855. His father, Rev. Joseph W. Lewis, was a Methodist Episcopal minister of Massachusetts for many years, of which State he was a native. His mother, Miss Dorcas K. Hoar, was a member of one of the most prominent families of the State. Their family consisted of three children—two sons and one daughter. Our subject was the eldest child, and while growing up received his education in the public and high schools of his native State. He prepared, by private instruction, for Boston University, and graduated in 1877 from the College of Liberal Arts, and four years later also graduated from the school of all science of the same university. He was professor of natural science in the Cincinnati Wesleyan College, has held the position of president of Little Rock University, and accepted his present position in 1886. In 1879 he married Miss Anna C. Sparks of Hamilton County, Ohio, who bore him two children, only one now living, Edward R. He and wife are both members and active workers in the Methodist Episcopal Church.

John E. Lloyd, is a native of Wales, and came to America in the spring of 1860. He spent the first two years, after landing in this country, in traveling quite extensively throughout the United States, prospecting for a company of mining capitalists at Philadelphia. He then settled at Dupont, Penn., as superintendent of mines belonging to Geo. Dupont & Co. He was with the Delaware Lackawanna & Western Railroad Company for three years as contractor. In 1872 and 1873 he was a member of the Tuscaloosa Mining and Transportation Company who were prospecting with a view to opening up some coal lands in Tuscaloosa County, Ala. He then moved to Rising Fawn, where he was engaged by a New York company, who were engaged in operating the Rising Fawn Iron Furnaces. He then came to Chattanooga and engaged in the real estate business. From here he went to Fort Payne, Ala., to open up the Beson Gap Coal Mines for a New York company, and this proved another failure. He afterward engaged in land surveying in DeKalb County, and moved from there to Soddy, where he has since remained. He was superintendent of the mines of Dayton in 1882 and 1883 under John H. Furgason, after which he went to Texas and Arkansas to open up mines for Carson & Louis, of Weatherford, Tex. For the past two years he has been located at Soddy, where he has been looking after the ventilation of the mines owned by The Soddy Coal Company. In 1886 Mr. Lloyd was the Democratic candidate for the Legislature from this Legistative district, cutting down the great majority by which the county is usually carried to 200. During the late war he commanded a company in Fitz John Porter's army corps. He engaged in all the battles and skirmishes in which his regiment took part up to the time of his separation from the army. He married Miss Annie Morgan in 1870. She was a native of Wales, and came to America, September, 1870. This union resulted in the birth of five children three of whom are living: Katie, Arthur, Emma, Eudora, Theophilus (deceased) and Elizabeth (deceased). Mr. Lloyd is a member of the Congregational Church as was also his wife. He has been quite a successful geologist and practical miner, and has walked over every foot of the mineral lands of East Tennessee, North Carolina and Alabama. His father lived and died in Wales. He was a soldier in the Peninsular war, engaged in the battle of Waterloo, and ranked as colonel in the British Army. He died when our subject was quite small.

A. Lloyd, general superintendent of the Soddy Coal Company, was born June 14, 1845, in South Wales. He came to America in the spring of 1863, and located first in Pennsylvania. He moved from there to Ohio, and in 1867 came to Soddy, where he has since remained. He was one of a company of twenty, mostly Welsh people, who organized a company, and our subject was sent to Soddy to prospect for coal, which being very promising, they at once opened up the coal mine. There being no railroad by which to ship their coal, they built a narrow gauge railroad to the river and shipped by steamboat. In 1874 it was reorganized, and the present company took charge. A. Lloyd and L. W. Morgan were the stockholders in the old company, the rest of the company were new members. It began with a capacity of 500 bushels per day, and it now has a capacity of 500 tons of coal and coke. Arrangements are now being perfected for a much greater capacity. Mr. Lloyd is principally concerned in this company's coal interest in Arkansas. Our subject received his education mostly by his individual application, having attended subscription schools only six months in his life. He is the fourth of five children, born to Evan and Catherine (Reese) Lloyd. The father was born about 1808 and died in 1875. The mother was born about 1814, and died in 1873. They came to America in 1870. Our subject began life as a day laborer, and by his industry and ability as a business manager and financier has accumulated quite a fortune. He married Miss Margaret Evans June 4, 1864. She is also a native of Wales, born in 1840, and the daughter f Morgan and Eliza Evans, natives of Wales. Mrs. Lloyd came to America in 1863, and by her union with our subject became the mother of six children: Elizabeth (deceased October 8, 1886), Evan (assistant bookkeeper at the Soddy Coal Company's office in Chattanooga), Morgan (deceased), Kate Helen, Maggie and Ida. Mr. and Mrs. Lloyd are members of the Welsh Congregational Church. Mr. Lloyd usually votes the Republican ticket, but votes more for principle and the best man. He is a Royal Arch Mason and is a member of the I. O. O F. The church with which Mr. Lloyd is connected was organized in 1871, and its congregation is composed of Methodists, Baptists and Congregationalists, principally the latter. It is in a very prosperous condition, has a splendid Sunday-school, and Rev. Morgan is the pastor. He is a native Welshman and preaches in both the English and Welsh languages.

William R. Lloyd, superintendent of the Sale Creek Coal Company, was born December 4, 1838, in South Wales, and came to America in 1861. He returned to Wales in 1862, and again in 1866. He worked on a farm until fourteen years of age, after which he worked at coal mining as a day laborer. He began life a poor man and owes his elevation to his present position to his own ability as a practical miner. He received his education in the subscription schools of South Wales, and at the age of twenty-one began working for himself. In 1859 he married Miss Margaret Thomas also a native of Wales, who came to this country with her husband. By this union they had these children: William T. (killed by a powder explosion at Soddy, in May, 1866), Evan (deceased), Catherine (Mrs. Thomas), Margaret Ann (Mrs. Price), Jane, Thomas, Rebecca and Taliesyn. Our subject's parents, Evan and Catherine (Reese) Lloyd, were natives of Wales, and they in company with Mrs. Lloyd's mother came to America in 1870. Our subject is a Republican in politics, and he and wife have been members of the Congregational Church for many years. He has been superintendent of the Sale Creek Mines since the fall of 1881, and has the respect and confidence of all who know him.

Morgan Llewellyn, secretary and treasurer of the Chattanooga Foundry and Pipe Works, is a native of Lehigh County, Penn., born January 20, 1846, and the son of William and Mary (Morgans) Llewellyn, both natives of Wales. Our subject was reared to manhood in his native State, and received a fair academic education. Early in life he engaged in the iron business, and later engaged in mercantile pursuits for himself at Alliance, Ohio. In 1869 he came to Tennessee, and engaged in the mercantile business at Knoxville, and then engaged in the coal business thirty miles above that city, being superintendent of the mines for eight years. He moved to Washington, D. C., in 1879, and accepted a position as clerk in the postoffice department, where he continued four years. In 1883, he resigned to re-enter the coal business at Oliver Springs, Tenn., owning an interest in the Winters Gap Coal Company of that place at the present time, and is secretary and treasurer of the same. June, 1884, he came to Chattanooga, and accepted a position as bookkeeper with the Chattanooga Foundry & Pipe Works, was elected secretary in July, 1885, and treasurer in July, 1886, being also one of its stockholders. In 1868 he wedded Sallie A. Powell of Pennsylvania, and four living children resulted from this union—two sons and two daughters. Mr. Llewellyn is a Republican, a Knight of Honor, a Royal Arch Mason, and a member of the Presbyterian Church.

The Loomis & Hart Manufacturing Co., saw mill, building material and wholesale manufacturers of furniture. The business was started in 1866 by J. F. Loomis and F. J. Bennett, under the firm name of Loomis & Bennett. In 1875 John A. Hart bought the interest of Mr. Bennett, and the business was conducted by Loomis & Hart until 1884, when J. T. Arnold, F. L. Winchester, A. J. Gohogan and A. G. Stivers purchased an interest in the business, and the same continued under the name of Loomis, Hart & Co., which firm extended their capacity and increased the business to such an extent that it was decided, on January 1, 1887, to incorporate as the Loomis & Hart Manufacturing Co. This company owns their manufacturing site at the foot of Pine and Cedar Streets, consisting of about fifteen acres. They employ about 150 men, and do an annual business approximating $250,000. The officers of the company are J. F. Loomis, president; J. T. Arnold, secretary; A. J. Gahagan, treasurer; F. L. Winchester, manager of mills and manufacturing department, and A. G. Stivers, manager of their sash, door and blind department.

D. B. Loveman & Co. This well-known wholesale and retail dry goods house was established in 1875 by D. B. and H. H. Loveman, who started the business on a small scale. In 1877 Mr. Ismar Noa became a member of the firm, Mr. H. H. Loveman retiring. In the fall of 1886 this firm completed its present large and commodious business block, where they have since carried on their business. In January, 1887, Mr. I. Noa retired from the firm, and Messrs. J. N. Mills and William McDonald were admitted. David B. Loveman is a native Hungarian, born July 29, 1844, and came to the United States in 1853. He was reared to manhood on a farm in Michigan, and in 1860 came to Tennessee, where he followed clerking in Nashville, Atlanta, Rome (Ga.), and Tuscaloosa, Ala. He engaged in business for himself at Atlanta from 1869 until 1875 in the firm of Friedman & Loveman, also in the firm of William Rich & Co., when he came to Chattanooga, where he has since been actively engaged in business. June 18, 1873, he married Miss Eva Wolfe, of Baltimore, Md., by whom he had three children—one son and two daughters. He is one of the incorporators of the Chattanooga, Rome & Charleston Railroad. He is the originator and is one of the largest stockholders of both building associations of Chattanooga, and is vice-president in both. He is a Republican in National politics and independent in local affairs. He is an ancient member of the Masonic fraternity, and a good citizen.

Capt. John Pomfret Long, of Chattanooga, was born at Knoxville, Tenn., November 25, 1807. His father was William Long, a native of Mecklenburg County, N. C., born February 19, 1775, settled at Knoxville in 1797, married Miss Jane Bennett in 1805, resided at Knoxville until 1813, when he removed to Washington, Rhea Co., Tenn., and staid there until November, 1836, when he removed to Chattanooga, where he died November 1, 1844. He was a house carpenter by trade. In the latter part of his life he was an elder in the Presbyterian Church. He was plain William Long but was so uniformly upright that it came to be a saying "as honest as Billy Long." He was one of the first settlers of Chattanooga, and assisted in organizing the Presbyterian Church there in 1840. Capt. Long's grandfather, John Long, was born in County Antrim, Ireland, settled in Mecklenburg County, N. C., participated in the Revolutionary war, married Miss Elizabeth Shields, of Mecklenburg County, and was drowned in 1799, while returning in the night from a Masonic lodge meeting. He came alone to America, leaving only a maiden sister in Ireland. During the Revolution, in Charlotte, N. C., some Tories were captured, from whom information was obtained that an attack was to be made on "Post Ninety-six," one hundred miles distant from Charlotte. The Whigs posted two couriers on horseback, taking different routes, to notify the garrison at "Post Ninety-six." John Long proposed to carry the information on foot, started at sunrise, and at sundown delivered his despatches at Ninety-six, and put the garrison on their guard—a remarkable record showing the patriotism of the man, the spirit of those times, and the pluck that is in the blood of the Longs. Capt. Long's mother, Miss Jane Bennett, was the daughter of Maj. Peter Bennett, a native of Virginia, who married Miss Elizabeth Pomfret, daughter of John Pomfret, of King William County, Va. Maj. Bennett was in the Revolutionary war, at the close of which he served as sheriff in Granville County, N. C. He died in 1822 in Knox County, Tenn., where he had settled in 1802, as a farmer. Capt. Long's maternal great-grandfather, John Pomfret, came from England, settled in King William County, Va., married a Miss Hunt, and died in Granville County, N. C., in 1802, at the age of eighty-four. Capt. Long's mother was born in Granville County, N. C., January 26, 1781, and moved with her father to Knox County, Tenn., in 1802. She was a Presbyterian. She died at Chattanooga, December 10, 1859, leaving three children: (1) Mary Long, now the widow of John A. Hooke, an attorney at law, who died at Chattanooga in 1865. She has five children, James, William, Robert, Jane and Elizabeth. (2) James Shields Long, a physician: married Jane Caldwell of Monroe County, Ga.; died in 1866, leaving two children, Mary and Virginia. (3) John Pomfret Long, subject of this sketch. The latter grew up at Washington, Rhea Co., Tenn.; finished his schooling at Knoxville when fourteen years old; engaged next in a tannery for three years; next clerked three years for

Col. Thomas McCallie, a merchant at Washington, then opened a store on his own account at that place, and from there moved to Ross' Landing (now Chattanooga), reaching there April 18, 1836. Here he opened a general store, which he continued, with varying success, until 1860. He was then elected city recorder of Chattanooga, and filled the position three years, until the city was evacuated by the Confederates. Prior to the evacuation, in 1862, he was appointed provost-marshal of Chattanooga by Gen. McCown, and served in that capacity several months. A few days after the battle of Chickamauga his house was torn down and his effects destroyed. He having gone South in the meantime, leaving his family in Chattanooga, they subsequently rejoined him at Griffin, Ga., where they remained until the close of the war. Capt. Long then returned to find himself without home or property, and a family to support. He began business as a real estate agent, and fortune favored him, for he soon was very successful. In 1868 he applied to Judges Trewhitt and Adams, at Chattanooga, for a law license, which was granted. His practice has been principally in the chancery court, where his knowledge of the land and titles in Chattanooga has been of great value to him. Notwithstanding his losses by war and going security, he has accumulated a nice property, mostly in real estate. When he first came to Ross' Landing—then a mere ferry and steamboat landing in an Indian country—he found no postoffice and no postroads. He made application to the postoffice department for a postoffice, which was granted, and he was appointed postmaster, without compensation. The name of the postoffice was changed to Chattanooga in 1838. Capt. Long held the postmastership until 1844, when he had to give way for one of the friends of President James K. Polk. In 1832 he cast his first vote for Gen. Jackson, his next was for Hugh L. White, and thenceforward he voted the Whig ticket from Harrison to Bell, since which time he has been a Democrat. He attended the Whig State convention at Murfreesboro in 1841, when Jones was nominated for governor against Polk. In February, 1861, he voted against secession, but when President Lincoln ordered out troops, he voted for secession. He was always a States' rights man, as was his father before him. He has, however, never been so warm a partisan as to vote the party ticket unless he liked the men; always considered it a duty to vote, but equally a duty to scratch objectionable names from the ticket. In 1845 he was elected to take his father's place as an elder in the Presbyterian Church, which he had joined in 1843. He was a commissioner of the town of Chattanooga when the land was subject to entry, and the occupants were entitled to preference of entry. The three commissioners, Aaron

M. Rawlings, George W. Williams and Capt. Long, entered the quarter-section, sold the lots, and made titles to the purchasers April 20, 1839, which was the day on which the town of Chattanooga had its birth. Capt. Long's staying power is illustrated by the fact that he has never yet seen the Mississippi River, and of the large cities only a few. Capt. Long was married to Miss Eliza Smith November 6, 1834, at Smith's Cross Roads (now Dayton), Rhea Co., Tenn. Mrs. Long was born January 25, 1813, at Washington, Rhea Co., Tenn. Her father was William Smith, a native of Massachusetts, who came to Knox County in 1808; was a school teacher, and had for one of his pupils Dr. J. G. M. Ramsey, the historian, who said of him. "He was one of the best common school teachers I ever saw." Mrs. Long's mother was Elizabeth Cozby, daughter of Dr. James Cozby, a man noted in the early history of East Tennessee as a physician and an Indian fighter. (See Ramsey's History of East Tennessee.) Mrs. Long's brother, Dr. Milo Smith, was an able physician, and for several terms mayor of Chattanooga, where he died in 1868. Mrs. Long was educated at Knoxville; made a profession of religion and joined the church in 1843, the same day her husband made profession and joined. She has been an invalid the greater part of her married life, but is beloved for her sweetness of temper. She is fond of the company of young folks; has an unconquerable will power that has carried her through all her troubles; is notably cheerful and pleasant, and, for one of her age, remarkably active, especially when "upon hospitable cares intent." To this union there were eleven children—all born in Chattanooga. Five of these died in infancy and childhood. The others are: (1) William Pomfret Long, died nineteen years old. (2) Elizabeth Jane Long, died sixteen years old. (3) James Cozby Long, born December 2, 1844; educated in the Naval Academy at Annapolis; resigned and joined the Confederate Navy in 1861, attaching himself to the fleet along the coast of North Carolina. He was in the fight at Roanoke Island, the second in command of the "Curlew," Capt. Hunter. He was then transferred to the "Merrimac," as midshipman, and was in the famous naval fights at Hampton Roads, and remained with his ship until she was burnt. He was then transferred to Drury's Bluff, and finally to Plymouth, N. C., and was on board the iron-clad "Plymouth," when she was blown up by the United States Navy. He next served under Capt. Moffit on a blockade runner. After the war he went into civil engineering, and had charge of the Government works at Mussel Shoals for a while. He is now a manufacturer of iron paint at Birmingham, Ala. He married, at Elyton, Ala., November 20, 1872, Miss Frances Walker, and has four children: William Walker, John

Pomfret, James Cozby and Mary. (4) John Pomfret Long, Jr., born March 4, 1847; joined Col. Walker's Nineteenth Tennessee Regiment in May, 1864, at Dalton, Ga.; participated in all the fights from there to Atlanta, and on July 22, 1864, was disabled by a shell taking his foot off; died March 1, 1880, unmarried. (5) Milo Smith Long, born May 10, 1850; graduated in medicine at Nashville, and is now in Dakota. (6) Marcus Bearden Long, born January 27, 1854; now a civil engineer, and was for a while engaged as engineer in Mexico on the Atchison, Topeka & Santa Fe Railroad; unmarried. One of the aims of Capt. Long's life has been to give his children something to start upon and to help them attain a standing in society, and he believes that every man ought to have a home and a family, and next, that he has duties to perform as a citizen. He has desired wealth, and has been sometimes up and sometimes down, but has always made it a rule to pay his debts. With one exception he has always made a profit on whatever he has sold. He never swore an oath in his life, and was brought up to regard the Sabbath. He has never been dissipated, though not always strictly temperate. He is a self-assertive man, and of quick temper. Being the oldest citizen of Chattanooga, he is often resorted to as an oracle on matters pertaining to the history of persons, families and property in that now important city. He has been a public-spirited man all along, and is uniformly spoken of as the best representative man of the city where he located when it was simply a river landing, and surrounded by the Cherokees. It was very appropriate that in 1881 he was selected to write the historical sketch of Chattanooga, on the occasion of representatives of the North and the South meeting at that city to shake hands over the bloody chasm. His article printed in the Chattanooga *Times* in September, 1881, is full of valuable history—local, personal and general.

J. T. Lynn, secretary, treasurer and superintendent of the Chattanooga Gas Light Company, is a native of Pittsburg, Penn., his birth occuring in the year 1856, son of James and Jane (Ferguson) Lynn, who were natives of Belfast, Ireland, and Glasgow, Scotland, respectively. The parents both came to America when young, and were married at Pittsburgh where the father died in 1857. The mother is yet living, and resides with her children, part of the time at Evansville, Ind., and part of the time with our subject. J. T. Lynn was educated, largely, in the public schools of Allegheny, and at about the age of fourteen years, began serving an apprenticeship at the machinist's trade on the Northern Pacific Railroad, being the first boy that worked on that railroad. From 1876 to 1881 he was connected with the gaslight company of Pittsburgh but at the latter date moved to Evansville, Ind., and from there to Chattanooga in 1883, where he has since resided. Mr. Lynn is a member of the Uniformed Rank, and major of the First Tennessee Regiment, is a Knight Templar in Masonary, and is the president of the Endowment Rank of K. of P., of this city. In November, 1881, he married Miss Emma Blackstock, a native of Pittsburg, Penn.

E. M. Martin, D. D. S. and M. D., is a son of J. A. and J. D. (Black) Martin, both of whom were born, reared and married in Pennsylvania. The father was a dentist by profession, having practiced about forty years. Their family consisted of three children—two sons and a daughter. The other son is paymaster in the United States Navy. Our subject was born October 23, 1860, in Lancaster County, Penn., and at the age of twelve began to extract teeth. His education was limited to the common schools, his health preventing a more thorough course. After following mercantile pursuits for some time he entered the dental department of the University of Pennsylvania, graduating in 1881. He also graduated from the medical department the following year. The same year he came to Chattanooga and practiced medicine a year, being one of those chosen to vaccinate the city, during the small-pox epidemic of 1882–83. He then practiced dentistry for over three years, when failing sight drove him from the profession. In 1886 he opened the drug store that he is now operating. He is a member of the Chattanooga Medical Association and of the East Tennessee Dental Association. In 1883 he married Miss Margaretta Harding, a native of Pennsylvania, and to them was born one child, McCloy. Dr. and Mrs. Martin are members of the Episcopal Church.

A. H. Marston, treasurer and manager of the Chattanooga Chair Company, is a native of the State of New York, and is a son and the only surviving child of Samuel F. and Carrie May (Blakely) Marston, who were natives of London, England. Realizing that America possessed far greater advantages over England for laboring people, and being only in moderate circumstances, the parents immigrated to this country and were married in New York State. Later they moved to Minnesota, the father now being a resident of St. Paul, where he is engaged in the manufacture of wagons, carriages, etc. A. H. Marston was reared and educated in the State of Minnesota, and was there engaged in saw milling until 1876, when he came to Chattanooga. From 1878 to 1885 he was an active member of the firm of Loomis, Hart & Co., but in December of the latter year, purchased an interest and assumed control of the Chattanooga Chair Company, continuing in that manner until the present time. Under Mr. Marston's management the company he represents has greatly improved in every way, and it is recognized as one of the leading manufacturing institutions of the city. April 30, 1876, Mr. Marston was united in marriage with Miss Carrie M. Everett, and to their union two children have been born—one now living.

J. W. Majors, keeper of the county jail at Chattanooga, is a native of Marion County, Tenn., born April 7, 1839, and the only child of Nelson and Penelope (Conner) Majors. Mr. and Mrs. Majors died when the subject of this sketch was quite small. He received his education principally at Strawberry Plains, East Tenn. He was deputy sheriff and jailor under A. B. Conner in 1867, after which he followed agricultural pursuits until September, 1886, when he was appointed to the position he is now holding. In June, 1862, he enlisted in the Sixth Indiana Cavalry, Company K, and was orderly sergeant of the same. He was in the Atlanta campaign and in the raid to Macon, under Gen. Stoneman. He was mustered out in 1864 at Indianapolis. In 1867 he married Miss Mary Smith, daughter of William and Jane M. (Macy) Smith. Three children were the result of this union: Cicero H., Jennie P. and John W. In politics Mr. Majors is Conservative, although reared a Republican. He has served the city as city and Metropolitan police, acting in the latter capacity six monts and the former twelve months. He was brought to Hamilton County when only two years old, where he has since resided. He is a good man as his many friends can testify.

George W. Martin, postmaster, is a son of Anderson C. and Louisa (Buchanan) Martin, both natives of Lincoln County, Tenn., and both of Scotch-Irish lineage. The father was a farmer by occupation, was a State senator, and also held various county offices. The mother died in 1861 and the father in 1882. Of their three children, a daughter is dead, and one son is an extensive wool grower in Texas. The other son, our subject, was born near Fayetteville, Tenn., January 20, 1854, and received the common education of the average farmer boy. He subsequently attended the University of Tennessee, aiding himself by working on the college farm, by driving an ice wagon on the streets of Knoxville during vacation, by filling the positions of janitor and tutor, and by doing anything that presented itself. He graduated with second honors in the class of 1877; after which he engaged with his brother in sheep husbandry in Texas. Through the influence of a college friend he secured the chief clerkship in the Chattanooga postoffice in 1880. Though under Republican rule, he retained that position, faithfully discharging the duties of his office, until 1885, when the change of administration opened the way to the position of postmaster for him. He has always been a firm supporter of Democracy. His promotion to the postmastership was a triumph of the principles of civil service reform, of which he is a stanch advocate. His appointment gave general satisfaction to the citizens of Chattanooga irrespective of party, and as a public servant he eschews politics and attends strictly to business. Referring to his management of his office, the civil service reformer said, "Postmaster Martin furnishes a good model for the President who appointed him." In 1882 he married Miss Flora C. Benton, of Coldwater, Mich., by whom he has three children: Mabel, Kenneth and Elaine. Both Mr. and Mrs. Martin are members of the Cumberland Presbyterian Church of which he is a ruling elder.

Rev. J. J. Manker, D. D., dean of the school of theology, and professor of systematic theology in Chattanooga University, was born December 24, 1839. His father was Rev. John Manker, who located in Ohio when a young man, and married Miss Sarah Wright. This union was blessed by the birth of seven children—four sons and three daughters. For a livelihood he followed mercantile and agricultural pursuits. Besides this he wielded great influence for good by locally ministering to the spiritual welfare of his fellow man. The mother, too, was a worthy Christian, both being of the Methodist persuasion. They lie buried in the Buckeye State. Our subject had good educational advantages. After completing his high school course he entered the Ohio Wesleyan University in 1858, but at the breaking out of the war he enlisted in Company B, Thirty-fourth Ohio Zouave as a private. Step by step he arose until he was commissioned captain of Company B, Fiftieth Ohio Regiment; his entire service extended over a period of nearly three years. After the war he entered East Tennessee Wesleyan University, from which he graduated in 1870 with the degree of A. B. In 1871 he received the honorary degree of A. M. from his first *alma mater*, the Ohio Wesleyan University, and in 1882 the degree of D. D. was conferred upon him by the University of Tennessee. During his course he had opportunities for teaching, and upon graduating was elected professor of Greek in that university, which position he filled for three years when he resigned and was made presiding elder of the Knoxville District. In 1880 he was sent to the Methodist Episcopal Church in Chattanooga, and during his pastorate the magnificent stone church was erected. He was afterward appointed presiding elder of Chattanooga District, and in 1886 took his present position. In 1864 he married Miss Julia Tarbell, only sister of Judge David Tarbell, of Georgetown, Ohio. She died in 1880, leaving five children—four sons and one daughter. Rev. J. J. Menker was a member of the general conference of the Methodist Episcopal Church in 1876 and 1884, and of the Centennial Conference of Methodism at Baltimore in 1884. He was a member of the General Missionary and Church Extension Committee from 1876 to 1880. He is a Knight Templar, being at present Grand Prelate of the State of Tennessee.

W. S. Marshall, of the law firm of Wheeler & Marshall, is a native of Richland County, Ohio, and is a son of John S. and Sarah (Stewart) Marshall who were natives of Pennsylvania and New York respectively, and whose respective deaths occurred in 1867 and in 1884. Until the year 1853 he remained in the State of his birth, attending the public schools, then entered Jefferson College of Pennsylvania, which graduated him in the year 1856. With the tide of immigration he drifted westward, and until the breaking out of the war made his home in Iowa. He volunteered his services for the preservation of the Union, and served until 1865, when he was honorably mustered out of the service with the rank of major in Gen. McPherson's corps. At the beginning of the war he held the commission of second lieutenant in the Fifth Iowa Volunteer Infantry. While in the South he became convinced of the healthfulness and future prosperity of Chattanooga, and at the close of the war moved to this city and embarked in the practice of his profession. In 1867 he became one of the firm of Stanley, Wheeler & Marshall, and later that of Wheeler & Marshall. This firm is one of the oldest, best known and most successful legal firms in Hamilton County. Mr. Marshall is a director of the Brush Electric Light Company, the Mount Lookout Railway Company, and is a member of the F. & A. M. and of the G. A. R. He has been twice married: first to Miss L. C. Bryant, a native of Iowa, in 1868, who died the same year. Kate S. Montague, a native of Ohio, became his wife in 1873 and by her he is the father of one son, Stanhope Stewart.

C. L. Magill, farmer in the Fourth District, was born March 12, 1845, in Hamilton County. He is one of ten children born to Hugh and Rebecca (Smith) Magill. The father was born in Roane County, Tenn., February 5, 1802. He was one of the best farmers in his locality and was forty years trustee and deacon in the Presbyterian Church. In 1834 he came to Hamilton County and settled on the farm where his son, C. L. Magill, now resides. At that time the country was full of Indians. The mother was born December 11, 1805, in Roane County, Tenn., and was an active worker in the Presbyterian Church. She died January 18, 1886. The father died January 9, 1873. Our subject received a fair education in the common schools of Hamilton County, and assisted on the farm until his marriage to Miss Cyntha Little. She was born October 31, 1844, and is the daugter of John and Mary (Marten) Little. Mr. Magill is a man who has succeeded under adverse circumstances; he is well known and universally respected. He has a fine farm of 230 acres, all under cultivation, located five miles from the corporate limits of Chattanooga. Mr. Magill is a stanch Democrat, and cast his first presidential vote for Horace Greeley. Mrs. Magill is a member of the Primitive Baptist Church.

Harry A. McQuade, plumber, gas-fitter and dealer in plumbers' and gas-fitters' supplies, is a native of Nashville, Tenn., where he was reared, and in 1860 began an apprenticeship to the plumbers' trade, serving five years Henderson Bros., of that city. He followed his trade there until 1870, when he came to Chattanooga, and was connected with the water company until 1881, when he established his present trade which has already grown to large proportions. He is also assistant chief of the fire department, being one of the charter members of the company. In 1868 he was united in marriage to Miss L. Chedbille, a native of France. To this union four children have been born, two daughters and one son now living. Michael and Margaret McQuade, the parents of our subject, were natives of Ireland, and came to the United States in 1845. They died in Nashville in 1862 and 1857 respectively. Our subject is a Knight of Pythias and served on the board of mayor and alderman in 1875, representing the Third Ward.

Joab L. McCollum, agent for the North Carolina, & St. Louis Railroad at Chattanooga, is a native of Dade County, Ga., born May 10, 1842; son of Joab and Sarah (Wood) McCollum, natives respectively of South Carolina and Georgia. Our subject was reared and educated in his native State. Upon the breaking out of the war he enlisted in Gen. John B. Gordon's (now governor) original company, known then as the "Raccoon Roughs," and served throughout the war, being promoted through the various grades to major. He was wounded at the battle of Seven Pines, Va., also at Chancellorsville, Spottylsvania and Petersburg, some of these were very severe wounds in the head and limbs. April 19, 1866, he married Miss Bettie A. Holmes, a native of Whitesburg, Ala., and they have two sons and five daughters living. Soon after the war Mr. McCollum began railroading on the Alabama & Chattanooga Road, in this city, served in various capacities as agent, acting treasurer, bookkeeper, master of transportation and superintendent of the road from 1868 to 1871. In the latter year he entered the employ of the North Carolina & St. Louis Railroad, as conductor. During the latter part of 1873 he entered the service of the S. & L. & S. E. Railroad as assistant superintendent, and served this road about one year, with headquarters at Nashville. He re-entered the employ of the North Carolina & St. Louis Railroad in the latter part of 1874 as train master at Chattanooga, and the following year was made agent at Chattanooga. Mr. McCollum is a

Democrat, a Mason, a member of the K. T., A. O. U. W., K. of G. R., and of the Methodist Episcopal Church.

Hugh L. McReynolds, M. D., is a native of Cass County, Mo., born July 2, 1848, and the son of Coleman C. and Mary (Callaway) McReynolds, both born, reared and married in East Tennessee, where they lived until 1844, and then moved to Missouri. In 1850 the father went to Colorado, and there died. His calling in life was that of a physician. Four years after the death of her husband, the mother died of cholera. In their family were five children, three of whom are living—two sons and one daughter, the other son is a Missionary Baptist minister. Our subject, when nine years of age, was brought to East Tennessee, where he received his literary education. In 1868 he began the study of medicine under Dr. A. D. Scruggs, and graduated from the Jefferson Medical College, Philadelphia, in 1871, and also at the same time, from the Philadelphia Lying-in Charity Hospital. For ten years he practiced at Mouse Creek, Tenn., and in 1882 came to Chattanooga. He is president of the United States Board of Examining Surgeons, a member of the Chattanooga and State medical association, and during 1883 he was physician of the Hamilton County jail. In 1871 he married Mattie L. Rice of East Tennessee, by whom he has three children—two sons and a daughter. Both Dr. and Mrs. Reynolds are members of the Missionary Baptist Church.

James P. McMillin, of Chattanooga, was born on Lookout Mountain in 1856, and is a son of the late Jonathan P. McMillin, who was a well known and prominent citizen of Chattanooga. He died in that city in 1882. Our subject was reared to manhood in Chattanooga, and educated at Emory and Henry College, Virginia. In 1876 he engaged in the general insurance and real estate agency business, in which he has remained continuously ever since, with excellent success. He also engaged in the drug business for four years of this time. In 1881 he married Miss Lizzie Armstrong, of Knoxville, who bore him two children—one son and one daughter. He is a Democrat in politics, a Royal Arcanum, and a worthy member of the Methodist Episcopal Church.

Arthur R. Melendy, D. D. S., is the son of A. B. and Anna B. (Rice) Melendy, natives of Vermont and Massachusetts respectively. They were married in Vermont and came to Tennessee in 1869. The father followed farming as an occupation, but is now retired from active life and lives in Knoxville, Tenn. Their family consisted of two sons. Our subject was born March 4, 1859, in Vermont and educated at the University of Tennessee. He received his dental education at Vanderbilt University, from which he graduated in 1883 taking the Morrison prize, on best general examination. He then went in partnership with Dr. S. B. Cook at Sweet Water, and afterward came to Chattanooga. In 1884 he married Miss Vallie Brewster, of Sweet Water, who bore him one child, Melvil. The Doctor is a member of the East Tennessee Dental Association of which he has been president, and he and wife are members of the Presbyterian Church.

I. B. Merriam, one of the leading wholesale grocery merchants of Chattanooga, was born in Syracuse, N. Y., in 1840. His parents, Noah and Mary A. (Brown) Merriam, were natives of New York, and the father was a farmer. Our subject grew to manhood on the farm, and secured a good academic education. In 1862 he enlisted in Company I, One Hundred and Twenty-second New York Infantry, Federal Army, and served until the close of the war, being sergeant the last year. At the battle of Winchester, he was wounded in the right arm which crippled him for life. After the war he engaged in mercantile pursuits in Michigan and Alabama until 1879, when he came to Chattanooga to engage in the wholesale business. Ever since Mr. Merriam has been one of the firm, although the firm title has undergone changes several times. In 1886 he took as partner, R. B. Davenport, who had formerly traveled for the house. They have two men on the road, and do an extensive business. In 1866 Miss Mary Saulsbury, of New York, became his wife, who bore him three children—all sons. After her death Mr. Merriam married Miss Bettie Dews, of Alabama. They have three children, two sons and a daughter. Mr. Merriam is director of the City Savings Bank, director of the Commercial Printing Company and also director of the *Baptist Reflector*. He is a Mason and a member of the Missionary Baptist Church.

P. A. Millard, assistant postmaster at Chattanooga, is the son of Hugh M. and Elizabeth (Preston) Millard. The father was born in Tennessee and the mother in Virginia, both near the line dividing these States. After marriage they settled in Virginia, where the father followed agricultural pursuits. Of their family of five children our subject was the eldest. He was born in Tennessee April 10, 1856, and educated in the public schools and King College. For about three years he assisted in the postoffice at Bristol, Tenn., and in 1880 came to the office at Chattanooga. He began as delivery clerk, but soon arose to the position of assistant postmaster, which he has filled acceptably for five years. In 1884 he married Miss Mary H. Drake, and to them was born one child, Myra. Mr. Millard is a member of the Christian Church, and his wife of the Presbyterian. They are highly respected citizens.

W. B. Mitchell, a member of the wholesale grocery firm of Mitchell

& Co., is a native of Marion County, Tenn., but spent most of his youth in Chattanooga. He left that city in 1863, and prior to his permanent location here, in 1882, was engaged in merchandising at Jasper, Tenn. The wholesale grocery firm of Merriam & Mitchell was formed in 1882, J. B. Merriam, our subject and J. A. Mitchell being the individual members. In 1884 W. B. and J. A. Mitchell withdrew and organized the present firm. They employ three traveling salesmen, and have a trade of about $200,000 annually, extending through Alabama, Kentucky, Georgia and Tennessee. In 1886 our subject married Miss Mintie Hall, a native of Sequatchie Valley. His parents, P. A. and Margaret (Griffis) Mitchell, were natives of Virginia and Marion County, Tenn., and died in that county in 1885 and 1877 respectively. The father came from his native State in childhood, and located in Marion County, where he resided until his death. Mr. Mitchell has been extensively engaged in real estate transactions during the past two years, and has been one of the most successful and judicious men in the city. He has acquired a fine competency by his pluck and energy.

R. J. Moore, a farmer of the Fifteenth District, was born March 25, 1818, in Bledsoe County, and came to Hamilton County in 1835, where he has since resided, excepting three years when he lived in Georgia. He is the fourth of twelve children born to Nimrod and Sarah (Jones) Moore. The father is of Irish descent, and a lineal descendant of Lord John Moore, of Ireland. The mother is of Welsh descent, and a member of the Baptist Church. Our subject received his education in the subscription schools of Bledsoe County principally, but also gained considerable knowledge from reading. He began business for himself when twenty-three and has made farming a success. In 1842 he married Miss Margaret Jane Pitner, a native of Sevier County, Tenn., born December 24, 1828, the daughter of John and Dorathy (Criswell) Pitner, both of Dutch descent. To our subject and wife were born thirteen children: Sarah D. (Mrs. Varnell), Richard D., Harriet A. (Mrs. Shelton), Mary A. (Mrs. Burns), Margaret J. (Mrs. Duncan, formerly Mrs. Gamble), Rebecca M., Marina E. (Mrs. Duncan), James R., Tennessee F. (Mrs. Burns), Thomas J. (deceased), Virginia V., John R. and Archibald H. Mr. and Mrs. Moore are members of the Cumberland Presbyterian Church of which Mr. Moore has been deacon for some time. He has also been an elder of the same since 1857. He is a Democrat in politics, and cast his first presidential vote for Martin Van Buren. He owns 623 acres of land near the East Tennessee, Virginia & Georgia Railroad. He has been trustee of the academy at Tyner for seven years, and takes a great interest in education. He is a Master Mason. His grandfather, Frederick Jones, was a soldier in the Revolutionary war, was a Whig at that time. His son, Jeremiah H., was a soldier in the Creek Indian war and was a clerk for Gen. Rufus Gaines. His eldest son, James Jones, was a sailor. Our subject's brother, Harberd H. Moore, was a soldier in the Seminole war twelve months. He was mustered out in Louisana at the close of the war.

Morrison & Woodward, proprietors of the planing-mill, lumber yard, sash, door and blind manufactory, succeeded Gillispie & Co. (who established the business in 1870) in January, 1881. The individual members of the present firm are Robert Morrison, Richard H. Woodward and John B. Nicklin. In 1884 their building on Market Street was destroyed by fire, but they had already commenced building their present works on King Street rear of East Tennessee freight depot. They have their own timber in central Alabama and manufacture building material almost exclusively. They employ on an average seventy men, and are doing an extensive business.

Theodore G. Montague, president of the First National Bank, of Chattanooga, Tenn., was born in Meigs County, Ohio, in 1836. Such advantages of education as were available he improved. His first business venture was to enter, as clerk, the leading store at the county seat, Pomeroy, where in the next two years he acquired some knowledge of goods and the ways of trade. He then taught school one term of four months, after which Mr. Montague spent two years at the Pomeroy Academy. On leaving this school he entered the bank of Daniel & Rathburn, where he put in practice the thorough business education he had acquired. The system of business in the bank was suited to his tastes, and although circumstances seemed to draw him into other lines he returned to this work the first favorable opportunity. For three years he was the bookkeeper of a large coal mining company, and from this office, in 1863, Mr. Montague entered the United States service, as adjutant of the One Hundred and Fortieth Regiment, Ohio Volunteer Infantry. When the civil war closed Mr. Montague went to such places in the Southern States as he thought might have advantages for future growth and development. Being favorably impressed with Chattanooga, Tenn., he easily induced the friends with whom he had been associated in the banking business to visit that section, and the result was the organization, in 1865, of the First National Bank, with W. P. Rathburn as president and Mr. Montague as cashier. The organization of this bank was a red-letter day in the young city's history. Mr. Montague was the cashier for nineteen years when, on the death of Mr. Rathburn he was chosen to the presidency. From the beginning the management was judicious in the use of this capital by fostering all worthy local enterprises. The history of the First National Bank for twenty-two years reflects the character of the men in control. Only $10,000 of the capital stock was originally subscribed by citizens of Chattanooga, now a majority of the stock is owned by them. The dividends paid to the stockholders have been larger than that of any bank in East Tennessee, and the capital and earnings now held by the bank and available for the wants of the ever increasing business is larger than that of any other bank in that section. Mr. Montague has not only officially but personally encouraged and assisted in the organization of most of the business enterprises that have contributed to make Chattanooga the most progressive manufacturing city in the South. Among the leading industries with which he has been connected we mention the Roane Iron Company, Lookout Water Company, Chattanooga Gas Company, Brush Electric Light Company, City Fire Insurance Company, Chattanooga Stove Company, Citico Furnace Company, Loraine Tool Company, Whitney (cotton) Mills, etc. Although prominently connected with the varied interests of this section, Mr. Montague has never been an aspirant for public or political honors. The only exception was to serve as alderman of the city one term. At this time the city finances were at a low ebb, and the board of aldermen refused to accept any pay for their services. In schools, churches and charities Mr. Montague is a recognized factor. In 1875 Mr. Montague married Miss Mary Thayer, of Boston, Mass., and by her is the father of four children. Mr. Montague and family are exemplary members of the Presbyterian Church.

Daniel E. Nelson, M. D., is the son of E. E. and L. E. (Fultz) Nelson, natives of Tennessee and North Carolina respectively. Soon after marriage, they moved to Rutherford County, where the father followed agricultural pursuits. The mother died in December, 1864, and the father four months later. Of their family of nine children, five are now living. Our subject was born April 5, 1859, in Rutherford County, Tenn. The close of the war found this family of children without parents and almost without means of subsistence. Our subject worked at all kinds of farm work, and supported himself even in childhood. Having learned the rudiments of education, he, by his own efforts, acquired a good education and taught a three months' school, studying medicine in the meantime. In 1879 he entered Vanderbilt University, and after one term, practiced his profession in Warren County for one year in order to enable him to obtain means to return and finish his medical course, which he did, graduating in 1882. At the completion of his course, he entered a competitive examination for a position in the city hospital of

Nashville, and was successful in obtaining it. After serving about eleven months he was chosen physician in charge of the small-pox hospital, and after the close of this institution in 1883, he came to Chattanooga, recommended by the authorities of the hospital. In 1886 he was one of six to apply for the position of coroner of Hamilton County, and succeeded in obtaining that position. Dr. Nelson is secretary of Hamilton County Medical Society, also a member of the State Medical Society, secretary and treasurer of the Christian Church, and medical examiner for the Manhattan Life Insurance Company.

Nixon & Wester, grain dealers and general storage and forwarding merchants of Chattanooga, established their business in 1877 on Market Street near Sixth. The firm is individually composed of William M. Nixon and Samuel D. Wester, who erected their large warehouse in 1883. It is situated on Convert Street near Montgomery Avenue, and covers about 45,000 square feet; capacity, 1,000 car loads grain, etc. They employ, on an average, twenty men, and buy and sell, principally grain and hay, shipping extensively, to all Southern States. They also store cotton and do a general storage business. William M. Nixon was born in Roane County, Tenn., July 8, 1850, son of George W. and Ann E. (McElwee) Nixon, natives respectively of Virginia and Tennessee. W. M. Nixon was reared and educated in his native county, came to Chattanooga in 1870, and was employed in the grain and grocery business as clerk and bookkeeper until he engaged in his present business in 1877. He is also director in the Third National Bank and of Forest Hill Cemetery, and president of the Chattanooga & Alabama Packet Company. December 3, 1874, he was united in matrimony to Miss Maggie G. Peak, of Meigs County, Tenn. Three living children are the result of this union—two sons and a daughter. He is a Democrat, a member of the Royal Arcanum, A. L. of H. and ex-president of the board of trade, and is now chairman of the transportation committee of the board of trade.

M. J. O'Brien, wholesale and retail merchant, was born in Ireland and brought to New York City when a boy. He received his education in the schools of that city and had started to college when his parents died. At the age of fourteen he was thrown upon his own resources. In 1867 he came to Chattanooga, and after working in a printing office a short time clerked in a store. About 1869 he engaged in the grocery business on a capital of $50, and by hard work and close attention to trade has succeeded in establishing his present business. He is now running a large wholesale house which extends from Market to Broad, has two traveling men, and is doing a flourishing business. He was first president of the board of trade, was president of the Iron and Coal Manufacturing Association, and was director in the Third National Bank. He is supreme treasurer of the Catholic Knights of America. In 1870 he married Mollie A. Horan, who died in 1884, leaving three children. For eighteen years our subject has been connected with the business interests of this city. He is a member of the Catholic Church as is also Mrs. O'Brien.

Daniel J. O'Connell, a member of the firm of O'Connell and Rogers, and secretary of the Union Railroad Company, is a native of the Buckeye State, born in the year 1851. He came to Chattanooga in 1880, and engaged in business with C. E. James until the building of the road was commenced, since which time he has been secretary of the same. He is a Democrat in politics, a member of the Catholic Church, and an energetic, thorough-going business man.

A. W. Palmer, D. D. S., is a son of John T. Palmer, a native of Dublin, Ireland, who came to America and settled in Georgia. He here married Elizabeth Barbour, a native of Georgia. He was a physician and a noted surgeon. During the late war he was surgeon of the Seventeenth Georgia Regiment. He was a graduate of Bellevue College of Surgeons, New York, was for two years surgeon of Chimborazo Hospital, Richmond, Va., during the war, and afterward surgeon of the Seventeenth Georgia Regiment. He was a graduate of the State University at Athens, Ga., and was also county judge. He died in 1865. Having lived in Georgia until 1873, the mother came to Chattanooga where she now lives. Their family consisted of seven children. Our subject was born in Wilkes County, Ga., May 5, 1845, and received his literary education at Oxford, Ga., and his dental education at the University of Tennessee in 1884, though he had practiced since 1872. In 1878 Miss Lizzie A. Brause, a native of Tennessee, became his wife. Her parents were natives of Saxony, and at an early day they came to this country. The result of our subject's union was one child: Albion Elizabeth. Dr. Palmer has held the office of president of the East Tennessee Dental Association twice, vice-president twice, and is now secretary.

Z. C. Patten is the secretary of the Chattanooga Medicine Company, which was organized in 1879. The company does a manufacturing business exclusively, and prepares proprietary goods which find ready sale in every State south of the Ohio and Missouri Rivers. Twenty-five to forty persons are employed, and traveling salesmen cover the extensive territory where the goods find a market. The company does a large amount of advertising in newspapers, and use more postage stamps than any other five establishments in Chattanooga, in mailing their pamphlets, etc. Mr. Patten was born in Jefferson County, N. Y., May 3, 1840, and is the son of John A. and Betsy (Cartter) Patten, both parents being of English descent and natives of New York. Their family consisted of four sons and one daughter. The father died in 1847. Our subject, in youth, received an academic education. When the late war broke out, being then a resident of Illinois, he entered the Federal service in Company H, One Hundred and Fifteenth Illinois Regiment. At the battle of Chickamauga he received a severe wound and was discharged, but after recovering, was commissioned second lieutenant of Company H, One Hundred and Forty-ninth New York Regiment. After three months, owing to the effects of his wound, he resigned, and in 1864 located in Chattanooga. For about ten years he was in the book business, and for two years conducted the Chattanooga Times. Since 1879 he has been secretary and treasurer of the above company. In 1870 he married Miss Mary M. Rawlings, and by her has one daughter, Lizzie O. In 1875 his wife died. He is a Knight Templar and was the first master of Temple Lodge.

Allen Parker, a farmer of the Fourth District, was born December 14, 1820, in Rhea County, Tenn., and is the eldest of a family of ten children born to Elisha and Martha (James) Parker. The father was of English descent and came to Hamilton County in 1821. His second wife was a Mrs. Schoolfield, formerly Miss Rice Bythe, who bore him six children. Mr. Parker was quite a prominent citizen of the county, and was justice of the peace for nearly twenty years. He was a soldier under Gen. Andrew Jackson in the Creek war. He died in 1866, seventy-seven years of age. Our subject received his education mostly by individual application. He assisted his father on the farm until nineteen years of age, when he married Miss Dovy Beeson, a daughter of Solomon and Margaret N. Beeson. This union resulted in the birth of these children, viz.: Minerva (Mrs. Fryar), Tandey (deceased), Wiley F., Lizzie (Mrs. Morris), Margaret N. (deceased), James (deceased), John and Jefferson. Mrs. Parker died in 1870, and Mr. Parker took for his second wife Miss Teressa Carden, in 1875 or 1876. She is a daughter of Robert Carden. The result of the last union was the birth of four children: Bobert, Dovy, Ida and Allen. In politics Mr. Parker is a Democrat. He began life as a day laborer; he now owns 1,200 acres of land two miles and a half southwest of the corporation line of Chattanooga. He followed farming until 1854, when he engaged in railroading as a day laborer, and afterward filled the position of contractor and conductor on construction trains, etc. He continued at the business until 1877, since which time he has followed farming. He was elected justice of the peace in 1876, and still holds the office. He has given universal satisfaction in the discharge of the duties of this office. His grandfather, Parker, was a soldier in the Revolutionary war.

William C. Payne, Esq., the subject of this sketch is descended from one of the oldest and most worthy families in Tennessee. His ancestors by both the paternal and maternal sides followed Sevier and Shelby from North Carolina and Virginia to the Watauga settlement about the year 1770; were with them at King's Mountain, and afterward with Gen. James Robertson across the mountains to the French Lick, now the city of Nashville. Josiah Payne, his great-grandfather, was among the first of the little army that penetrated the wilderness to that frontier settlement, and his name appears upon the first tax list that was ever prepared for Davidson County. William Payne, his grandfather, and Elizabeth Payne, his grandmother, both being of the same name and distantly related, were married about the year 1787, and soon thereafter removed to a point on the Cumberland River, about forty-five miles by land east from Nashville to what is now Smith County, cut the cane and built a home in the bend of that river which took its name from his settlement as Payne's Bend, and is still known by that name. John Payne his father, son of William and Elizabeth Payne, was born on this old homestead in the year 1800, grew to manhood, and in 1823 was married to Eunice Graham Chambers, who was born in the year 1805, and was the worthy daughter of John Chambers another early immigrant to that settlement. John Payne died at the old home in April, 1848, his wife Eunice Chambers Payne surviving him many years, and died in the year 1883 at the age of seventy-eight years. William C. Payne our subject, was born to John and Eunice Payne in Smith County, Tenn., on the 9th of August, 1831, being the fourth of six children. He grew up on the old farm, and secured his education first at the country school near his father's home, was afterward sent to Oakland Academy, at Dixon's Springs, in Smith County, Tenn., from there he went to Irving College in Warren County, Tenn., and thence to Cumberland University at Lebanon in Wilson County, Tenn., graduating from the law department of that institution in the year 1855. On the 27th of November, 1852, he was married to Miss Mary Joliffe Bruce, daughter of Dr. Edward H. and Harriet Martin Bruce. Dr. Edward Bruce and wife were Virginians by birth and education, who had moved to and settled in Smith County some years before. Dr. Bruce was the son of Robert Bruce, a Scotch gentleman, who came from Scotland at an early day, and settled in the valley of Virginia near Winchester. He was a lineal descendant from Robert Bruce of Scotland. Our subject, after spending a year in the West, looking about, returned to his native State, and began the practice of law at the town of Sparta in White County, Tenn., in the early part of the year 1857. He at once took good rank in his profession, and was in a few months elected attorney-general for his district, which position he held until the breaking out of the civil war between the States. Being an ardent Southern man, and much attached to his native State, which a long line of honorable ancestry had helped to settle and build up, he entered the Confederate Army in September, 1861, serving first in the infantry, and afterward as a staff officer on the staff of Gen. George G. Dibrell. Though never having sought military honors or preferment, he was an earnest supporter of the Southern cause, until the close of the war. In November, 1866, Mr. Payne moved with his family to the city of Chattanooga, where he has since resided, engaged in the practice of his profession. He has two sisters living: Mrs. Minerva Price, of Hartsville, Trousdale Co., Tenn., and Mrs. Lucy Williams, of East Nashville, Tenn., who with himself compose all that is left of his father's family, the others dying in infancy. He and his estimable wife have had seven children, four of whom only are living: Lucy, Herbert, Margie and Alice. The family are members of the First Presbyterian Church at Chattanooga. In politics he is a Democrat, having ever believed in the teachings of Mr. Jefferson, and a strict construction of the fundamental written law.

Thomas Parkes, vice-president of the Daisy Coal Company, first began prospecting for coal in 1880, and as soon as coal was discovered in paying quantities, opened up the mine and increased the capacity of the mines to one hundred tons daily average. In 1881 a stock company was organized known as the Daisy Coal and Coke Company. Mr. Parkes was born April 16, 1840, in Williamson County, and is the second of six children of Thomas and Elizabeth (Field) Parkes. Mrs. Parkes was a lineal descendant of Lord Scales, one of the early governors of Virginia, and she and her husband were both of English ancestry. Our subject received his education at Franklin Academy. He was united in marriage to Miss S. E. Smith, of Nashville, Tenn., who is a daughter of George W. and Susan Smith. Mr. Smith was of German and Mrs. Smith of English descent. The result of our subject's marriage was the birth of three children: Daisy, George and Thomas. Mr. Parkes was chairman of the board of police commissioners of Nashville for seven years. In May, 1861, he enlisted in Company H, Twentieth Tennessee Infantry of which he was lieutenant and afterward major on Gen. J. Wheeler's staff. He served during the war, was captured but made his escape three weeks afterward. After the war he opened up the Daisy Coal Mines, and was a cotton commission merchant at Nashville, Tenn., style of the firm being

Thomas Parkes & Co. Thomas Parkes, Sr., came to East Tennessee in 1833 to prospect for coal and iron. At that time he purchased land at and near Chattanooga and predicted that that city would be the future Pittsburg of America. He built the first cotton factory in Middle Tennessee, and owned the first steam cotton factory in Middle Tennessee. He was the inventor of the nail cutter now in use, but did not get it patented. Fifteen years later he went to Wheeling, Va., and found his machine in use. It is now about the latest improved nail cutting machine in use. He was the projector and president of the first railroad running south from Nashville, and was a remarkable man in foreseeing the future manufacturing possibilities of the country. The railroad of which he was the projector, running south to Sheffield from Nashville, is now one of the principal routes South. Our subject is a Democrat in politics, and he and wife are members of the Methodist Episcopal Church South.

J. A. N. Patterson, a farmer and merchant at Sale Creek, was born June 17, 1838, in Hamilton County, Tenn., and is the fifth of eleven children born to Lewis and Mary Y. (Pearson) Patterson, eight of whom are now living. Both parents were of Scotch-Irish descent. The father was born in 1796 in Tennessee, and came to this locality before Hamilton County was organized. He was magistrate for many years and died in 1867. He took a great delight in hunting in his earlier days, being considered the best shot and the champion turkey hunter on many occasions. The mother was born in 1806 in Monroe County, Tenn., and died in 1872. Our subject was educated in Sale Creek Academy principally, and assisted his father in farming until twenty-two years of age. July 26, 1860, he married Miss E. S. Coulter, daughter of T. J. and M. J. (Gamble) Coulter, and this union was blessed by the birth of five children, four of whom are living: William Preston, Robert Jefferson, Alfred L., John T. and J. N. (deceased). Mrs. Patterson died in 1877, and in 1879 Mr. Patterson married Margaret H. Wallace, a daughter of Benjamin and Mary Wallace. Mr. and Mrs. Patterson are members of the Presbyterian Church of which he has been an elder since 1868. He is a Democrat and cast his first presidential vote for John Bell. He has been a very successful farm manager and stock raiser. He began life in ordinary circumstances and lost most of his personal property during the late war. In 1862 he enlisted in Company C, First Tennessee Cavalry, and was discharged in 1863. He participated in all the battles and severe skirmishes in which his company took part. In the fall of 1885 he opened a general store at Sale Creek, where he still continues. He is a successful farmer and an excellent citizen.

Starling C. Peeples, of Chattanooga, was born in Gordon County,

Ga., October 25, 1850, and is a son of Drewry and Mary (Collier) Peeples, natives of North Carolina and Georgia respectively. Our subject grew to manhood and received his education in Georgia. In 1870 he came to Chattanooga, and was in the employ of his brother, William O., in the grocery business until the year 1880, when he became a member of the firm of W. O. Peeples & Bros. October 29, 1874, he married Miss Evaline Gregory, of Murray County, Ga., who died October 20, 1885, leaving two daughters: Mary E. and Sarah A. Mr. Peeples is a Democrat in politics, a Knight of Pythias, a member of the Royal Arcanum, A. L. of. H. and the F. L. of H. He is also a member of the Methodist Episcopal Church South.

W. O. Peeples & Bros., wholesale grocers, is individually composed of William O., S. C. and R. B. Peeples. This firm was established in 1868 by W. O. Peeples and W. W. Jackson, succeeded by W. O. Peeples, later by W. O. Peeples and J. C. Edmondson, and still later by W. O. Peeples. About 1880 the present firm was established. In the spring of 1887 the firm erected the large brick hotel and business block at the intersection of Ninth, Chestnut and Carter Streets. It is a triangular shaped building, 140x275 feet at one end, four stories high and a basement. The hotel has 140 rooms, exclusive of office, dining-rooms, parlors, etc., and is estimated to have cost $85,000. There are eight business rooms on the ground floor, besides the hotel office. Two rooms, 50x140 feet, and basement are occupied by W. O. Peeples & Bros., who have two traveling men on the road in the general grocery trade. This trade extends over Alabama, Tennessee and Georgia. They employ four men in the house, besides three of the firm. Their business averages $250,000 per annum, and is one of the most successful wholesale establishments in Chattanooga.

John H. Peebles, superintendent of the union passenger depot and union ticket agent at Chattanooga, was born in Petersburg, Va., June 30, 1849, and is the son of William L. and Rebecca (Harrison) Peebles, both natives of Virginia. Our subject grew up and was educated in his native State. In 1865 he came South, located in Nashville, and was in the employ of the North Carolina & St. Louis Railroad, as baggage master, but later was passenger conductor until 1876, when he came to Chattanooga and was ticket agent at this place for the Western & Atlantic and North Carolina & St. Louis Railroads until 1882, when he accepted his present position. April 18, 1878, he was united in marriage to Elizabeth B. Lanier, a native of Nashville, Tenn., and the fruits of this union were the births of three children—two sons and one daughter. Mr. Peebles is a Democrat in politics, a Knight Templar, a Mason and a member of the Methodist Episcopal Church.

Allen M. Pennock, manager of the Western Union Telegraph office, is a son of William A. and Harriet (Barnes) Pennock, both natives of Pennsylvania, where they grew up and were married. They were Quakers in their religious views. Having lived in Pennsylvania until about 1856 they moved to New Jersey and made that their home. The father was by occupation a tailor. In 1883, while going home from collecting money he was waylaid and killed. After his death the mother moved back to the old home in Philadelphia, where she is now living. To them were born six children, only, three of whom are living— two sons and a daughter. The other son is the inventor of the Pennock Underground Conduit Telegraph System of Brooklyn. Our subject was born September 9, 1857, near where Washington crossed the Delaware in New Jersey. He received his education in the common schools, and when nine years of age learned telegraphy. At the age of fourteen he attended New Jersey College at Bordentown, after which he returned to his former business and worked for several years under a train dispatcher. He was then made manager of Bordentown Western Union office where he continued two years and then accepted the position of manager of the office at Chester, Penn. He was night manager of all the telegraph lines that ran to the Centennial grounds. He was with the Baltimore & Ohio Railroad as operator nine months; was also operator at New York until 1878, when he came to Chattanooga. The following year he became day chief, and in 1885 was appointed manager, which position he is holding at present. In the latter year he married Miss Maggie Ragsdale. Mr. Pennock has under his charge three clerks, nine operators, five messengers, two line men and one battery man. He is a Knight of Pythias and a member of the Baptist Church. Mrs. Pennock is a member of the Methodist Episcopal Church.

H. H. Poe, farmer at Daisy, was born November 24, 1845, on the farm where he now resides. He is the second of eight children born to Samuel P. and Mary (Bryant) Poe. The father was born in Virginia and came to Daisy, Tenn., with his father when only eight years old. He raised a regiment for the Mexican war and was elected major, but before starting received orders not to come as the war was at an end. He engaged in business at old Dallas, the first county seat, and was one of the first men to sell goods in Hamilton County. He died in November, 1866. The first county court was held at the house of H. Poe, grandfather of our subject. He (H. Poe) was a soldier in the war of 1812. The mother of our subject was born near Daisy, Tenn., and died in 1863. H. H. Poe received his education in the common schools of Hamilton County. He assisted his father on the farm until twenty-one years of age, after which he began working for himself. He now has 250 acres of the best land in the Tennessee Valley and is quite comfortably fixed. In 1878 he married Miss Ruth Champion, who was born August 11, 1845. The fruits of this union were three children: Myrtle, Porter and Edgar. Mr. and Mrs. Poe are members of the Cumberland Presbyterian Church, of which he has been deacon for two years. He is a Democrat in politics. Mr. Poe's grandfather got the first charter for and built the first turnpike in Hamilton County, the one running from the Tennessee to the Sequatchie Valley, known as the Poe Turnpike.

Dr. E. H. Price, physician, of Chattanooga, and son of Joel and Edith (Martin) Price, was born May 31, 1833, in Baltimore County, Md. He secured an academic education and, after teaching a short time, began the study of medicine, but was interrupted by the breaking out of the late war. Having moved to Ohio, he helped raise Company C, Eleventh Ohio Infantry (United States Army), and at first was first lieutenant, but in 1862 was promoted to the rank of captain of the same company. The last year of his service he was brigade inspector on the staff of Gen. John B. Turchon. After the war he took a course of lectures at Cleveland Homœopathic Medical College, and in 1869 came to Chattanooga and practiced until 1872. One year later he graduated at Pulte Medical College at Cincinnati, Ohio, and since then he has practiced at Chattanooga. Previous to the war in 1856 he married Sarah C. McConnell, a native of Maryland, who bore him two children—both daughters. The Doctor is a successful physician, and is doing well in his profession. He was one of the first police commissioners of Chattanooga, was a member of the first board of health, was school commissioner of his ward several years, and is universally respected. His parents were natives of Maryland and Pennsylvania respectively. The father was a farmer, and died in Ohio while on a visit to that State. The mother died a few years later. Three of the father's brothers were soldiers in the war of 1812, but at that time he was too young to participate.

Dr. John R. Rathmell was born in Franklin County, Ohio, August 6, 1853, and is one of eight children—three sons and five daughters—born to the union of John and Susan (Frank) Rathmell, natives of Ohio and Pennsylvania respectively. The father was a farmer and followed agricultural pursuits all his life. Our subject graduated from the classical course of Ohio Wesleyan University in 1880, and from the Starling Medical College, Columbus, Ohio, in 1883. The same year he came to Chattanooga, where he has practiced his profession ever since. As a physician he has been successful, being progressive, studious, candid and practical. Soon after coming to Chattanooga he was made secretary of the board of health, and was president of the same board in 1887. He is a member of the Chattanooga Medical Association and of the Medical Society of the State of Tennessee. In 1883 he married Miss Edith Beach of West Jefferson, Ohio, and the result of this union was one child, Maude. Dr. Rathmell is a Free Mason, being Worshipful Master for 1887 of Chattanooga Lodge, No. 199. In 1885 the degree of A. M. was conferred upon him by his *Alma Mater*. He and Mrs. Rathmell are members of the Methodist Episcopal Church.

Rev. G. C. Rankin, D. D., pastor of the Centenary Methodist Episcopal Church South, is a native of Jefferson County, Tenn., born November 19, 1849, and the son of Creed W. and Martha J. (Clark) Rankin, both natives of East Tennessee. The Rankin family has produced twenty-three preachers—twenty-one Presbyterians, one Congregational and one Methodist Episcopal. Creed W. was a farmer by occupation and died in 1862. The mother is still living. Our subject is the only living child of a family of seven children. He was educated in the common schools and at Hiwassee College from which institution he graduated in 1874. Since that time he has been engaged in his ministerial duties at the following places, respectively: Abingdon, Va; Asheville, N. C.; Knoxville, Tenn., and Chattanooga, where he is at the present time. In 1875 he married Miss Fannie Denton, of Dalton, Ga., who bore him five children—one son and four daughters. Mrs Rankin is also a member of the Methodist Episcopal Church. Mr. Rankin is a mason, and has been preaching the gospel for twelve years. He came to Chattanooga in 1883, and is an able and faithful minister. He received the degree of D. D. from the University of Tennessee in the year 1879.

Dr. William E. Raht, a retired physician of Chattanooga, is a son of Julius E. and Matilda (Dombois) Raht, both natives of Germany, where they were reared. The parents came to America thirty-five years ago, and found a home in Tennessee. For many years the father was superintendent of the Coffer Mines in Polk County. He was a mining engineer and a graduate of a German college. He died in 1879. The mother is still living. Their family consisted of eight children, our subject being the third. He was born in Polk County, Tenn., February 6, 1858, and while growing up had good educational advantages. He paid considerable attention to mathematics. He spent three years at Sheffield Scientific School of Yale College, and graduated in medicine from the University of Pennsylvania in 1883 as an allopathic physician. He also took a post graduate course at Hahnemann Homœopathic Medical College, after which he came to Chattanooga and entered into partnership with Dr. D. G.

Curtis with whom he practiced until 1886. In 1883 he married Alice Edmiston, a native of Logan County, Ohio, by whom he had one son, Theodore. Dr. Raht is a Knight of Pythias, and since retiring from his profession, has been devoting his energies to surveying.

J. Foster Rogers, miller and farmer near St. Elmo, was born September 26, 1849, in the Second District of Hamilton County, and is the youngest of nine children born to Joseph and Rebecca (Hixon) Rogers. The father was born in Greene County, Tenn., about 1801, and died about 1854. He was of Irish descent, and a farmer and stock raiser by occupation. He began life in very ordinary circumstances, and succeeded in accumulating quite a handsome fortune. The mother was born in Greene County in 1803, and was of Dutch descent. She was a member of the Methodist Episcopal Church, and died in 1882. Our subject received his education in the Hamilton County common schools, and in 1866 he studied law with Richard Arnet, a lawyer in Hamilton, now James County. He moved to the Eighth District in the fall of 1868. In December of the next year he moved to his farm in the Seventeenth District where he now resides. January 14, 1869, he married Miss M. J. Kirklen, who was born October 8, 1849, and who is the daughter of Elisha, Sr., and Susan Kirklen. To Mr. and Mrs. Rogers were born three children, two of whom are living: Ida and Arra. He was assistant tax collector during the years 1872 and 1873, was elected and has served as tax assessor eleven years. He was elected justice of the peace of the Seventeenth District in 1876 and re-elected in 1882, but resigned in October, 1886. He has been a successful farmer, and a very successful real estate and stock dealer. He now owns forty-three acres near St. Elmo, sixty-four acres in the Sixteenth District, and also half interest in the flour-mill near Hixon Station, the individual members of the firm being P. A. and J. Foster Rogers. Besides his land and mill property Mr. Rogers has mortgages due him to the amount of $17,000. He also owns four acres of land in St. Elmo. He is a Democrat in politics, and is an enterprising citizen.

Jesse C. Roberson, farmer of the Fifteenth District, was born February 10, 1820, in Bledsoe County, and came to Hamilton County in June, 1862. He is the ninth of twelve children born to James and Margaret (Worthington) Roberson. The father was born in Anderson County, Tenn., in 1784, on Clinch River, and was of Scotch descent. He moved to Bledsoe County in 1805, was the first settler in Sequatchie Valley and suffered all the hardships and privations incident to pioneer life. At first he had to go eighty miles to mill. He represented Bledsoe and Marion Counties in the State Legislature in 1829 and 1830. He was a very successful farmer and trader, accumulating a large fortune, and was a prominent citizen of the county. He was a major in the State Militia, a deacon in the Baptist Church, and was the first man in that county to send his children away to school. He died in August, 1851. Mrs. Roberson was born in 1785, and died January 28, 1828. She was of English descent. He married, the second time, Miss Sallie Hutchinson, by whom he had four children. Our subject received his education in the University of Knoxville, and at the age of eighteen was thrown upon his own resources. He wedded Miss Mary Shepherd February 15, 1863. She is the daughter of Lewis and Margaret (Donohoo) Shepherd. Mr. Shepherd was born in Newberry District, S. C., in 1796, and died November 2, 1856. Mrs. Shepherd was born in Monroe County, Tenn., in 1811, and is still living. Mrs. Shepherd's father, Mr. Charles Donohoo, came to Monroe County at quite an early day, locating first in a fort. He was sheriff of that county for many years. His father was an Irish weaver, and was quite prominent in Ireland. Our subject's great-grandfather, on his mother's side, came from England to America with Lord Baltimore, and settled in Baltimore County, Md. Many of his descendants now live there, wealthy and prominent citizens. Our subject began life a poor man, and when twenty-seven years of age his father gave him $600 and he received some property by his wife, the balance has been acquired by his own industry and splendid management. During the late war much of his property was destroyed and taken by the armies which infested the neighborhood quite frequently. The war left him $28,000 in debt, which he has about liquidated. He now owns a fine farm of over 2,900 acres in Hamilton County, and also owns 1,600 acres in the Sequatchie Valley. To Mr. and Mrs. Roberson were born four children: Sallie M., Lewis Shepherd, Mary Worthington and Jessie Kankin. Mr. and Mrs. Roberson are of Baptist belief, and their daughters are members of that church. Mr. Roberson is a Royal Arch Mason, was a Whig in politics before the war, a Republican afterward, and is now a stanch Prohibitionist. He is a man well known for his honest dealings, has never pleaded usury nor taken advantage of the bankrupt law. His children have had good educational advantages for the last twelve years in the city of Chattanooga.

J. C. Roberts, farmer, is a native of Tennessee, born June 1, 1835. He is the youngest of five children born to the union of Thomas and Sarah J. (Kennedy) Roberts, both natives of North Carolina. The father was born in North Carolina in 1801, came to Tennessee in 1832 and settled on Buffalo River. He removed to Hamilton County in 1838, and was a very successful farmer. He died about 1879. The mother was born about 1795. She was an active and devoted member of the Methodist Episcopal Church for many years. She died in 1863. Our subject received his education in the common schools of Hamilton County. He wedded Miss Arabella Pickett, June 24, 1855, daughter of Mrs. Margaret Pickett. One child was the result of this union, who died in infancy. Mrs. Roberts died in 1857, and for his second wife Mr. Roberts took Miss Nancy Adaline Moreland in October, 1858. She is a daughter of Pleasant and Margaret Moreland. Mrs. Roberts was born in May, 1836, and this last union resulted in the birth of eleven children: Malinda (deceased), Thomas (deceased), John W., James M., Mattie, Cynthia, Sallie, Bell, Mary, Willie and Lulla. Mr. and Mrs. Roberts and the eldest five children are members of the Methodist Episcopal Church. In politics Mr. Roberts is a Democrat. He has followed farming all his life, excepting time spent in the late war. He enlisted in September, 1862, in Lookout battery, which operated principally in Mississippi. He was in the fights at Jackson (Miss.), Resaca and Atlanta, and was mustered out of service after the fight at Atlanta. He served the people of his district as justice of the peace for four years, and was a member of the county court, giving universal satisfaction. He takes quite an interest in education, and his children have had good educational advantages. Starting in life with very little, he now has property valued at $35,000. His grandfather, Roberts, came from Ireland to America about the time of the Revolutionary war, and settled shortly after in North Carolina.

P. A. Rogers, miller and farmer of the Second District, was born March 2, 1846, in Hamilton County, the son of Joseph and Rebecca (Hixon) Rogers. The father was born in 1803, in the Sequatchie Valley, and died in August, 1855. The mother was born in 1806, also in the Sequatchie Valley, and was for over sixty years a zealous Christian worker in the Methodist Episcopal Church. She died in 1882. Our subject received his education mostly in the country schools of Hamilton County, and attended Sequatchie College one term. He worked on the farm until the breaking out of the late war, when he enlisted in Company I, Second East Tennessee Infantry, and served until the latter part of February, 1865, when he was mustered out at Knoxville. He was engaged in all the battles and skirmishes in which his command took part, the principal battle being Stone River. After the cessation of hostilities our subject returned home and engaged in agricultural pursuits, which he followed until 1875. He then engaged in the milling business with his brother, under the firm name of Rogers & Bro. Our subject also owns 500 acres of fine land on the Tennessee River, in addition to his interest in the mill, and is in very comfortable circumstances. In 1869 he married Miss Mary E. Rogers, a native of Hamilton County, born in 1845, and the daughter of Henry and Charity (Wingo) Rogers. To our subject and wife were born seven children: Lenora E., Earnest A., Arabell, Volney E., Garance A., Leon A. and Gertie. Mr. Rogers is a Democrat in politics, casting his first presidential vote for H. Seymour.

J. C. Rogers, farmer and blacksmith, was born in Hamilton County, Tenn., April 11, 1834, and is the second of eight children born to George W. and Catherine (Jackson) Rogers. He attended school but very little in his life, and his education was received principally at the family fireside. He married Miss Mary W. Smith in March, 1854, but remained on the farm with his father until 1855. Mrs. Rogers was born in Hamilton County in 1833, and is the daughter of Elijah and Nancy Smith. To our subject and wife were born these children: Elijah W. (deceased), James M., George A. (deceased) and William M. Mrs. Rogers died July 18, 1867, and September 5, 1867, he married Miss Lydia Barker, a native of Sequatchie County, born November 3, 1837, and the daughter of John H. and Nancy Barker. They have two children: Ransom, born June 27, 1868, and Emma, born August 27, 1870. Mr. and Mrs. Rogers are members of the Methodist Episcopal Church South. In politics Mr. Rogers is a Democrat. He was elected justice of the peace in 1872, and held the office the following six years after which he resigned. He was school commissioner of his district for twenty years and has been steward of his church for twelve years. In 1862 he enlisted in Company D, Fourth Georgia Mounted Infantry (Confederate Army), and went out as orderly sergeant. After the battle of Chickamauga he was promoted to the rank of second lieutenant. He came home in May, 1864, and afterward volunteered for home protection, but was forced into service in the regular army of the United States. Mr. Rogers was a brave, obedient soldier, and had the confidence of his superior officers. Our subject has always lived in Tennessee with the exception of about eighteen months in Illinois, where his father moved when J. C. was about fourteen. He has followed farming all his life, but being a natural mechanic can turn his hand to most any kind of work in wood and iron. He is now quite comfortably fixed to enjoy life. His father was born in Monroe County, Tenn., in 1812, was justice of the peace of his district for several years, and was also deputy sheriff of Hamilton County the term beginning in 1840. He was a licensed exhorter in the Methodist Episcopal Church. He was a very zealous and devoted Christian worker from the time he joined the church until his death in February, 1886. The mother was born in Sequatchie

County in 1810. She died about October, 1880. She was a helpless cripple from rheumatism the last eight years of her life. She was an exemplary Christian from early womanhood.

W. B. Seymour & Co., proprietors of the planing-mill and lumber yards, Chattanooga, established their business in September, 1883. The company is individually composed of Walter B. Seymour and Henry T. Olmstead, who have their mills and yards located between Burton and East Streets and East Tennessee, Virginia & Georgia Railroad tracks. They employ seventy to eighty men, and handle on an average 4,000,000 feet of lumber annually. Walter B. Seymour was born in Connecticut in November, 1858, and came to Chattanooga in 1882. He traveled for the Southern Lumber Company, of Chattanooga, for one year, and then established the present business in which they are succeeding unusually well. Mr. Seymour is a Republican in politics, a member of the Masonic fraternity, and is an active business man.

Hon. Alonzo G. Sharp, present mayor of Chattanooga, is a native of Fulton County, N. Y., his birth occurring January 2, 1841, son of John and Victoria Sharp, who were natives of Manchester, England. The parents immigrated to America in 1831 and until 1847 resided at Fulton County, N. Y., engaged in farming; then moved to Franklin County, Ohio, where the father died, leaving a widow, three sons and eight daughters to mourn their loss. About this time, and while yet a mere boy, the subject of this sketch started out into the world to act and do for himself. He succeeded in securing a good practical education by much perseverance and industry, and at the time of the breaking out of hostilities between the North and South was acting in the capacity of book-keeper in the commission house of J. R. Paul & Co., of Columbus, Ohio. In April, 1861, immediately after the assault upon Fort Sumter, he enlisted as a private in Company C, Second Ohio Volunteer Infantry, and was a participant in the first battle of Bull Run. When his term of enlistment had expired he organized a new company for the service of which he was elected captain. This was Company B, Forty-sixth Ohio Volunteer Infantry. The regiment was ordered to Paducah, Ky., under command of Gen. W. T. Sherman, and from there up the Tennessee River to Shiloh, Corinth, Memphis and on into Mississippi. Before starting on the campaign against Vicksburg, Capt. Sharp was compelled to resign from the service on account of ill health, and he returned to Ohio to recuperate. November 17, 1864, he united in marriage with Miss Jennie Cushman, of Columbus, Ohio, and shortly after this event located in Chattanooga, Tenn., where he has since mostly resided, closely identified with the city's business interests and prosperity. His career as a civil officer began in 1867 when he was elected city treasurer, and from that time until the present he has been almost continuously in public life. In 1867-68 he was city treasurer, and in 1869 was mayor of the city, also serving as director in the Tennessee penitentiary at the same time. In 1870 he served about six months as clerk and master of Hamilton County Chancery Court under appointment of Chancellor D. C. Trewhitt. The fall of 1870 he was elected city recorder, and after serving two elective terms, was elected city attorney, serving one year. At the close of his second term of recorder he formed a legal partnership with Judge D. C. Trewhitt, and practiced law until 1873, when he was appointed by President Grant internal revenue collector for the Third Tennessee District, in which position he served until they were consolidated. In March, 1877, he was appointed an inspector in the postoffice department by Postmaster-General D. M. Key, and in charge of a force resided with his family at San Francisco four years. He then returned to Chattanooga, but removed to Washington, D. C., to fill the appointment of chief inspector of the United States. He resigned this position in September, 1885, and again returning to his old home in Chattanooga was, the month following, elected mayor of the city to serve two years. Mr. Sharp is one of the Republican leaders of Tennessee.

C. E. Shelton, farmer of the Fifteenth District, is the youngest of five children born to C. E. and Sarah (Williams) Shelton. The father was born about 1788, probably in Virginia, and moved to Rhea County about 1820. He was an officer in the Creek Indian war, serving nearly two years. He was sheriff of Rhea County one term and also trustee for two terms. He served one term as county surveyor, and was justice of the peace of his district for twelve years. He was one of Rhea County's most prominent citizens, and was highly respected by all. He died in 1833. The mother was born in Virginia in 1790, and moved to Granger County, Tenn., where she married. She died in 1862. Our subject was born in Rhea County, Tenn., in 1822, and moved to Hamilton County in 1849, settling near where he now resides. He received his education in the subscription schools of Rhea and Hamilton Counties. He took charge of his mother's farm and supported her after he became twenty years of age. In December, 1846, he married Miss Nancy Walker, daughter of William and Rachel Walker, the first settlers of Bledsoe County, Tenn. Mrs. Shelton was born in 1829 in Bledsoe County, and to her and Mr. Shelton were born ten children: Matilda (deceased), Azariah (now trustee of Hamilton County for the second term), William, Martha (Mrs. Selcer), Mira (deceased), Sallie (Mrs. Fryar), Tennessee (deceased), Mary A., McKinney and Jane. Mr. and Mrs. Shelton and all their children but one, are members of the Cumberland Presbyterian Church, of which Mr. Shelton has been elder for ten years. He was reared a Whig, and is now a Republican in politics. He is also a Master Mason. He was elected justice of the peace in 1853, served one term, and was elected again in 1877. He was deputy sheriff of Hamilton County two years. He has a fine farm of 240 acres in one tract, and 340 acres about two miles from where he resides, both well cultivated. Mr. Shelton's father-in-law, Mr. William Walker, was trustee of Bledsoe County for twelve years, was highly respected, and an influential citizen. His wife was of Dutch descent, as were also Mr. and Mrs. Shelton, Sr. Our subject has always been ready and willing to aid in the advancement of educational interests in his neighborhood, being one of the five who furnished the greatest bulk of funds required in building the academy near his residence.

Azariah Shelton, the present efficient trustee of Hamilton County, is descended from one of the old pioneer families of the State. He is a native of the county in which he now resides, and was born on the 24th of January, 1850. His early education was quite limited, the ordinary three months' country schooling being all the advantages accorded him, but with the energy and perseverance characteristic of the subject of this sketch, managed to acquire more than an average education, which he has in later years steadily improved. When quite young he was apprenticed to a blacksmith, which trade he fully mastered, but this occupation was abandoned for that of the teacher's profession. He soon took the lead in his chosen profession, and in a creditably short time was elected to the office of county superintendent of public instruction on the first day of January, 1878, entered upon his second term in 1880, and in August, 1882, was elected trustee and tax collector for his native county, and is at present serving his third term. As a business man Mr. Shelton has no superior, and enjoys an enviable reputation throughout the State, and the State accounting officers are loud in their praises of his method of conducting the business of his office, and is exceedingly popular with all who enjoy an acquaintance with him. When but eighteen years old, August 27, 1868, he formed a happy union with Miss Hattie A. Carper, a native of Hamilton County, and by her is the father of one son and four daughters. He is a leading member of this county in the Masonic and Odd Fellow fraternities.

C. C. Shelton, manufacturer of flour and meal, and dealer in grain and feed, is a native of Jackson County, Ala., where he was reared and educated. He resided in that locality until 1871, when he came to Chattanooga and embarked in the grocery trade, at which he continued until

1876, when he built and began the operation of his present mills, situated at 136, 138 and 140 Market Street. He is doing a large business, manufacturing about 150 barrels of flour per day, and for this he finds a ready wholesale market in Tennessee, Alabama and Georgia principally. Mr. Shelton is a member of the board of trade of Chattanooga, and is one of the city's most respected and enterprising citizens. In 1866 he united in marriage with Miss Mary J. Baker, a native of the same county as himself, and to their union two sons and one daughter (deceased) have been born: George M. and Clement Lee. The parents of the subject of this sketch, Shepherd and Rose (Chapman) Shelton, were natives of the Old Dominion; were reared in North Carolina, from where they removed to Middle Tennessee, thence to Jackson County, Ala., where they followed farming until their respective deaths in 1875 and 1885.

G. M. Sherwood was born July 14, 1839, in New York, and is the eighth of nine children born to Amos and Mary (Campbell) Sherwood. They were of English and Scotch descent, respectively. The father was born in 1802 in Connecticut, and moved to the suburbs of Syracuse, N. Y., when a young man. He was quite a prominent man of the locality where he resided, taking part in all questions pertaining to the public interest. He died in the year 1858. The mother was born in Onondaga County, N. Y., in the year 1804, and was a member and an active worker in the Presbyterian Church. She died in the year 1867. Our subject received his education principally at Onondaga Academy; began business for himself at the age of eighteen, and in 1862 married Miss Fannie Butts, daughter of Nelson and Prudence Butts, who were old and prominent citizens of Onondaga County, N. Y. Mr. Sherwood had the misfortune to lose his wife in 1862, and in 1866 he married Miss Sarah M. Woodbury, a daughter of Francis and Maria P. Woodbury. To this union were born five children: Mary C., George W., Clara, Juliet and Edward Marshall. After marriage our subject engaged in the boot and shoe business in Jackson, Mich., where he moved in the year 1864, the style of the firm being Sherwood Bros. He sold his stock of boots and shoes, and came to Chattanooga in April, 1870, where he engaged in the same business for six years. He was elected city recorder, serving in that capacity for four years; he was out one year and then was re-elected and served one year. He was a member of the county court about seven years, after which he moved out to Mission Ridge, purchased 80 acres of land, and since then has engaged extensively in buying and selling real estate. Mr. Sherwood is a Republican in politics. His brother, Harvey C. Sherwood, has been a member of the State

Senate of Michigan, and was a Democratic candidate of the Fourth District for Congress, but was defeated by a prominent Republican. Although the district was strongly Republican, he led his competitor a hot chase. Mr. and Mrs. Sherwood are members of the Second Presbyterian Church of Chattanooga, of which Mr. Sherwood is an elder.

P. D. Sims, M. D., is a native of Jackson County, Tenn., and one of five children, three of whom are living, born to the marriage of Martin and Nancy (Smith) Sims. They were married in Jackson County, Tenn., and the father has followed agricultural pursuits all his life. He is still living and is eighty-seven years of age. The mother's parents came from Scotland and settled in North Carolina, but later moved to Tennessee. She died in 1851. Our subject was born October 22, 1828, was reared on a farm and educated in Alpine Institute, private school. After taking some private instruction in professional studies he graduated from the medical department of the University of Nashville in 1856. The same year he came to Chattanooga, where he has remained ever since, passing through the several epidemics. He is a member of the county and state medical societies and also of the American Medical Association. He was at one time mayor of Chattanooga. Six children, three of whom are living, were born to his union with Miss Mary Randall in 1857. She was a native of Middle Tennessee, a member of the Cumberland Presbyterian Church, and died in 1879. Dr. Sims is also a member of the Cumberland Presbyterian Church, a Royal Arch Mason, and has practiced his profession for thirty-one years.

F. W. Skillern, M. D., is a native of Bledsoe County, born July 19, 1851, a graduate of Sequatchie College in 1868, and also a graduate of the medical department of Vanderbilt University in 1876. The following year he moved to Texas, where he remained until 1883, and then returned to Tennessee. In 1875 he married Miss Alice Williams, a native of Tennessee, but reared in Texas. Two children were the result of this union: Mattie J. and Willie Maud. Mrs. Skillern is a consistent member of the Methodist Episcopal Church South. In 1886 Dr. Skillern located in Chattanooga. He is a Mason, Knight of Pythias, and for twelve years has been engaged in the practice of his profession. He is the son of William and Martha (Farrar) Skillern. The father was born in Bledsoe County, Tenn., and his ancestors came from the Emerald Isle. The mother was born in Bath County, Va. She descended from an old English family. After their marriage they settled in Rhea County, Tenn., where the father was quite an extensive stock trader. The mother died in 1865, after which the father married Miss Sarah

Henninger; he is still living. To his first marriage were born four children—two sons and two daughters—and to his last union only one child was born.

J. P. Smartt, senior member of the firm of Smartt Bros. & Co., wholesale boot and shoe dealers, was born in Warren County, Tenn., in 1844. His parents, George M. and Anna (Waterhouse) Smartt, were natives of Tennessee. The father was a farmer, and a man who took an active interest in the welfare of his community. In 1857 he was sent by the people of his county to represent them in the General Assembly. In 1871 the mother died, but the father is still living. To them were born nine children—four sons and five daughters. After the death of his wife the father was again married, with the result of three children. Our subject was reared on the farm, and educated at McMinnville College, and also at Hannah Highland College. In 1862 he volunteered in Company C, Sixteenth Tennessee Infantry, Confederate Army, and during three years of service never missed a day. At the cessation of hostilities he returned and taught at Hannah Highland College, where he had received the principal part of his education. In 1868 he went to Nashville, where he was engaged respectively in the wholesale drug, boot and shoe and hat business. In 1875 he came to Chattanooga, and has since been a prominent factor in the business progress of the city. In 1879 Rowena Kennedy, of Chattanooga, became his wife, and the fruits of this union were three children—two sons and one daughter. Mr. Smartt is director, and formerly vice-president of the Third National Bank; is director of Mountain City First Marine City Insurance Company; is director and vice-president of the Chattanooga Investment Company; has been president of the board of trade; is director in the Chattanooga Springs Company, and is a member of the Cumberland Presbyterian Church, having been an elder in the same since 1866.

Hon. H. J. Springfield, farmer, was born September 15, 1841, in Murray County, Ga., and is the youngest of six children born to Solomon Langston and Catherine (Bradley) Springfield, both natives of Greenville County, S. C. The father was born August 15, 1807, and was of English descent. He was a soldier in the Indian war, and assisted in their removal from Georgia. He died March 23, 1842. He was one of the best school teachers of his day and excelled in penmanship. He had the reputation of being the most courageous and muscular man of the State. The mother was born September 15, 1809, and is still living, making her home with her son. Our subject received his education in the common schools of Georgia and in St. Clair County, Ala. He has also a good business education. He lived eighteen years in St. Clair

County, Ala., and then moved to Chattanooga, after which he went to Chickamauga station and then to Tyner, where he engaged in merchandising eight years, the style of the firm being H. J. Springfield & Bro. He was elected sheriff of Hamilton County in 1878, after which his brother took entire control of the business, and in 1880 they sold the entire stock. Our subject was twice elected to the office of sheriff by the people, and, in 1882, after being out of office thirty days, was elected by the county court to fill a vacancy caused by murder. While sheriff he was one of the bravest and most courageous officers ever in Hamilton County. He filled the unexpired term of the sheriff who was murdered by the Taylor brothers, desperadoes, and played a very important part in apprehension and execution of Andy Taylor. He captured John Taylor in the northeastern part of Tennessee, and lodged him in the jail at Chattanooga. He was a member of the Constitutional Convention in Alabama, in 1867, which effected the reconstruction of and restoration to the Union of Alabama, Georgia and Florida. He was appointed by the State superintendent of registration as a member and chairman of the board of registration in his district. He also represented his district in the State Legislature of Alabama in 1868-69; was appointed United States marshall by Gen. Grant in 1870, but declined the appointment because of his having previously decided to move to Tennessee. December 24, 1861, he married Miss Mary C. Masteller, of St. Clair, Ala., who died in 1864. They had one child, James Henry (deceased). He married his second wife, Miss Joicey L. Simpson, in 1866, and she died the same year. In 1869 he married Miss Mary E. Franklin, of St. Clair County, Ala., and five children have blessd this last union: Willard J., Charles, Almera, Walter M. and Edgar C. Mr. and Mrs. Springfield are members of the Methodist Episcopal Church, and he is a Master Mason. He enlisted in the spring of 1863 in the Federal Army and served as captain. He has been a life-long Republican, casting his first presidential vote for Gen. Grant.

N. C. Steele, M. D., is a successful physician of Chattanooga, and the fourth child of a family of seven children born to J. N. and Mary A. Steele, natives respectively of South Carolina and Alabama. At the age of seven his father left his native State and came to Alabama, where at the age of twenty-nine he married Miss Steele, a native of that State, though not a relative. Three of their four boys are ministers of the gospel. Our subject was born September 20, 1849, near Athens, Limestone Co., Ala., and at the age of five was taken to Mississippi. Living near Corinth, that State, one of the great military stations of the war, and in the vicinity of the famous battles of Corinth and Shiloh, his father's fortune was almost totally swept away. This and the impaired condition of his health seriously interfered with his studies, but at the age of twenty-one he began the study of medicine under Dr. J. M. Taylor, of Corinth, one of the most prominent physicians of Mississippi. After studying there a year he took one course of lectures in the medical department of the University of Louisville, Ky., and a second course in the medical department of the University of Nashville, from which latter institution he graduated with honor, in February, 1873, having taken the prize for the best thesis on "The Action of Quinine," and divided the prize for standing the best examination on the principles and practice of surgery. After practicing in Mississippi for thirteen years he went to Europe in 1886, to make a special study of the diseases of the eye, ear and nose, to which he had for several years been devoting much attention. In that year he was a highly endorsed and strong applicant for the chair of eye and ear in the medical department of the University of Nashville and Vanderbilt University, made vacant by the death of Prof. V. S. Lindsley. On returning from Europe, wishing a large city in which to practice his specialties, he removed to Chattanooga in the latter part of 1886. In 1875 Miss Frances E. Jones, of Mississippi, became his wife. To them have been born three children, two of whom are living: Mary T. and Willard H. Both he and wife are members of the Cumberland Presbyterian Church, he being a ruling elder in that church. The Doctor is an honorary member of the Mississippi State Medical Society, a member of the Tri-State Medical Association of Mississippi, Arkansas and Tennessee, and of the Chattanooga Medical Society. In 1884 he graduated from the Chautauqua Literary and Scientific Circle. He is a Mason, a good citizen, a total abstainer from all intoxicating liquors, and a Prohibitionist.

Theodore F. Stewart, of Chattanooga, was born in Atkins County, Ohio, March 12, 1846, and is the son of Hiram Stewart, of that State. Our subject was reared under the parental roof, and educated in his native State. In 1861 he enlisted in the Thirty-ninth Regiment Ohio Volunteer Infantry, United States Army, and gave four years' service to his country's cause. In March, 1866, he came to Chattanooga, and accepted a position as teller in the First National Bank, where he continued eighteen years. Failing health obliged him to abandon this sedentary employment, and he then engaged in the insurance business until 1887. Mr. Stewart has been prominently identified with various manufactories in Chattanooga, and was secretary and treasurer of Lookout ice factory, also a director in the wood and dish factory. He was connected with the cotton-mills, and with Mr. Blair operated a roller corn meal mill (roller process) one year, during 1886. He is at present director in the First National Bank. In January, 1887, he engaged in the real estate business, to which he is now giving most of his attention. November 1, 1870, he married Miss Celia M. Shaffer, of Delaware, Ohio, who bore him one child, Bessie M. Mr. Stewart is a Republican in politics, a member of the G. A. R., and the Methodist Episcopal Church.

Arthur G. Stivers, of the firm of Loomis, Hart & Co., was born in Meigs County, Ohio, September 23, 1855, and is the son of Washington and Caroline (Fisher) Stivers, natives respectively of New York and Ohio. Our subject was reared to manhood in his native county, and received his education in the schools of his native State. He came South in 1878, and located at Chattanooga, where he has been connected with the firm of Loomis, Hart & Co. ever since. He has charge of the office at 115 and 117 West Eighth Street, also has charge of the sash, door and blind departments at the above numbers. May 8, 1883, he was united in marriage to Miss Fannie Pickens, of Racine, Ohio, who bore him one son. Mr. Stivers is a Republican in politics, a Knight Templar, and a Mason, being High Priest of Hamilton Chapter of this city. The firm of Loomis, Hart & Co. is individually composed of J. F. Loomis, John A. Hart, James T. Arnold, F. L. Winchester, A. J. Gohagan and A. G. Stivers. The business was established in 1866 by J. F. Loomis and F. J. Bennett who conducted the saw mill and lumber business at the foot of Pine and Cedar Streets until 1875. John A. Hart succeeded Mr. Bennett. The firm of Loomis & Hart inaugurated the manufacture of furniture, which they continued until 1884, when the present company became proprietors. The mill and works cover sixteen acres of ground on the bank of the Tennessee River, and at the foot of Pine and Cedar Streets. In 1887 they erected a large, three-story frame warehouse at the corner of Pine and Water Streets. The dimensions of this building are 60x180 feet. The up-town office and large sash, door and blind warehouse is situated at 115 and 117 West Eighth Street. They employ on an average 150 men, and the business will approximate $200,000 per year. They saw and handle about 12,000,000 feet of lumber per year.

M. E. Stone, merchant and postmaster at Divine, Tenn., was born July 3, 1850, in Chattooga County, Ga., and is the second of seven children born to William and Annie (Junkins) Stone. The father was born in North Carolina about 1823, and was captain of the State militia of the district in which he resided. He taught school and has been bailiff of the county for two terms. The mother was born about 1832 in South Carolina, and her parents were J. W. and Annie Junkins, who came from Ireland to South Carolina about 1820, settling in Franklin County, where Mrs. Stone was born. She died in 1865. Mr. and Mrs. Stone were active Christian workers in the church since early in life. Mr. Stone has always been a member of the Methodist Episcopal Church, and Mrs. Stone first joined the Cumberland Presbyterian Church but after marriage joined the Methodist Episcopal Church. Mr. Stone is a licensed minister in the church, and has served the organization to which he belongs as a class leader and in other capacities for some time. He is of German and Holland descent. Our subject received his education in the Chattooga County common schools principally. He assisted his father on the farm until nineteen years of age, when he was thrown upon his own resources. Mr. Stone is a very promising young man. He followed farming until 1880, when he engaged in business at his present location. One year from that date, there being need of a postoffice at this place, Mr. Stone was commissioned to fill the position of postmaster under Thomas L. James, the postmaster-general at that time. Mr. Stone commenced life in very limited circumstances, but by energy and enterprise he has succeeded in a very creditable manner. He has as fine a stock of goods as is to be found in any country store. He built the first store in this locality, and has increased his business until his sales amount to $9,000 per year. He is a Democrat in politics, casting his first presidential vote for Horatio Seymour. Besides his store building and stock of goods Mr. Stone owns five acres of land, two and a half miles from the corporation limits of Chattanooga, and is a valuable piece of property. His grandfather, Stone, was a very prominent citizen of the German Government before immigrating to this country.

Stoops & Brown, proprietors of the popular Natural Bridge Hotel on Lookout Mountain, took charge of the same in 1885. The grounds belonging to the hotel comprise fourteen acres on which is the Natural Bridge, Telephone Rock and numerous other attractions. There are also several fine springs of both free-stone and chalybeate water. The association of spiritualists purchased the property in 1881 for $7,000. The hotel as it is now improved and arranged contains forty-five rooms. H. E. Stoops is a native of Hamilton County, Ohio, came to Chattanooga in 1871, and was connected with the Florentine Hotel from 1876 until he became interested in the management of the Natural Bridge Hotel. He was also treasurer of the Chattanooga Opera House Company, from 1879 to 1886, and during the latter year was postmaster of Lookout postoffice. His parents, A. J. and Nannie A. (Cox) Stoops, are natives of Pennsylvania and Franklin County, Ind., they are now residing in Chattanooga, the father following the occupation of a contractor. J. N. Brown is a native of Washington County, Tenn., where he was reared and educated. He came to Chattanooga in 1878, and was also connected with the Florentine Hotel until he and Mr. Stoops took charge of their present hotel. In 1885 he married Miss Nettie Stoops a native of Covington, Ky. James F. Brown, father of J. N., was born in Washington County, Tenn., and died in the same county in 1863. Margaret (Harvey) Brown, the mother, is also a native of Washington County, Tenn., of Irish descent, and now resides in Jonesboro, Tenn.

Berry Talley, a farmer in the Fifth District, was born in South Carolina in 1827, and moved to Georgia with his parents in 1832, in which State he lived twenty-six years. He then moved to Hamilton County, in 1856, locating where he has since resided. He is the youngest of six children born to Stephen and Polly (Pool) Talley. The father was born in North Carolina in 1788. While living in Georgia he was coroner for one term. He died in 1872. He was a soldier in the war of 1812 under Gen. Jackson, and was a genial good man. The mother was born in 1803 in South Carolina, and died about 1829. Our subject began business for himself at the age of seventeen, and was fifty years old before he learned to write his name, with very little means at his command, he now owns 107 acres of land well cultivated, on the Bird Mill road. He married Mrs. Ellender Langston, formerly Miss Gay, and six children blessed this union: Stephen (deceased), Mary (Mrs. Petty), Nancy (Mrs. Biggs), John, William (deceased) and an infant (deceased). Mrs. Talley died in 1862, and in 1863 Mr. Talley married Miss Celina Olliver, who presented him with one child: Kesiah (Mrs. Lee). Mrs. Talley died in 1874, and he then married Miss Martha Wright, who bore him seven children: Alice, Tennessee (Mrs. McDowel), Berry, Margaret and three infants deceased Mrs. Talley departed this life in 1879, and in 1881 he married Mrs. Betters, formerly Miss Lee, by whom he had two children, only one living, Thomas Wesley. Mr. and Mrs. Talley are members of the Baptist Church in which he is a deacon. In politics Mr. Talley was a Democrat before the war, but since that event has been conservative, voting for principal instead of party. Mr. William Talley, the eldest brother of our subject, is living with him at the present time. He (William) assisted in collecting the Indians from the surrounding country for removal to the Indian Territory. Two years before he served as a soldier in the Creek Indian war. Our subject owned the second cotton-gin ever put up in Hamilton County, and is a man who has taken a decided interest in all public improvements.

Henry F. Temple, of Chattanooga, was born in Utica, N. Y., September 14, 1840, son of John F. and Cornelia (Morris) Temple, natives respectively of Germany and New York. In 1852 Henry F.

removed with his parents to Chicago, and in 1861 enlisted in the Federal Army, serving in the Twenty-first Kentucky Regiment, first as private, and through all the grades to captain of Company D., and adjutant-general on the staff of Gen. W. C. Whitaker. After the war he was engaged in the manufacture of pumps in Chicago for some time, but came to Chattanooga in January, 1874, and engaged in his present business viz.: the manufacture of furniture, pumps, pipe and lumber. He is also vice-president and general manager of the Lookout Incline Railway Company. He has also been prominently identified with other enterprises in Chattanooga real estate, etc. January 28, 1868, he married Sarah A. Egan, of Chicago, who bore him seven children—five sons and two daughters. Mr. Temple is a Democrat, and was mayor of Chattanooga in 1879 and 1880. He is a member of the G. A. R., and is an excellent citizen.

Joseph F. Shipp was born in Jasper County, Ga., February 3, 1844, and is a son of Gustavus V. and Caroline (George) Shipp, natives respectively of North Carolina and Georgia. Joseph F. was reared and educated in his native State, and in 1861 enlisted in the Confederate Army, serving with the Fourth Georgia Regiment two years. He then served in the transportation department until the close of hostilities, when he followed the mercantile business in Social Circle, Ga., until 1873, when he and Maj. Temple established the present business in Chattanooga. He has also been largely engaged in real estate transactions in Chattanooga. August 12, 1866, he married Lillie E. Eckles of Walton County, Ga., who bore him nine children—six sons and three daughters. He is a Democrat, and has served on the board of mayor and aldermen. He was the Democratic candidate for mayor in 1883, and is a member of the city school board. He is also commander of N. B. Forrest's camp of Confederate Veterans. Singularly enough the firm of Temple & Shipp is composed of an ex-Federal soldier and an ex-Confederate soldier, each having faithfully served the cause he deemed right. They dwell in harmony together notwithstanding this fact and are reasonably prosperous.

W. G. M. Thomas, attorney and counsellor at law, a member of the firm of DeWitt & Thomas, situated in the McConnell Block, is a native of London, Canada, and is a son of William and Grace (Keiler) Thomas, who were natives of England and Canada respectively, and who are now residents of Spring City, Rhea Co., Tenn. At the age of three years the subject of this sketch became a resident of Tennessee by reason of the removal of his parents to Bledsoe County, and he was there reared to manhood and received his early education. He afterward entered

Vanderbilt University, studied law, was admitted to the bar in 1882 and then came to Chattanooga, where he has since resided practicing his profession. He was first connected with the firm of DeWitt, Shepherd & Thomas, then accepted the position of attorney for the Cincinnati Southern Railroad until 1884, when the present firm of DeWitt & Thomas was organized. Mr. Thomas is one of the city's most progressive citizens, is a first class lawyer and is a member of the local lodge of Knights of Pythias. DeWitt & Thomas are attorneys for Hamilton County, Tenn.

A. J. Thomas, a retired farmer, at Hixon, was born March 10, 1825, in Bledsoe County, and came to Hamilton County in 1833, settling first at Georgetown. He has been living at or near Hixon since 1854. He is the sixth of nine children born to Abraham and Sarah (Kosy) Thomas. The father was born in Virginia December 20, 1789, and came to Sequatchie Valley at a very early period, where he married. He afterward moved to Hamilton County, and here died, December, 28, 1859. He was a soldier in the war of 1812, and was discharged at Mobile, at the close of the war. The mother was born in Marion County, and died September 7, 1846. She was of English descent. Our subject received his education at the subscription schools of Hamilton County. He lived with and assisted his father on the farm until his twenty-ninth year, when he married Miss Louisa Gann, a native of Hamilton County, born in 1834, the daughter of Preston and Mary Gann, who were of Irish and Dutch extraction respectively. To our subject and wife were born eight children: Sarah (Mrs. Barker), Mary (Mrs. Powell), Martha (deceased), James A. (deceased), Matilda (Mrs. Dr. W. F. Skillern), William (deceased), George and Florence (deceased). Mrs. Thomas is a member of the Methodist Episcopal Church. Mr. Thomas is a Democrat in politics although in early life he voted with the Whig party. He is a member of the Masonic fraternity. He was elected justice of the peace in 1865, and served in that capacity with universal satisfaction until 1871. Not one of his decisions was ever reversed. The grandfather of our subject, John Thomas, was a soldier in the Revolutionary war, and shortly after being discharged moved his family into the Sequatchie Valley.

Hon. D. C. Trewhitt, judge of the circuit court, is a native of Morgan County, Tenn., born in 1823. In the year 1836 he moved to Cleveland, Tenn., where he was reared and educated. He was admitted to the bar in that city in 1848, and four years later he moved to Harrison, Hamilton Co. (now in James County), Tenn. He was a member of the Legislature in 1859 and 1860, and was elected to the Senate in 1861 but resigned;

went to Kentucky and enlisted in the First Tennessee Infantry, where, at the time of his resignation, in March, 1862, he occupied a prominent position in the army. From the above date until the close of the war he was chancellor of this district, and then practiced law until elected to his present position in the year 1878. July 4, 1865, he was united in marriage to Miss Mary M. Hunter, a native of Hamilton County. This union resulted in the birth of four children. Levi and Harriet (Lavender) Trewhitt, the parents of our subject were natives of North Carolina, where they died in the years 1862 and 1855 respectively.

Francis E. Tyler was born in Ireland July 13, 1838, and came with his parents to the United States in 1849. He was reared and educated in Pittsburgh, Penn., and was in the employ of a wholesale grocery in that city a number of years, and also in the employ of the Pittsburgh, Fort Wayne & Chicago Railroad eight years. In 1861 he enlisted in the Union Army and served first as second lieutenant but was afterward promoted to the rank of lieutenant-colonel of the Seventy-fourth New York Regiment. He came South in 1870 and was paymaster and bookkeeper with the Roane Iron Company for five years. In 1876 he engaged in the general insurance agency business, which he has continued up to the present, representing a great many well known fire insurance companies. Mr. Tyler is secretary and treasurer of the Mutual Real Estate and Home Building Association of Chattanooga. He is notary public and magistrate of the Fourteenth District, and president of the Chattanooga Board of Underwriters. December 25, 1865, he married Mary F. Fleeson, of Pittsburgh, Penn., and to them were born six children, all living. Mr. Tyler is a Republican in politics, is Past Grand of the local lodge of the I. O. O. F., and Past Chancellor of Damon Lodge, No. 2, K. of P., also a member of the military order of Loyal Legion (Cincinnati, Ohio, Commandery), also of the G. A. R., Lookout Post, No. 2, of this city, and a member of the Second Presbyterian Church. The above mentioned Mutual Real Estate and Home Building Association, of which Mr. Tyler is secretary and treasurer was incorporated in September, 1885, has a capital of $200,000, with R. M. Barton, Jr., president, and F. E. Tyler, secretary and treasurer. The board of directors are R. M. Barton, H. M. Ward, F. E. Tyler, R. Whigham, A. S. Ochs, W. Heron, L. O. Read, H. C. Beck and C. E. Smith. This company own and buy large tracts of property in and about the city which they lay off in lots and sell on eight years' terms, 10 per cent cash and $12 per $1,000 monthly rental. They also build residences on lots on same terms, thus offering unequaled inducements to laboring men. This is the only company of the kind in the Southern States.

Troutt & Coxon (firm), dealers in marble furniture slabs, and manufacturers of monuments and general cemetery work, was established in September, 1885. They employ two traveling salesmen and seventy-five work hands, and have a flourishing business. They use both foreign and domestic marble and granite. John Troutt was born in the Keystone State in 1843 and grew to manhood there. He followed masonry and stone cutting until 1868, after which he followed the same trade in Montana, Utah, Arkansas and Texas, until he came to Chattanooga in 1878. He was then a member of the firm of Renwick & Troutt, masonry contractors, and remained such until the death of his partner in January, 1885. He then continued alone until the present firm was formed. His parents, Daniel and Mary (Loudmilish) Troutt, were natives of Pennsylvania, where they died in 1851 and 1854 respectively. Our subject, John Troutt, is a member of the K. of H., and a genial, pleasant citizen. William Coxon is a native of Montreal, Canada, born in 1849, and came to New York in infancy where he was reared and educated. In 1873 he moved to South Carolina, where he remained one year, then went to Washington, D. C., and from there to Chattanooga in 1875. He has always followed the stone cutters' trade. In 1878 he married Miss Jennie Morgan, a native of Illinois. Mr. Coxon is a member of the Masonic fraternity and an excellent business man. His parents, James and Susan (Watts) Coxon, are natives of England. They came to Canada in childhood, were married there, and in 1849 moved to New York, where they still reside.

Benjamin Truxal was born in Westmoreland County, Penn., March 22, 1842, and is a son of Henry and Elizabeth (Searly) Truxal, both natives of Pennsylvania. Our subject was reared and educated in that State, learning the machinist's trade in Pittsburg, Penn. In 1862 he enlisted in Company L, One Hundred and Second Pennsylvania Volunteer Infantry as private, was seriously wounded in the left shoulder in front of Petersburg, June 18, 1864, and disabled for further service. He came to Chattanooga in 1870, and established what is now the Enterprise Machine Works. In 1870 he married Miss Mary Locke, of Pennsylvania, who presented him with one child—a daughter named Eva. Mr. Truxal is a Republican, a Mason, and a Knight of Pythias.

Ambrose Wagner was born in Baltimore, Md., October 2, 1856, and is the son of John M. and Mary A. (Kirshuer) Wagner, both of whom were natives of Bavaria. Our subject was reared and received a fair education in the city of Baltimore, where he also learned the pattern and model making trade. At the age of twenty-one, he left his native State, came to Tennessee, and located in Chattanooga where he worked at his trade one year. In June, 1878, he established his present foundry machine shops (a sketch of which appears elsewhere in this work). The January previous, of the same year, he was united in marriage to Miss Annie M. Zinkand, of Baltimore, Md., and to them one daughter, Agnes (deceased) was born. Mr. Wagner is a Democrat, a member of the Catholic Knights of America and of the Catholic Church, and is one of the enterprising and reliable business men and manufacturers of Chattanooga.

Dr. Leonard Walden is a son of Bishop J. M. and Martha (Young) Walden, both of whom were born and reared in Ohio. Of their family of five children our subject was the eldest. He was born April 20, 1860, at Lynchburg, Ohio, and received his literary education at Cincinnati and Delaware, Ohio. In 1884 he graduated from the Ohio Medical College. After practicing a short time in Covington, Ky., he came to Chattanooga, and in less than a year was elected city physician. He was connected with the board of health, is a member of the Sons of Temperance and other secret orders. He is a very successful practitioner. His father, Bishop J. M. Walden, was born in Lebanon, Ohio, on a farm. He received his literary education at Farmer's College, College Hill, Ohio, and graduated at the age of twenty-one. He was a correspondent of the *Commercial Gazette*, Cincinnati, Ohio, and during the year 1853 started a paper in Illinois, but this proved a failure. In 1855 he left Illinois and moved to Kansas, where he started a paper, but this also proved a failure. He was elected to the office of commissioner of education of that State in 1856, and in 1858 he returned to Ohio and entered the Cincinnati Conference. His first circuit was near Cincinnati. He afterward went to Lynchburg, Ohio, where he was stationed three years and was then sent to Cincinnati. He was connected with the Freedmen's Bureau until 1868, when he was elected junior member of the Methodist Book Concern. In 1880 he was elected senior member of the same, and in 1884 was elected bishop.

Dr. R. F. Wallace is a son of John and Rose (Lamar) Wallace, both natives of Anderson County, Tenn., where they are now living, the father engaged in agricultural pursuits. In their family were nine children—six sons and three daughters. Two of the sons are physicians. Our subject was born in the same county as his parents, February 12, 1859, and was the sixth child. He attended college in Jefferson County, where he received a good education. Having read medicine with Dr. J. P. Wallace, he took a course at the medical department of the University of Tennessee where he graduated in 1886, receiving the first prize, faculty medal, for general proficiency.

Isaac A. Wallace, farmer, was born in December, 1841, in the Twelfth

District of Hamilton County. He is the sixth of ten children born to Benjamin and Mary (Anderson) Wallace. The father was born in Blount County, and educated at Marysville College of that county, for the ministry. He was one of the first Presbyterian preachers of the Twelfth District, and was a successful minister of the gospel. He has two sons who are ministers in the same church. Both father and mother were of Scotch-Irish descent, the former born about 1808 and died about 1855, the latter was born in 1811 and is still living. Our subject was educated in the common schools of the Twelfth District. He began life a poor man, has accumulated considerable property and is quite comfortably fixed. He owns 200 acres of land which is considered the best farm near Soddy. He married Miss Nancy McDonald, a granddaughter of Col. William Clift, and also a granddaughter of James McDonald, one of the early settlers of the county. Mrs. Wallace was born in December, 1844, in Hamilton County, and by her marriage became the mother of six children: Benjamin E., James P. (deceased), Joseph W., Albert E., Fannie B. and Mary A. Mr. and Mrs. Wallace are members of the Presbyterian Church of which he has been an elder for ten years. Mr. Wallace is a Democrat and cast his first presidential vote for H. Seymour. He is at present clerking in the Soddy Coal Company's grocery department. His father was an early settler of this part of the county, and was a very successful school teacher. J. Albert Wallace, a brother of our subject, is one of the leading educators of Sullivan County. He is president of King's College at Bristol, where Isaac A.'s oldest son is attending school.

P. A. Wall, a school teacher in the Twelfth District, was born October 18, 1844, in Spartansburg, S. C., and is the eldest of nine children born to J. and S. L. (Jackson) Wall. The father was born in South Carolina June 24, 1817, and died June 20, 1884. The mother was born July 29, 1820, in South Carolina, and is of Scotch descent. Our subject was educated in the common schools and at New Prospect Academy in South Carolina. He engaged in agricultural pursuits until the breaking out of the war. He then enlisted in Company K, Fifth South Carolina Infantry, in October, 1864, and took part in all the battles and severe skirmishes in which his regiment participated. He surrendered with Gen. Lee's army April 9, 1865. For the first two years after the war he attended school, then up to 1870 he tilled the soil. He then began school teaching, and has made that his life's work. He has taught the school at Soddy for the past seven years, and is holding that position at present. This alone speaks well of his efficiency as a teacher. December 12, 1875, he married Miss Sarah Copeland, a native of Walker County, Ga., born December 27, 1849, and the daughter of Alexander and Malissa (Sartain)

Copeland. Mr. Copeland was of Irish and Mrs. Copeland of Scotch descent. Our subject and wife are members of the Presbyterian Church. In politics Mr. Wall is Democratic, casting his first presidential vote for H. Seymour. He is a Master Mason and a good citizen. To Mr. Wall and wife have been born six children: Bertha L., Jasin A., Robert W. (deceased), Walter (deceased), Lizzie C. and Anna L. Mr. Wall's foreparents on his father's side, came from Pennsylvania to South Carolina about 1800. On his mother's side they came from Scotland to America about 1750, and settled in South Carolina about 1776.

T. H. Walker, superintendent of the southern division of the Baltimore & Ohio Express Company, was born in Washington, D. C., January 19, 1857, and educated in the public schools of Baltimore and Washington, D. C. His father, William Walker, was a native of Virginia, and a contractor on public works. He died in 1861, at the breaking out of the late civil war. His widow, Sue (Michael) Walker, was born in Maryland and still lives. Our subject began with the Baltimore & Ohio Company many years ago, and has held the positions of depot manager, cashier, traveling auditor, and in 1886, when they ran a line into Chattanooga, he took his present position. By our subject's marriage to Miss Ella Taylor in 1884, he became the father of one child, Josette. Mrs. Walker is a daughter of Samuel H. Taylor, of Indiana. Our subject is a live business man, and is well respected by all who know him.

G. M. Walker, a physician and druggist of Soddy, was born in 1847, and is a son of Harvey and Sarah Walker. He was born in Lookout Valley, and in 1856 moved to the State of Arkansas. In 1858 his father moved to Texas and left our subject at Cane Hill to finish his education. In 1861 the trouble between the States caused him to leave Cane Hill and join his father in Texas. In 1863 he enlisted in the Confederate Army, in the Fourth Missouri Cavalry. His company operated principally in Missouri and Arkansas. He participated in the following battles: Arkansas Post, Jenkinson Ferry and Poison Spring; went on a raid through north Arkansas and south Missouri; thence through the Indian Territory, the Cherokee and Choctaw Nations, and went into winter quarters on Red River. He was in all the severe skirmishes and minor engagements in which his command took part. He was captured at Arkansas Post, and three days afterward made his escape. In 1865 our subject was surrendered with the army of E. Kirby Smith, in Texas, and went from there to Honduras, with a company composed of some of the chief officers commanding in the trans-Mississippi department, but returned in the fall of the same year, when he again joined his father in northwest Texas, and left there for this State where he arrived in

1866. In 1868 he attended a course of lectures at Louisville, Ky. In 1869 he was at McMinnville and went to Beersheba Springs, where he completed his studies in the Latin language under a private instructor; he then traveled one year. While engaged in the life insurance business, in 1871, he married Margaret Hackwarth, daughter of Jasper Hackwarth, of Marion County, and in the fall of the same year, 1871, located near Soddy. Margaret presented him with one child, Thomas Dick. Mrs. Walker died in September, 1880, and in November, 1882, Dr. Walker married M. M. Clift, who was born in 1861. She is a daughter of R. B. Clift, of Hamilton County. This union resulted in the birth of two children—both girls: Sallie (deceased) and Tinque Nay. Dr. Walker is a Democrat, a Master Mason, and in 1880 was appointed notary public, which position he now holds. Mrs. Walker is a member of the Presbyterian Church at Soddy. Our subject's father was of English and his mother of Scotch descent. His grandfather, Walker, came from Virginia, settled in Warren County (now Grundy), and was one of the earliest settlers in that region. His father and mother were Baptists.

Joseph H. Warner, of Chattanooga, was born in Sumner County, Tenn., September 5, 1842, the son of Jacob L. and Elizabeth J. (Cartwright) Warner, natives respectively of Virginia and North Carolina. Our subject's maternal grandfather, James Cartwright, immigrated to Tennessee in 1780, and was one of the pioneer settlers and Indian fighters of Middle Tennessee. Our subject was reared and educated in his native county. In 1862 he enlisted in Company A, Nineteenth Tennessee Regiment Confederate Infantry, serving as private and non-commissioned officer until captured at Missionary Ridge, and was held in the Federal prisons until the close of the war. He then engaged as clerk in a wholesale hardware store in Davenport, Iowa, and in the latter part of 1865 he engaged in the business for himself in Nashville. In December, 1866, he removed to Chattanooga and started his present hardware business on a limited scale. His trade now extends to Georgia, Alabama, Mississippi, Tennesssee and Kentucky. He employs twenty men in the house which is located on the southwest corner of Seventh and Market Streets. It is five stories high, and is a commodious structure. He also employs five traveling salesmen. Mr. Warner is one of the original founders of the Chattanooga Street Railroad Company, and has been its president for four years. He was one of the organizers of the Third National Bank, and its president some years. June 20, 1867, he married Miss Alice G. Hood of Rutherford County, Tenn., and has five living children by this union—two sons and three daughters. Mr. Warner is independent in his political views but has affiliated with the Democratic party. He is a Knight of Pythias.

T. C. Warner, D. D., pastor of the Methodist Episcopal Church at Chattanooga, was born December 11, 1843, in Medina County, Ohio. His father, Lorenzo Warner, was a native of Connecticut, and in early life moved to Ohio, where he was educated in Western Reserve College and at Ohio Medical College. For about fifteen years he practiced medicine and then turned his attention to the ministry, in which he became eminent. He was a representative in the Ohio Legislature, and for seven years was chaplain of the Ohio penitentiary. He was chaplain of the Fourth Ohio Infantry two years during the late war. The mother, Mary O. Kingsbury, was born in New Hampshire, and in girlhood moved to Ohio. The parents were members of the Methodist Episcopal Church, as are also their five children. Our subject received his early education in the common schools, and was well advanced in his course at the Ohio Wesleyan University, when the stirring events of the war put a stop to further study. In 1861 he enlisted in Company C, Fourth Ohio Infantry, and after serving two years was discharged on account of wounds received at Fredericksburg, Va. He then returned home, and engaged in mercantile pursuits for some time. He entered the ministry in 1866 and for eighteen years was a member of the Northern Ohio Conference. In 1884 he was called to Chattanooga, and under his able management the church has increased rapidly in prosperity and numbers. While in Ohio Dr. Warren gave public lectures on a variety of subjects. Since coming here the Doctor has thoroughly identified himself with the interests of the South in helping to solve the social and other difficulties that have arisen. In 1864 he married Miss Frances, daughter of Alex. Laughlin of Ohio, and by her became the father of ten children, seven of whom are living. In 1885 he received the degree of D. D. from Little Rock University. He is a member of the G. A. R., was chaplain of the department of Ohio a year, also of the department of Tennessee and Georgia a year and is now chaplain in chief. He is a member of the executive committee, and trustee of Chattanooga University.

C. A. Warren (deceased) was a native of London, Canada, born November 7, 1837, and at the age of thirteen moved with his parents to Detroit, Mich. At the age of nineteen he enlisted in the United States naval service, where he continued two years, after which he followed railroading in Michigan two years. He was then in the employ of the Louisville & Nashville Railroad until May, 1867, when he was transferred to the M. & C., serving as conductor for five years.

In 1873 he accepted the position of passenger and traveling agent for the A. G. S., and after one year was appointed passenger and traveling agent for both the A. G. S. and C. S., which position he held until the time of his decease. September 25, 1867, he married Miss Louisa Seaman, a native of Cincinnati, Ohio, after which they resided one year at Memphis, and then located in Chattanooga. Mr. Warren was one of the most popular citizens of Chattanooga, and had many warm friends, being loved and respected by all who knew him. He was a charter member of the K. of P., A. O. U. W. and K. of H. lodges of Chattanooga, each of which, by his death, March 25, 1886, lost a valuable and efficient member. He left but one child, William, aged fifteen. He and his wife were members of the Episcopal Church, and he departed this life with a full realization of the Christian hope. His parents, William A. and Pauline (Charles) Warren, were natives of Canada. The father's death occured at Detroit, Mich., where the mother still lives. Mrs. Warren is still a resident of Chattanooga, but was a resident of Cincinnati, Ohio, up to the time of her marriage. Her parents, Joseph C. and Louisa C. (Arnold) Seaman, were natives of Ohio and Kentucky respectively, but resided in Cincinnati the greater part of their lives, the father being engaged in the mercantile trade. Their death occurred in 1861 and 1879 respectively.

Alfred Webb & Co., one of the prominent manufacturing firms of Chattanooga, is individually composed of Alfred Webb and F. I. Stone. The business was established in 1880 by J. M. Wilson, who started on a small scale with all hand tools and a force of six men. He conducted it one year when Alfred Webb, James Hagie and John McVey purchased his outfit. They conducted the business about four years when the other members of the firm withdrew, leaving Mr. Webb, who conducted it alone for one year. In 1886 the present firm became proprietors, and have put in the most improved steam-power tools used in boiler making. In February, 1887, they completed their present new and elegant works on Cowart and Market Streets. The boiler shop proper being 60x150 feet, and the warehouse being 40x150 feet, is used by Mr. Stone for general wholesale hardware business. The machinery department, which will be conducted by the company, will carry a full line of all kinds of wood and iron making machinery, viz.: engines, boilers, saw mills, etc. They employ on an average fifty men. Their machine agency is superintended by Mr. W. A. L. Kirk, late of Kirk Machine Co., who is an able and efficient manager. Outside of the regular business they are also building stand pipes extensively for use in Southern States as water works. They are energetic, wide-a-wake business men.

Dr. W. B. Wells, a successful surgeon and practitioner of medicine at Chattanooga, is the son of John and Mary (Stewart) Wells, both natives of South Carolina. They came to Georgia when young, and here passed the remainder of their days. The father followed the occupation of a farmer. Of their family of eight children—four sons and four daughters—our subject was the eldest. He was born June 8, 1838, in Habersham County, Ga., and received a good academic education. At the age of twenty-one he began the study of medicine, and took a course in the Atlanta Medical College. During the war he served in the medical department of Hardee's corps, Walker's division and Gist's brigade. After returning from the war he entered the Atlanta Medical College, and graduated from that institution in 1866. Dr. Wells has practiced his profession for twenty-six years, and twenty of those years were passed in practicing in one locality in Georgia. In 1885 he went to New York, and graduated in the Polyclinic, a school of clinical medicine for graduates from other schools, and afterward came to Chattanooga. He is a member of the Georgia Medical Association and also of the American Medical Association. Four children were the result of his marriage to Miss M. E. Pope in 1867. The Doctor is a Mason and he and his wife are members of the Missionary Baptist Church as are also his children.

Samuel D. Wester, of Chattanooga, was born in Roane County, Tenn., January 10, 1849, son of Christopher C. and Mary (Johnson) Wester, both natives of Roane County, Tenn., and members of pioneer families of East Tennessee. Our subject was educated at Wesleyan University (now Grant Memorial), Athens, McMinn Co., Tenn. He came to Chattanooga in 1877 and engaged in the grain business, in company with Mr. William M. Nixon, which he has continued up to the present time. He married Miss Lelia A. Rice, of McMinn County, Tenn., and three children are the fruits of this union. Mr. Wester is a Republican, a member and trustee in the First Methodist Episcopal Church of Chattanooga, and trustee in the Chattanooga University.

F. O. Wert, attorney and counsellor at law, is a native of the State of Alabama, where he was reared and educated. He is a son of M. and E. C. (Cowen) Wert, who were natives respectively of Harrisburg, Penn., and Alabama. They are yet living and are now residing in the latter State. After acquiring his literary education, the subject of this biography studied law and was admitted to practice his chosen profession at Decatur, Ala., where he continued until the fall of 1880, when he removed to Chattanooga which has since been his home. He takes an active interest in all public matters, and is deservedly popular because of his enterprise and liberality. He is the present Vice-chancellor of the local lodge of K. P. In 1882, the solemnization of his marriage with Miss Lucy Crow occurred, and to them two children have been born: Aubin and Louise. Mr. Wert and wife are members of the Methodist Episcopal Church.

Xenophon Wheeler, senior member of the law firm of Wheeler & Marshall, is a native of Licking County, Ohio, where he grew to man's estate. After securing the common-school education conferred upon all who attended the district schools, he entered Yale College, which graduated him in 1860, and at the commencement of the war he enlisted in the Sixty-seventh Ohio Volunteer Infantry. He was mustered out at Cleveland, Ohio, with the rank of captain in the One Hundred and Twenty-ninth Ohio Volunteers. While on a leave of absence in 1863, two very important events occurred in the life of Mr. Wheeler—his marriage with Miss A. E. Knowlton, a native of the Buckeye State, and his admittance to the bar at Newark, Ohio. When the war ended, in 1865, he came to Chattanooga, and associated himself in the practice of his profession as a member of the firm of Stanley, Henderson & Wheeler. In 1867 the firm name changed to Stanley, Wheeler & Marshall, which was dissolved in 1869, Mr. Wheeler practicing alone one year. In 1871 the present firm of Wheeler & Marshall was organized, and their long practice at the bar of Hamilton County has placed the firm among the first of the State. The parents of Mr. Wheeler, Salmon and Gillin (Chipman) Wheeler, were natives of Vermont, and their respective deaths occurred in 1874 and 1868.

George T. White, of Elder & White, attorneys, located in the White Building at the corner of Seventh and Walnut Streets, was born in North Carolina in December, 1849, and is a son of Col. J. F. White. A brief sketch of the father here would not be inappropriate: He was a native of Hawkins County, this State, but removed to Hamilton County in 1850, and a few years prior to the commencement of the war was judge of the county court. He raised a company of cavalry for the Confederate service, of which he was afterward made lieutenant-colonel; was taken prisoner near Knoxville; was paroled, but before being exchanged went to Florida where he continued, after being paroled, in the employ of the Confederacy. His wife, formerly Miss Martha Faw, a native of North Carolina, died June 3, 1865. Col. White is now living at Live Oak, Fla., practicing law, and has held the position of criminal court judge. George T. White, the immediate subject of this sketch, although a native of North Carolina, was raised until fourteen years of age in this county, then went with his parents to the Peninsula State where he made his home until twenty-four years of age. In 1870 he entered Emory and

Henry College, Virginia, and in 1872 graduated at the law school at Lebanon, Tenn. In 1873 he located in Chattanooga for the practice of his profession, at which he has been a decided success. May 23, 1884, the present firm of Elder & White was organized, and on the same date he married Miss Annie Henegor, a native of Charleston, Tenn., by whom he is the father of one son. Mr. White is a member of the Masonic fraternity.

Hon. Hugh Whiteside, ex-mayor of Chattanooga, enjoys the distinction of being the first native of that city, who has held the office of mayor, and the first native of that city who has attained political prominence since the war. He was born in Chattanooga in 1854, and is a son of Hon. James A. Whiteside, one of the most distinguished men who has lived in this section since it was first settled. Our subject entered college at Sewanee in 1869, and graduated in 1873 at the age of nineteen. In 1877 he entered Washington Law University at St. Louis, graduating in the ensuing year, and began to practice in 1879. After serving as an alderman he was nominated for mayor by the Democrats by acclamation in 1883, and with a majority of 500 to 750 against him, was elected by nine votes, after one of the strongest fights ever made in the city. Mr. Whiteside's administration of the city's affairs has been characterized by public spirit, prudence and a fine sense of duty. In 1880 he married Miss Gertrude Staley, one of the city's most accomplished young ladies, and they have an interesting and happy family. In August, 1886, he was elected county judge for a period of eight years, and is now filling that office. His father, Col. James A. Whiteside (deceased), was a native of Kentucky, born September 1, 1803, and the son of Jonathan and Thankful Whiteside. He came to the Sequatchie Valley in early childhood, and carried mail to Chattanooga when a young man. In 1840 he moved to Chattanooga, and practiced law until about 1850, after which he devoted his whole time, studying internal improvements of the States. He was in the State Legislature one term, and for many years was manager and vice-president of the North Carolina & St. Louis Railroad, being instrumental in extending the St. Louis branch from Nashville. He was also the originator of the Atlantic Great Southern & Missouri Central Railroads. He was first married, February 5, 1829, to Mary J. Massengill to whom five children were born, two now living. She died in April, 1843, and February 1, 1844, he married Harriet L. Stran, a native of Virginia, who bore him nine children, one, Ann Newell, dying in infancy, the balance are still living, viz.: James Leonard, of Chattanooga; Florence, of Boston, Mass.; Helen, Mrs. R. Walkins, of Chattanooga; Vernon, of Chattanooga; Hugh, William, Charles and Glenn, all of Chattanooga. The Colonel at the time of his decease, November 1, 1861, had great confidence in the future of Chattanooga, and was a very large land holder at that place. Our subject's mother, Harriet L., resides in Chattanooga, and is one of the wealthy and enterprising business citizens.

C. S. Wight, M. D., is a son of Seth and Barbara A. (Bean) Wight, both natives of Maine, and both of English descent. The father in early life was salesman, but has spent the greater portion of his life engaged in agricultural pursuits. He and wife are still living, and both are three score and ten years of age. Of their family of ten children, consisting of five sons and five daughters, three of the sons were physicians. Eli M. and Jarvis S., both served in the late war, the former as lieutenant and afterward as surgeon, and the latter as private and corporal-sergeant. The elder attended both Yale and Harvard Colleges, from the latter receiving the degree of M. D. Jarvis S. prepared himself at a school of pharmacy. Both located in Chattanooga, where the former practiced medicine about eighteen years, and was twice mayor of the city. The latter engaged in the drug business. They have both been dead some years. Our subject was born November 13, 1855, in Eastern Maine, and received a good academic education. In 1876 he came to Chattanooga, and studied medicine under his brother. Having attended the medical department of the State University, from which he graduated in 1879, he returned and became a partner of Dr. Eli Wight, who died a year later. For two years our subject was city physician, and two years county physician. He is a member of the State and county medical societies, and for eight years has been in active practice. He passed through the yellow fever epidemic of 1878, and was himself prostrated by the fever. Eli M. Wight held the chair of diseases of the chest and throat, in the medical department of the University of Tennessee, was Republican candidate for governor, and was appointed a member of the State board of health.

William J. Williams was born March 11, 1845, in South Wales, and came to America in 1869, settling in Pennsylvania. He was educated in the subscription schools of Wales. At the age of seventeen he left the parental roof. In 1868 he married Miss Mary Ann Davis, a native of Wales, born in 1850, and the daughter of John and Mary (Howell) Davis. To our subject and wife were born six children: Mary, John, David, Gwenie, Thomas and Griselda. In 1872 Mr. Davis left Pennsylvania, and came to Soddy, Tenn., where he has since resided. He worked in the coal mines for one year, after which he was given the position of contractor to blast the roof of the mines, which position he held for twelve years. He was then elected bank boss, which position he now holds. He has under his supervision about 250 men. He owns his present position to his own ability as a practical miner and overseer. He has the entire confidence of his employers, and is an honest, industrious man. He and his wife and eldest two children are members of the Congregational Church. In politics Mr. Williams is a Republican.

William A. Willingham, of Chattanooga, was born in Beaufort County, S. C., July 6, 1837, son of Thomas and Phœbe S. (Lawton) Willingham, both natives of South Carolina. Our subject was reared and educated in his native State. In 1859 he married Miss Emilie F. Dews, of Daugherty County, Ga. She died in 1868 leaving four children, three now living: John T., Edward G. and Maxie Belle (wife of J. K. Nuckells, wholesale shoe merchant, of Columbus, Ga). In 1862 our subject enlisted in the Third South Carolina Cavalry, and served one year as a non-commissioned officer. In 1865 he left South Carolina, and spent three years in agricultural pursuits in southwest Georgia. In 1869 he engaged in the lumber business at Forsyth, Ga., where he continued until 1876, after which he engaged in the same business at Columbus, Ga. In January, 1885, he established a sash, door, blind and general lumber business at Chattanooga. In 1869 Mr. Willingham married his present wife, Mary J. Woodruff, of Columbus, Ga., who bore him three children: Furman D., Florence and Ruby. (Mary the eldest is deceased.) Mr. Willingham is a director in the Chattanooga Savings Bank, a Democrat, an ancient Mason, a member of the A. O. U. W. and K. of P., and a deacon in the First Baptist Church of Chattanooga.

Hon. H. M. Wiltse, a legal practitioner of the firm of Wiltse & McLean, is a native of Michigan, in which State he was reared and educated, graduating in law from the University of Michigan in 1874. He came to Chattanooga in 1870 and was admitted to the bar in 1873. He did not begin practicing until after his return from law school, when he practiced alone until the present firm was formed January 7, 1887. He is president and attorney for the Lookout Homestead Association, and secretary of the Iron, Coal and Manufacturers Association. He was a member of the Legislature during the years 1879-82, and was assistant postmaster of Chattanooga from July 1876 until July 1877. He was alderman three terms and city attorney four years. He was also editor of the daily and weekly *Commercial* about two years. In 1877 he was united in marriage to Miss Emma Fairfield, a native of Michigan, who bore him three children, only one now living. Mr. Wiltse is Chancellor Commander of Damon Lodge, No. 2, K. of P.

His parents, Henry and Mary A. (Huggins) Wiltse, are natives of New York and Massachusetts, respectively. They reside in Michigan and the father is a retired farmer.

David Woodworth, Jr., manager of the Fayeryweather & Ladew Tannery, Chattanooga, was born in New York in 1838, where he was reared and educated. He was brought up in the tannery from boyhood, having been connected with this company throughout. He came South in 1870 and established a tannery for the company at Paw Paw, on the Baltimore & Ohio Railroad, in western Virginia. In 1876 he came to Chattanooga and established the tannery of which he has since been manager. In November, 1862, he married Mary North, of New York, who bore him one son, Clement N. Mr. Woodworth is a Republican in politics, a member of the Methodist Episcopal Church, and a director of the First National Bank. He has engaged extensively in the real estate business and has built largely in the city. He is a good citizen and a wide-awake business man.

W. T. Worley, station agent at Chickamauga, also farmer and lumber dealer at the same place, was born July 14, 1847, in Cherokee County, Ga., and is the fourth of twelve children of Lodson and Evaline (Clayton) Worley. The father was born in North Carolina in 1812, and is now living in Cherokee County, Ga., where he has resided for the past fifty years. He is of French descent. He has been postmaster for nearly forty years. The mother was born in Forsyth County, Ga., in 1822, and is of Scotch descent. Her father, Seward C. Clayton is still living in Cherokee County, Ga., and is eighty-eight years old. Our subject received his education in the common schools of Cherokee County, and began working for himself at the age of twenty-two. He was baggage master on the Western & Atlantic Railroad for nine years and conductor on a through run for over a year. After marriage he engaged in farming, merchandising and milling, and, although he commenced life a poor man, he now owns 326 acres on the Western & Atlantic Railroad, well improved and well cultivated. Besides this he owns a saw mill in the Fifteenth District. In 1875 he married Miss Georgia A. Kaiser, a daughter of W. J. and Nancy (Howell) Kaiser. The father was born in North Carolina in 1815, and died in 1881. Mrs. Kaiser was born in North Carolina March 11, 1811, and died March 24, 1884. Mr. Worley is a Democrat in politics, and cast his first presidential vote for Horatio Seymour. By his marriage he became the father of three children: Mabel N., Clara M. and James Clark. Mrs. Worley was born October 8, 1851, and is an active worker in the Missionary Baptist Church.

Henry D. Wyatt, M. D. and A. M., and superintendent of the city schools of Chattanooga, is a son of Daniel and Phebe (Palmer) Wyatt, both natives of New Hampshire, where they are now living. Of their family of eight children, five are now living,—four sons and one daughter. Our subject was born in Grafton County, N. H., September 24, 1836, grew to manhood on the farm and received his rudimentary education in the common schools and in an academy. Having early imbibed a fondness for teaching he taught several terms during the winter season and worked on the farm during the summer. The war broke out about this time, and in 1862 he enlisted as a private in Company B, Fifteenth New Hampshire Infantry, United States Army, but soon arose to the rank of first lieutenant, which position he held until 1863, when he was wounded at Port Hudson, and mustered out of service in August of that year. He soon turned his attention to teaching and the study of medicine, attending lectures at Harvard College, and in 1865 became assistant surgeon of a regiment of heavy artillery, which position he filled until May, 1866. After cessation of hostilities he graduated from the medical department of Dartmouth College, and then, having a desire to engage in teaching as a profession, he took the classical course at Dartmouth College, graduating in 1871. He then taught in the North until late in 1872, when he was called to take charge of the Chattanooga schools, which he organized and has brought to their present advanced condition. In 1875 he wedded Miss Alice J. Polsey, of Rhode Island. Both are church members and respected citizens.

Charles C. Wynne, manager and partner of the Chattanooga Storage & Forwarding Company, was born in Gadsden, Ala., January 19, 1861, son of William B. and Mary A. (Cowden) Wynne, natives respectively of South Carolina and Georgia. Our subject removed to Atlanta, Ga., in 1870, where he was reared and educated. He learned the machinist's trade, at which he worked for some time, but afterward engaged in the directory business in the Southern States. He came to Chattanooga February 1, 1886, and engaged in his present business, being the cotton buyer and handler of the firm. December 10, 1882, he was united in marriage to Miss Julia E. Janes, a native of Greene County, Ga., and one son, Leroy F., was the result of this union. Mr. Wynne is a Democrat and a member of the Baptist Church. The Chattanooga Storage & Forwarding Company is individually composed of S. A. Cunningham and C. C. Wynne, who are lessees of M. H. Clift's warehouse, No. 1321 Market Street. This building is 75x160 feet, with a gallery running entirely around it. The firm is engaged in a general storage and brokerage business, and sells fertilizers.

INDEX

Prepared by
Colleen Morse Elliott
Fort Worth, Texas

HAMILTON COUNTY, TENN.

Abbot...875
Abbott, Willard 843,849
Abel, E. L. 909
  Mary 909
  Perry 909
Abell, G. W. 852
Abrahams, H. S. 863
Ackerman, Hattie 849
Adair...803
Adams...963
  Frank R. 846
  Laura J. 957
  M. 831
  McKinney 834
  Melville 900
  William L. 835
  W. L. 832,865
Agey, Calvin 903
  Carrie 904
  D. M. 903,904
  Hoite M. 904
  J. W. 903,904
  Susan 904
  Thomas G. 904
Aiken, J. N. 898
Albert, Paul 904
  Paul R. 904
  Sophia 904
Alexander, Catherine 907
  H. C. 835
Allen, J. A. 861,904,905
  James 835,902
  Louis 905
  Lucy 905
Allin, John B. 901
Allison, A. 852
  Jesse B. 859,861
Ames, Orson 901
Anderson, Fannie I. 905
  J. M. 816
  John 830
  John C. 905
  John W. 905
  Joseph M. 816
  J. S. 905
  Mary 1006
  Matthew 831
  W. W. 848
Armitage, Margaret 956
Armstrong, Lizzie 971
Arnet, Richard 986
Arnett, George W. 831
Arnold, Elizabeth 906
  G. W. 903
  James T. 905,906,998
  J. T. 881,961
  Lettie 906
  Louisa C. 1010
  Margaret 906
  William 906
Ashley, Mary S. 957
Atkins, James 851
Aultman, C. 929
Avery...863

Bachman, J. W. 849,892
Baker, Mary J. 993
Balch, E. 860,861
Baldwin...850
  A. A. 906
  C. H. 906
  Dudley 871
  Isaac 856
  W. W. 906
Ball, Sarah J. 934

Banks, Aviline 907
  Caroline 907
  Charles H. 906
  Ella 907
  Hugh R. 907
  John 906
  John C. 906
  Laura 906
  Martha 906
Barbour, Elizabeth 977
Barker, Henry 900
  John H. 989
  Lydia 989
  Nancy 989
  Sarah 1002
Barkley, Hiram 907
  Martha Bettie 907
  Thomas E. V. 907
Barnes, Clarence A. 907
  George A. 907
  Harriet 983
  Jeannette 907
Barnett...937
Barrett...863
Barton, R. M. 815,892,899,
  1003
  R. M., Jr. 884,1003
Baskette, W. E. 877,883
Bate, William B. 831
Bates, W. H. 850
Battle, Miss M. A. 943
Baxter, Bruce 908
  Catherine 907
  Douglas 908
  Ellen 908
  G. A. 907,908
  George W. 907
  John 908
  William 869
Bayes, Hattie 927
Bays, W. W. 851
Beach, Edith 985
Beam, Susan 904
Bean, Barbara A. 1014
  W. H. 831
  William H. 831
Bearden, Richard 807
Beasley, John R. 831
Beck, David 805
  H. C. 831,833,1003
  Henry C. 908
  Joshua 908
  Margaret 908
  Rhoda D. 908
Beddo, Albert W. 901
Beene, W. M. 841
Beeson, Dovy 978
  Margaret N. 978
  Solomon 978
Bell...866
  B. B. 861
  David N. 882
  E. L. 909
  John 815
  J. T. 909
  Nancy 909
  William H. 909
  W. S. 859
Benge, John 811
Bennett, Celia 940
  Elizabeth 962
  F. J. 961,998
  Jane 961,962
  L. G. 913
  Maria J. 913

Bennett, Peter 962
  Mrs. P. M. 913
  Sarah J. 913
Benton, Flora C. 968
Berlin...907
  C. H. 909
  Charlotte 910
  H. 909
  Henry 910
  Mary 910
Berry, James 858
Best, Catherine 948
  Daniel 949
Betters...1000
Bettis, Alfred 834
Bidwell, Eliza P. 917
Biese, Charles W. 880,910
  Eliza A. 910
  Narcissa 910
  Robert 910
Biggs, J. R. 852
  Nancy 1000
Billingsly, John 816
Billmeyer, Joseph 910
  Lida 911
  Margaret 910
  U. D. 910
Bird, Philamon 813
  S. H. 813
Black, J. D. 966
Blackburn, A. 849
Blackstock, Emma 966
Blaine, James G. 830
Blair...997
  A. R. 950
  Mary A. 911
  Samuel 880,911
Blakely, Carrie May 966
Block, Leo 912
  M. 911,912
Bloomfield, C. C. 876
Blunt, Ainsworth E. 812,
  813,848
Blymyer, J. S. 880
Boggess, Mollie B. 914
Bohanan, Miss M. J. 902
Bohr, A. 859
Boltman, Peter 836
Bolton, Annie 912
  Peter 830,898,912
  Robert 912
  Selena L. 912
  William B. 898
Bonaparte, Napoleon 932
Born, Elizabeth 913
  Fannie 913
  Minerva 913
  Samuel 913
Boudinot, Elias 810
Bowman, J. H. 890
Brabson, Ada E. 926
  Reese B. 832,840,926
Bradfield, John H. 901
Bradford...838
  Tipton 924
  William M. 837
  W. M. 836
Bradley, Catherine 995
Bradshaw, J. N. 849
Bragg...818,819,820
Brainerd, David 812
Branes, John M. 931
Branham, G. W. 898
Brauner, Mrs. P. A. 830
Brause, Lizzie A. 977

Brayfield, Daniel B. 901
Breckenridge, John C. 815
Breckinridge, S. P. 892
Brennan, R. V. 897
Brewster, Vallie 972
Bridges, George W. 834,835
Bright, L. P. 884
   Lucius P. 884
Brock, L. N. 854
Brooks, Edward M. 901
   Nancy A. 923,925
Brown, Aaron V. 815
   Eunice 921
   Foster V. 833
   Green A. 902
   Henry Vincent 852
   James 804,807
   James F. 1000
   J. C. 830
   J. E. 873
   J. H. 836
   J. N. 999
   John 804,807
   Margaret 1000
   Mary A. 972
   M. S. 836
   Neill S. 815
   Nettie 1000
   Robert 807
   Susanna 807
   William B. 849
   W. R. 835
Brownlow, John A. 834
   W. G. 830
Bruce, A. C. 814
   Edward H. 979
   Harriet Martin 979
   Mary Joliffe 979
   Robert 979
Brundage, Georgie V. 913
   Jonathan W. 913
   Nora E. 913
   Permelia 913
   Sarah J. 913
   William M. 913
Bryan, J. J. 859
Bryant, Catherine 936
   Miss L. C. 969
   Mary 983
   M. C. D. 836
Buchanan, James 815
   Louisa 967
   W. J. 831
Buck, D. T. 852
Buckler, Miss E. L. 853
Buckner...819
Buford, Cyrena 937
Bunch, Jane 933
Buntley, Frederick 829
Burch, J. C. 816
   John C. 816
Burchell, Ellen 915
Burgert...915
Burns, Allen C. 882
   Mary A. 973
   Tennessee F. 973
Burroughs, T. F. 941
Bush...850
Bushyhead (Chief) 811,812
Butler, J. W. 885
   P. H. 831
   T. D. 852
Buttolph, Bessie 914
   David L. 913
   James D. 913,914,937
   Laura 913
Butts, Fannie 993
   Nelson 993
   Prudence 993
Bynum, I. G. 866
Bythe, Rice 978

Cahill, Ellen 914

Cahill, John T. 914
   Margaret 914
   William 914
Caldwell...937
   Elizabeth S. 921
   James A. 920,921
   Jane 921,962
   O. H. P. 921
   W. A. 850
Calhoun, John C. 864
Callaway, Mary 971
Calloway, Thomas 882
Campbell, Andrew 914
   J. A. 879
   John A. 914
   Martha Bettie 907
   Mary 993
   Mary J. 914
   Mollie B. 914
   Sarah 914
   Thomas J. 816
   W. A. 879
   William A. 914
   William B. 815
Cannon, B. B. 805,831
   George R. 901
   Newton 815
Cape, Ailsey 856
Capps, F. M. 834
Card, Edward S. 899
   George 899
   George S. 900
   William H. 899
Carden, Minerva 913
   Robert 978
   Teresa 978
Carey, A. C. 921
   A. M. 921
   E. H. 921
Carlile, Eliza B. 903
   Marion A. 903
   Thomas J. 887
   T. J. 860,884
   W. E. 886
   W. R. 886
Carnahan...915
   Margaret 910
Carpenter, Anna 916
   Asa 916
   C. A. 916
   Charles C. 903
   Clara E. 916
   Clarence A. 916
   D. A. 883
   D. T. 879,916
   Ella 916
   Ella M. 941
   Flora B. 916
   George E. 916
   Grace L. 916
   Jesse 916
   Jettie A. 916
   Miranda 916
   S. M. 872
Carper, Foster 902
   Hattie A. 992
Carr, David J. 893
   D. C. 859
Carroll, C. T. 851
Carson...958
Carter, Langdon 806
   T. C. 852,890
   William B. 806
Cartter, Betsy 978
Cartwright, Elizabeth J. 1008
   James 1008
Cary, Aaron 915
   Alberta 916
   Arthur M. 916
   Estella E. 916
   Hugh Aaron 916
   Lewis 915

Cary, M. 915
   Nancy 915
   Winifred Alice 916
Case...895
   Caroline E. 918
   Eliza P. 917
   Frank Luther 919
   Halbert B. 917,918
   H. B. 830,833,836,838
   Janie M. 919
   Joseph L. 917
Cash, Eunice 921
   Henry 921
   J. B. 921
Cass, Lewis 815
Castle, Maggie 944
   Mary 944
   Samuel 944
Caswell, Richard 806
Cate, A. M. 830
   William T. 836,893
   W. T. 833
Cathey...856
Caulkins, Douglas 920
   John G. 919
   Laura D. 920
   Nancy 919
   Wilford 846,919,920
Chadick, William D. 849
Chamberlain, Amelia I. 922
   Hiram S. 922
   Hiram Sanborn 922
   H. S. 869,871,880,882,
     883,884,892
   Leander 922
   Louise A. 922
   Mary Hattie 922
   Minnie Morrow 922
   Morrow 922
   Peleg 922
   Susanna 922
   Susie Willey 922
Chambers, Eunice Graham 979
   John 979
Champion, Charles B. 831
   Ruth 984
Chandler...866
   D. J. 892
Chapman, Carrie B. 923
   Henry Z. 923
   Milton L. 922,923
   M. L. 884,907
   Rose 993
Chappell, Absalom 862
Charles, Pauline 1010
Chase, D. W. 852,890
Chedbille, Miss L. 970
Cheek, Elijah 923
   Mary 923
   Mary M. 923
   Thomas H. 913,923,937
Cheeves, J. B. 890
Chester, J. S. 905
Childres, James 834
Chipman, Gillin 1012
Christian, J. T. 854
Clark, B. F. 832
   L. M. 831,833
   Martha L.
   Martha J. 985
Clay, Henry 815
Clayton, Evaline 1016
   Seward C. 1016
Cleage, Alexander 924
   Jemima 924
   J. H. 924
   Sarah 928
   Tipton 924
Cleburne...819
Clements, James 836
Cleveland, Grover 830
   Lettie 906
Cleudup, D. G. 899
Clift...861

Clift, A. C. 925
  Bruce 925
  Elizabeth J. 924
  Elizabeth L. 924
  Florence 925
  James 831,925
  James W. 814,832
  J. J. 923,924
  Joseph W. Aldine 924
  J. W. 899,924
  M. H. 815,882,883,884,
    899,925,1017
  Miss M. M. 1008
  Nancy A. 923,924,925
  Nancy E. 924
  Nina Wallace 924
  R. B. 1008
  William 899,923,924,925,
    1006
  Wingenund 925
  W. Robert 924
Cobleigh, N. E. 890
Cohen...863
Colburn, Ada E. 926
  Albert T. 926
  Betsey 926
  W. J. 838,860,883,891
  Webster J. 925,926
Collier, Mary 982
Collins, Anna 927
Colonus, B. A. 799
Colyar, L. L. 873
Conner, A. B. 967
  Alfred 832
  B. C. 831
  G. C. 869
  Mrs. G. C. 894
  Jane 926
  J. E. 833,927
  Penelope 967
  Wesley P. 926
Connor, A. B. 831
  G. C. 830,884
  James C. 831
  Louise B. 830
  Wilson B. 902
Conway, J. J. 836,861
Coody, James 813
  Joseph 803
Cook, Anna 927
  John 927
  S. B. 972
  S. C. 972
Cooke, Miss A. C. 925
  J. B. 897
  Mary 830
  Penelope M. 830
  Richard J. 920
Coolidge, Charles H. 927
  Elisha 927
  Ella 927
  Hattie 927
Cooper, J. L. 843
Copeland, Alexander 1006
  Malissa 1006
  Sarah 1006
Cowden, Mary A. 1017
Cowen, Miss E. C. 1011
Coulter, Miss E. S. 981
  John J. 897
  Milo 831
  M. J. 981
  Thomas 804,898
  T. J. 981
Cox, Austin 936
  Georgiana Mary 936
  Nannie A. 999
Coxon, James 1004
  Jennie 1004
  Susan 1004
  William 1004
Cozby, Elizabeth 964
  James 804,807,964

Cozby, Robert 804
  Woods 804
Craigmiles, John 882
  P. M. 882
Cravens, Robert 840,859
Crisman, John 849
Criswell, Dorathy 973
Crittenden...818,819,820
Croft, R. H. 859
Crote...955
Crouch...894
Crow, Lucy 1012
Crowder, W. H. 831
Crutchfield, Courtney 929
  Frances A. 929
  Mary Jane 929
  Medora 929
  Nancy Jane 929
  Oscar 929
  Sarah 928,929
  Stapleton 929
  Thomas 813,814,817,862,
    928,929
  Thomas, Sr. 859
  Thomas Williams 929
  Tom 882,901
  William 817,832,859,
    866,927,928,929
Cummings, John 831
Cunningham, Alice 929
  David 804
  Hugh 804
  James 804
  S. A. 1017
  Samuel A. 929
  Samuel B. 929
  William 849
Cunnyngham, W. G. E. 850
Curry, George 831
Curtis, David G. 930
  D. G. 880,985,986
  Eleanor Eames 930
  H. W. 930
  Sarah R. 930
Cushman, George H. 932
  Jennie 990
  Mary Octavia 932
Cutler, Temple 854

Dahlgren...934
Dale, W. P. 861
Dallas, Alexander James
  814
Daly, Patrick C. 950
  P. C. 876
Daniel...974
Darling, Henry W. 887
Darnall, William H. 849
Davenport, R. B. 972
Davis, C. G. 861
  Jefferson 816,928
  John 1014
  Mary 1014
  Mary Ann 1014
  Samuel H. 856
  Tabitha 835,836
  T. H. 830
  William M. 856
  W. R. 834
Dawson, William B. 849
Dayton, Laura 937
Dean...861
De Beck, J. 859
Dennison...918
Denton, Fannie 985
de Sabla, Catherine Helen
  932
  Eugenie 932
  Fielding Eugene 932
  James Theodore 932
  Joseph Ernest 932
  L. J. 932
  Marquis de Joly de Bla-

de Sabla (cont'd.)
  yon 932
  Mary Octavia 932
  Matilda Alice 932
  Paulene Nancy 932
Dewees, Thomas 930
  Warren A. 930,931
  Wilhelmina 930
De Witt...1001,1002
  Elizabeth 932
  Emilia 932
  Samuel 931
  William Henry 931,932
Dews, Bettie 972
  Emilie F. 1015
Dibrell, George G. 980
  G. G. 833
Dickens, M. E. 832
Dickerson...945
Dickinson...910
  Mrs. L. T. 830
Dismukes, Miss...843
Dixon...858
Doak, George M. 890
  Samuel/S. S. M. 856,901
Dobbs, Anna 933
  David 934
  Gorden 933
  James M. 933
  J. D. 933,934
  John 933
  Joseph D. 933
  Lewis David 933
  Maria 933
  Minnie S. 933
  Nancy 933
Dodan...899
Dodge, Mrs. S. C. 894
Dody, Mary 944
Doherty...808
Dolan, T. J. 815
Dombois, Matilda 985
Donaldson, Nancy 836
Donelson, Stockley 805,806,
  807
Donohoo, Charles 987
  Margaret 987
Dorsey, A. 932
  Barbara L. 933
  Charles S. 933
  D. 932
  Dimmon A. 933
  Hattie 933
  John 933
  Louvina 933
  Mary 933
  Willie N. 933
  W. M. 932,933
Doty, D. M. 860,861
Doud, Edward 880,884
Douglas, Ellen 908
  Stephen A. 815
Douglass, Hiram 849
Drake, Elmira 934
  George M. 890
  G. W. 934
  Laura 934
  Mary H. 972
  M. F. 915
  Samuel B. 933
  Sarah J. 934
Drinnon, Willey J. 903
Drum, Richard C. 821
Duckworth, A. 932
  John 933
Dugger, Eliza J. 944
  W. L. 849
Dumbell, George W. 935,936
  George William 936
  Georgiana Mary 935
  Howard Murray 936
Duncan, J. M. 874
  Marina E. 973

Duncan, Margaret J. 973
Dunham, Joseph 807
Dunlap, A. S. 935
  James 935
  Margaret 935
Dunmeyer, Catherine 934
  Jacob 934
  Lottie 934
  Louis 875,934
Dunscomb, Alexander H. 936
  Anna M. 936
  John McK. 936
Dupont, Geo. 958
Durand, Addie 939
  Harry W. 934,935
  Jessie Lee 935
  J. J. 935
Dutton, T. H. 836
Dyer, Adda 936
  Catherine 936
  C. H. 836,861,936
  David B. 936

Eager, Sarah J. 937
  William H. 936,937
Eakin...956
  Albert 937
  Cyrena 937
  John 937
  Laura 937
  Lucretia 937
East, Sarah J. 937
Eaton, E. G. 884
Eckles, Lillie E. 1001
Edmiston, Alice 986
  Sarah R. 930
Edmondson, J. C. 982
Edwards, A. L. 850
  R. M. 831
Egan, Sarah A. 1001
Elder...1012
  Harriet N. 938
  Henry L. 938
  John W., Jr. 938
  L. M. 891,937,938
  Martha G. 938
  Mary 938
Eldridge, Simeon 835
Elliott, Bessie 914
  Bishop 914
  W. L. 828
Ellis, A. C. 854
  John M. 902
  Joseph 856
Ellsworth, John C. 813
Ensign, C. E. 891
Etheridge, Emerson 830
Evans, Addie 939
  Anna 938
  Eliza 959
  H. C. 834,843,860,861,
    869,871
  H. Clay 884,938,939
  Jesse B. 938
  Margaret 959
  Mary 945
  Morgan 959
  Nellie 869
Evarts, William M. 897
Everett, Carrie M. 967

Faidley...850
Fairfield, Emma 1015
Farmer, J. O. 861
Farrar, Martha 994
Father John 887
Faw, Martha 1012
Fayerweather, D. B. 875
Fayerweather...1016
Feehan, P. A. 945
Fellers, Jeannette 907
Feltz, Lucy 905
Ferguson, Jane 965

Ferguson, Martha 913
Field, Elizabeth 980
Fillmore, Millard 815
Finley, J. W. 902
Fischer, Otto 836
Fisher, Caroline 998
Fleeson, Mary F. 1003
Fleming, Andrew 939
  Anna 939
  Martin 939
  Mary 939
  P. 939
Flippin, T. D. 883
Folkerth, Margaret 906
Ford, John W. 860
  Rachel 948
Forrest, N. B. 1001
Forsyth, A. R. 871
Fort, Tomlinson 830,884,
  860,892
Foster, Ephraim H. 815
  P. 860
Foute, Mary A. 952
Fox, H. L. 874
Fraer, Celia 940
  J. M. 940
  Julia 940
  Peter 940
Francis, J. C. 831
Francisco, Adda 936
Frank, Susan 984
Franklin, Mary E. 996
Frazier, Alleck 942
  Annie 942
  Beriah 858
  James B. 939
  Lou 940
  Margaret M. 940
  Matthew 856
  Sallie 942
  S. J. A. 942
  Thomas M. 940
Freeman, A. A. 830
  Charles B. 942
  E. H. 856
  J. P. 942
  T. J. 938
French, Ella 916
  Ella M. 941
  G. D. 851
  John H. 940
  Jessie V. 940
  L. Virginia 940
  May L. 940
  Walter Scott 940
  W. S. 879,916
Friar, John 805
Friedel...879
Friedman...961
  W. 861
Fryar, Minerva 978
  Sallie 991
Fuller...808
  E. Q. 890
Fulton, W. D. 859
Fultz, L. E. 975
Furgason, John H. 958
Fussell, Joseph H. 831

Gahagan, A. J. 881,883,961
  Andrew J. 943,944
  Eliza J. 944
  George W. 943
  Mary E. 943
Gaines, Rufus 974
Gallois, Eugenie 932
Gamble, Charles 797,803,
  831
  John C. 902
  Margaret J. 973
  Miss M. J. 981
  Robert L. 902
Gann, Louisa 1002

Gann, Mary 954,1002
  Preston 804,954,1002
  Rebecca 954
Gardenhire, Frank 814
Garfield, James A. 830
Gaskell, V. A. 884
Gaskill, Annie Lee 943
  C. R. 883,942,943
  M. A. 943
  Sallie 943
  V. A. 943
Gaston, Celestia 943
  Fred 943
  Harry 943
  Jane 943
  J. L. 830
  Joseph L. 943
  Mitchel 943
Gaut, John C. 832,834,865
Gay, Ellender 1000
Gentry, Meredith P. 815
George, Caroline 1001
Gibbs, Carrie B. 923
Gibson, F. 891
  Fillmore 886
  Thomas 808
Giles, David 877,945
  Mary 945
  Thomas 945
Gillaspie, Jacob 944
  Jane 944
  Maggie 944
  Marcus 944
  William 944
Gilleland, William B. 856
Gillespie, Elizabeth S. 921
  James W. 816
  John C. 879
  John M. 879
  Joseph S. 858
Gilliland, M. J. 902
Gillmore...956
Gilmour...873
Given, Joseph C. 834
Glass, E. A. 831
  Elbert A. 865
Gleeson, Patrick J. 945
  P. J. 853
Glenn, W. C. 942
Gohagan, A. J. 998
Gohogan, A. J. 961
Golden...875
Goldsmith, Abigail 949
  Caroline 949
  Oliver 949
Goodman, Frank 941
Gordon, John B. 970
Gossett, F. M. 933
  Maria 933
Grant, Marcus 884
  Ulysses S. 830
Gray, John 798
Greeley, Horace 830
Green, Augustus P. 946
  Mattie 951
  William T. 946
Greene, James I. 816
Gregory, Evaline 982
Grenville, Charles E. 859
  C. E. 863,866
Griffin, J. C. 883
Griffis, John C. 948
  Margaret 973
  Mary E. 948
Griffiss, J. C. 883,892
  John C. 884
Griffiths, Annie 947
  David 947
  D. R. 946,947
  Richard 947
  Ruth 947
  Thomas 947
  William 947

Grigsby, Aaron 849
  Charles 856
Grimer, John E. 903
Griscom, Harry F. 893
  H. F. 833,890
Guild, George B. 946
  Georgie 946
  J. C. 945,946
  Jo. C. 946
  Mary 946
Gunn, W. A. 864
Gurhauer, Sophia 904
Guthrie, R. H. 831,839
Gwathmey, George B. 856

Hackett, John 806,807
Hackwarth, Jasper 1008
  Margaret 1008
Hagie, James 1010
Hair, Larkin 859
Hale, William C. 900
Hall, Caswell 834
  Moody 812
Hamill, Benjamin 948
  Catherine 948
  Daniel 948
  David 949
  James Buchanan 948
  J. F. 948
  John 948
  John F. 831
  Lizzie 948
  Mary 948
  Mollie J. 948
  Mollie John 948
  Rachel 948
  Samuel 948
Hamilton, Alexander 797
Hammond, Ella 907
Hampton, Wade 897
Hancock, W. S. 830
Handy, T. R. 851
Hanna, John 804
Hannah...915
Hardie, J. H. 831,841
Hardin...808
Harding, Margaretta 966
Harris, Isham G. 815
  J. W. 885
  Nathan 856
Harrison...874
  Rebecca 982
  William Henry 814,815, 901
Hart...915,944
  J. A. 883
  John A. 860,877,880, 881,883,947,961,998
Hartman, David 836
  Jacob 804
Harvey, Margaret 1000
Hatton, Robert 815
Haven, Gilbert 920
  Mary 920
Havron, John M. 816
Hawkins, Alvin 831
  F. M. 852
  S. 852
Hayes, Burchard 897
  Rutherford B. 830
  Webb 897
Hazelton...874
  J. C. 884
  J. N. 872
Hazen...817,818
Hazlehurst, George H. 891, 947
  G. H. 872
  Irene W. 947
  James N. 947
  J. N. 872
  Mary E. 948
Headrick, L. B. 832,899

Heard, Caroline 949
  Charles W. 949
  Charles Wallace 949
  Clio 949
  G. M. D. 949
  Lillie 949
  Lois Goldsmith 949
  Rawlings 949
  Walton 949
Helmuth, William T. 940
Henderson...970,1012
  Daniel 831
  Jane 856
  J. C. 929
  J. W. 861
  Medora 929
  R. 831,860
  Richard 860
  Richardson 859
Henegor, Annie 1013
Henninger, Mary J. 914
  Sarah 994,995
Henry, Gustave A. 815
  Patrick 817
Hensel, Amelia 950
  Casper H. 949,950
Henson, G. H. 850
  G. N. 879
Heron, W. 1003
Hewitt, Abram S. 871
Heywood, H. B. 841
Hickey, R. M. 850
Hickman, Henry 834
  John R. 898
  William 834
Higgins, William 901
Hight, Anna F. 830
Hill, Alice B. 950
  Catherine 950
  Hannah 903
  Jesse T. 950
  J. T. 860,876,877,883
  Robert T. 950
  William 856
Hillas, R. B. 883
  John 806
Hillsman, Matthew 856
Hindman...819
Hixson, E. 900
  E. F. 900
  Ephraim 804
  Ephraim F. 900
  G. W. 900
  H. 900
Hixon, Margaret 908
  Rebecca 986,988
  Susan 957
Hoagland, Amelia 951
  Cynthia 950
  E. M. 950
  J. W. 950,951
  Mariah 950
Hoar, Dorcas K. 957
Hodge, W. C. 830,861
Hogan, D. 859
  Daniel 852
Holland, C. S. E. 891
  G. Allison 891
  H. P. 952
  Sarah 952
Holley, Thomas C. 902
Holmes, Bettie A. 970
Holt, Annie 912
Holtzman, Mary 923
Hood, Alice G. 1008
  James R. 830,889,893
Hooke, Elizabeth 962
  James 962
  Jane 962
  John A. 859,962
  Mary 962
  Mary L. 848
  Robert 962
  Robert M. 848

Hooke, William 962
Hooper, Elizabeth 951
  Frank 951
  Jacob 951
  Mabel 951
  Mary 951
  Mattie 951
  W. W. 846,852,951
Hope, Kate Welcker 952
  Lizzie L. 952
  Mary A. 952
  M. M. 952
  W. B. 952
  William T. 951,952
Hopson...852
Horan, Mollie A. 977
Hoskins, W. A. 897
House, G. W. 902
Houser, Daniel F. 834
Houston, Harriet N. 938
  Martha G. 938
  R. G. 882
Howard, Nathan 834,835
  O. O. 828
Howell...850
  Charles 859,861
  D. C. 861
  Mary 1014
  Nancy 1016
Hoyl, John B. 832,835,836, 865
Hoyt, Ard 813
  C. A. 892
  J. B. 875
Huffaker, Addie 953
  H. D. 952
  Jesse T. 952
  Sarah 952
Huffine, William S. 901
Hudgins, B. K. 856
Huggins, Mary A. 1016
Hughes...873
  David W. 953
  D. W. 878
  John 806
  Lizzie 953
  Thomas 897
  William 953
Hunt...962
  T. A. 843
Hunter...964
  Addison P. 837
  A. P. 831
  James A. 954
  Mary M. 1003
  Sophronia 954
Huntington...880
Hurst, Jemima 924
Huston, Elizabeth F. 924
Hutchinson, Sallie 987
Hyde, Mrs. A. 894
  Charles 850

Icely, Elizabeth 913
Ingle, W. J. 833
Ingraham, Mary 920
Irwin, J. C. 849
Isbester, Caleb 953
  Caleb B. 953,954
  C. B. 877,945
  C. P. 877
  Elizabeth 953
  Virginia 954
Izen, Samuel T. 901

Jack, Robert 898
Jackson, Andrew 815,978
  Ardelia 954
  Catherine 989
  Ephraim 955
  James LaFayette 954
  J. J. 954,955
  Jonathan 835,954

Jackson, Lizzie 957
   Martha A. 954
   Mary Ann 954
   Nancy 954
   Rebecca 954
   Rufus 954
   S. L. 1006
   Sophronia 954
   Tennessee 954
   Willie 954
   W. W. 982
James, C. E. 883,977
   Charles E. 955
   E. A. 830,893
   Elbert A. 889
   Franklin A. 903
   George R. 830
   Jesse J. 955
   J. F. 884
   John W. 833,857,860
   J. W. 870
   Kate R. 955
   Martha 978
   Sarah M. 955
   Thomas L. 999
   Walter M. 903
Janes, Julia E. 1017
Jarnagin, G. H. 883
Jenkins, Abram 955
   Ann 955
   Catherine 955
   Elenor 955
   Evan 955
   Hester 955
   John 955
   Maggie 955
   M. L. 955
Johnson, A. A. 906
   A. M. 843,870,872,883
   Amasa 956
   Andrew 804,815,837
   A. S. 852
   Delpha 956
   H. A. 955,956
   Hannah 916
   John 831
   Mary 1011
   R. C. 834
   Rosa 956
   William 834
Johnston, Elizabeth 906
   Jane 921
Jones...938
   Abigail 949
   A. R. 833
   Benjamin 797
   Berry 856
   Cary A. 856
   Clinton A. 901
   Elizabeth 848
   Frances E. 997
   Frederick 974
   Henry 848
   James 974
   James C. 815
   Jeremiah H. 974
   J. H. 831
   J. S. 852
   J. T. 899
   Rufus G. 865
   Sarah 973
Julian, George W. 831
Junkins, Annie 998
   J. W. 998
Juvinal, A. M. 921

Kaiser, Georgia A. 1016
   Nancy 1016
   W. J. 1016
Kamerer, Paul 891
Karrigan, Mary 939
Kauffman, John 949,950
Keely, John B. 882

Keeney, John 856
Keiler, Grace 1001
Keith, Annie 942
   Thomas 834
Kelley, J. J. 898
Kelly...850
   Thomas 816
Kellyhouse, Fannie 913
Kendrick, Robert S. 893
Kennedy...808
   Allen 856
   Allen A. 849
   Rowena 995
   Sarah J. 987
   S. H. 879
   T. L. 833
   V. J. 898
Kerley, Richard M. 901
Kerr, Milnan 913
Kesterson, A. 859
   John 836
Key...861
   David M. 832,956
   D. M. 832,836,837,840,
     871,897,991
   Elizabeth 956
   John 956
   Margaret 956
   S. A. 830,860,869,877,
     883
Kibbee, Caroline E. 918
Kimbrough, D. K. 835
Kincheloe, John F. 902
King, Alfred 831
   John 882,900
   Mary 956
   Thomas 956
   Thomas S. 956,957
   W. R. 881
Kingsbury, Cyrus 812,813
   Mary O. 1009
Kirk, R. A. 929
   W. A. L. 873,1010
Kirklen, Abraham 957
   Elisha 957
   Elisha, Sr. 986
   George 957
   Joseph 957
   Laura L. 957
   Lizzie 957
   Martha J. 957
   Mary 948
   Mary S. 957
   Miss M. J. 986
   Nancy 957
   Susan 957
   William 957,986
Kirshuer, Mary A. 1004
Knowlton, Miss A. E. 1012
Kosy, Sarah 1002
Kroft, R. H. 861
Krutch, E. 943
Kuhlmann, George 904
   Sophia 904
Kunz, Jacob 859

Ladew...1016
   H. S. 875
Lafferty, Mary A. 911
Lamar, Rose 1005
Lamon, Celestia 943
Langston, Ellender 1000
Lanier, Elizabeth B. 982
La Roche, J. H. T. 853
Lauderdale, William 797,803
Laughlin, Alex. 1009
   Frances 1009
Lavender, Harriet 1003
Lawson, Henry 836
Lawton, Phoebe S. 1015
Layman, James 832
Laymen, Mary 954
Lazard, Prosper 886,911,912

Lee...937
   Gordon 886
   J. N. 850
   Kesiah 1000
   Nancy 919
   Sallie 943
Legg, M. W. 856
Lenoir, Albert S. 856
   Elizabeth 956
Lenois, B. B. 952
Lewis, Ann 955
   Anna C. 958
   Charles E. 859
   Dorcas K. 957
   Edward R. 958
   E. S. 846,852,957,958
   Elizabeth 951
   Joseph W. 957
Lindsay, C. O. 891
Lindsley, V. S. 997
Line, J. E. 872
Little, Cynthia 969
   John 969
   Mary 969
Livingston, P. V. 845
Llewellyn, M. 877
   Mary 960
   Morgan 960
   Sallie A. 960
   William 960
Lloyd, A. 899,959
   Abraham 899
   Annie 958
   Arthur 958
   Catherine 955,959,960
   Elenor 955
   Elizabeth 958,959
   Emma 958
   Eudora 958
   Evan 955,959,960
   Ida 959
   Jane 960
   John E. 958
   J. T. 899
   Kate Helen 959
   Katie 958
   Maggie 959
   Margaret 959,960
   Margaret Ann 960
   Morgan 959
   Rebecca 960
   R. P. 830
   Taliesyn 960
   Theophilus 958
   Thomas 960
   William R. 960
   William T. 960
Locke, Jesse 831
   Mary 1004
Lodor, Mrs. B. D. 830
Lomenick, Prealey R. 831,
   832
Long, Eliza 964
   Elizabeth 962
   Elizabeth Jane 964
   Frances 964
   James Cozby 964,965
   James Shields 962
   Jane 961,962
   J. M. 900
   John 962
   John P. 805,808,848,855,
     856,857,859,860,893
   John Pomfret 961,962,
     965
   Marcus Bearden 965
   Mary 962
   Milo Smith 965
   Virginia 962
   William 856
   William "Billy" 961,962
   William Pomfret 964
   William Walker 964

Loomis...944,947
  Mrs. E. E. 894
  J. F. 843,880,883,961,998
  Julius F. 881
Lord, Henry C. 871
  John M. 871
Loudmilish, Mary 1004
Louis...958
Love, Robert 808
Loveman, David B. 961
  D. B. 850,884,885,892,961
  Eva 961
  H. H. 961
Lowe, S. B. 874,883,884,873
Lowrie...803
Lowry, J. J. 860,861
  John J. 859
Lyle, George W. 840
Lynn, Emma 966
  James 965
  Jane 965
  J. T. 869,965,966

Mac Gowan, J. E. 890,891
Macy, Jane M. 967
Maddox, Robert H. 900
Magill, C. L. 969
  Cynthia 969
  Hugh 969
  Rebecca 969
Maher, Margaret 914
Majors, Cicero H. 967
  Jennie P. 967
  John W. 967
  J. W. 967
  Mary 967
  Nelson 967
  Penelope 967
Mallalieu, W. F. 846
Maney, George 831
Manker, J. J. 846,851,852,968
  John 968
  Julia 968
  Sarah 968
Mann, J. 859
Marks, A. S. 831
Marquet...873,953
  F. E. 880
Marsh...866
Marshall...935,1012
  John S. 969
  Kate S. 969
  L. C. 969
  R. M. 852
  Sarah 969
  Stanhope Stewart 969
  W. S. 869,969
Marston, A. H. 966
  Carrie M. 967
  Carrie May 966
  Samuel F. 966
Marten, Mary 969
Martin, Anderson C. 967
  Edith 984
  Elaine 968
  E. M. 966
  Flora C. 968
  George W. 893,967,968
  J. A. 966
  J. D. 966
  J. M. 898
  John A. 885
  Joseph 803,808
  Kenneth 968
  Louisa 967
  Mabel 968
  Margaretta 966
  McCloy 966
  Patrick 797,803

Marye, L. S. 830
Massengale...863
  Henry W. 859
Massengill, Mary J. 1013
Masteller, Mary C. 996
Mathis, I. T. 856
Maxwell, Laura 913
May, E. F. 879
Mayfield, W. D. 890
Mayhew, Joseph F. 902
Maynard, Horace 831
Maysey, Jane 926
McCallie...866
  Mrs. E. D. 894
  T. H. 849,892,893
  Thomas 848,963
McClung, Charles 806
McCollum, Bettie A. 970
  Joab 970
  Joab L. 970
  Sarah 970
McConnell, Sarah C. 984
  T. M. 895
McCook...818
McCorkle, Mrs. S. D. 894
McCown...963
McCoy, Daniel 803
McCrary, Robert 902
McCroskey, E. J. 850
McCullom, J. L. 883,884
McDonald...803
  Benjamin 804
  James 804,1006
  Mary 899
  Nancy 1006
  Narcissa 910
  Roland 804
  William 961
McDowell, Tennessee 1000
McElwee, Ann E. 976
McFarland, Lucy A. 848
  Thomas 803
McGhee, C. M. 871
McGill, Hugh 849
  Newton 831
  William 804
McGlohon, J. J. 860
McGowan, J. E. 864
McGuffey, C. D. 892
McIlroy, Lizzie L. 952
McKee, Carrie 904
  R. C. 899
McKenzie, Elizabeth F. 924
  Samuel 924
McKey, D. 932
McLean...1015
McLemore, A. G. 861
McMillin, Miss B. 938
  D. C. 859,860,882
  D. C., Sr. 938
  James P. 971
  Jonathan P. 850,971
  Lizzie 971
McMinn, Thomas 859
McNabb, Robt. L. 832
McNair, Daniel 803
McPherson...803,969
McQuade, Harry A. 970
  Margaret 970
  Michael 970
McRee, R. C. 839
  R. C., Jr. 832
McReynolds, Coleman C. 971
  Hugh L. 971
  Joseph 898
  Margaret M. 940
  Mary 971
  Mattie L. 971
McVey, John 1010
McWhirter...931
Melendy, A. B. 971
  Anna B. 971
  Arthur R. 971,972

Melendy, Melvil 972
  Vallie 972
Merriam, Bettie 972
  I. B. 972
  J. B. 883,885,973
  Mary 972
  Mary A. 972
  Noah 972
Merriman, Bryant 912
  Martha 913
  Selena 912
Michael, Sue 1007
Miles, Nancy E. 924
Millard, Elizabeth 972
  Hugh M. 972
  Mary H. 972
  Myra 972
  P. A. 972
Miller, I. V. 852
  Thomas W. 885
  T. V. B. 886
Milliken, Alexander 900,901
  James 902
Mills, E. R. 863
  J. N. 961
  Permelia 913
Milton, G. P. 897
Minnis, J. A. 816
  John A. 840
Minturn, Mrs. John 853
Minty...818
Mitchell, C. D. 849,876
  J. 863
  J. A. 973
  James C. 816
  John 814
  Margaret 973
  Mintie 973
  P. A. 973
  W. B. 972,973
Moe, S. B. 843
Moffat, R. 852
Moffit...964
Molleston, W. J. 850
Montague, D. P. 875,880
  Kate S. 969
  L. E. 875
  Mary 975
  T. G. 871,872,882
  Theodore G. 974
Montgomery, John 808
  W. F. 836
Moore, Archibald H. 973
  A. W. 831
  Harberd H. 974
  Harriet A. 973
  H. S. 902
  James 835
  James R. 973
  John 973
  John R. 973
  Margaret J. 973
  Margaret Jane 973
  Marina E. 973
  Mary A. 973
  Nimrod 973
  Rebecca M. 973
  Richard D. 973
  R. J. 973
  Sarah 973
  Sarah D. 973
  Tennessee F. 973
  Thomas J. 973
  Virginia V. 973
Moreland, Margaret 988
  Nancy Adaline 988
  Pleasant 988
Morgan, Annie 958
  Gideon T. 898
  Jennie 1004
  L. W. 959
  Mary 956

Morgans, Mary 960
Morrill, F. F. 872
  W. C. 873
Morris, Cornelia 1000
  Lizzie 978
  William 891
Morrison, J. L. 891
  Robert 974
Morrow, Amelia I. 922
  William 883
Mosy, W. R. 835
Motheral, N. W. 849
Munger, Peter 834,839
Munsey, Thomas W. 856
  W. E. 850
Murphy, James 829
Myers, Nancy 915

Nail, N. P. 859
Narramore, Paulene Nancy 932
Neal, John R. 830
Negley...819
Nelson, Alice 929
  Daniel E. 975,976
  D. E. 852
  E. E. 975
  L. E. 975
  Mrs. S. E. 894
  Thomas R. 929
Netherland, John 815
Newton, Charles 834
  Elizabeth 953
  John H. 863
Nicholson, G. B. 799
Nicklin, B. S. 860
  J. B. 879
  John B. 974
Nisbet, Irene 947
Nixon, Ann E. 976
  George W. 976
  Maggie G. 976
  William 885
  William M. 976,1011
  W. M. 886
Noa, Ismar 961
Noel, May L. 940
Nuckells, J. K. 1015
  Maxie Belle 1015

O'Brien, M. J. 860,884,885, 976,977
  Laura D. 920
  Mollie A. 977
Ochs, Adolph 889
  Adolph S. 891
  A. S. 1003
  Julius 853
O'Connell, Daniel J. 977
O'Donnell, Anna 939
Oehmig, Mrs. W. G. 830
Older, Betsy 926
Olliver, Celina 1000
Olmstead, Henry T. 990
Orr, Mary 946

Packard, O. L. 872
Pahmyer, W. L. 898
Paine, Joseph 804
Palmer, Albion Elizabeth 977
  A. W. 977
  Elizabeth 977
  J. M. 828
  John T. 977
  Lizzie A. 977
  Phebe 1017
Parham, F. A. 889
  Louis L. 884
  L. P. 862
  N. B. 859
Parker, Allen 978
  Dovy 978

Parker, Elisha 978
  Ida 978
  James 978
  Jefferson 978
  John 978
  Lizzie 978
  Margaret N. 978
  Martha 978
  Minerva 978
  R. H. 851
  Rice 978
  Robert 978
  Tandey 978
  Teresa 978
  W. H. 872
  Wiley F. 978
Parkes, Daisy 980
  Elizabeth 980
  George 980
  S. E. 980
  Thomas 980,981
Parkhurst, Hannah 916
  John 916
  Miranda 916
Parks, Daisy 899
  Thomas 899
Parlin, Ella 927
Parrott, Florence 925
Patten, Betsy 978
  John A. 978
  Lizzie O. 978
  Mary M. 978
  Z. C. 977,978
Patterson, Alfred L. 981
  E. S. 981
  Jacob A. 898
  J. A. N. 981
  J. N. 981
  John T. 981
  Lewis 981
  Margaret H. 981
  Mary Y. 981
  Robert 797,803,804,806
  Robert Jefferson 981
  William Preston 981
Patton, C. C. 830
Patty, Josiah 856
Paul, Franc M. 867
  J. R. 990
Payne, Alice 980
  Elizabeth 979
  Eunice Graham 979
  Herbert 980
  J. C. 889
  John 979
  Josiah 979
  Lucy 980
  Margie 980
  Mary Joliffe 979
  Minerva 980
  Oliver 918
  William 979
  William C. 979
Peak, C. S. 892
  Maggie G. 976
  W. F. 885
Pearl, E. G. 859
Pearson, A. A. 830
  Abel A. 898
  Lucretia 937
  Mary Y. 981
Peebles, Elizabeth B. 982
  John H. 982
  Rebecca 982
  William L. 982
Peeples, Drewry 982
  Evaline 982
  Mary 982
  Mary E. 982
  R. B. 982
  Sarah A. 982
  S. C. 982
  Starling C. 981,982

Peeples, William O. 982
  W. O. 883,885,886
Pendegrass, Hiram 834
Pendergrass, J. C. 850
  Nimrod 804
Pennock, Allen M. 983
  Harriet 983
  Maggie 983
  William A. 983
Pennypacker, Wilhelmina 930
Perry, Abram 856
  David G. 856
Peters, C. H. 909
  J. B. 831
Petty, Mary 1000
Phillips, George 835
  G(eorge) R. 902
  Henry T. 893
  Sewell 850
Pickens, Fannie 998
Pickett, Arabella 988
  Margaret 988
Pierce, D. J. 885,886
  Franklin 815
  George F. 850
Pitner, Dorothy 973
  John 973
  Margaret Jane 973
Poe, A. 836
  A. W. 929
  Edgar 984
  H. 983
  Hasten 804,814
  H. H. 983,984
  J. H. 833
  John 804
  Mary 983
  Mary Jane 929
  Myrtle 984
  Porter 984
  Ruth 984
  Samuel P. 899,983
Polk, James K. 815
Polsey, Alice J. 1017
Pomfret, Elizabeth 962
  John 962
Pool, Polly 1000
Pope, Miss M. E. 1011
  O. C. 890
Porter, Fitz John 958
  James D. 831
  John A. 856
Post...852
Powell, Mary 1002
  Sallie A. 960
  William 849
Presnell, Mary M. 846
Preston, Elizabeth 972
  James 816
Price, Edith 984
  E. H. 843,984
  Emilia 932
  Ezekiel 856
  Joel 984
  Margaret Ann 960
  Minerva 980
  Sarah C. 984
  Thomas 932
Prowell, Alexander T. 831
Pryor, Eliza A. 910
Puckett, A. G. W. 831,832, 839
Pulliam, Martha 906
Purcell, John Baptist 945
Pyron, J. B. 885

Quarles, Robert 798

Ragsdale, D. B. 831
  J. H. 860
  Maggie 983
  William F. 893
Raht, Alice 986

Raht, Julius E. 985
  Matilda 985
  William E. 985
Rainy, Nancy 909
Ramsey...866
  J. G. M. 964
  Joseph 863
  R. A. 856
Randall, Mary 994
Rankin, Creed W. 985
  Fannie 985
  G. C. 851,985
  Martha J. 985
Rathburn, Joseph H. 882
  W. P. 814,815,860,871,
    882,883,884,898,974
Rathmell, Edith 985
  John 984
  John R. 984
  Susan 984
Raulston, H. L. W. 830
Rawlings, Aaron M. 901,963,
  964
  A. M. 856
  Asahel 804,901
  Daniel R. 816,860
  John T. 902
  Lizzie 949
  Mary M. 978
  N. L. 902
  Resin M. 831
Ray, James 835
Read, L. O. 1003
Reade, Sue E. 903
Reckter, Charlotta 957
Reed, Mrs. C. A. 894
Rees, D. B. 872
  D. E. 871,883,884
Reese, Annie 947
  Catherine 959,960
Reid, Frank T. 831
  Mary M. 923
Reiley...915
Renwick...1004
Reveley, Elizabeth L. 924
Reynaud, A. G. 880
Rhodes, A. G. 924
Rice, Anna B. 971
  Joseph 856
  Lelia A. 1011
  Mattie L. 971
  W. A. 849
Rich, William 961
Richards, Margaret 947
  Ruth 947
  William 947
Richmond, Theodore 877
Riddle, Terrill 831
Rider, George W. 814,834
  G. W. 831
Ridge, John 809,810
Ristine...879,914
Roberson, Jacob 807
  James 986
  Jesse C. 986,987
  Jesse Kankin 987
  Lewis Shepherd 987
  Margaret 986
  Mary 987
  Mary Worthington 987
  Sallie 987
  Sallie M. 987
Robertson...915
  C. P. 884,885,886,892
  Edward A. 846
  Isaac 816
  James 979
  J. M. 836,890
  John H. 831
Roberts, Arabella 988
  Bell 988
  Commodore 933
  Cynthia 988

Roberts, James M. 988
  Jane 933
  J. C. 987,988
  John W. 988
  Lulla 988
  Malinda 988
  Mary 988
  Mattie 988
  Nancy 933
  Nancy Adaline 988
  Sallie 988
  Sarah J. 987
  Thomas 987,988
  Willie 988
Robinette, J. J. 852
Robinson, Kate Welcker 952
Rockwood, W. E. 872,884
  W. O. 871
Roddy, James 831
Rodgers, Nancy 954
Rogers...977
  A. H. 832
  Arabell 989
  A. M. 831
  Arra 986
  Asahel 831
  Catherine 989
  Charity 989
  Earnest A. 989
  Elijah W. 989
  Elisha 804
  Emma 989
  Ephraim 900
  Garance A. 989
  George A. 989
  George N. 902
  George W. 989
  Gertie 989
  Henry 805,989
  H. F. 841
  Ida 986
  James 831
  James M. 989
  J. C. 989
  J. Foster 986
  Joseph 805,986,988
  Lenora E. 989
  Leon A. 989
  Lydia 989
  Mary E. 989
  Mary W. 989
  M. J. 986
  P. A. 986,988,989
  Ransom 989
  Rebecca 986,988
  Volney E. 989
  William 804,831
  William L. 860
  William M. 989
  William T. 831
Rollins, James 843
Rosecrans...817
Ross, F. A. 849
  Andrew 803
  Daniel 803
  Eliza 803
  John 803,809,810,811
  Lewis 803
Rowden, Isaac C. 903
  Samuel 903
Rowles, George W. 834
Rubedeaux, C. E. 874
Ruble, George S. 903
Rule, W. 833
Ruohs, Joseph 889
Russell, Eliza 856
  John 797,804,807
  Samuel R. 831
  Thomas R. 805
Ryan, P. 853

Saffarans, Mary 938
Sanders, Newell 861,876

Sartain, Malissa 1006
Satterlee, D. 883
Saulsbury, Mary 972
Sawyer, George 804
  W. J. 833
Sayles, Lottie 934
Scales, Helena M. 902
  John S. 902
  (Lord) 980
  N. D. 813
Schermerhorn, J. F. 809
Schofield, L. 872,883
Schoolfield, Rice 978
Schrieber, E. 853
Schuein, Amelia 950
Schwartsenburg...887
Schwartz...860
  Henry 836,861
Sciveley, Daniel 804
Scott, Winfield 811,815
Scruggs, A. D. 971
Scuddy, A. C. 924
Seaman, Joseph C. 1010
  Louisa 1010
  Louisa C. 1010
Searly, Elizabeth 1004
Seeman, J. 904
Selcer, A. 831,834
  Martha 991
  Richard F. 900
Sellers, E. B. 854
Seney, George I. 920
Senter, D. W. C. 830
Sevier, E. F. 884
  E. T. 850
  John 808
Seymour, Horatio 830
  Walter B. 990
Shaffer, Celia M. 998
  Miss S. E. 894
Sham, James P. 902
Sharp, A. G. 861,884
  Alonzo G. 990
  Jennie 990
  John 990
  Victoria 990
Sharpe, A. J. 860
Sheffield, C. J. 846
  G. S. J. 846
  Joseph E. 846
Shelby, Evan 808
Shelley, Anna M. 936
Shelton, A. 833,841
  Azariah 991,992
  C. C. 881,992,993
  C. E. 834,991
  Clement Lee 993
  George M. 993
  Harriet A. 973
  Hattie A. 992
  Jane 991
  Martha 991
  Mary A. 991
  Mary J. 993
  Matilda 991
  McKinney 991
  Mira 991
  Nancy 991
  Rose 993
  Sallie 991
  Sarah 991
  Shepherd 993
  Tennessee 991
  William 991
Shepard, Miss M. H. 843
Shepherd, Lewis 836,987
  Margaret 987
  Mary 987
Sherman, W. T. 990
Sherwood, Amos 993
  Clara 993
  Edward Marshall 993
  Fannie 993

Sherwood, George W. 993
  G. M. 891,942,993
  Harvey C. 993
  Juliet 993
  Mary 993
  Mary C. 993
  Sarah M. 993
Shultz, Martha J. 957
Shields, Elizabeth 962
Shiflett, Sarah 914
Shingle, Anna 938
Shingler, J. J. 852
Shipley, Jesse 834
  Nathan 804
  Orson 835
Shipp, Caroline 1001
  Gustavus V. 1001
  J. F. 874
  Joseph F. 1001
  J. T. 860
  Lillie E. 1001
Shirley, Thomas 805
Simmerman, Philip 859
Simpson, Jane 944
  Joicey L. 996
  Nancy 915
Sims, Martin 994
  Mary 994
  Nancy 994
  P. D. 860,994
Sister Angela 887
Sister Bernadin 887
Skillern, Alice 994
  F. W. 994,995
  Martha 994
  Matilda 1002
  Mattie J. 994
  Sarah 994
  W. F. 1002
  William 994
  Willie Maud 994
Sladen, James 798
Slayton, J. R. 861
Smartt, Anna 995
  George M. 995
  J. P. 883,886,995
  Rowena 995
Smith, Beryl 805
  Caroline L. 848
  C. E. 1003
  Cynthia 950
Smead, Delpha 956
Smith, E. Kirby 1007
  Elijah 989
  Eliza 964
  Elizabeth 964
  George W. 980
  James 804,835,836
  James W. 856
  Jane 926
  Jane M. 967
  John 950
  Joseph E. 854
  J. P. 877
  L. Virginia 940
  Mary 948,967
  Mary W. 989
  Milo 858,859,964
  Morgan L. 826
  Moses 834
  Nancy 989,994
  Rebecca 969
  Miss S. E. 980
  Susan 980
  W. F. 823
  William 848,964,967
Snapp...850
Sneed, H. H. 843
Snow, T. A. 877
  William 831
Snyder, Laura 906
Sparks, Anna C. 958
  Sarah 929

Sparks, William G. 856
Spicer, T. W. 839
Spooner, Janie M. 919
Springfield, Almera 996
  Catharine 995
  Charles 996
  Edgar C. 996
  Henry B. 902
  H. J. 902,995,996
  James Henry 996
  Joicey L. 996
  Mary C. 996
  Mary E. 996
  Solomon Langston 995
  Walter M. 996
  Willard J. 996
Squire, H. C. 882
Squires, James 901
Staley, Gertrude 1013
Standifer, James 816
  William I. 865
  Wm. J. 816
Stanley,...969.1012
  Lewis 934
  Maria 933
  T. R. 859
State, Mariah 950,951
Stately, Jane 921
  William M. 921
Steele...892,894
  Frances E. 997
  J. N. 996
  Mary A. 996
  Mary T. 997
  N. C. 996
  Willard H. 997
Steudel, Mrs. R. G. 846
  Robert 846
Stewart, Bessie M. 998
  Celia M. 998
  Hiram 997
  Margaret 935
  Mary 1011
  Sarah 969
  T. C. 849
  Theodore F. 997
Stiff, Thomas 831,901
Stivers, A. G. 961
  Arthur G. 998
  Caroline 998
  C. E. 883
  Fannie 998
  Washington 998
Stockard, E. J. 849
Stockton, Charlotta 957
  Nancy 957
  William 957
Stone, Annie 998
  E. I. 879
  F. I. 1010
  M. E. 998
  William 998
Stoneman...967
Stoops, A. J. 999
  Harry E. 903
  H. E. 999
  Nannie A. 999
  Nettie 1000
Stout, Catherine 950
Strahle...879
Stran, Harriet L. 1013
Strang, S. B. 871
  W. B. 891
Suiteman, Christian 835
Sullins, David 850
Sundquist, Charles 815

Tabler, J. H. 899
Tade, E. O. 841,854,882
  Ewing O. 903
Taft, J. B. 829
Talley, Alice 1000
  Berry 1000

Talley, Celina 1000
  Ellender 1000
  John 1000
  Kesiah 1000
  Margaret 1000
  Martha 1000
  Mary 1000
  Nancy 1000
  Polly 1000
  Stephen 1000
  Tennessee 1000
  Thomas Wesley 1000
  William 1000
Tankesley, R. M. 833,885
Tarbell, David 968
  Julia 968
Taylor...955
  A. C. 901
  Alfred A. 831,861
  Andy 836,996
  Bob 836,837
  Dick 803
  Ella 1007
  Fox 803
  G. 851
  J. M. 997
  John 836,837,996
  R. L. 920
  Robert L. 831,861
  Samuel H. 1007
  Thomas 893
  Zachary 815
Temple, Cornelia 1000
  Henry F. 1000,1001
  H. F. 874,883,884,891
  J. F. 874
  John F. 1000
  Sarah A. 1001
Templeton. A. 849
Thatcher, L. P. 891
Thayer, Mary 975
Thomas...818
  Abraham 805,1002
  A. J. 839,1002
  Catherine 960
  Dorsey B. 831
  Florence 1002
  George 1002
  Grace 1001
  James A. 1002
  John 1002
  Louisa 1002
  Margaret 960
  Martha 1002
  Mary 1002
  Matilda 1002
  Sarah 1002
  W. G. N. 1001
  William 1001,1002
Thomasson, L. L. 863,883,
  885
Thompson, Georgie 946
  G. W. 883
  Ruth 947
  William 849
Thornbrough, Allen 902
Thornburg, Jacob 869
Thornton, J. W. 870,872
  Virginia 954
Thrailkill...856
Thurman, William 856
Tilden, Samuel J. 830
Timberlake, Richard 807
Todd, David 918
Toney, Thomas 849
Torbett, John H. 831
Tounnel, Noble J. 831
Townsend, William S. 848
Travers...905
Treece...873
Treice...956
Trewhitt...963
  Chancellor 837

Trewhitt, Daniel C. 816,835, 837
  D. C. 814,832,991,1002, 1003
  Harriet 1003
  Levi 1003
  Mary M. 1003
Trigg, J. N. 886
  Mary 830
Trimble, W. J. 849
Trindle, John 829
Trousdale, William 815
Troutt, Daniel 1004
  John 1004
  Mary 1004
Truxal, Benjamin 1004
  Elizabeth 1004
  Eva 1004
  Henry 1004
  Mary 1004
  Benjamin 875(Truxall)
Tummall, Robert 831
Tunnell, James W. 856
Turchon, John B. 984
Turner, Anna 916
Turney, H. L. 921
Tutt, Benjamin F. 949
  B. F. 863
  Lillie 949
  Lizzie 949
Tyler, F. E. 1003
  Francis E. 1003
  Mary F. 1003
Tyner...902

Vail, John 812,813,848
Van Buren, Martin 815
Vance, J. C. 882
Vandegriff, Gilbert 804
  William 834
Van Deman, J. H. 815
Van Dyke, T. Nixon 837,865
  W. D. 814,815,843,883, 884
Vanhorn, M. D. 883
Varnell, Addie 953
  G. W. 953
  Lafayette 902
  Lizzie 952
  Louvina 933
  Sarah D. 973
  Thomas B. 902
Varner, George 835
  James 804
Vaughn, F. 831
Vernon, J. M. 890
  Mills 816
Vetter, J. W. 880
Vincent, Jessie Lee 935
  Sarah M. 955
Vinson, A. A. 831
  Charles W. 831,834
  C. W. 831,832,833
Von Aldehoff, H. W. 841
Von Podiwils, Mary 909

Wagner...818
  Agnes 1005
  Ambrose 877,1004,1005
  Annie M. 1005
  G. D. 866
  John M. 1004
  Mary A. 1004
Walden, J. M. 846,1005
  Leonard 1005
  Martha 1005
Walker, Ella 1007
  Frances 964
  Francis M. 840
  Frank M. 946
  G. M. 1007
  Harvey 1007

Walker, Josette 1007
  Maggie 946
  Margaret 1008
  M. M. 1008
  Nancy 991
  Rachel 991
  Sallie 1008
  Sarah 1007
  Sue 1007
  T. H. 1007
  Thomas Dick 1008
  Tinque Nay 1008
  William 991,992,1007
Walkins, Helen 1013
  R. 1013
Wall, Anna L. 1007
  Bertha L. 1007
  J. 1006
  Jasin A. 1007
  Lizzie 1007
  P. A. 842,899,1006,1007
  Robert W. 1007
  Sarah 1006
  S. L. 1006
  Walter 1007
Wallace, Albert E. 1006
  Benjamin 981,1006
  Benjamin E. 1006
  Fannie B. 1006
  Isaac A. 1005,1006
  J. Albert 1006
  James P. 1006
  John 1005
  Joseph W. 1006
  J. P. 1005
  Lida 911
  Margaret H. 981
  Mary 981,1006
  Mary A. 1006
  Nancy 1006
  R. F. 1005
  Rose 1005
Wallick, Lavina 933
Walling, John 805
Wamboldt, M. M. 854
Ward, H. M. 1003
  M. H. 880
Warner, Alice G. 1008
  Elizabeth J. 1008
  Jacob L. 1008
  James 850
  J. C. 859
  J. H. 877,883,885,926, 946
  Joseph H. 1008
  Lorenzo 1009
  Mary O. 1009
  T. C. 851,852,1009
Warren, C. A. 1009,1010
  Frances 1009
  Louisa 1010
  Pauline 1010
  William A. 1010
Washington, W. M. 854
Wason, Charles 872
Wassman, Joseph 886,892
Waterhouse, Anna 995
  Richard 816
Waters, Esther A. 903
Watkins, R. L. 883
Watson, John M. 899
  Mary 951
Watts, Susan 1004
Weaver, J. B. 830,869
Webb, Alfred 879,1010
  Lewis 856
Webster, Kate R. 955
  Thomas 860,866
Welcker...956
  A. G. 837,840
Wells, John 1011
  Mary 1011

Wells, W. B. 1011
Wert, Aubin 1012
  E. C. 1011
  F. O. 1011,1012
  Louise 1012
  Lucy 1012
  M. 1011
West, Mary E. 943
Wester, Christopher C. 1011
  Lelia A. 1011
  Mary 1011
  Samuel D. 976,1011
Westmoreland, Shade 836
Wexler, E. C. 850
  Rhoda D. 908
Wheeler...935,969
  Gillin 1012
  J. 980
  Joseph 937
  Salmon 1012
  Xen. 869,871,884
  Xenophon 1012
Wheland, George W. 876
  G. W. 874
Whigham, R. 1003
Whitaker, W. C. 1001
White...937
  Annie 1013
  George T. 938,1012
  Hugh L. 815
  J. F. 1012
  J. W. 816
  Martha 1012
Whitehead, Laura 934
Whiteside, Ann Newell 1013
  Charles 1013
  Florence 1013
  Gertrude 1013
  Glenn 1013
  Harriet L. 1013,1014
  Helen 1013
  Hugh 839,860,861,1013
  James A. 816,839,840, 848,856,1013
  James Leonard 1013
  Jonathan 1013
  Mary J. 1013
  Thankful 1013
  Vernon 1013
  William 1013
Whitman, Maggie 946
Wiehl, F. F. 871
Wiggins, Amelia 951
  Charles F. 951
Wight, Baraba A. 1014
  C. S. 1014
  Eli M. 1014
  E. M. 831,843,860
  Jarvis S. 1014
  Mrs. M. M. 894
  Seth 1014
Wilbur, N. W. 859,860,861
Wilder...818
  John T. 814,834,860, 871,873,893
  J. T. 869,883,884,899
Wilds, D. A. 856
Wiley...851
Wilkins, A. S. 933
  Barbara L. 933
  Lavina 933
Wilkinson, Mrs. J. P. 894
Williams, Alice 994
  David 1014
  George 805
  George W. 856,964
  Griselda 1014
  Gwenie 1014
  Jeremiah 929
  John 1014
  J. T. 861,899

Williams, Julia 940
   Lizzie 948
   Loring S. 812,813
   Lucy 980
   Mary 1014
   Mary Ann 1014
   Mathias 856
   Nancy Jane 929
   Samuel 856
   Sarah 929,991
   Thomas 1014
   Thomas L. 837
   Thomas R. 929
   William 859
   William J. 1014
Willey, Susanna 922
   W. 810
Willingham, Edward G. 1015
   E. G. 878
   Emilie F. 1015
   Florence 1015
   Furman D. 1015
   John T. 1015
   J. T. 878
   Mary 1015
   Mary J. 1015
   Maxie Belle 1015
   Phoebe S. 1015
   Ruby 1015
   Thomas 1015
   W. A. 878,883
   W. G. 878
   William A. 1015
Wilson, C. T. 882
   D. W. 898
   Elizabeth 932
   Jane 943
   J. M. 879,1010
   P. C. 885,941
   S. F. 831
   W. H. 898
Wiltse, Emma 1015
   Henry 1016
   H. M. 830,884,1015,1016
   Mary A. 1016
Winchester...956
   F. L. 881,961,998
   S. M. 871,873
Wingfield, A. B. 948
   Nisbet 871
Wingo, Charity 989
Wise, R. M. 853
Wisener, W. H. 830
Witt, Abner 856
Wolfe, Eva 961
Wood, Elmira 934
   Mrs. G. A. 894
   Sarah 970
   Thomas J. 821
Woodburn...894
Woodbury, Francis 993
   Maria P. 993
   Sarah M. 993
Woodruff, Fannie I. 905
   Mary J. 1015
Woodward...956
   Alice B. 950
   Richard H. 974
Woodworth...861
   Mrs. D. 894
   D., Jr. 892
   David, Jr. 875,1016
   G. B. 852,873
Worcester, Samuel 813
Worley, Clara M. 1016
   Evaline 1016
   Georgia A. 1016
   James Clark 1016
   Lodson 1016
   Mabel N. 1016
   Winfield T. 902
   W. T. 1016
Worthington, Margaret 986

Wright, John V. 831
   Martha 1000
   Rosa 956
   Sarah 968
Wyatt, Alice J. 1017
   Daniel 1017
   H. D. 843,891
   Henry D. 1017
   Phebe 1017
Wynca (Indian Chief) 808
Wynne, Charles C. 1017
   Julia E. 1017
   Leroy F. 1017
   Mary A. 1017
   William B. 1017

Yardley, W. F. 831
Yardly, E. 870
Yarnall, Jmaes S. 901
Yarnell, Elvira 835
   James S. 831
   Joseph 831,834
Yonge, William 891
Young, Martha 1005
Younglove, M.C. 871

Zinkand, Annie M. 1005

#

www.ingramcontent.com/pod-product-compliance
Lightning Source LLC
Chambersburg PA
CBHW020646300426
44112CB00007B/255